# The Nature of Corporate Governance

CORPORATIONS, GLOBALISATION AND THE LAW

**Series Editor**: Janet Dine, *Director, Centre for Commercial Law Studies, Queen Mary, University of London, UK*

This uniquely positioned monograph series aims to draw together high quality research work from established and younger scholars on what is an intriguing and under-researched area of the law. The books will offer insights into a variety of legal issues that concern corporations operating on the global stage, including interaction with the World Trade Organization (WTO), international financial institutions and nation states, in both developing and developed countries. While the underlying foundation of the series will be that of company law, broadly-defined, authors are encouraged to take an approach that draws on the work of other social sciences, such as politics, economics and development studies and to offer an international or comparative perspective where appropriate. Specific topics to be considered will include corporate governance, corporate responsibility, taxation and criminal liability, amongst others. The series will undoubtedly offer an important contribution to legal thinking and to the wider globalisation debate.

Titles in the series include:

National Corporate Law in a Globalised Market
The UK Experience in Perspective
*David Milman*

Transnational Corporations and International Law
Accountability in the Global Business Environment
*Alice de Jonge*

The Corporate Objective
*Andrew Keay*

Secured Credit and the Harmonisation of Law
The UNCITRAL Experience
*Gerard McCormack*

A Legal Framework for Emerging Business Models
Dynamic Networks as Collaborative Contracts
*Emily M. Weitzenboeck*

Directors' Duties and Shareholder Litigation in the Wake of the Financial Crisis
*Edited by Joan Loughrey*

Governance of Distressed Firms
*David Milman*

The Nature of Corporate Governance
The Significance of National Cultural Identity
*Janet Dine and Marios Koutsias*

# The Nature of Corporate Governance

## The Significance of National Cultural Identity

Janet Dine

*Professor of International Economic Development Law, Centre for Commercial Law Studies, Queen Mary, University of London, UK*

Marios Koutsias

*Lecturer in EU Commercial Law, School of Law, University of Essex, UK*

CORPORATIONS, GLOBALISATION AND THE LAW

**Edward Elgar**

Cheltenham, UK • Northampton, MA, USA

Published by
Edward Elgar Publishing Limited
The Lypiatts
15 Lansdown Road
Cheltenham
Glos GL50 2JA
UK

Edward Elgar Publishing, Inc.
William Pratt House
9 Dewey Court
Northampton
Massachusetts 01060
USA

A catalogue record for this book
is available from the British Library

Library of Congress Control Number: 2013936167

This book is available electronically in the ElgarOnline.com Law Subject Collection, E-ISBN 978 1 78100 612 2

MIX
Paper from responsible sources
FSC® C013056
FSC www.fsc.org

ISBN 978 1 84542 700 9

Typeset by Columns Design XML Ltd, Reading
Printed and bound in Great Britain by T.J. International Ltd, Padstow

# Contents

# Preface

The thesis of this book argues that national corporate governance is extremely important for societies. Recently many scholars have said that a convergence of corporate governance is inevitable. We believe that this is true, but as Mark Twain said, 'the reports of my death are greatly exaggerated'. We show that although there is some convergence, national law of corporate governance is thriving. We also believe that it is necessary for the identity of each country. The reason that national diversity in corporate governance is still widespread is because of the history, philosophy and economy of each country as shown in its cultural heritage, and which gives its identity. The cultural heritage in each state is identifiable in the company law and corporate governance codes. We consider that this is crucial for the well-being of democratic nations. Convergence in corporate governance is a threat to ordered commercial regulations because of the power of the pre-eminent economic paradigm in the West which is the neo-liberal model. The neo-liberal agenda that predicates deregulation, privatisation and the liberalisation of markets is moulding many jurisdictions into an Anglo–American model of corporate governance which is dangerous for a number of reasons:[1]

- It is an extreme sort of utilitarianism without significant ethical principles.
- It allows the growth of mega-companies backed by powerful international institutions including the International Monetary Fund (IMF), the World Bank (WB), the Organisation for Economic Co-operation and Development (OECD) and the World Trade Organization (WTO).
- It changes the balance of power between states, individuals and countries and the mega-companies, including the financial sector ('the markets') and the international institutions.
- It is disastrous because of the burgeoning inequality between nations and individuals.

---

[1] Talbot, L., *Progressive Corporate Governance for the 21st Century* (Routledge, Abingdon 2013).

- It is profoundly anti-democratic because of the powerful actors.
- It is disastrous for the environment.

Against the power of large companies, multinational companies (MNCs) and the financial institutions, national policy-makers are disadvantaged because of the imbalances. Chapter 1 is concerned with global issues emerging from the pre-eminence of the neo-liberal agenda. Corporate governance matters because of the sort of society that each state wants. Imbedded in each nation's issues of board structures and general meetings is the whole structure of the economic management in the country. Western capitalism is always a compromise between ethical principles and pragmatism, God and Mammon, God against the Devil. We will consider in each section the tensions between these concepts in corporate governance. Modern discourse uses different words to express a concept of God. We use terms like human rights, corporate social responsibility, ethical principles, communitaire, sustainability, democracy, public interest or bona fide. On the other side there are terms like efficiency, growth, development and necessity. In each chapter of our book we highlight the tension between these powerful ideas and the compromises that policy-makers have made in different jurisdictions to reach a balance between them. We contemplate the neo-liberal paradigm as a rigid contractual model for an economic system unable to imagine the value of real equality rather than simulated equality, leading to significant consequences. A rigid contractual model will always involve significant advantages for the powerful unless law or regulation can rebalance the equation. The neo-liberal prescription involves a number of crucial tenets, including rigid interpretation of property rights and ownership. In Chapters 1 and 2 we show how important these tenets are, although these concepts can be reinterpreted in a different light depending on the historical and philosophic foundation of each nation. We show that property rights and ownership are chameleon-like constructs; the definition of ownership and property rights depends on whether there a rigid interpretation of these terms, which allows special interests to flourish, or a looser interpretation which allows ethical and communitaire ideas to flourish in corporate governance.

In Chapter 5 we consider the German political consensus model which allows a common understanding of the interests of the community including companies. The opposite theory is the neo-liberal model which is predicated on contract which is rigidly contractual. We assess the differences first in Chapter 1 where the different definitions of property rights are starkly exposed when the Indians lost their lands, but throughout the book it pervades all aspects of corporate governance. The stakeholder versus the shareholder debate is about ethical principles versus profit, and the ownership of companies is part of this argument. The German consensus of politics is about the ownership of the 'commons', a public interest concept which has resonance in corporate governance. On the other hand the individualism of the American political system with its rigid adherence of property rights is a reason why maximisation of profit is a key part of corporate governance in the US. In the UK there is an uneasy compromise between neo-liberal corporate governance and a stakeholder model embedded in the Companies Act 2006, section 172 where there is a fig leaf for stakeholders other than shareholders. Throughout the book we show these tensions between individual shareholders and the public interest in different jurisdictions. We wish to scrutinise the foundation of key concepts of corporate governance because each country understands these concepts slightly differently, and if policy-makers wish to amend the law these tenets need to be thoroughly examined. We hope that this might be particularly useful for policy-makers in the transition countries including countries that are applying to join the European Union (EU), but also when each jurisdiction reviews its corporate governance systems.

Our research shows that although the neo-liberal paradigm is extraordinarily powerful, so much so that many scholars expect that all corporate governance systems will be converged eventually, there is divergence particularly in important details. The ongoing Western recession might trigger a revolution of corporate governance,[2] allowing a stakeholder model to thrive. In the meantime national policy-makers need to see the global picture before drafting laws and corporate governance systems which reflect as much as possible the culture of their country, adapting it to the international 'standards' promoted by global institutions. Chapter 1 considers the history and philosophy of neo-liberalism and the colonisation of the neo-liberal paradigm on corporate governance, particularly the way in which it is promoted in codes, templates and standards. The contractual model of bargains and companies is discussed, showing why a contractual model leads inevitably to inequality. When

---

[2] Dignam, A. and M. Galanis, *The Globalization of Corporate Governance* (Ashgate, Farnham 2009): 'the rule of the free-market radicals that started with Margaret Thatcher and Ronald Reagan has ended with a big bang'. If that is so, then the price of that bang will be high, indeed the down payment has already by early 2009 been exorbitant, but perhaps in a more regulated demand-managed world, stability and incremental innovation may come to be valued once more over excess profitability, and in turn the insider corporate governance model may once more have its day in the sun (p. 419).

inequality is predominant, this leads to a democratic deficit because of the imbalance between actors. Democracy is not just a matter of voting; imbalance between powerful interests is crucial. Trying to balance the powerless and the powerful is a fundamental tenet for democracy. A stakeholder model of corporate governance tends to iron out some of the imbalances. There is no doubt that a principal reason for the 2007–2008 financial crash is the imbalance between the financial sector and governments. A bank too big to fail is inevitably a risk because of a conflict of interests between a society and the financial sector. The situation was morally hazardous because the risk of gambling was high. The neo-liberal contractual model followed by the banks allowed them to become powerful because there were not enough checks and balances in the companies. The shareholders wanted the profit, the governments wanted investments in the economy, and other stakeholders were powerless. Eventually this led to bail outs by the taxpayers. We see now the consequences of reckless borrowing which is linked to the bank crisis in the Eurozone. Unfortunately national policy-makers cannot significantly influence the corporate governance of big banks because the corporate governance of banks is regulated internationally; however, a system of scrutinising public companies in each jurisdiction is important to make sure that stakeholders have sufficient information.

Environmental protections by companies have become essential because of the need to live sustainably. The threat of climate change is enormous. Here the tensions are immense because all companies consume resources in their trading and manufacture. The neo-liberal theory is particularly dangerous here because of its rooted dislike of regulation and also the ability to use extraterritoriality especially in switching assets between companies. Chapter 2 discusses the convergence and divergence in corporate governance in each jurisdiction and why public policies matter. We believe it is crucial to reflect the history and political ideology of each society. Differences matter if communities are to be comfortable and find their identity. In Chapter 2 we identify four streams of corporate governance, which of course have many tributaries. Roughly we have identified: (1) legal-based corporate governance scholarship focusing on shareholder rights, agency problems between shareholders and the management on companies and different models of boards;[3] (2) an economic analysis of corporate governance trying to assess the efficiency of

[3] Andenas, M. and F. Wooldridge, *European Comparative Company Law* (Cambridge University Press, Cambridge 2009); du Plessis, J.J., A. Hargovan and M. Bagaric, *Principles of Contemporary Corporate Governance* (Cambridge University Press, Cambridge 2011).

different models of company structures;[4] (3) the debate between the shareholder primacy model versus the stakeholder design of company and whether the models are converging;[5] (4) a soft-law focus which involves wider issues including ethical principles in companies, such as issues of sustainability and corporate social responsibility. This category includes the concession theory of companies.[6] Chapters 3, 4 and 5 consider these four streams of corporate governance in the context of a detailed knowledge of the structures of companies in the USA, the UK and Germany, demonstrating their diversity. Amending or drafting company law or principles of corporate governance needs detailed consideration of the structure of boards or the rights of stakeholders, while simultaneously considering the cultural identity of each nation.

---

[4] Dignam and Galanis (2009).

[5] Hansmann, H. and R. Kraakman, 'The End of History for Corporate Law' (2000), *Harvard Law School John M. Olin Center for Law, Economics and Business Discussion Paper Series*, paper 280.

[6] For example: Parkinson, J., 'The Socially Responsible Company' in M. Addo (ed), *Human Rights Standards and the Responsibility of Transnational Corporations* (Kluwer, The Hague 1999); Boeger, N., R. Murray and C. Villiers (eds), *Perspectives on Corporate Social Responsibility* (Edward Elgar Publishing, Cheltenham 2008); Keay, A., *The Corporate Objective* (Edward Elgar, Cheltenham 2011).

# Table of cases

# Table of legislation

# 1. Corporate governance global economics: the neo-liberalism paradigm

This chapter discusses the neo-liberal economic paradigm from several angles. We start with the anxiety that there is a crisis of capitalism because of growing inequalities globally and within countries. We believe that the increasing convergence of corporate governance into a neo-liberal paradigm is one of the causes of growing inequality.[1] This chapter traces the historical antecedences of neo-liberalism. We find that it is predicated on contracts which should be individually fair but unfortunately bargains are inevitably unequal because of differences between the parties. A rigid adherence to contractual rules does not allow a fair balance between parties where there are stark differences and imbalances of power or riches. The uneven playing field can only be levelled by regulation allowing ethical and communitaire ideas to flourish in corporate governance. We show where powerful neo-liberal ideas are spreading into international institutions via codes and international standards, influencing other jurisdictions. The WB and the OECD are promoters of a number of these initiatives, which are almost overwhelming the societies who wish to adhere to a stakeholder's model of corporate governance. This is dangerous because if the contractual model of corporate governance becomes pre-eminent there will be inherent powerful actors able to challenge democratic legitimacy.

The chapter traces the history of the inherent inequality involved in contracts, back to the foundation of the contractual model of companies. A contractual model of corporate governance has allowed the flourishing of Multinational Enterprises (MNEs) which are often more powerful than national governments. The MNEs are helped by international law which shelters them from some risks by structuring their enterprises in a

[1] BBC, 27 January 2012, accessed on 22 January 2013 at www.bbc.co.uk/news/business-16757564, Jasmine Whitbread, 'Will Inequality Finally Top the Agenda at Davos?', 22 January 2013, accessed on this date at www.huffingtonpost.com/jasmine-whitbread/davos-inequality_b_1235591.html.

number of jurisdictions. Enforcing harms against MNEs is extremely complex partly because of the structure of the company veil, international norms and extraterritoriality. The power of the global financial sector was one of the causes of the 2007 financial crisis which is ongoing. We consider the links between the IMF and private banks which fuelled the Asian crisis of 1997 and the current Eurozone emergency, which meant that the taxpayers had to bail out the banks because they were so powerful and 'too big to fail'. The crisis was powered by a corporate governance failure; the contractual model of companies was unable to incorporate other stakeholders into the model. The accountability of large companies is a threat to democracy, not only in a crisis but generally. Democracy is not only about voting: a vibrant democracy does not have actors which are too powerful which undoubtedly MNEs are. The growing risk of pollution and particularly climate change is something that corporate governance policy-makers need to consider, and the structure of companies may need to be adapted to encourage sustainability.

## THE SIGNIFICANCE OF NATIONAL CULTURAL IDENTITY

One would think that the issue of corporate governance would be a purely technical and slightly legalistic one, falling within the ambit of what we define rather strictly as company law. Therefore, the issue in question would fall within the interests of mainly academics or corporate lawyers. The truth however is very different. Corporate governance found itself at the centre of a debate that relates to the very cultural identity of a society and its basic political and ideological choices. This clearly revealed the true parameters of the issue and its far-reaching effects. The reason behind the debate that has generated hundreds of academic articles and books,[2] a very lively exchange of ideas and opinions on the

---

[2] Riley, A.C., 'Understanding and Regulating the Corporation' (1995) 58 *Modern Law Review* 4, 595, 595; Stiglitz, J.E., 'Multinational Corporations: Balancing Rights and Responsibilities' (2007) 101 *Proceedings of the Annual Meeting* (American Society of International Law); Attenborough, D., 'Giving Purpose to the Corporate Purpose Debate: An Equitable Maximisation and Viability Principle' (2012) 32 *Legal Studies* 1, 4; Parkinson, J.E., *Corporate Power and Responsibility: Issues in the Theory of Company Law* (Clarendon Press, Oxford 1993) at 237; Keyes, A., *The Corporate Objective* (Edward Elgar, Cheltenham 2011); Cheffins, B., *Company Law: Theory, Structure and Operation* (Clarendon

part of politicians, industry and society and sometimes a rather overt confrontation between important parts of the society such as the employees and the employers, is the fact that corporate governance requires the effective engagement of actors with the most important issues for humanity. To consider corporate governance is also to consider competing models of capitalism and competing global economic models. There is no doubt that that we are living in an age when capitalism is in crisis. Many academic commentators believe that there is 'a rapidly accelerating and potentially fatal human crisis of global proportions';[3] and if there is such a crises, are 'the systemic forces nurturing the growth and dominance of global corporations … at the heart of the current human dilemma?'[4] Escalating recent scandals in the financial sector, press manipulation of communications,[5] the increasing anomie in our societies, the burgeoning inequality between individuals and between states shows that our model of capitalism is in trouble. Former Archbishop of Canterbury Dr Rowan Williams argued that 'no one can any longer regard the free markets as a natural beneficent mechanism'.[6]

If there is a crisis of capitalism today it is important to consider the root causes of the problems economically, philosophically and legally. It is not good enough to divide specialities into watertight compartments. Many scholars[7] argue that powerful companies are a central part of a system which exacerbates poverty and inequality:

> The world has become a dangerous unequal place – even for the rich[8] in the major cities of the West. Debt services alone accounts for $200 billion a year

---

Press, Oxford 1997) at 1999; Bottomley, S., *The Constitutional Corporation* (Ashgate, Farnham 2007).

[3] Korten, D., *When Corporations Rule the World* (Kumarian Press, San Francisco 1995), p. 3.

[4] Ibid., p. 9.

[5] www.levesoninquiry.org.uk, accessed on 26 September 2012.

[6] Interview by David Hare with Archbishop Dr Rowan Williams, *The Guardian,* 9 July 2011. See note 144 for the longer quotation.

[7] Dine, J., *Companies, International Trade and Human Rights* (Cambridge University Press, Cambridge 2005); Clapham, A., 'The Question of Jurisdiction under International Criminal Law over Legal Persons' in Kamminga, M and S. Zia-Zarifi (eds), *Liability of Multinational Corporations under International Law* (Kluwer, The Hague 2000); Bakan, J., *The Corporation: the Pathological Pursuit of Profit and Power* (Free Press, New York 2004).

[8] UNDP, *Beyond Scarcity; Power, poverty and the global water crisis,* Human Development Report 2006.

> in currency flows from the South to the North. … while 1.2 billion people – nearly a fifth of the world's population – have to manage on less than a dollar a day.[9]

The first decade of this century did not reveal a better world for the poor; rather research shows that inequality was rampant,[10] and studies suggesting that powerful companies should have responsibilities to the planet and to stakeholders other than shareholders are now legion.[11] However, there are comparatively few arguments[12] linking these problems to the structure of company law and corporate governance itself. The links between company law and corporate governance, deepening poverty and the structure of company law have not yet been fully drawn. Add the multifaceted environmental crisis,[13] including climate change and pollution, and we then need to question all of our institutions, including

---

[9] Beck, U., *Power in the Global Age* (Polity Press, Cambridge 2005), pp. 24–5. See also Green, D., *From Poverty to Power* (Oxfam, Rugby 2008); Stiglitz, *The Price of Inequality* (Allan Lane, Penguin, London 2012); Wilkinson, R. and K. Pickett, *The Spirit Level* (Penguin, London 2009).

[10] United Nations Development Programme, Report, 2010, www.worldhunger.org/articles/Learn/world%20hunger%20facts%202002.htm, www.oxfam.org.au/refugee/public/issues/…/statistics.php, . Both accessed on 28 July 2012.

[11] For a few see: Ruggie, J., Human Rights Council, Seventeenth session, 'Report of the Special Representative of the Secretary-General on the issue of human rights and transnational corporations and other enterprises', A/HRC/17/31; Zerk, J., *Multinational and Corporate Social Responsibilities: Limitations and Opportunities in International Law* (Cambridge University Press, Cambridge 2006); Eroglu, M., *Multinational Enterprises and Tort Liabilities* (Edward Elgar, Cheltenham 2008); Boeger, N., R. Murray and C. Villiers, (eds), *Perspectives on Corporate Social Responsibility* (Edward Elgar, Cheltenham 2008).

[12] But see Dignam, A. and M. Galanis, *The Globalization of Corporate Governance* (Ashgate, Farnham 2009), Zerk (2006), and Eroglu (2008).

[13] Hulme, M., *Why We Disagree about Climate Change* (Cambridge University Press, Cambridge 2009); Barbier, E.B., *A Global Green New Deal* (United Nations Environment Programme (UNEP), 2010), *www.unep.org/*, accessed 25 October 2012; Helm, D. and C. Hepburn (eds), *The Economics and Politics of Climate Change* (Oxford University Press, Oxford 2009); Stern, N., *The Economics of Climate Change* (Cambridge University Press, Cambridge 2007); Chossudovsky, M., *The Globalisation of Poverty* (Pluto, Halifax, Nova Scotia 1998); Harrison, P., *Inside the Third World*, 3rd edn (Penguin, Harmondsworth 1993); Hertsgaard, M., *Earth Odyssey* (Abacus, London 1999); Karliner, J., *The Corporate Planet* (Sierra Club, San Francisco 1997); *Oxfam Global Finance, Tax Havens: Releasing the Hidden Billions for Poverty Eradication* (Oxfam, Boston 2001), http://policy-practice.oxfam.org.uk/our-work/aid-development-financ, accessed on 25 October 2012; *Oxfam America Oil gas and mining: Poor*

companies and the related issue of corporate governance. Companies are not a natural phenomenon; they were crafted by societies whether by individuals or together in regional pacts (like the EU) and influenced by global players like the IMF, the WB, the WTO[14] or OECD. Their behaviour and structures must be examined and scrutinised.

As mentioned in the Preface, this book charts details of corporate governance in the USA, UK and Germany. It is not possible to consider *all* of the global influences which have led to the current international system of corporate governance, but there is a pressing reason to examine four issues: the international neo-liberal economic model, international inequality, democracy, and (briefly) the negative impact on the environment. To examine corporate governance without considering these issues would be negligent. The thesis of this book is that national policy-makers should be supported against powerful companies and the international institutions which promote them. Corporate governance laws and codes should be drafted with democracy in mind, considering the national history and philosophy. Democracy will never thrive if rich agents are able to subordinate citizens. Our research shows that although the neo-liberal paradigm is extraordinarily powerful, there is divergence particularly in important details. The ongoing Western recession might trigger a revolution of corporate governance,[15] allowing a stakeholder model to thrive. In the meantime national policy-makers need to see the global picture before either only considering national corporate governance in a watertight compartment which is now almost impossible, or drafting laws and corporate governance which reflect as much as possible the culture of their country and adapting it to the international 'standards' promoted by global institutions. However, we start by considering the dominant economic model, the neo-liberal paradigm.

## THE NEO-LIBERAL ECONOMIC MODEL

> In the 'old political game of national (welfare)' the aim was to achieve the greatest possible security … against a background of national homogeneity … The neo-liberal agenda is an attempt to capture the momentary historical gains of global and political mobile capital and fix them institutionally …

---

*Communities Pay the Price* (Oxfam, Boston 2001); Redclift, M., and T. Benton (eds), *Social Theory and the Global Environment* (Routledge, London and New York 1994).

[14] Dignam and Galanis, 'Corporate Governance and the Importance of Macroeconomic Context', (2008) *Oxford Journal of Legal Studies* 28, 201.

[15] Dignam and Galanis (2009), 419; see Preface, footnote 2.

> according to this scheme, what is good for capital is good for all: everyone will get richer, and ultimately even the poor will benefit, or so the promise goes. The seductiveness of this neo-liberal ideology, then, lies not in giving selfishness a free rein or in maximizing competition, but in the promise of global justice. The implication is: maximizing the power of capital is *ultimately* the better way towards socialism. *That* is why the (welfare) state is superfluous.[16]

The neo-liberal philosophy 'allocates to states the function of a guardian of free, spontaneous markets through the instrumentality of the "rule of law"'.[17] The foundation of this theory is dubious for many reasons, including the concept of the 'rule of law' which can be bent into a number of shapes.[18]

The neo-liberal economic paradigm was first invented by the Chicago University economists, the so-called Milton Friedman 'Chicago Boys' who were recruited by the Central Intelligence Agency (CIA) to help with the reconstruction of the Chilean economy following the Pinochet coup in 1973.[19] Although Milton Friedman is the author of the modern neo-liberal school, there is a long tradition of right-wing scholars who wanted to disparage the state and promote markets. Skidelsky and Skidelsky[20] traced the history of the neo-liberal paradigm back to the enlightenment philosophers who believed that man (not women, of course) were rational.[21] They propounded a theory of utilitarianism. Skidelsky and Skidelsky used the 'Faustian Bargain' fable to illustrate the point. The issue was that utilitarian theories can be good for economic growth but often the instruments that are used are immoral, and in Christopher Marlowe's play *Dr Faustus*, the eponymous hero lost his soul.[22] Some other authors augmented the fable to allow Faust to go to

---

[16] Beck (2005), pp. 4–5.

[17] Birch, K., and V. Nykhnenko, 'Introduction – A World Turned Right Way Up' in Birch and Nykhnenko (eds), *The Rise and Fall of Neo-liberalism: The Collapse of an Economic Order?* (Zed Books, London and New York 2010), p. 3.

[18] Tamanaha, B., *The Rule of Law* (Cambridge University Press, Cambridge 2004), arguing that should be a universal norm for the benefit for humankind.

[19] Klein, N., *The Shock Doctrine: The Rise of Disaster Capitalism* (Allen Lane, London 2007) pp. 7, 25–38.

[20] Skidelsky, R. and E. Skidelsky, *How Much is Enough?* (Allen Lane, London 2012).

[21] Schous, P.A., *Reasoned Freedom* (Cornell University Press, London 1992).

[22] Marlowe, Christopher, *The Tragicall History of the Life and Death of Doctor Faustus* (1604).

heaven because he did good deeds; now this is what is meant by a 'win-win situation'!

> By the early nineteenth century, in Goethe's classic retelling (1808 and 1832) Faust has become a symbol of endlessly striving modern man, fallible but ultimately worthy of love. Goethe's *Faust* can be seen as the literal expression of the *felix culpa* of the political economist. With the help of Mephistopheles, Faust does all kinds of terrible things, but at the end his soul goes to heaven because he has 'striven greatly'. Faust's elevation from wicked prankster to world-historic hero reflects the weakening of Christian orthodoxy and its absolute prohibition on evil. It insinuates the heretical thought that in our dealing with the Devil it is *we* who can come off winners.[23]

John Maynard Keynes was also ambivalent about capitalism, saying that 'It was a civilization which unleashed bad motive for the sake of good results. Morality had to be put in cold storage till abundance was achieved, for abundance would make possible a good life for all'.[24] Keynes also wrote:

> we must pretend to ourselves and to every one that fair is foul and foul is fair; for foul is useful and fair is not. Avarice and usury and precaution must be our god for a little longer still. For only they can lead us out of the tunnel of economic necessity into daylight.[25]

The Skidelskys show us that Christian theology had a simple dichotomy of evil and good, but this was lost when the Reformation softened the orthodoxy.[26] This allowed utilitarianism doctrines to be followed without retribution by the devil:

> The Renaissance invented – or rediscovered – the idea of *using* human desires to govern societies rather than castigating them as wicked. The wise prince, wrote Machiavelli, treats people as they are, not as they should be: he exploits their fickleness, hypocrisy and greed to attain his ends.[27]

---

23 Skidelsky and Skidelsky (2012), p. 55.

24 Ibid., p. 43.

25 Keynes, J.M., *Essays in Persuasion*, *The Collected Writings of John Maynard Keynes*, vol 9 (Cambridge University Press, Cambridge 1978), p. 372, and see Skidelsky, R., *Keynes; The Return of the Master* (Penguin, London 2009).

26 Skidelsky and Skidelsky (2012), p. 47.

27 Ibid.

Both doctrines are simplistic because we now know much more about the human brain and the complexity of the networks connecting the desires and emotions in the human mind.[28] However the dichotomy of evil and good continues to be a powerful narrative and against this utilitarian principle, theories were propounded by merchant class who found a powerful voice in Bernard Mandeville (1670–1733). The Skidelskys cite Mandeville's best-known work, *The Fable of the Bees, or the Private Vices, Publick Benefits*: 'Mandeville's bees are addicted to "Fraud, Luxury and Pride", yet succeed, through "State's Craft", in transforming these "private vices" into the public benefit of commerce and industry':

> The Root of Evil, Avarice,
> That damn's ill-nature's baneful Vice
> Was Slave to Prodigality,
> That Noble Sin; whilst Luxury
> Employ'd a Million of the Poor,
> And odious Pride a Million more:
> Envy it self, and Vanity,
> Were Ministers of Industry.[29]

The authors show us how vice is slowly turned into a colourless sin of self-interest by a breathless public relations coup. The stage is set for Adam Smith's *The Wealth of Nations*.[30] The Skidelskys argue that the paradigm shift was possible because Adam Smith presents

> humans as driven by natural desire from self-improvement, which under conditions of free competition leads them 'as if an invisible hand' to promote the public well-being. … This was a revolutionary invention. Traditional morality had conceived of society as an enterprise devoted to the common good … Smith's doctrine of self-interest did more than just turn avarice into a virtue; it turned classical virtue into a vice … In Smith's political economy, asceticism becomes the virtuous form of self-interest, the efficient cause of capital accumulation. Alms-giving was discouraged because it promotes idleness.[31]

---

[28] Eagleman, D., *Incognito: The Secret Lives of the Brain* (Cannongate, Edinburgh 2011), particularly Chapter 5: 'The Brain as a team of rivals' where the author posits the idea that the brain is similar to a democracy.

[29] Skidelsky and Skidelsky (2012), p. 49.

[30] Smith, A., *The Wealth of Nations* (Prometheus Books, New York 1991), originally published in 1776.

[31] Skidelsky and Skidelsky (2012), p. 50 and see the recent debate in the UK, especially by right-wing Conservative politicians, Kwarteng, K., P. Patel, D. Raab, C. Skidmore and E. Truss, *Britain Unchained* (Palgrave Macmillan, London 2012), Stiglitz (2012), especially p. 229.

The theology of the beatitudes was eclipsed: 'Thou shalt love thy neighbour'[32] was redundant. Utilitarian doctrines are very dangerous, as Pogge writes:

> moral norms, designed to protect the livelihood and dignity of the vulnerable, place burdens on the strong. If such norms are compelling enough, the strong make an effort to comply. But they also, consciously or unconsciously, try to get around the norms by arranging their social world so as to minimise their burdens of compliance.[33]

The Utopian vision of a win-win situation is a rosy vision but it is not reality. Instead the neo-liberal theology has given us MNCs which are so powerful that governments are nearly powerless.[34] Neo-liberal economic theory is the dominant force fuelling the convergence theory which says that all company governance should be run on the Anglo–American, contractual model.[35] For multinationals and their subsidiaries it is efficient in monetary terms, but also significantly flawed, leaving many externalities in its wake. One of the externalities is the erosion of democracy. This is why Beck[36] realises that not only has power shifted from governments and people but also that ethical principles are absent, including justice.[37] An excellent synopsis of neo-liberalism is found in Glinavos:

> How, then, did a specifically neoliberal version of capitalism built on an essentially American model of 'laissez-faire' become the strand of Western free market ideology that won the day? … [this has become] the theoretical

---

[32] Matthew, 5:43, although the Puritans were ambivalent about capitalism; see Sedgwick, P.H., *Christian Ethics* (Cambridge University Press, Cambridge 1999).

[33] Pogge, T., *World Poverty and Human Rights* (Polity Press, Cambridge 2002 and 2008), p. 5.

[34] Ainger, K., 'A Financial Coup d'Etat: The Spanish government may be happy to sacrifice sovereignty for a bailout. But not the Indignos', *The Guardian*, 26 September 2012.

[35] Hansmann, H. and R. Kraakman, 'The End of History for Corporate Law' (2000) *Harvard Law School John M. Olin Center for Law, Economics and Business Discussion Paper Series*, paper 280 but see a powerful contra-argument by A. Keay, *The Corporate Objective* (Edward Elgar, Cheltenham 2011) and Parkinson, 'The Socially Responsible Company' in M. Addo (ed), *Human Rights Standards and the Responsibility of Transnational Corporations* (Kluwer, The Hague, 1999).

[36] Beck (2005).

[37] Green (2008); Kwa, A., *Power Politics in the WTO* (Focus on the Global South, Bangkok January 2003); Dine (2005), especially Chapter 3.

underpinnings of neoliberalism, focusing in particular on its underlying assumptions that markets are natural; that the rationality of their operations is threatened by governments' intervention; that the role of law is limited; that law should be subordinate to markets' needs; that the 'invisible hand' of the market not only ensures efficiency but also distributive justice.[38]

The recent history of neo-liberalism is to found in the scholarship propounded by the Austrian economist Ludwig Von Mises and social philosopher Friedrich Von Hayek.[39] Von Mises's axiom that 'egoism is the basic law of society'[40] led him to conclude that unrestricted laissez-faire, free markets and governments that are confined to the defence of unhampered private property rights comprised the only viable policy for the human race.[41] The neo-classicist doctrine is that rational actors will, if left undirected, make maximally efficient economic decisions which will maximise their welfare, leading to an efficient economy where all will eventually benefit:

For more than 20 years economists were enthralled by so-called 'rational expectations' models which assumed that all participants have the same (if not perfect) information and act perfectly rationally, that markets are perfectly efficient, that unemployment never exists (except when caused by greedy unions or government minimum wages) and where there is never any credit rationing.[42]

That this model is becoming increasingly discredited does not alter the fact that faithful adherents to this model are acting on the theory and now it is the dominant economic paradigm for the world:

At the time of writing, markets have assumed mythological proportions. Like the Gods of ancient days, their displeasure looms over popular protestations. In places such as Greece and Italy, governments stand or fall by their ability to respond to divine dictates. Translated into modern discourse, what is being witnessed is the practice of neo-liberal national and transnational governance.[43]

---

38 Glinavos, I., *Neoliberalism and the Law in Post Communism Transition* (Routledge, Abingdon 2010), p. 12.

39 Birch and Nykhnenko (2012), p. 3.

40 Ibid.

41 Rothbard, M.N., 'Biography of Ludwig Von Mises (1881–1973)' (Ludwig Von Mises Institute), accessed 16 August 2012 at http://mises.org/about/3248.

42 Stiglitz, *The Guardian*, 20 December 2002, and see Stiglitz (2012).

43 Rercival, Y., forthcoming phd thesis, Queen Mary, University of London, 2012.

The consequences are dire for the populations of these countries:[44] the denigration of the environment and increasing inequality but also the decrease of democracy, including the hollowing out of national states.

> The neo-liberal regime provides for globally binding decisions against individual states' resistance, and a universally valid and application 'policy mix' is propagated accordingly. This means that political reforms should be oriented towards economic objectives – low inflation, a balanced budget, the removal of trade barriers and foreign currency controls, maximum mobility for capital minimum regulation of the labour market and a lean, adaptable welfare state that orders its citizens to work. These are *the* reform objectives of the neo-liberal regime … it is supposed to be apolitical but of course it is highly political.[45]

This project has fundamental consequences for corporate governance because of the idea that convergence of systems of corporate governance is inevitable. It is clear that corporate governance 'reforms' follow the neo-liberal agenda orchestrated by powerful institutions including the WB and OECD:

> As part of the Reports on the Observance of Standards and Codes (ROSC) initiative, the World Bank has established a program to assist its member countries in strengthening their corporate governance frameworks. The objectives of this program are to
>
> - Benchmark the country's corporate governance framework and company practices against the OECD Principles for Corporate Governance.
> - Assist the country in developing and implementing a country action plan for improving institutional capacity with a view to strengthening the country's corporate governance framework.
> - Raise awareness of good corporate governance practices among the country's public and private sector stakeholders.

---

44 Hellenic Observatory, European Institute, 'The Greek Crisis in focus, Austerity, Recession and the path to Recovery', accessed 21 August 2012 at www2.lse.ac.uk/europeanInstitute/research/hellenicObservatory/pdf/GreeSE/GreeSE%20Special%20Issue.pdf; GlobalPost, 'Greek unemployment soars with one fifth out of work', accessed 21 August 2012 at www.globalpost.com/dispatch/news/business-tech/debt-crisis/120412/greek-unemployment-soars-over-one-five-out-work.

45 Beck (2005), p. 79.

## Promoting the Neo-liberal Agenda in Corporate Governance: Standards, Codes and Templates

The World Bank conducts corporate governance country assessments under the Reports on the Observance of Standards and Codes (ROSC) initiative at the invitation of country authorities. The World Bank uses a diagnostic tool – a Template – that it has developed to gather pertinent information for preparing the Corporate Governance ROSC.[46]

It is very clear that the WB's template of corporate governance is significantly tilted against stakeholders other than shareholders; the template propagates the canard[47] that the shareholders are the owners[48] of the company.[49] The template considers the most important issues of corporate governance to be the rules about shareholders' rights and particularly their property rights. It is in the form of a questionnaire and the first section is entitled 'Ownership and Control'; the first question asks about the 'ownership and its concentration'.[50] Later in this template a key concept of neo-liberal axioms appears, that is, the message that markets should be 'efficient' without properly defining efficiency: it is certain that the template prefers a shareholder primacy or insider model.[51] On these terms many externalities are not included in the definition of 'efficiency', in particular, a fair wage for employees: 'A Corporate governance framework should be developed with a view to its impact on overall economic performance, market integrity and the incentives it creates for the market participants and the promotion of transparent efficient markets.'[52] Chapter II details the importance of shareholders' rights: 'The title is "The rights of shareholders and key ownership functions": The corporate governance framework should protect and facilitate the exercise of shareholders' rights.'[53] The questions in this section are extensive (numbers 141 to 201), after which there is a wide-ranging set of (19) questions about the market for corporate

46 www.worldbank.org/ifa/rosc_cg.html, accessed 17 August 2012.

47 Ireland, P., 'Company Law and the Myth of Shareholder Ownership' (1999) *MLR* 62. See also J. Hill, 'Visions and Revisions of the Shareholder' (2000) *American Journal of Comparative Law* 39.

48 Keay (2011) considers this issue several times including when he cites the UK's Cadbury committee in its *Report on the Financial Aspect of Corporate Governance,* p. 66, and see the ownership debate in Chapter 2.

49 See Ireland (1999) and Chapter 2 on this point.

50 www.worldbank.org/ifa/CG_template.pdf, accessed on 20 August 2012.

51 See Chapter 2 for definitions of these terms.

52 www.worldbank.org/ifa/CG_template.pdf, accessed 20 August 2012.

53 Ibid.

controls, which is neo-liberal speak for takeovers which allow the powerful companies to dominate the international agenda and often states:[54] 'Markets for corporate control should be allowed to function in an efficient and transparent manner.'[55] Chapter III returns to the equitable treatment of shareholders' rights, with another 31 questions. The template only mentions stakeholders at question 277, Chapter V: 'Do any laws provide rights to stakeholders (employees, trade unions, creditors, customers, suppliers, consumers, and the community) to participate or have input in the corporate governance of the company?' Although the section is headed 'Stakeholders', its definition is telling; it 'includes constituencies *other than shareholders*,[56] such as employees, trade unions, creditors, customers, suppliers, consumers, and the community'.[57] The divisions between stakeholders and shareholders are very glaring, and the template clearly separates the sheep from the goats. Shareholders are a privileged class, not part of the company's community. They are 'owners', and the rest of the stakeholders of the enterprise are not part of the polity.

It is interesting that the term 'corporate social responsibility' is not included, although many scholars believe that the convergence of corporate social responsibility and corporate governance is one of the ways that accountability and responsibility in companies could be fostered. Responsible capitalism and neo-liberal capitalism are at odds. Corporate governance and corporate social responsibility (CSR) is where competing philosophies divide. This division is illustrated in the OECD's Corporate Governance Code (2004) and the OECD Guidelines for Multinational Enterprises (2011) which are significantly different and, some would say, contradictory.[58] The OECD's Corporate Governance Code is about regulating the internal management of companies; the Guidelines are concerned about external pressures on companies including ethical, social and environmental issues. These two competing codes can be aligned by considering the risk for companies who ignore externalities, external stakeholders and the wider community. This means contemplating global

---

54 See the takeover debate, later in this chapter.

55 www.worldbank.org/ifa/CG_template.pdf, accessed 20 August 2012.

56 Our italics.

57 www.worldbank.org/ifa/CG_template.pdf,,question 277, accessed 20 August 2012.

58 The sources rely on the earlier version of the Guidelines: Chatterjee, C., 'The OECD Guidelines for Multinational Enterprises: an analysis' (2002) *Amicus Curiae* 18; Karl, J., 'The OECD Guidelines for Multinational Enterprises' in Addo (1999).

issues, ethical and intergenerational externalities which should be internalised by companies. Zerk argues that CSR and corporate governance are distinct but related:

> It is not surprising, but these are actually two separate concepts. Corporate governance is generally taken to refer to issues relating to ownership and control of companies, and covers topics such as decision-making, reporting and transparency, whereas CSR … is concerned with a wider sets of relationship – with employees, suppliers, communities, consumers and interested NGOs.[59]

In *Companies, International Trade and Human Rights*[60] Dine attempted to show that corporate governance, CSR, property rights and risks are symbiotic terms, bound in with the way that society orders its economy and justice. It is very distressing that the discipline of corporate governance is often considered as a separate speciality from CSR. If the two concepts are to be merged, much research is necessary to implement concrete proposals,[61] turning them into a solid foundation from which legislators can draft company laws rather than vague statements like those appearing in the OECD's Code. Further, having identified society's concessional boundaries,[62] these need to be fed into the decision-making machinery of a company and extracted from the public relations departments of companies.[63] In Chapter 5 the authors argue that in a small way this could be done by drafting a law which could allow government and individuals to sue multinational companies in their own jurisdiction including foreign subsidiaries. If this could be done in some jurisdictions there could be a significant change of culture, allowing better accountability for powerful companies.

---

[59] Zerk (2006), p. 31.

[60] Dine (2005).

[61] The Ruggie report is trying to 'operationalise' principles which are central to company governance and human rights: accessed 28 September 2012 at http://198.170.85.29/Ruggie-report-2010.pdf.

[62] See later considering the concession theory and Chapter 5.

[63] Tench, P., and L. Yeoman, *Exploring Public Relations* (Pearson, Harlow 2012).

## Synergies and Disparities between the OECD Guidelines for Multinational Enterprises (the Guidelines) 2011 and Principles of Corporate Governance 2004

If corporate governance should be about providing an ethical framework for companies including advising how they can be expected to comply with laws and soft-law initiatives, a vital step in making corporate governance norms effective is to marry corporate governance codes with ethical principles.

At present those concerned with the *methods* of decision-making within companies and the enforcement mechanisms to ensure proper decision-making appear to be inhabiting a different planet from those drawing up guidelines and codes of conduct. Principally the neo-liberal 'governance' debate accepts the primacy of shareholders whereas many CSR codes have been extended far into stakeholder territory without considering how implementation may change the governance rules. The disparities between the OECD Guidelines for Multinational Enterprises (the Guidelines) 2011[64] and Principles of Corporate Governance 2004[65] (the Principles) can certainly be seen in this light. The Articles of the OECD Convention promotes policies designed:

– to achieve the highest sustainable economic growth and employment and a rising standard of living in member countries, while maintaining financial stability, and thus to contribute to the development of the world economy;
– to contribute to sound economic expansion in member as well as non-member countries in the process of economic development; and
– to contribute to the expansion of world trade on a multilateral, non-discriminatory basis in accordance with international obligations.

For those who believe that this is impossible because of the 'constraints of the limits of the planet's resources', this is not a good start. If growth is to be limited for reasons of sustainability, this principle should be integrated into corporate governance.[66] After this the issue is how the resources should be distributed, and this is where corporate governance

---

[64] Accessed on 22 August 2012 at www.oecd.org/…/0,3746,en_2649_34889_2397532_1_1_1_1,00.htm.

[65] Accessed on 22 August 2012 at www.oecd.org/daf/corporateaffairs/corporategovernanceprinciples/oecdprinciplesofcorporategovernance.htm.

[66] Meadows, D., J. Randers, D. Meadows, *Limits to Growth* (Earthscan, New York and London 2010).

principles should start to incorporate the key elements of the Guidelines, especially the concept of sustainability.

The Principles are the foundation of the WB template, consideration of which above has already shown the provenance of the ideas. This section analyses the Principles and the Guidelines. Both start from the premise that 'One key element in improving economic efficiency is corporate governance'.[67] The Principles also commence with 'the Rights of Shareholders',[68] and contain the principles that 'markets for corporate control should be allowed to function in an efficient and transparent manner'[69] and 'Anti take-over devices should not be used to shield management from accountability'.[70] The 2000 formulation only nodded to such 'stakeholders' as are 'established by law';[71] the 2004 formulation has changed this, expanding the 'stakeholder section' and increasing the rights of stakeholders by recognising mutual agreements.[72] However there is no prescription as to which constituencies should be regarded as stakeholders. The 2000 formulation stated: 'The degree to which stakeholders participate in corporate governance depends on national laws and practices, and may vary from company to company as well.'[73] This has been dropped in the 2004 version,[74] and stakeholders have a slightly enhanced status:

> A key aspect of corporate governance is concerned with ensuring the flow of external capital to companies both in the form of equity and credit. Corporate governance is also concerned with finding ways to encourage the various stakeholders in the firm to undertake economically optimal levels of investment in firm-specific human and physical capital. The competitiveness and ultimate success of a corporation is the result of teamwork that embodies contributions from a range of different resource providers including investors, employees, creditors, and suppliers. Corporations should recognise that the contributions of stakeholders constitute a valuable resource for building competitive and profitable companies. It is, therefore, in the long-term interest of corporations to foster wealth-creating cooperation among stakeholders. The governance framework should recognise that the interests of the corporation

---

67 OECD Code, Preamble.
68 OECD Code, Principle IA.
69 OECD Code, Principle I IIE.
70 Ibid.
71 OECD Code, Principle IV A.
72 OECD Code, Principle IV A.
73 OECD Code, Principle III D.
74 OECD Code, Principle IV A.

are served by recognising the interests of stakeholders and their contribution to the long-term success of the corporation.[75]

As we argued earlier, the Principles and also the OECD Template[76] intended to promulgate the UK/US neo-classical model of corporate governance. They envisage a model of corporation law which

1. relies heavily on the fiction of shareholder control over management
2. adopts the view that shareholder control over management will in some way be beneficial rather than simply increase the pressure for profit maximisation at all costs
3. adopts the 'market forces' model of ownership control; this model would limit or prevent the adoption of corporate structures mentioned elsewhere in the Code such as the representation of employees on boards, and hinder takeovers.[77]

Although the Principles do recognise employee participation in a significant shift from the earlier version, this change is therefore baffling and incoherent given the neo-liberal tenor of the document. The 2004 version is also more employee-friendly: 'Examples of mechanisms for employee participation include: employee representation on boards; and governance processes such as works councils that consider employee viewpoints in certain key decisions.'[78]

From the international perspective, the most glaring omission in this document is the absence of any recognition that a drive for economic efficiency on an international basis is at the root of many of the malpractices in which transnational corporations have been implicated.[79] Indeed the excessive reliance on the existing models of corporate governance in member states could be seen as using subsidiary principles to shirk the responsibility to suggest best practice so far as the adoption of governance models. In that respect, it is extremely interesting that 'Corporate governance is only part of the larger economic context in

---

[75] OECD Code, Principle IV, introduction.

[76] OECD *Template for Country Assessment of Corporate Governance*, 2007.

[77] Co-determination has long been accepted as a barrier to takeovers. See Dine, J. and P. Hughes, *EC Company Law* (Jordans, looseleaf, 1991–2004), Chapter 12, especially 12.19.

[78] OECD Code, Principle IV, C.

[79] Dine, *The Governance of Corporate Groups* (Cambridge University Press, Cambridge 2000); Muchlinski, P., *Multinational Enterprises and the Law* (Blackwell, Oxford 1995).

which firms operate that includes, for example, macroeconomic policies and the degree of competition in product and factor markets'. A clear distinction is drawn between ethical and societal concerns and commercial objectives of companies. Ethical concerns seem to be the last issue: 'In *addition,*[80] factors such as business ethics and corporate awareness of the environmental and societal interests of the communities in which a company operates can also have an impact on its reputation and its long-term success.'[81]

Both the international dimension and the 'ethical, environmental and other issues' are treated more explicitly in the OECD Guidelines for Multinational Enterprises. The two documents read very differently. While neither document purports to be legally binding, the extreme difference of tone may perhaps be explained by the distinction between the suggested standards (Guidelines) and the methods of achieving those (Principles of Corporate Governance). Because of an underlying philosophical difficulty in the structure of the marketplace, there is an insufficient match between the exhortations to achieve moral probity and the suggested governance methods. The Guidelines were written in 2000 and reviewed in 2011. There is shift on emphasis in the 2011 text. Both versions adhere to the attitude that 'suggests that the Member Countries may have a moral duty to ensure that the activities of their MNEs in host states *do not contribute* to the detriment of those states' economies, particularly if they are less developed'.[82] However the 2000 Guidelines were mostly negative, trying to limit the damage that the enterprises were doing but at the same time trying to stimulate economic growth in the developed nations *and* in the developing countries. Thus 'The common aim of the governments adhering to the Guidelines is to encourage the positive contributions that multinational enterprises can make to the economic, environmental and social progress and to minimise the difficulties to which their various operations may give rise'.[83] A small positive note is struck in supporting sustainability: the processes are to take place within the framework of 'sustainable development'. The puzzle is why there are two documents rather than one, and the answer may be of more fundamental importance than would first appear. If the standards articulated in the Guidelines are to be delivered, this can surely only be through corporate governance mechanisms. One difference between the Principles of Corporate Governance and Guidelines may be

---

80 Our italics.
81 OECD Code, Preamble.
82 Muchlinski (1995), p. 579 (our italics).
83 Ibid., Preface, paragraph 10.

in the fact that the OECD is dealing with MNCs. This is one difference from the Principles, which are intended to guide national corporate governance implementation. Perhaps the Guidelines were drafted without much hope because MNEs have so much power that even the OECD are reluctant to lecture them. Alternatively they know that there is no legal entity known as a 'multinational company' and therefore it is extremely complex to regulate (even in a soft-law way) all of the subsidiaries[84] of the parent company[85] in an MNE. Yet there is an evident reluctance to see the sustainable development and environmental issues as a 'corporate governance' concern; this is particularly pertinent for the later argument about growth and the sustainability of the planet, but as well for ethical problems besetting all companies.[86] The Principles of Corporate Governance state that the board of a company has responsibility to 'promote transparent and efficient markets, [and] be consistent with the rule of law'.[87] This is in contrast to this statement:

> Enterprises should, *within the framework of laws*, regulations and administrative practices in the countries in which they operate, and in consideration of relevant international agreements, principles, objectives and standards, take due account of the need to protect the environment, public health and safety, and generally to conduct their activities in a manner contributing to the wider goal of sustainable development.[88]

Despite the fact that both documents urge the setting up of systems to monitor environmental performance, it remains clear that the governance model requires adherence to *the rule of law*, whereas the Guidelines exhort adherence to *the wider principle of 'sustainable development'*. The only paragraphs in the Principles which have a wider reach than proper compliance with law appear in the Disclosure and Transparency

---

[84] This is using a simplistic model of MNCs; there are a multiplicity of patterns of arrangements, including franchises, cross-shareholder arrangements, joint ventures etc,, see Eroglu (2008), E.M. Weitzenboeck, *A Legal Framework for Emerging Business Models: Dynamic Networks as Collaborative Contracts* (Edward Elgar, Cheltenham 2012).

[85] Dine, 'Jurisdictional Arbitrage by Multinational Companies: a national law solution', *Journal of Human Rights and the Environment*, vol 3 (March 2012), pp. 44–69; Zerk (2006); Muchlinski, *Multinational Enterprises and the Law* (Blackwell, Oxford 2007).

[86] Helm and Hepburn (2009); Meadows, Randers, Meadows (2010); Sandel, M., *What Money Can't Buy: The Moral Limits of Markets* (Allen Lane, Abingdon 2012).

[87] OECD Principle, 1, p. 17.

[88] OECD Guideline VI (our italics).

section.[89] On the basis that 'Disclosure … helps improve public understanding of the structure and activities of enterprises, corporate policies and performance with respect to environmental and ethical standards, and companies' relationships with the communities in which they operate', companies are urged to 'disclose policies relating to business ethics, the environment and other public policy commitments' and 'risks relating to environmental activities'. However, 'Disclosure requirements are not expected to place unreasonable administrative cost burdens on enterprises. Nor are companies expected to disclose information that may endanger their competitive position unless disclosure is necessary to fully inform the investment decision and to avoid misleading the investor'. So far as environmental damage is concerned, only problems that will affect the decisions of *investors* are material, and informing the consumer is not necessary where a competitive disadvantage may be feared. This disclosure regime will only work to the benefit of the environment if we assume that all investors have an ethical approach. Thus a statement that 'mahogany trees are being felled at a significant rate and turned into garden furniture, netting a huge profit for investors' will be unlikely to deter non-ethical investors, whereas the other side of the story 'we are chopping down ancient forests and creating a desert' could be withheld on the basis that it is not material for investors and it would put the company at a competitive disadvantage. The Guidelines are much more positive in the environmental field, requiring the maintenance of systems of environmental management, consultation with local communities, adoption of a precautionary principle and the preparation of environmental impact reports.

There are several other problems with the approaches in the Principles and Guidelines. Apart from their non-binding nature[90] and the controversy over the status of corporations in international law (addressed above), it is also problematic that the Guidelines represent a form of 'outside the company exhortation' and it will be unlikely to be effective unless mechanisms to achieve sustainable development can become part of the internal governance systems of companies rather than outside encouragement. A third, and most fundamental problem is that it will not be possible to enlist company support for the wider meaning of 'sustainable development' until the underlying social objectives of companies is changed. At the moment the term 'sustainable development' in the context of the purposes of companies is an oxymoron. If sustainability is

---

[89] Ibid., Part V.

[90] See Zerk (2006).

to be mentioned in the Guidelines at all, the purpose of companies must be altered especially if 'sustainable development' is to retain its original ambience which included a significant redistributive agenda.[91] The principal aim of MNEs is to maximise shareholder profit. It is for this reason that the mahogany statement may be regarded as acceptable disclosure to investors. Further, since the vast majority of the shareholders of MNEs live in the developed world, the repatriation of profits made in environmentally damaging ways represents a regressive redistribution of wealth which is the precise opposite of the aim of sustainable development.

Before leaving the debate about corporate governance and the WB's Template which was based on the revised OECD Principles of Corporate Governance 2004, it is important to remember that the template was 'designed for use as the diagnostic tool for assessing the strengths and weaknesses of the corporate governance framework in a particular country'.[92] Some small points should be noted. Question 378 asks, 'Do board members have to act in good faith and in the interest of the company?' This makes a bland assumption that everyone knows what the interest of the company is, which is a key question for the rest of this book. We know that there is a major debate about the inequality of directors' remuneration and other less well paid employees, but the template says nothing about ordinary employees, nothing about the wages or conditions of the median worker or the proportional wage rates in the company. Again this is of great consequence in our quest to understand the difference between corporate governance systems. What the template confirms is that the management is more powerful than other stakeholders. In the title section about remuneration, the template asks, 'Aligning key executive and board remuneration with the longer term interests of the company and its shareholders. … Is board remuneration *high enough*[93] to ensure that board members devote sufficient time to their duties?'[94] This suggests that the only problem about remuneration is whether the pay should be high enough, although Stiglitz argues that corporate governance as practised by the neo-liberal institutions are part of the rise of inequality.[95]

---

91 Brundtland, H., *Our Common Future* (Oxford University Press, Oxford 1987).

92 World Bank *Template*, 2007, introduction.

93 Our italics.

94 Accessed on 20 August 2012 (our italics) on www.worldbank.org/ifa/CG_template.pdf.

95 Stiglitz (2012), p. 66.

The assumptions in the WB corporate governance project are an insidious way of controlling states' culture into a global corporate governance system for the convenience of the MNCs, including the multinational banks and their subsidiaries. The neo-liberal corporate governance paradigm has not yet tipped into a slave trade mentality but history shows that terrible suffering can be perpetrated by a free trade approach. Laissez-faire economics led to the Atlantic slave trade,[96] probably the worst example of the Faustian Bargain where England was enriched on the back of terrible suffering: 'Sugar and tobacco production ... developed hand-in-hand with co-erced and degraded labor: grasping for wealth, profit-maximising English planters relentlessly sought overseas markets, ruthlessly exploited fellow humans, accumulated narrowly concentrated power, and resonated very little to liberal ideas and higher values.'[97] Corporate governance matters because it is a fundamental building block of the governance of commerce, and therefore the economy of states and eventually the international economy. If companies are run with no compassion, the international economy will implode because of the endemic inequality which is the legacy of neo-liberal policies.

## CONTRACT, FREEDOM, INEQUALITY, DEMOCRACY AND REGULATIONS

The neo-liberal paradigm is a contractually based system. In a market economy contract is a crucial tool, but there are some fundamental problems in a *free* contractual market. A market economy is based on the theory that each individual has freedom to trade and this leads to each person getting their needs and desires satisfied. An economy which is mostly arranged on a contractual design means that there will be inevitably people who are disadvantaged. Where this happens contract can be a malign construct and eventually there will be a paradox: people will be limited in their choices although the whole idea of a contractual model economy was to enhance freedom. Where this happens in grossly unequal societies this is also a danger for democracy. If individuals are so poor that they are fighting to get enough food or water democracy will

---

[96] Thomas, H., *The Slave Trade* (Picador, Phoenix 2006).

[97] Nash, G., 'Foreword' in R. Dunn, *Sugar and Slaves: The Rise of the Planter Class in the English West Indies, 1624–1713* (University of North Carolina Press, Virginia 1972 and 2000).

not be their first priority, nor can they access information or debate the political issues in the nation.[98]

While at first sight an agreement between two individuals to buy and sell might seem a politically neutral transaction and therefore politically uncontroversial, as soon as any disparity of bargaining power is taken into consideration it becomes clear that the arrangement will tend to benefit the party who started in the more powerful position. This is a simple example to illustrate the way in which inequality can quickly exacerbate divisions between people:[99] on a cold day I had half an hour to kill before meeting my daughters from school. I went to buy a minor electrical item in a large electrical superstore. As I had some time I read (for the first time ever) the small print of terms and conditions of the sale, and found a term which I considered to be outrageous. I presented the item to the young person at the till, announcing that I would like to buy the item but mentioning that I had crossed out this particular term as I did not accept it. This caused a delightful chaos. Of course, the person at the till could not accept the changed bargain, so he called the supervisor, who called the store manager, who called the area manager. At this point, I ran out of time and left without the item.

What the interlude illustrates is that large companies are used to dictating the terms on which they will deal. Such a contract is very far from being a contract between equals. Only if safeguards (such as unfair contract terms legislation) are enacted can the equation be rebalanced. Teubner illustrates the notion of contractual unfairness in a consumer marketplace as follows: 'A contractual term is unfair if "contrary to the requirement of good faith it causes a significant imbalance in the parties' right and obligation arising under the contract, to the detriment of the consumer"'.[100] Of course, this leaves unexplained the intractable question of which imbalances are 'fair' and what, therefore, is meant by 'good faith'. Teubner has pointed up some of these questions in his work on transplanting laws between countries. He argues that transplanting laws into a different jurisdiction is usually disastrous unless each country is philosophic attuned, and uses contractual concepts to illustrate his concepts of fairness, particularly unfair terms contracts legislation. He illustrates the way that the UK courts rejected the requirement of good faith, saying: 'The British courts have energetically rejected this doctrine on several occasions treating it like a contagious disease of alien origin.'

---

98 Shue, H., *Basic Rights* (Princeton University Press, Chichester 1996).

99 Dine, Inaugural Lecture at Queen Mary, 15 June 2008.

100 Teubner, G., 'Legal Irritants: Good Faith in British Law or How Unifying Law Ends up in New Divergences' (1998) *MLR* 62, p. 11.

He cites *Walford v Miles*,[101] where the judge said that good faith is 'inherently repugnant to the adversarial position of the parties'.[102] For Teubner this shows that the judicial system in the UK is imbued with contractual cultural connotations. The German understanding of good faith is more generous and inclusive, involving the whole of society and not just the parties. Similarly, company governance in Germany tends to follow a communitarian model. Arrangements for economic enterprises were profoundly different within continental Europe before the creation of the European Economic Community (EEC), but when the UK joined the EEC, the existing divisions were exacerbated. German capitalism, for example, has a philosophical concept of 'good faith' which is the reverse of the UK-contractual paradigm. Teubner argues that arrangements in Rhineland capitalism are predicated on trust between all of the individuals in the company, its suppliers and their financial backers:

> Economic action is closely coordinated by business association and by informal business network … These regimes give considerable autonomy to employees within the hierarchy of the organisation and to suppliers and deliverers within long-term cooperative networks. This opens opportunities for production prone to long-term cooperation, but creates simultaneously considerable risks that are typical for high autonomy and high trust relations.[103]

Transition countries are particularly prone to legislate using 'experts' from other countries, and great care is needed to align the fundamental philosophy of the state with all of the legal structures including the constitution, judicial system and commercial law, or it will be dysfunctional.[104]

## Economic Contractualism and the Rise of the Multinationals

Later we will consider in detail the corporate models which are found in America, Germany and the UK. However, the most important and influential companies in the Western world use a contractual model. This means that trade bargains are always asymmetrical because of the

---

[101] Ibid., p. 25.
[102] Ibid., p. 26.
[103] Ibid., p. 25.
[104] Dine, M. Koutsias and M. Blecher, *Company Law in the New Europe: Acquis. Comparative Methodology Law* (Edward Elgar, Cheltenham 2007).

imbalance between individuals' bargaining position.[105] This is the well-understood difference between the Pareto theory and the Kaldor–Hicks notion of efficiency. Pareto efficiency requires that someone gains and no one loses in a contract. In contrast, the Kaldor–Hicks test accepts as efficient 'a policy which results in sufficient benefits for those who gains such that *potentially* they can compensate fully all the losers and still remain better off.'[106] Ogus explains this difference very simply and tellingly, using the following example:

> Bill agrees to sell a car to Ben for £5,000. In normal circumstances it is appropriate to infer that Bill values the car at less than £5,000 (say £4,500) and Ben values it at more than £5,000 (say £5,500). If the contract is performed, both parties will gain £500 and therefore there is a gain to society – the car has moved to a more valuable use in the hand of Ben ... this is said to be an 'allocatively efficient consequence'.[107]

Everyone is a gainer, which is an illustration of the Pareto efficiency test. This win-win situation is a Utopian vision and extremely rare because of the number of disadvantages that can be envisaged. The most obvious ones are power or money, therefore bargains are usually rigged because of imbalance between the parties. Because of the rarity of Pareto bargains a different test was designed, the Kaldor–Hicks principle, where the good bargains and the bad are averaged in an economy.[108] Unfortunately, in the Kaldor–Hicks test there is no reason why the gainer should compensate the loser, and therefore in a contract where the loser is already disadvantaged he will probably become further deprived. This is a reason for the growth in global inequality.

There is a sliding scale of contractual freedom in Western economies which allows some commercial laws to be enacted without proper consideration of the risk borne by the disadvantaged. Because of the

---

[105] The fictive nature of companies is also crucial: 'Denial of a separate personality to the entity form by the human group of actors is a necessary foundation for the application of market theories, since the underlying assumption is the creation of maximum efficiency by individual market players bargaining with full information. Taking the view that free markets are the most effective wealth creation system neo-classical economists including Coase have analysed companies as a method of reducing the costs of a complex market consisting of a series of bargains among parties.' Dine (2012).

[106] Greenfield, K., 'From Rights to Regulation' in F. Macmillan Patfield (ed), *Perspectives on Company Law: vol 2* (Kluwer, London 1997), p. 10.

[107] Ogus, A.I., *Regulation: Legal Form and Economic Theory* (Clarendon Press, Oxford 1994), p. 24.

[108] Ibid.

power of MNCs they can dictate terms to employees and suppliers but also to governments. A contractual design of a free market appears to be good for individual freedom but it is a chimera; freedom is disguised as a form of neutrality and equality:

> Every stable social system possesses an order of power and wealth, but unlike historically prior distributive schemes, the market order avoids the imposition of a detailed pattern. Instead of a structure of rank and privilege fixing entitlements to wealth and power, the distributive mechanism of the market allocates resources to those persons able and willing to pay the highest price for them … The market order avows blindness to claims of privilege or force, so it recognises no claims of an inherent right to govern or to possess superior wealth … The market order lets fly the centrifugal forces of radical individualism, permitting philosophers to celebrate the relative fluidity of its distributive outcome and to legitimate it by appeals to the impervious mask of market forces. No other order so successfully disguises the fact that it constitutes an order at all.[109]

The same argument works in exactly the same way at an international political level. An agreement between states with equal bargaining power may be considered to be politically neutral, but when they are of disparate power the 'contract' is of profound political importance. In this respect it is significant that thc first quasi-judicial enforcement mechanisms at international level have been designed and operate to enforce international commercial law, and clearly favour richer nations with more diverse economies. The neo-liberal design with which the world is imbued is an aggressive sort of capitalism but it is not completely new. It has an uncanny resemblance to the way in which the English colonised North America.

> The English could congratulate themselves on the honourable way they were populating North America. They could see the Indians growing poorer but they did not conceive that they were the agents of the Indian's impoverishment. They were not taking the Indian's land by force of arms, after all. They were buying it on the open market.[110]

There were transactions called 'Treaties', but of course they were not genuine contracts, because the Indians did not *consent* to sell their land.

---

[109] Collins, H., *The Law of Contract* (1986), cited in D. Campbell, 'Reflexivity and Welfarism in the Modern Law of Contract' (2000) *Oxford Journal of Legal Studies* 477.

[110] Banner, S., *How the Indians Lost their Land* (Harvard University Press, Cambridge MA 2005).

They had different conceptions of property from European settlers, so they could not have understood what the settlers meant by a sale. The Indians were really conquered by force, but Americans and their British colonial predecessors papered over their conquest with these documents[111] to make the process look proper and legal.[112] What was happening for the Indians was that they completely missed the importance of a key concept. They had a concept of property in which land was community-owned, therefore the individual-contract idea was entirely foreign for them.[113]

When we consider corporate governance in detail for each jurisdiction, we will see how decisive are the language and concepts. Perhaps this can be best illustrated by the differences between the Anglo–American contractual model which accentuates the fictive nature of companies, born from negotiation by individuals agreeing a contract, and an organic understanding of company as a living entity which is prevalent in German jurisprudence.[114] This latter theory is more conducive to CSR practitioners and academics who promote stakeholder models.[115] However on the global stage, the contractual model of companies has been used by MNCs to enhance their prestige and power with devastating consequences.[116] The argument starts with single companies using a

---

[111] William Crashaw's 'A Sermon Preached in London before the Right Honorable Lord La Warre, Lord Gouenour and Captaine Generall of Virginea, and others of his Maiesties Counsell for that Kingdome, and the rest of the Aduenturers in that Plantation', given for the Virginia Company on 21 February 1610.

> 'A Christian may take nothing from a Heathen against his will, but in faire and lawfull bargaine'

[112] Banner (2005), p. 1.

[113] See also the tensions between collectivism and individualism in the Soviet system: Hill, J., 'Corporate Corporate Governance and Russia – Coming Full Circle' in G. Doeker-Mach and K.A. Ziegert (eds), *Law, Legal Culture and Politics in the Twenty-First Century – Essays in Honour of Erh-Soon Tay, Alice*, (Franz Steiner Verlag, Stuttgart 2004), p. 153.

[114] Keay (2011), pp. 33–5, and see also Edward, V., *EC Company Law* (Oxford University Press, Oxford 1999), p. 35.

[115] Keay (2011), p. 201, Chapter 3; Teubner, 'Enterprise Corporatism; New Industrial policy and the "essence of the Legal Person"' (1988) 36 *American Journal of Comparative Law* 130; Worthington, S., 'Shares and Shareholders: Property, Power and Entitlement (Part 2)' (2001) *The Company Lawyer* 307. Dine (2005).

[116] Dine (2000), p. 152. See also for example Larsson, T., *The Race to the Top; The Real Story of Globalisation* (Cato Institute, Washington 1999), Irwin, D., *Free Trade Under Fire* (Princeton University Press, Princeton NJ 2002), a

contractual model and turns into the giant MNEs of today's society. The rise of the mega-companies was engineered by the neo-liberal paradigm using contract, free market philosophy and deregulation. On the international stage states were often pressured by the neo-liberal institutions including the World Bank, the IMF and the WTO to believe that growth and development was crucial for all nations, including the developed countries. This is now being challenged by a growing number of thinkers who believe that continuing the pattern of unlimited growth is damaging the earth and is simultaneously bad for human health, mental and physical.[117] These authors cite different reasons for their beliefs, with some using utilitarian theories while others cite spiritual reasons. However if they are right, it is important to incorporate these ideas in corporate governance and embed them in national jurisprudence. From the global perspective this is particularly difficult because of the international traditional understanding of the sovereignty of states; nations jealously guard their own interests even though their prerogatives are more and more compromised by globalisation and the power of the multinational companies.[118] To construct a global corporate governance system which balances not only national stakeholders' interests but also governmental interests and global environmental issues is a true challenge.[119] So far there is no possibility of such agreement. Absent an international agreement national corporate governance might be improved to ameliorate inequality. The MNEs use the limits of national sovereign jurisdiction for their advantage often incorporating subsidiaries in countries where the government cannot control the company. The quirks and priorities of national corporate governance will be explained in Chapters 3, 4 and 5. We will see that although the neo-liberal paradigm

---

slightly more balanced approach in Moore, M., *World Without Walls* (Cambridge University Press, Cambridge 2002), Glinavos (2010).

[117] Skidelsky and Skidelsky (2012); Stigliz (2012); Wilkinson and Pickett (2009 and 2010); Sandel (2012); Green (2008); Dine (2005).

[118] Beck (2005).

[119] However, designing a corporate governance system is challenging not only because of their power but also because of the fictive nature of multinational companies. In legal parlance TNCs are not recognised as a legal entity, they are not able to own property or to sue or be sued. MNEs are only a set of linked companies. Individual companies are legal persons but MNEs are not legal persons; of course, society recognises them as viable groups, but MNEs are a group of companies linked either by shareholders' rights in each company or, more radically, by power (one company might be subordinate to another). This legal flexibility is one reason why they have become so powerful.

is very powerful, there are significant differences between national corporate governance systems.

## Multinationals' Legal Structures and Extraterritoriality

It is odd that many corporate governance texts ignore groups of companies, even though MNCs are becoming more powerful than some states and governments.[120] We have seen the intractable problems set by MNEs including the democratic deficit, environmental damage and the growing gap of inequality. We charted the strict jurisprudence in the UK and the USA which adheres to a stringent separation between shareholders and the company. In the case of *Salomon*[121] in the House of Lords, Lord MacNaughten stated:

> The company is at law a different person altogether from [those forming the company]: and, though it may be that after incorporation the business is precisely the same as it was before, and the same persons are managers, and the same hands receive the profits, the company is not in law the agent of the subscribers or trustee for them. Nor are the subscribers as members liable, in any shape or form, except to the extent and in the manner provided by the Act … If the view of the learned judge were sound, it would follow that no common law partnership could register as a company limited by shares without remaining subject to unlimited liability.

The idea is that the company is an entity separate from the people actually involved in it. This fictional 'legal person' owns the property of the business, owes the debt to business creditors and is in full position to become a party in legal relations; it can sue and be sued on its own, it can become a party to a contract and very significantly it retains its identity and business despite radical changes in the composition, number or identity of its founders and at times membership. This translates into the international context allowing MNEs to play 'jurisdiction arbitrage'.[122] Frequently, in the case of environmental hazards, a parent company can hive out risky or dirty business abroad. Problematically, if there is a violation of the environment the subsidiary company will generally not be sued, either because the venture is in a state which is politically

---

[120] See Chapter 1, but also see Dine (2000) and Andenas, M. and F. Wooldridge, *European Comparative Company Law* (Cambridge University Press, Cambridge 2009).

[121] *Salomon v Salomon* [1897] AC 22.

[122] Dine (2012).

unstable and/or lacking in effective environmental regulation or enforcement practices, or because the subsidiary can be starved of finance by the parent and placed in danger of insolvency. Meanwhile, suing the parent company is problematic because each company in the MNC group is constructed as being completely separate. Each jurisdiction, moreover, has a limited jurisdictional reach, while in effect each company in the MNC group is insulated by the operation of the 'corporate veil' isolating the companies making up the group. In this sense, the MNC makes a particularly complex target for the imposition of liability: there is no single MNC 'entity', as such. Constructing a form of 'enterprise liability', however, would potentially mean that the whole MNC enterprise could be sued simultaneously, making it simpler to force the directors of each company to respect standards of environmental probity and any relevant fiduciary duties. The growth of MNCs has been possible precisely because most legal systems regard one company holding shares in another in exactly the same way as if the company were a human individual shareholder.[123] Most legal systems take no account of the reality of the accumulation of power represented by a large number of companies related by interlocking shareholdings, despite the fact that many companies are organised in a 'group' structure wherein control is exercised over a number of subsidiaries through shares held by a 'parent' company. While the simplest case is a hierarchy with 100 per cent shareholding by a parent company, there are numerous other ways of creating effective control of one company over others through a range of share structures and other contractual devices such as franchises and joint ventures.[124]

The fictive nature of companies gains a new level of complexity, therefore, in the case of MNCs, and the fundamental 'non-existence' of the MNC as an 'entity' is arguably intimately related to the problem presented by the extraterritoriality of national jurisdiction. Each nation state has equal sovereign power to regulate the territory that it owns, and enacts its own laws. Companies are a legal *fiction*[125] invented by national law. Each state possesses the power (and usually the exclusive power) to regulate the company and to enforce its liabilities. However, as has been suggested already, MNCs do not exist as an 'entity' defined or recognised by law. Rather, they are complex structures made up of individual

---

123 Dine (2000); Blumberg, P., 'The American law of Corporate group' in J. McCahery, S. Picciotto and C. Scott (eds), *Corporate Control and Accountability* (Clarendon Press, Oxford 1993).

124 Weitzenboeck (2012).

125 Zerk (2006); Muchlinski (2007); Dine (2005).

companies in a variety of interrelationships.[126] While globalisation means that the world appears to be a smaller place, and while goods and people can move freely across borders, companies remain legally tied to the country where they are formed. The operation of equal sovereign power, however, normally means that regulations made in one jurisdiction, in the normal course of events, cannot have any impact on corporate liability in another. This is the problem of extraterritoriality. The fact that MNCs are series of companies formed in different national legal systems and tied together in various legal ways, either by holding shares in each other or by various legally binding agreements between them, presents genuine complexity. This complexity, moreover, is exploited by MNCs. There are numerous cases, for example, of parent companies exporting dirty and dangerous business to poor countries where regulations are minimal or not enforced; or of paying exploitatively low wages; and/or ignoring the environmental effects of corporate operations.[127] Poorer countries, meanwhile, are often desperate for any foreign investment – and thus rendered especially vulnerable to such practices.

The practical implications of MNC complexity can be devastating. Suppose, for example, that damage is done to the health of employees of a company. The employees will find it difficult or impossible to claim against the local operator in some countries, especially if the legal system is structured to favour the MNC because of the need to attract foreign

---

[126] See the US Third Restatement, ALI 'restatement of the Law, Third, Foreign Relations' para 213; 'For purposes of international law, a corporation has the nationality of the state under the law of which the corporation is organised'. And 'Multinational Corporations': 'The Multinational enterprise or corporation … is an established feature of international economic life, but it has not yet achieved special status in international law or in national legal system. A multinational corporation generally consisted of group of corporations, each established under the law of some state, linked by common managerial and financial control and pursuing integrated policies'; see also Zerk (2006), pp. 149–150.

[127] Just some of them are Simms, A. and D. Boyle, *Eminent Corporations* (Constable & Robinson Ltd, London 2010); Monbiot, G., *Captive State: The Corporate Takeover of Britain* (Macmillan, Basingstoke 2000); Korten (1995); Klein, *No Logo* (Picador, London 1999); Klein, *Fences and Windows* (Picador, New York 2002); Hertz, N., *The Silent Takeover* (Heinemann, London 2001); Chomsky, N., *Profit over People* (Seven Stories Press, New York 1999); Palast, G., *The Best Democracy Money Can buy* (Pluto, Halifax, Nova Scotia 2002); Ehrenreich, B., *Nickel and Dimed* (Granta, London 2002); Schlosser, E., *Fast Food Nation* (Penguin, London 2002); Toynbee, P.., *Hard Work* (Bloomsbury, London 2003); Hutton, W., *The World We're In* (Little, Brown, London 2002); Chossudovsky (1998); Harrison (1993); Hertsgaard (1999); Karliner (1997).

investment and/or if the legal system is corrupt or dysfunctional. Moreover, the layers of the corporate veil mean that the employees will find it impossible to claim against the foreign 'parent' company, because it is a separate company, structured according to the laws of a different jurisdiction, and not *legally* responsible for the acts of other companies in the MNC group even if they are very closely tied together through shareowning or by contractual arrangements. Drafting a law which encapsulates the complex range of legal structures of MNCs[128] presents an extremely intricate challenge, for as we can see, each MNC is a complex of companies founded and governed by the commercial laws of different nation states. The companies can be connected in a multitude of ways, by contract, by franchising agreements and by cross-shareholding, yet, despite this density of interconnection, there is no overall legal regulation of the whole commercial enterprise.

Only in very exceptional cases will the courts in rich countries break with general practice and 'lift the veil', that is, look to the reality of the situation.[129] Perhaps the most egregious example of the problem of extraterritoriality was the English case, *Adams v Cape Industries.*[130] Several hundred employees of the corporate group headed by Cape Industries had been awarded damages for injuries incurred as a result of exposure to asbestos dust in the course of their employment. Many of them were dying an unpleasant and lingering death. The damages had been awarded by a court in Texas, but Cape Industries had no assets in Texas, so the claimants could obtain no monetary compensation there. The claimants sought to enforce the claims in England, where Cape had its head office and considerable assets. The English Court of Appeal held that the awards could not be enforced in England against Cape even though one of the defendants was a subsidiary of Cape's and despite the fact that the group had been restructured in order to avoid liability. The purpose of restructuring, moreover, was blatant: the US subsidiary (which had been responsible for marketing in the US (North American Asbestos Corporation (NAAC)) was put into liquidation and ceased to

---

[128] See Zerk (2006) at p. 51; E.M. Weitzenboeck, *Between Contract and Partnership: Dynamic Networks as Collaborative Contracts and More* (PhD Thesis, Oslo University, April 2010).

[129] Zerk (2006): see p. 55 to illustrate some examples of lifting veil legislation. Interestingly she uses the UK Companies Act 1985, section 751, to show that parents might be responsible for subsidiaries if the parent was a 'shadow director' now superseded by the Companies Act 2006.

[130] 1990 BCLC 479.

exist. Instead, two new companies were formed: a company in Liechtenstein whose shares were held by a subsidiary of Cape, and an Illinois company (Continental Productions Corporation (CPC)) whose shares were held by the ex-president of NAAC. The two companies were also put in charge of US marketing. As a result of this, while there remained no *legal* link between Cape and CPC because Cape no longer held any shares, the reality was that the ex-president (who held all the shares) remained loyal to Cape's interests and controlled CPC. Additionally, in the case of CPC, a new legal link was introduced to add to the chain which connected Cape to its marketing operation. These moves were clearly and openly intended to avoid liability for the outstanding claims for asbestosis injury which Cape knew were in the pipeline. Yet, Slade J reasoned that:

> Our law, for better or worse, recognises the creation of subsidiary companies, which, though in one sense the creation of their parent companies, will nevertheless under the general law fall to be treated as separate legal entities with all the rights and liabilities which would normally attach to separate legal entities … We do not accept as a matter of law that the court is entitled to lift the corporate veil as against a defendant company which is the member of a corporate group merely because the corporate structure has been used so as to ensure that the legal liability (if any) in respect of particular future activities of the group … will fall on another member of the group rather than the defendant company. Whether or not this is desirable, the right to use a corporate structure in this way is inherent in our law.

And

> If a company chooses to arrange the affairs of its group in such a way that the business carried on in a particular foreign country is the business of the subsidiary and not its own, it is, in our judgment, entitled to do so. Neither in this class of case nor in any other class of case is it open to this court to disregard the principle of *Salomon v Salomon* [1897] AC 22 merely because it considers it just so to do.[131]

Such a legal outcome is commonplace throughout the world. This means that companies can export potentially liability-attracting activities away

---

[131] A recent case, *Chandler v Cape plc* [2012] EWCA 525 gives some scholars a reason for optimism. The Court of Appeal broadened the concept of assumption of responsibility and devised a novel test to hold a parent company liable for injuries sustained by one of its subsidiary's employees using tort law. See Chapter 5 considering the German law on company groups.

from the rich world to poverty-stricken areas where *any* sort of employment, including scavenging from rubbish tips, is welcome and there are fewer, or no, inconvenient checks on health and safety, environmental or labour standards. The fact that in theory the subsidiary company in the poor country could be held legally answerable, there is, as we have seen, no comfort. Quite apart from the possibility of corruption or dysfunction in the relevant national legal system, two further difficulties arise: first, the parent company can simply cause its creature in the poor country to disappear by instructing it to liquidate and if necessary transfer any funds to the parent company, leaving the employees with a blank space – they have no company to sue, it has just disappeared; secondly, any regulatory controls are frequently bargained away, in any case, before the company agrees to set up a business. These realities mean that MNCs can play regulatory or jurisdictional arbitrage, seeking out the jurisdiction with the fewest protections in order to maximise profit. This is the well-known 'race to the bottom', encouraged and protected by commercial law, just as was the slave trade in earlier times.

There are some exceptions to the strict doctrine of national sovereignty, though rare (the MNC lobby keeps a tight rein on legislation).[132] Perhaps the best instance of a law purporting to tighten MNC accountability is the Foreign Corrupt Practices Act (FCPA) in the US.[133] However, this Act failed to deliver on the early promise of its preceding Bill. Zerk records that:

> In relation to 'foreign corrupt practices', for example, an early proposal to apply legislation directly to foreign subsidiaries of US-owned countries was rejected because of concerns about 'the inherent jurisdictional, enforcement and diplomatic difficulties raised by the inclusion of foreign subsidiaries of US companies in the direct prohibitions of the Bill'. … This is despite concerns that a failure to extend the law to foreign subsidiaries would create a 'massive loophole through which millions of bribery dollars would continue to flow'. A form of parent-based regulation of foreign companies is used instead: US parent companies can themselves be held liable under the Foreign Corrupt Practices Act (FCPA) for the acts of foreign subsidiaries outside the USA where the US parent company has authorised or directed 'corrupt payments' to be made.[134]

While the new Act is a significant step forward, it fails to live up to the promise of its Bill because disgorgement is the normal remedy, meaning

---

132 Zerk (2006), Chapter 3.
133 15 USC 78dd-1.
134 Zerk (2006), p. 108.

that individual victims will not normally benefit from the legislation.[135] This suggests that the profits of redress for corporate malfeasance will accrue to the state rather than individual victims, leaving a huge blank space in which they will have no redress, particularly in tort cases.

Enforcement, as already implied, is in any case extremely complex. The problems are multiple. Extraterritoriality is one problem, but there is genuine difficulty in finding approaches able to hold MNC power effectively to account. Often, for example, reliance is placed, unsuccessfully, upon soft power.[136] In the field of corporate accountability, for example, there is a widespread commitment to voluntarism, reflected in certain codes or principles and in the discourse of CSR, which still offers little in the way of direct enforcement despite its potential future promise for generating more diffuse forms of corporate accountability.[137]

Zerk[138] has documented the range of methods used by society to address the most egregious violations of human rights by MNCs: methods deploying a huge variety of pressure points, including codes, norms, reports, boycotts and internet activism.[139] MNCs themselves, however, are becoming involved in the debate,[140] and opinion on the promise of such initiatives, including scholarly opinion, remains sharply divided. A genuine question concerns the continuing influence of the Anglo–American neo-liberal philosophy, with its rampant individualism

---

[135] Weiss, D.C., 'The Foreign Corrupt Practices Act, SEC Disgorgement of Profits, and the Evolving International Bribery Regime: Weighing Proportionality, Retribution, and Deterrence', (2009) 30 *Michigan Journal of International Law*, p. 471. Available at SSRN: http://ssrn.com/abstract=1319814.

[136] Charlemagne, 'If Obama's America can't make soft power work, what hope does Europe have?' *The Economist*, 11 March 2010.

[137] Although the author has revised her assessment of CSR as a 'moral deflection device' which she wrote in frustration in Dine (2005) (from Pogge's concept), she now believes that the academic and NGO community have made significant inroads on MNCs' violations, and it may be possible to enact a hard law in an international law context; it will however be a slow process, and using national law could be another channel to use (see next section).

[138] See also for example de Jonge, A., *Transnational Corporations and International Law* (Edward Elgar, Cheltenham 2011); Bottomley, S., and D. Kinley (eds), *Commercial Law and Human Rights* (Dartmouth, Aldershot, 2002); Woodroffe, J., 'Regulating Multinational Corporations in a World of Nation States' in M. Addo (1999); Skolgy, S. and M. Gibney, 'Transnational Human Rights Obligations' (2002) *Human Rights Quarterly* 781. See also Dine (2005), especially pp. 3–10.

[139] Zerk (2006), especially pp. 21 and 94–101.

[140] Ibid., especially at p. 99.

and consumerism.[141] As we have seen, the neo-liberal, Chicago economic model values individualism over all ethical principles and rests on rationality, efficiency and information. This theory posits that a person acting rationally will enter a bargain which will be to his or her benefit.[142] The most aggressive version of this model posits that a rational person wants maximisation of her assets.[143] The whole structure of Western society is predicated on this hegemonic value system[144] and all individuals are imbued with some version of the theory. Since companies are manmade they are not immune from the prevailing culture. Because of this, ethical businesses and CSR initiatives are faced with a powerful contraindication. In the light of this, it is unsurprising that Zerk argues that

> it is still extremely difficult to tell how far the core ideals of the CSR communities have become embedded in corporate culture. There is still plenty of scepticism within 'civil society' about the level of commitment of multinationals to self-regulatory schemes and social and environmental reform in general. Some multinationals have seen their environmental initiatives dismissed as 'greenwash', while others have been accused of using CSR-related initiatives as a way of diverting attention away from bad press elsewhere or as a tactical concession to avoid stringent legislation at some later stage.[145]

CSR seems even more limited when placed against the background of the operation of limited liability and the weakness of international legal enforcement mechanisms. (In international trade law, in fact, there are only WTO enforcement mechanisms, widely seen as being counterproductive for the strengthening of labour conditions and for the protection of the

---

[141] UN Development Progress, *Human Development Report 1996* (Oxford University Press, New York 1994); Third World Network, 'A World in Social Crisis: Basic Facts on Poverty, Unemployment and Social Disintegration', *Third World Resurgence* (No. 52) (1994).

[142] Williamson, O.E., 'Contract Analysis: The Transaction Cos Approach' in P. Burrows and C. Velanovski (eds), *The Economic Approach to Law* (Butterworth, London, 1981).

[143] Ayres, I. and J. Braithwaite, *Responsive Regulation* (Oxford University Press, Oxford 1992), p. 23.

[144] Interview by David Hare with Archbishop Dr Rowan Williams (2011): 'no one can any longer regard the free market as a natural beneficent mechanism, and how more sophisticated financial instruments have made it even harder to spot when the market's causing real hurt'.

[145] Zerk (2006), pp. 100–101.

environment.[146]) However, it may just be that the huge CSR effort to counter environmental transgressions by MNCs may be bearing some limited fruit, though the evidence remains difficult to assess. It has been suggested that CSR standards are slowly becoming part of a normal societal understanding, and that CSR norms are becoming harder, a sort of middle way between hard law and 'voluntary' law.[147] Braithwaite and Drahos, for example, argue that 'when many different types of actors use many dialogic mechanisms of this sort, both impressive regime regime-building and impressive compliance have been repeatedly demonstrated'.[148] This kind of accountability is arguably what Ruggie means when he uses a 'social licence'[149] concept for MNC accountability.[150] The search for effective accountability, particularly in the face of the challenges of extraterritoriality, however, goes on.[151] Ruggie's final report,[152] moreover, offers little to overcome the problem. His 'three pillars' (which mirror the 'protect, respect and fulfil' motif of human rights standards with 'protect, respect, remedies'), and his focus on 'operationalizing' seem to produce an unsatisfying lack of effective sanctions or reparations.[153] Paragraph 25 of his report says that '[a]s part of the duty to protect against business-related human rights abuses, States must take appropriate steps to ensure, through judicial, administrative, legislative or other appropriate means, that when such abuses occur within their territory and/or jurisdiction those affected have

---

[146] Revesz, R.L., P. Sands and R.B. Stewart (eds), *Environmental Law, the Economy and Sustainable Development* (Cambridge University Press, Cambridge 2000).

[147] Braithwaite, J. and P. Drahos, *Global Business Regulation* (Cambridge University Press, Cambridge 2000).

[148] Ibid., p. 32.

[149] Human Rights Council, *Report of the Special Representative of the Secretary-General on the issue of Human Rights and Transnational Corporations and other Business Enterprises: Guiding Principles on Business and Human Rights Implementing the UN 'Protect, Respect and Remedy' Framework* (2011).

[150] Zerk (2006), p. 95: CSR norms are usually bottom-up concepts. Slaughter has suggested that international law should be replicated in a similar form including 'reordering [the] relative priority [of] sources of international order'. This will change the way that MNCs are viewed; any reorganisation must start from a perception that they are crucial in an international context. Slaughter, A., 'A Liberal Theory of International Law' (2000) *American Society of International Law Proceeding*, 240.

[151] Zerk (2006). Rehearsing the many initiatives by NGOs, parliamentarians and other groups to get a grip with extraterritoriality issues, see pp. 160–96.

[152] Accessed on 9 August 2011 at www.business-humanrights.org/media/documents/ruggie/ruggie-guiding-principles-21-mar-2011.pdf.

[153] Ibid.

access to effective remedy',[154] while paragraph 26 details the principles of judicial mechanisms. None of this, however, appears to amount to detailed, robust standards for effective MNC accountability, and extraterritoriality remains a stubborn barrier. We have also noticed the disjunction of corporate governance and CSR and the synergies and disparities between the OECD Guidelines for Multinational Enterprises (the Guidelines) 2011[155] and Principles of Corporate Governance 2004.[156]

The relative failure to hold MNCs accountable remains troubling. There are two remaining alternative approaches that this analysis will now consider: the first is based on the concept of universal jurisdiction, and the second, more promising, based on the idea of building a network of national laws enshrining 'enterprise' liability for MNCs. The first alternative is embedding an international law rule which lays down a principle of universal jurisdiction. There is no prospect of this solution ever working, or at least only in the long term. The 'revival' of the Alien Tort Claims Act (ATCA) 1789 as a way of challenging corporate abuses has been claimed as a 'beacon of hope' by human rights activists.[157] Unfortunately, even this beacon of hope has now been extinguished or at least significantly doused. In *Kiobel v Royal Dutch Petroleum*[158] the judges by a majority said that a company could not be a sole defendant in a claim in an ATCA suit. There is still litigation in the US Supreme Court but it is likely that this avenue will be blocked.[159] However a different possibility could be opened if the German Law of Groups and the EU competition rules were to be extended by national legislation (see

---

[154] Ibid., para 25.

[155] Accessed on 22 August 2012 at www.oecd.org/.../0,3746,en_2649_34889_2397532_1_1_1_1,00.htm.

[156] Accessed on 22 August 2012 at www.oecd.org/daf/corporateaffairs/corporategovernanceprinciples/oecdprinciplesofcorporategovernance.htm.

[157] Earthright press release, 29 June 2004.

[158] On 17th April 2013 the US Supreme Court restricted the application of the Alien Tort Claims Act in cases involving allegations of abuse outside the United States. The Court's decision significantly narrows the range of human rights cases that can be brought under the ACTA in US courts based on alleged abuses outside the USA. It requires a closer connection to the United States than many US courts interpreting the ATS have required in the past. However the Court did not address the question of corporate liability under the ATCA, although this had been the original question before the Court when the Court first agreed to hear Kiobel.

[159] Accessed on 30 October 2012 at www.business-humanrights.org/Documents/SupremeCourtATCAReview. The Supreme Court's decision expected in the summer term of 2013.

Chapter 5). Next we need to extend our parameters to consider the consequences of a contractual economic model by considering the consequences of inequality and the democratic deficit.

## Inequality

'The extent of global inequality is breathtaking. The income of the world's 500 richest billionaires exceeds that of its poorest 416 million people.'[160] An increasing chorus of academic literature and evidence from Non-Governmental Organisations (NGOs), the WB, and the United Nations Development Programme (UNDP) shows that inequality is becoming worse and exacerbating a range of problems from health issues (especially mental health) to obesity, life expectancy and happiness.[161] The causes are extremely difficult to pinpoint accurately but so far many believe that at least some of the blame points to the neo-liberal, loosely labelled 'Washington Consensus' and its programme of deregulating the market, privatising public services and cutting the state. This in turn gives private companies, particularly the large MNCs, more power because they have more financial resources and therefore more power than national governments. As early as 2000 the WB's *World Development Reports* were uncompromising. Setting out the numbers for trying to live on less than $2 or $1 dollar a day, one report (2000–2001) notes that

> This destitution persists even though human conditions have improved more in the past century than in the rest of history – global wealth, global connections and technological connections have never been greater. But the distribution of these gains is extraordinarily unequal … And the experience in different parts of the world has been very diverse. In East Asia the number of people living on less than $1 a day fell from around 420 million to around 280 million between 1987 and 1998 – even after the setbacks of the financial crisis. Yet in Latin America, South Asia, and sub-Saharan Africa the numbers of poor people have been rising. And in the countries of Europe and Central Asia in transition to market economies, the number of people living on less than $1 rose more than twentyfold.[162]

---

[160] UNDP *Human Development report*, 2005 and 2006, accessed on 25 October 2012 at http://econ.worldbank.org/external/default/main?pagePK=64165259&theSitePK=478060&piPK=64165421&menuPK=64166093&entityID=000112742_20050920110826.

[161] Wilkinson and Pickett (2009 and 2010); UNDP *Human Development Reports*, 2005–2011; Green (2008); Stiglitz (2012); Mount, F., *Mind the Gap* (Short books, London 2004 and revised edition 2012).

[162] WB, *Development Report 2000–2001* (Oxford University Press, Oxford 2001), p. 3. See also Hertz (2001), pp. 40–1.

And, as we have already seen, some scholars argue that these figures underestimate the problem.[163] Similar conclusions about growing inequality were reached by the International Labour Organization (ILO) in its 2004 report *A Fair Globalisation*;[164] while recognising that globalisation has great potential for good,

> we also see how far short we still are from reaching this potential. The current process of globalisation is generating unbalanced outcomes, both between and within countries. Wealth is being created but too many countries and people are not sharing in its benefits … Many of them live in the limbo of the informal economy without formal rights and in a swathe of poor countries that subsist precariously on the margins of the global economy. Even in economically successful countries some workers and communities have been adversely affected by globalization. Meanwhile the revolution in global communications heightens awareness of these disparities.[165]

Transnational companies (TNCs) are the driving force behind globalisation. Through their production, trade and investment activities, they are integrating countries into a global market. Through their control over resources, access to markets, and development of new technologies, TNCs have the potential to generate enormous benefits for poverty reduction. However, that potential is being lost. The weakness of international rules, bad policies and weak governance in developing countries, and corporate practices which prioritise short-term profit over long-term human development are undermining the capacity of poor countries – and poor people – to benefit from international trade.[166]

The immense power of corporations is indicated by a comparison between the economic wealth generated by corporations, measured by sales, compared with a country's Gross Domestic Product (GDP). On this basis 'the combined revenues of just General Motors and Ford … exceed the combined GDP for all of sub-Saharan Africa'[167] and 51 of the largest

---

[163] Reddy, S. and T. Pogge, 'How not to Count the Poor', accessed on 21 December 2012 at www.socialanalysis.org.

[164] ILO, *A Fair Globalisation* (Geneva, 2004).

[165] Ibid.

[166] Oxfam Report, *Rigged Rules and Double Standards* (Oxfam 2002), p. 175. Accessed on 16 April 2013 at http://policy-practice.oxfam.org.uk/publications/rigged-rules-and-double-standards-trade-globalisation-and-the-fight-against-pov-112391.

[167] Karliner (1997); Fortune Global 500: The World's Largest Corporations (7 August 1995); WB, *World Development Report 2000–2001* (2001).

100 economies are corporations.[168] Further, the number of transnational corporations jumped from 7,000 in 1970 to 40,000 in 1998, and they account for most of the world's trade. They also stand accused of creating the current trade rules by their influence on government. Drahos and Braithwaite note that US trade representatives ask the large corporations what they want from a trade negotiation and then negotiate accordingly.[169]

> These corporations and their 250,000 foreign affiliates account for most of the world's industrial capacity, technological knowledge and international financial transactions. They mine, refine and distribute most of the world's oil, gasoline, diesel and jet fuel. They build most of the world's oil, coal, gas, hydroelectric and nuclear power plants. They extract most of the world's minerals from the ground. They manufacture and sell most of the world's automobiles, airplanes, communications satellites, computers, home electronics, chemicals, medicines and biotechnology products. They harvest much of the world's wood and make most of its paper. They grow many of the world's agricultural crops, while processing and distributing much of its food. All told, the Transnationals hold 90% of all technology and product patents worldwide and are involved in 70% of world trade.[170]

Anna Grear also charts the recent changes of globalisation, including the opening of electronic communications, transport links, influential brands and scientific advances, and realises that the picture is one of transformation because of the power of transnational corporations. She believes that mega-banks are clearly crucial in the world economy, and the financial crash of 2008 (and continuing instability) has been a central pillar of the problems, saying that 'there are reasons to suspect that the current crisis is not so much a crisis *of* neoliberalism but a crisis *within* neoliberalism concerning the best way to retain and protect of its fundamental tenets, structures and institutions'.[171]

---

[168] Anderson, S. and J. Cavanaugh, *The Rise of Global Corporate Power* (Institute for Policy Studies, Washington DC, 1996).

[169] Braithwaite and Drahos (2000).

[170] Karliner (1997), p. 5; UNCTAD, *World Investment Report 1995: Transnational Corporations and Competitiveness* (United Nations Conference on Trade and Development, Division on Transnational Corporations and Investment: New York 1995), pp xix–xx.

[171] Grear, A., *Redirecting Human Rights* (Palgrave Macmillan, Basingstoke 2010), p. 9.

Along with other commentators,[172] Grear argues that the financial crisis has crystallised further a situation which is 'socialised' by a strategy in which the private risk of the owners of capital are underwritten by the state, the losses of corporations and banks are mitigated by the ordinary tax-payer and are 'left holding future debts that in effect, simply pass the impact of the crisis to ordinary citizens'.[173] Originally MNCs made products but as Stiglitz has shown us, the next wave of consolidation was by the financial sector led by the IMF and the WB. The first attack was in the developing countries, but now even the developed states fear the market and in those countries politicians are only puppets. The Eurozone has been particularly damaged, with Greece, Spain, Italy and Cyprus especially affected.

## The Financial Crisis 2008 – Risk-free Banking, Neo-liberal Policies and National Strategies

Till the 2008 financial crash it was a strange aspect of the 'globalisation debate' that MNCs were in the forefront of the debate and that the biggest banks were able to escape scrutiny. Originally attention focused on companies which produced tangible items bought by consumers. Activists focused on the wage conditions of employees, the violation of human rights or the pollution of the environment. This meant that there was an extra veil of invisibility over the operations of giant banks. Even though by 2003 the total assets of the top five banks were estimated at US$4,807,294 million,[174] their activities were frequently left off the globalisation agenda. This changed radically in 2008 when the financial crash came, and the numbers look very different now.[175] However, there has not been a rigorous global reinvention of financial regulations and the IMF certainly has not changed its structural adjustment programmes; rather, in Europe it is merely supported by other institutions like the

---

[172] Ha-Joon Chang, 'We must stop protecting the rich from market forces', *The Guardian*, 25 October 2012: 'Gore Vidal … famously quipped that the US economic system is "free enterprise for the poor and socialism for the rich"', and see Ha-Joon Chang, *23 Things They Don't Tell About Capitalism* (Penguin, Allan Lane, London 2010).

[173] Grear (2010), p. 9 and see also Beck (2005).

[174] Figures issued by Bank of America and reported in *The Guardian*, 28 October 2003.

[175] Accessed on 11 October 2012 at www.federalreserve.gov/econresdata/statisticsdata.htm.

European Central Bank and the European Commission (the Troika).[176] There is no doubt that the way in which the global financial architecture has managed financial matters in a number of recent crises (including the ongoing crisis in the Eurozone) has given rise to unprecedented opportunities for banks to make huge profits while running virtually no risks. This is in part because of the response that the IMF has made to those crises. Underhill and Zhang see the rise of multinationals as a threat to domestic political legitimacy by weakening states' authority over macroeconomics and social policy, and by being significant in the formulation of national economic policy: 'integration with global financial structures has strengthened the position of private market actors over public authority. Powerful private actors come to dominate the formulation of national economic policies which, in their attempts to extract benefits from global integration, tend increasingly to serve the interests of market agents'.[177] (See more on this in the next section of this chapter.)

However, the IMF has largely (and rightly) been vilified for the conditionality policies which it pursues, demanding severe cutbacks in social services in return for its loans,[178] rather than the financial policies which it has pursued. Recently, however, the financial policies behind its activities have been questioned, as well as the effect that its structural adjustment policies and their successors have had on the poorest within creditor nations. Stiglitz writes:

> The IMF is pursuing not just the objectives set out in its original mandate of enhancing global stability and ensuring that there are funds for countries facing a threat of recession to pursue expansionary policies. It is also pursuing the interests of the financial community … Simplistic free market ideology provided the curtain behind which the real business of the 'new' mandate could be transacted. The change in mandate and objectives, while it may have been quiet, was hardly subtle: from serving global *economic* interests to serving the interests of global *finance*.[179] Capital market liberalisation may

---

[176] Accessed on 11 October 2012 at www.ekathimerini.com/4dcgi/_w_articles_wsite2_1_11/10/2012_465595.

[177] Underhill, G., and Zhang, X., 'Global Structures and Political Imperatives; in search of normative underpinnings for international financial order' in Underhill and Zhang (eds), *International Financial Governance under Stress: Global Structures versus National Imperatives* (Cambridge University Press, Cambridge 2003), p. 78.

[178] See Dine (2005), Chapter 3.

[179] Italics in original.

> not have contributed to global economic stability, but it did open up vast new markets for Wall Street.[180]

This reassessment of the IMF turns partly on the 'bail out' policies it has pursued. The allegation is that loans to risky areas are encouraged and underpriced because it is known that the IMF will support the country's currency when a crisis threatens (see below). Eichengreen and Ruhl describe the 'moral hazard' thus:

> Investors, it is argued, have been able to escape the financial costs of crises through the extension of international rescue loans. These 'bailouts' (as they are described by their critics) give governments the funds they require to pay off their creditors, who are then able to exit the country free of losses. Not being subject to the cost of crises, investors disregard the risks of lending, and the consequent lack of market discipline allows feckless governments to set themselves up for a painful fall.[181]

The allegation that the IMF is in the service of international finance essentially flows from the insistence by the IMF on liberalisation, in particular capital account liberalisation. The intended result of this is to permit capital flows to take place freely across the world. However, while this may be good for the financial community, it is not necessarily good for developing countries. '[T]he cocktail of free capital flows, floating exchange rates, domestic financial liberalisation in G3 countries, and unregulated innovations in financial instruments and institutions such as derivatives and hedge funds has dramatically increased financial instability after the collapse of the Gold-Dollar standard.'[182] The instability is a result of a system of liberalisation based on neo-classical assumptions, including perfect information flows.

> If one asks which of the neo-classical assumptions fail in a way that permits [financial] crises to develop, it is the information structure on the basis of which lending decisions are made. Rather than each investor deciding individually his or her expectations on the basis of their estimate of the

---

[180] Stiglitz, *Globalisation and its Discontents* (Allen Lane, London 2002), pp. 206–7.

[181] Eichengreen, B. and C. Ruhl, 'The Bail-in Problem: Systematic goals, Ad Hoc Means', http:://emlab.berkeley.edu/users/eichengr/.

[182] Taylor, L. and J. Eatwell, *Global Finance at Risk* (The New Press, New York 2000), cited in Oxfam, *Global Finance* (2001), p. 26.

> fundamentals, investors make their decisions on the basis of what others are expected to do, resulting in herd behaviour.[183]

This assessment is based on Keynes' beauty contest analysis, referring to a game in the UK tabloid press in the 1930s in which readers were asked to assess from pictures which women would be judged as the most beautiful by the entire readership:

> in other words, readers would not win by giving their own opinion about the women's beauty, not even by assessing what others' personal opinions would be, but by guessing what people would, on average, believe average opinion to be. In financial markets, a trader will not bid a price according to what he or she believes an asset's fundamental value to be, but according to what he or she assesses average opinion to be about average opinion of the asset's value. The beauty contest analogy helps understand why market participants tend to engage in 'momentous trading' (i.e. herd behaviour) and why market valuations are subject to sudden shifts in 'market sentiment'.[184]

Underhill and Zhang point out that 'more than seventy financial and monetary crises of different proportions and characteristics have occurred in both developed and developing countries over the past two decades'.[185] They see as

> a common background to these developments … the intensifying process of global financial liberalisation and integration … As financial crises have become more frequent and more severe over the past two decades, this has raised the question of whether the growing frequency and severity of crises correlate with the emergence of this liberal and transnational financial order.[186]

While domestic policies have a large part to play in countries' financial crises, many studies now show that two other factors have great significance. One is the role of speculators and the second is '"crony capitalism" at the global level, in the form of IMF bailing out Wall Street'.[187] Opportunities for speculators increase every time markets are opened, as do opportunities for the most powerful multinational banks. The role of the bail out mechanism is discussed below. Following the Asian crisis of

---

183 Williamson, J., 'Costs and Benefits of Financial Globalisation' in Underhill and Zhang (2003), p. 44.

184 Oxfam, *Global Finance* (2001), p. 26.

185 Underhill and Zhang (2003), p. 1.

186 Ibid.

187 Oxfam, *Global Finance* (2001), p. 28.

1997–8, a flurry of reports sought to identify the root causes.[188] Story identifies two distinct interpretations; an internalist explanation which sought to blame the governments suffering the crises, and an externalist argument focused on the international financial markets.[189] It is important to be aware of the possibility of 'explanatory nationalism' leading the international financial institutions (IFIs) to the most convenient explanation, exonerating them from blame. A classic proponent is Moore: 'most of the responsibility for these [Asia 1997, Argentina 2002] collapses lies with domestic policy-makers, of course', despite in the same paragraph admitting that the very magnitude of money flows create forces so great that 'they are difficult for all but the most powerful nations to resist'.[190]

The 'internalist' explanation of the Asian crisis sees the cause of the collapse thus:

> as lying in the close connections established within the states between politics and bank-centred financial systems. The states provided implicit guarantees to banks, encouraging the banks to lend to corporations with good political contacts. As capital controls were eased, foreign creditors lent to the banks and credit exploded despite multiple warning signals ahead of June 1997. Externally, the inflow of capital to the East Asian countries was stimulated by the near zero interest rates prevailing in a moribund Japan, and by continued investor pessimism about business prospects in Europe. Consumption and imports boomed, just as volume export growths plummeted. With China's accelerated move into world markets, foreign investors switched their attention to opportunities on the mainland, so that East Asian balance of payments' dependence on short-term capital flows increased. When the Thai 'wake-up call' came, alerted investors withdrew in haste from one currency after another.[191]

---

[188] IMF, *International Capital Markets* (IMF, Washington DC 1998); *World Economic Outlook*, (IMF, Washington 1998); Group of 7, *Declaration of G-7 Finance Ministers and Central Bank Governors* (G7, Washington 1998), www.imf.org/external/np/g7/103098dc.htm; Group of 22, *Report of the Working Group on International Financial Crises* (G-22, Washington 1998); *Report of the Working Group on Transparency and Accountability* (G-22, Washington 1998); United Nations Executive Committee on Economic and Social Affairs, *Towards a New International Financial Architecture* (Economic Commission for Latin America and the Caribbean, Santiago 1999).

[189] Story, J., 'Reform: What has been Written?' in Underhill and Zhang (2003), p. 27.

[190] Moore (2002), p. 32.

[191] Story (2003), p. 27.

The externalist explanation focused more sharply on the instability inherent in liberalisation followed by 'herd behaviour'.[192]

Recent crises have involved twin banking and financial crises.[193]

> They were initially attributed to poor financial regulation and supervision as well as poor monetary policy, thereby putting the blame back on national governments and their 'crony capitalist' clientele … It is now recognised that third generation crises are more complex, and may also include multiple equilibria effects, originate from abroad due to contagion effects or involve 'crony capitalism' at the global level, in the form of IMF bailing out Wall Street.[194]

Analysing the East Asia crisis, Stiglitz writes:

> in retrospect, it became clear that the IMF policies not only exacerbated the downturns but were partially responsible for the onset: excessively rapid financial and capital market liberalisation was probably the single most important cause of the crisis, though mistaken policies on the part of the countries themselves played a role as well.[195]

The most significant of those policies is the liberalisation of capital flows. The Eurozone crisis has followed the same path as the developing countries, including the structural adjustments of government policies. The Greek bail out cost £23 billion, and the conditionality conditions were protracted and bitter with tough budget cuts. However,

> Despite the bailout, the ongoing fragility of the Greek economy was underlined by the latest unemployment statistics, which showed the country's jobless rate jumped to a record 20.7pc in the fourth quarter of 2011. Young people have been worst affected, with almost four in ten people aged between 15 and 29 out of work, up from 28pc a year earlier. The Spanish economy is also struggling. House prices in the country fell by 11.2pc in the final three months of last year, compared with the same period a year earlier. It was the fastest pace of decline since 2007 when the National Statistical Institute's series began, and left prices around 22pc lower than their pre-crisis peak.[196]

---

[192] Soros, G., *The Crisis of Global Capitalism: Open Society Endangered*, (Public Affairs, New York 1998).

[193] Sharma, S., *The Asian Financial Crisis* (Manchester University Press, Manchester 2003).

[194] Oxfam, *Global Finance* (2001), p. 28.

[195] Stiglitz (2002), p. 91.

[196] Monaghn, A., 'IMF gives formal approval for Greek Bailout', *The Daily Telegraph*, 15 March 2012.

Loans from either the IMF or World Bank come not only at a financial price, but at the cost of agreement to 'structural reforms'. While the IMF denies absolutely that it has any role in political matters, many have argued the contrary case. Stiglitz puts the matter succinctly: 'The IMF took rather an imperialistic view … since almost any structural issue could affect the overall performance of the economy, and hence the government's budget or the trade deficit, it viewed almost everything as falling within its domain.'[197] There is now a significant democratic deficient in Europe.

> The sheer reality of global corporate dominance has produced a situation in which human rights discourse struggles to retain critical distance from the human rights-colonising activities of formations of global capital … Quite simply, it is essential not to underestimate the influence of [Transnational Companies] TNCs in the current world order.[198]

Since the foundation of the human rights movement was the attempt to free people from the dominance of the state, human rights discourse is struggling with the new dominance of TNCs which are supreme in world politics and economic influence.[199] This persuades some scholars that the human rights movements are being captured by international capital or are at least complicit with it, particularly in increasing inequality.[200]

We will see some national corporate governance solutions in other chapters which could lessen the impact of financial crisis by short-term strategies in companies including twin boards, employee participation and quotas of non-executive directors. Policy-makers should study these solutions carefully and simultaneously make sure that these solutions fit in the national psyche. The solutions will not be found only in corporate governance but also in tightening the ethical standards of lawyers and accountants.

---

[197] Stiglitz (2002), p. 96.

[198] Grear (2010), p. 9.

[199] Beck (2005); Korten (1995), p. 3.

[200] Douzinas, C., *Human Rights and Empire: The Political Philosophy of Cosmopolitanism* (Routledge-Cavendish, Abingdon 2007); Evans, T., and A.J. Ayers, 'In the Service of Power; The Global Political Economy of Citizenship and Human Rights' (2006) 10 *Citizenship Studies* 239.

## DEMOCRATISING AND DE-DEMOCRATISING

Now we have seen how the neo-liberal theories of free markets, privatisation and a small state have been constructed, we need to consider the implications for states, their governments, their populations and democracy. Beck argues:

> We are witnessing one of the most important changes there has been in the history of power. Globalisation needs to be decoded as a creeping, post-revolution, epochal transformation of the national and international state-dominated system governing the balance of power and the rules of power. A *meta-power game* is in progress in the relationship between global businesses and the state, a power struggle in which the balance of power and the rules of power governing the national and international systems of states are being radically changed and rewritten.[201]

Of course the new power in the game is wielded by the enormous companies, especially the financial mega-banks, hedge funds and other speculators. It is not only the state that has been hollowed out; governments and political parties have also been affected. Beck argues that the neo-liberals have hijacked the arguments:

> This is why national governments and political parties are so bland because the neo-liberal agenda are seduced by the neo-liberal concepts. The global economic aims and principles of neo-liberalism breaks through national specificities and borders from the inside and accelerate processes of reform aimed at opening up the national to interdependencies.[202]

In particular, such views lead to the undermining of the state as a responsible entity, the purpose of which is to represent a collective morality and achieve a fair distribution of goods. It also inevitably points to the individual as providing the salvation for all, most importantly through the use of property transactions. The consumer as saviour is a direct descendant of these ideas. Globalisation is thus both driven by philosophies of open markets and fuelled by the consumerist, individual culture which operates at citizen level. Thus the citizen becomes a consumer with considerable impact on our understanding of democracy. If the state exists merely to mend 'market failure' so that the invisible hand of the market can create paradise for all, what use is a vote at nation state level? Further, if the 'market' can manipulate politicians in the

---

[201] Beck (2005), p. 52.
[202] Ibid., p. 79.

shape of threats and bribes from powerful companies, where is the citizen to exercise any influence?

Many contend that for a variety of reasons, democracy needs to mean more than churning almost identical politicians every few years.[203] The ability of such politicians to represent a wide range of possibilities has been severely eroded by a number of factors, some stemming from the 'willing capture' of the state,[204] others from globalisation[205] and the ability of MNCs to evade and supersede state regulation.[206] These twin forces mean that the state is 'on the side' of the multinationals and, if state authorities deviate from subservience to corporate interests they are able to evade regulation[207] or leave. One of the consequences of the overwhelming consensus about the 'proper' economic path to success (the Washington Consensus) has been the 'dumbing down' of politics to a narrow centrist band which is obsequious to 'the market' and consequently to large market players, most notably transnational corporations. This has led not only to the 'market state'[208] but also to the fragmentation of power away from the traditional monolithic state structures. It has also led to the blurring of the boundaries between public and private realms, including public and private law.[209] Regional and international agreements have also achieved fragmentation.[210] This has

---

[203] Teubner argues that merely elevating actors such as MNEs into traditional governance is flawed as the designers 'cannot free themselves of the fascination of nation-state architecture'; 'Societal Constitutionalism: Alternatives to State-centred Constitutional Theory', *Stoors Lectures* (Yale Law School, 2003/4), p. 54.

[204] Dine (2005).

[205] Ochoa, C., 'The Relationship of Participatory Democracy to Participatory Law Formation' (2008) *Indiana Legal Studies* research paper No. 101, January; (2008) 15 *Indiana Journal of Global Legal Studies* 1. Available at SSRN: http://ssrn.com/abstract=1085355 or http://dx.doi.org/10.2139/ssrn.1085355, accessed on 16 April 2013; Stiglitz (2012), p. 118 et seq.

[206] Beck (2005), p. 52.

[207] Just one example is the extensive use of offshore tax havens; Alldridge, P. and A. Mumford, 'Tax Evasion and the Proceeds of Crime Act 2002' (2005) 25 *Legal Studies* 253.

[208] Archbishop Dr Rowan Williams's phrase in *The Guardian*, 27 February 2003.

[209] Teubner argues that private law has become simply 'juridification of economic action': 'The public/private dichotomy: After the critique?', paper given at the European University Institute seminar 'Governance, Civil Society and Social Movements', 30 June 2007.

[210] Bernard, N., *Multilevel Governance in the European Union* (Kluwer, Dordrecht, Netherlands 2000). Joerges, C., 'Integration through de-legalisation?

made governance structures more complex and less responsive to democratic pressure. Power has become multicentric rather than monolithic.[211] Beck believes that 'Globalisation … has introduced a new space and framework for acting: politics is no longer subject to the same boundaries as before'.[212] For him, the pieces of the jigsaw of global politics have been rearranged partly by MNCs.[213]

> The world to-day behaves like a madhouse. The worst of it is that the values we had more or less defined, taught, learned, are thought of as archaic as well as ridiculous. Respect for the world: who is that important to? The human being should be the absolute priority. And it isn't. It's becoming less and less so. It seems that it's more important to reach Mars than prevent 13 million Africans dying of hunger. Why would I want to know if there's water on Mars if we're polluting the water here on Earth, doing nothing to avoid it? Priorities need to be redefined, but there's no chance of redefining those priorities if we didn't confront the need to know what democracy is. We live in a very peculiar world. Democracy isn't discussed, as if democracy had taken God's place, who is also not discussed.[214]

Perhaps the discussion should begin with the understanding that markets are not all-powerful.

Charles Tilly rejects the argument that it is possible to identify a 'borderline' between democracy and non-democracy by an assessment of chosen factors such as those identified by Freedom House.[215] Instead, Tilly focuses his definition on state–citizen relations and argues that democracy is always in a state of dynamic movement with constant pressures towards democratisation and de-democratisation.[216] 'Democratization means net movement towards broader, more equal, more protected and more binding consultation. De-democratization, obviously, then means net movement towards narrower, more unequal, less protected, and less binding consultation.'[217] In seeking to uncover the causes of movement in either direction, he argues that there is a crucial

---

An irritated heckler', paper given at the European University Institute seminar 'Governance, Civil Society and Social Movements', 30 June 2007.

[211] Aarte-Schole, J., 'Reconstructing Contemporary Democracy' (2007) 15 *Indiana Journal of Global Legal Studies* xxx, accessed on 16 April 2013 at http://myuminfo.umanitoba.ca/Documents/1470/ScholteJABGD.pdf.

[212] Beck (2005), p. 3.

[213] Ibid., pp. 52–3.

[214] Saramago, J., *The Guardian*, 28 December 2002.

[215] Accessed on 8 August 2007 at www.freedomhouse.org.

[216] Tilly, C., *Democracy* (Cambridge University Press, Cambridge 2007).

[217] Ibid., p. 14.

difference between *capacity* of states and the health of their democracy. Here, capacity relates to states' ability to implement their policies: '*State capacity* means *the extent to which interventions of state agents in existing non-state resources, activities, and interpersonal connections alter existing distributions of those resources, activities and interpersonal connections as well as relations among those distributions*.'[218] Democratisation depends on a complex interaction between the democracy in the sense of broader, more equal, more protected and more binding consultation and capacity to deliver. Tilly's central tenet is that democracy cannot be measured in the traditional ways which employ '*idealist, structuralist* or *instrumentalist* approaches'.[219] These, he explains, as

> democracy as an idea that someone (the Greeks?)[220] invented, starting a centuries-long effort to implement the idea. We might take the opposite tack, arguing that only the conditions of industrial capitalism could support broad, equal, protective, and mutually binding political relations between states and citizens. We might also think that competing models of government, once familiar to national elites, attracted different sorts of ruling classes, and that some of those chose dictatorship and others democracy.[221]

Rather, Tilly argues that attention should be paid to *processes* to identify the movement towards or away from democracy. The processes he identifies are 'increasing integration of trust networks into public politics, increasing insulation of public politics from categorical inequality and decreasing autonomy of major power centres from public politics'.[222] The first of these and its relationship with his definition of democracy is encapsulated by the following:

> of breadth, equality, mutually binding consultation and protection, integration of trust networks into public politics most directly affects mutually binding consultation. To the extent that people integrate their trust networks into public politics, they come to rely on governmental performance for maintenance of those networks. They also gain power, individual and collective, through the connections to government that those networks mediate. They acquire an unbreakable interest in governmental performance. The political stakes matter. Paying taxes, buying governmental securities, yielding private information to officials, depending on government for benefits, and releasing

---

218 Ibid., p. 16. Italics in original.

219 Ibid., p. 48. Italics in original.

220 Although he points out that the Greeks were slave-owners and excluded women from politics so the breadth of participation is extremely suspect.

221 Tilly (2007), p. 49.

222 Ibid., p. 50.

network members for military service cement that interest and promote active bargaining over the terms of its fulfilment.[223]

Trust networks 'contain *ramified interpersonal connections, consisting mainly of strong ties, within which people set valued, consequential, long-term resources and enterprises at risk to the malfeasance, mistakes, or failures of others*'.[224]

It is clear that the trust between citizens in Greece, Spain and the UK and their governments has recently been strained.[225] However even before the financial crisis, inequality, particularly in the US and the UK, has damaged democracy. Tilly argues that it is possible to have significant inequality and rely on political magic tricks to isolate political decision-making from that inequality by mechanisms which do not reflect those inequalities in formal arena. We have argued elsewhere that this is only true to a very limited extent. Those who are starving do not vote and even marginalisation can breed despair as having any influence. Where there is a dominant actor, such as the financial sector, governments are subordinated and unable to help its citizens. This is particularly cogent for the inequality debate. Inequality fuels de-democratising forces, the poor often do not vote but society can be split by divisions between classes, a new apartheid. Both Ehrenreich and Toynbee vividly portray the 'invisibility' factor as part of the experience of poverty due to low pay in the US and UK respectively.[226] Fallows notes the lack of shared spaces and services. In the US,

> [a]s public schools and other public services deteriorate, those who can afford to do so send their children to private schools and spend their off-hours in private spaces – health clubs, for example, instead of the local park. They don't ride on public buses and subways. They withdraw from mixed neighbourhoods into distant suburbs, gated communities or guarded apartment

223 Ibid., p. 95.

224 Ibid., p. 81. Italics in original.

225 Bawdon, F., 'Verdict on UK Riot; people need a "state in society", says report', *The Guardian*, 28 March 2012, at www.guardian.co.uk/uk/2012/mar/28/verdict-uk-riots-stake-society; 'Antonis Samaras, says Greece's democracy is in danger', at www.guardian.co.uk/world/greece; Tremlett, G., 'Spain reels at violent tactics by riot police', *The Guardian*, 29 September 2012, at www.guardian.co.uk/world/2012/sep/29/spain-riot-police. All accessed on 11 October 2012.

226 Ehrenreich (2002). Toynbee (2003) and see Grear (2010), p. 174.

> towers; they shop in stores that, in line with prevailing 'market segmentation' are designed to appeal to the affluent alone.[227]

Toynbee writes:

> London was a sadder, duller, more impoverished place ... Wherever I walked, everything I passed was out of bounds, things belonging to other people but not to me ... This is what 'exclusion' means, if you have ever wondered at this modern wider definition of poverty. It is a large No Entry sign on every ordinary pleasure.[228]

This polarisation of society is neatly summed up in Klein's metaphor of *Fences and Windows* to describe the separation of the haves and have-nots (Fences) and the opportunities for hope (Windows).[229]

Such exclusion does not readily lead to political participation. Tilly apparently discounts the effects of the way in which inequality and discrimination are built into political systems in an institutional way, an issue discussed below in relation to institutional racism and corruption. One process identified by Tilly is the antithesis to the inequality issue. That is the way that a process decreases the autonomy of major power centres from public politics. A revealing part of the discussion of this issue comes when Tilly deals with the de-democratisation of Russia by President Vladimir Putin: 'Yet in one regard Putin may surprisingly have been promoting longer-term changes that will eventually facilitate Russian democratization. Although he was permitting Russian military dangerously broad autonomy in the Caucasus, he was also subordinating capitalists who had acquired extraordinary independence from state control.'[230] Here Tilly has missed the point and appears to be operating in a pre-transnational corporate world. Corporations not only *Rule the World*[231] but they have bought the politicians, if not with money then with economic argument and sheer economic power. The result of this is to corrupt the whole system. So democratisation can only happen by

---

[227] Ehrenreich (2002), p. 216, citing J. Fallows, 'The Invisible Poor', *New York Times*, 19 March 2000.

[228] Toynbee (2003), p. 239.

[229] Klein (2002). Klein argues that global society has created many fences; 'barriers separating people from previously public resources' (p. xviii), both physical barriers and virtual ones such as education being restricted by the charging of fees. Windows are signs of hope of breaking down barriers such as the World Social Forum and reclaiming public spaces.

[230] Tilly (2007) p. 137.

[231] Korten (1995). Pilger, J., *The New Rulers of the World* (Verso, London 2002).

decreasing the autonomous power of corporations while finding an alternative approach to the current economic system. A new economic system which decreases the reach of corporate power and its elites can only be achieved by popular pressure. It is therefore arguable that the US, UK and Europe have significantly de-democratised in recent years because of increasing inequality and because of the 'willing capture' by companies of the 'market state' giving significant autonomous power to corporations.

The second process identified by Tilly as an indicator of democratisation is equality: 'Democracy works better, and democratization is more likely to occur, when political processes reduce translation of everyday categorical inequalities into public politics'.[232] Thus the argument is not that democracy cannot exist where there is significant inequalities but that these must not appear in the political arena. By categorical inequalities Tilly means 'organized differences in advantages by gender, race, nationality, ethnicity, religion, community and similar categories ... Democracy thrives on a lack of correspondence between the inequalities of everyday life and those of state-citizen relations'.[233] 'Any substantial increase in categorical inequality also affects democracy's prospects. Any substantial increase in categorical inequality that occurs without some compensating adjustment in public politics poses a serious threat to existing democratic regimes.'[234]

> Increasing categorical inequality threatens democracy because it gives members of advantaged categories means and incentives to:
>
> * Opt out of democratic bargains
> * Create beneficial relations with state agents
> * Shield themselves from onerous political obligations
> * Use their state access to extract more advantages from unequal relations with non-state actors
> * Use their influence over the state for further exploitation or exclusion of subordinate categories, and thus
> * Move their regimes even further away from broad, equal, protected, mutually binding consultation.[235]

Here the corporate governance is key, company law, social movements, human rights activism and corporate social responsibility must go hand

232 Tilly (2007), p. 111.
233 Ibid., pp. 111 and 118.
234 Ibid.
235 Ibid., p. 137.

in hand with democracy and the arbitrary distinction between corporate governance and CSR should be demolished. This is particularly crucial because of the growing danger for the environment. The EU Acquis Communautaire should truly be a binding commitment to democracy, not an administration of the elites. Consensus politics as found in Germany could allow more participation in government and corporate governance.

## THE ENVIRONMENT AND CORPORATE GOVERNANCE

For some time there has been a problem of pollution from companies because they are not internalising their waste and costs. There is also no doubt that there has been a significant export of 'dirty' industries and pollution from the activities of mining and manufacturing operations masterminded by TNCs across the world.

> One of the keys to understanding the global problem of waste and pollution, is that much of its incidence in the developing world is due to developed nations' illegal shipment of their own waste to these regions … trucks entering Eastern Europe [from Germany] export hundreds of thousands of tons of waste that Westerners find too expensive or too inconvenient to dispose of themselves. The pressure is mostly financial. Under US and European environmental laws today, the cost of disposing of hazardous industrial and mining waste can be as high as several thousand dollars per ton … Shipping such materials abroad is often much cheaper.[236]

The exporting nations can pose as environmentally aware:

> Japan has reduced its aluminium smelting capacity from 1.2 million tons to 149,000 tons and now imports 90% of its aluminium. What this involves in human terms is suggested by a case study of the Philippine Associated Smelting and Refining Corporation (PASAR). PASAR operates a Japanese-financed and constructed copper smelting plant in the Philippine province of Leyte to produce high grade copper cathodes for shipment to Japan. The plant occupies 400 acres of land expropriated by the Philippine Government from local residents at give-away prices. Gas and waste water emissions from the plant contain high concentrations of boron, arsenic, heavy metals, and sulfur compounds that have contaminated local water supplies, reduced fishing and rice yields, damaged the forests, and increased the occurrence of upper respiratory diseases among local residents. Local people whose homes,

---

[236] Czinkota, M., I. Ronksinen and M. Moffett, *International Business*, 4th edn (Dryden, Fort Worth 1996).

> livelihoods and health have been sacrificed to PASAR are now largely dependent on the occasional part-time or contractual employment they are offered to do the plant's most dangerous and dirtiest jobs.[237]

David Leigh has written on the Trafigura disaster where a ship unloaded cargo in the Ivory Coast in 2006. The ship was loaded with toxic chemicals from Europe. 'The UN human rights special rapporteur, Professor Okechukwu Ibeanu, wrote: "According to official estimates, there were 15 deaths, 69 persons hospitalised and more than 108,000 medical consultations ... there seems to be strong prima facie evidence that the reported deaths and adverse health consequences are related to the dumping".'[238] According to Leigh, 'The documents reveal that the London-based traders hoped to make profits of $7m a time by buying up what they called "bloody cheap" cargoes of sulphur-contaminated Mexican gasoline. They decided to try to process the fuel on board a tanker anchored offshore, creating toxic waste they called "slops"'.[239] A number of company internal emails were found:

> One trader wrote on 10 March 2006: 'I don't know how we dispose of the slops and I don't imply we would dump them, but for sure, there must be some way to pay someone to take them.' The resulting black, stinking, slurry was eventually dumped around landfills in Abidjan, after Trafigura paid an unqualified local man to take it away in tanker trucks at a cheap rate.[240]

Recently there has been disquiet with 'fracking'.[241] There are many reports of environmental violations perpetrated by large companies.[242] Simultaneously the amount of extraction of minerals and other materials from the ground rises exponentially. On the eve of India's independence,

---

[237] Korten (1995).

[238] Leigh, D., 'How UK oil company Trafigura tried to cover up African pollution disaster', *The Guardian*, 16 September 2009, accessed on 17 October 2012 at www.guardian.co.uk/world/2009/sep/16/trafigura-african-pollution-disaster.

[239] Ibid.

[240] Ibid.

[241] http://quitcoal.org/natural-gas-hydraulic-fracking, accessed on 16 October 2012: 'Hydraulic fracture methods ("fracking") are associated with a range of environmental impacts, some of which are not fully understood. It's possible that the carbon footprint of shale gas may be significantly greater than for conventional gas.'

[242] See Oxfam, *Global Finance Hurts the Poor* (Oxfam America, Boston 2002), especially p. 46; also, Oxfam, *Oil, Gas and Mining*: *Poor Communities Pay the Price* (Oxfam America, Boston 2001).

Mahatma Gandhi was asked whether he thought the country could follow the British model of industrial development. His response retains a powerful resonance in a world that has to redefine its relation to the earth's ecology: 'It took Britain half the resources of this planet to achieve its prosperity. How many planets will India require for development?' We ask the same question for a world edging towards the brink of dangerous climate change.

## Climate Change

'There is "a looming environmental crisis, which poses a threat to the basic of our very existence.'[243] The Intergovernmental Panel on Climate Change (IPCC) believes:

> There is *high confidence* that neither adaptation nor mitigation alone can avoid all climate change impacts … Unmitigated climate change would, in the long term, be *likely* to exceed the capacity of natural, managed and human systems to adapt. Reliance on adaptation alone could eventually lead to a magnitude of climate change to which effective adaptation is not possible, or will only be available at very high social, environmental and economic costs.[244]

There has been for some time a pollution epidemic but the climate change crisis has eclipsed this. The corporate governance debate has not included the issues of climate change, rather shied away from internalising environmental costs including carbon emissions. The sustainability industry is large but is beset by spin doctors.[245] The Stern Review said that the negative effects of externalising greenhouse gasses are 'the greatest and widest-ranging market failing ever seen'.[246] Using the annual ceiling of 14.5 Gt $CO_2$, if emissions were frozen at the current level of 29 Gt $CO_2$ we would need two planets to sustain our current lifestyles.

---

[243] Sjafjell, B., *Towards a Sustainable European Company Law* (Wolters Kluwer, Alphen aan Rijn, Netherlands 2009), p. 3, Helm and Hepburn (2009).

[244] IPCC Core Writing Team, R.K. Pachauri and A. Reisinger (eds), *Climate Change 2007: Contribution of Working Groups I, II and III to the Fourth Assessment Report of The Intergovernmental Panel on Climate Change* (IPCC: Geneva 2008), accessed on 16 October 2012 at *www.ipcc.ch/pdf/assessment-report/ar4/syr/ar4_syr.pdf.*

[245] www.eiris.org/files/research%20publications/EIRISGlobalSustainabilityReport2012.pdf.

[246] Stern on the 'Economics of Climate Change: Executive Summary 2006', accessed on 16 October 2012 at www.sternreview.org.uk.Stern *The Economics of Climate Change: The Stern Review,* Cambridge University Press, 2007.

However, some countries are running a less sustainable account than others. With 15 per cent of the world's population, rich countries are using 90 per cent of the sustainable budget. How many planets would we need if developing countries were to follow the example of these countries?[247]

At last we believe that anthropogenic climate change is real: 'we have slowly, and at times reluctantly, realised that humanity has become an active agent in the reshaping of physical climates around the world, so our cultural, social, political and ethical practices are reinterpreting what climate change means'.[248] Principle 12 of the Rio Declaration requires states to cooperate to promote a supportive and open international economic system, and demanded that 'trade policy measures for environmental purposes should not constitute a means of arbitrary or unjustifiable discrimination or a disguised restriction on international trade'.[249] Agenda 21 of the Rio Declaration also says that international trade has been inequitable and this has been one reason for environmental degradation of the planet. It is a paradox that the Declaration also believed in the logic of trade liberalisation particularly because it would be good for the world. Elliott argues that one reason for the argument is a semantic one; the rhetoric of international trade does not allow 'protection' against nations. She asks:

> Can environmental protection issues be accommodated within the logic of trade liberalisation? Can trade liberalisation contribute to overcoming environmental degradation or is it likely to contribute to further environmental degradation? Is it possible in trade liberalisation discourse, to distinguish between environmental protection and environmental protectionism? … These are important because trade rules and agreements are a major determinant of how natural resources are used, what pressures are placed on the environment and who benefits from the huge money flows … that cross borders with the exchange of goods … At a normative level, answers to these questions rest in part on different views about 'protection' – a 'pejorative term' for the trade community.[250]

---

[247] UNDP, *How Many Planets,* accessed on 16 October 2012 at http://hdr.undp.org/en/statistics/data/climatechange/planets/. Helm and Hepburn (2009).

[248] Hulme (2009), p. xxv.

[249] UNCED, *Report of the UN Conference on Environment and Development Annex 1, Rio Declaration and Development,* A/CONE. 151/26 (Vol 1), 12 August 1992.

[250] Elliott, L., *The Global Politics of the Environment,* 2nd edn (Palgrave Macmillan, Basingstoke 2004), citing. S. Postel and C. Flavin, 'Reshaping the global Economy' in L.R. Brown et al. (eds), *State of the World* (Norton & co,

For corporate governance this matters because of the importance of the macroeconomic context. The WTO is heavily influenced by neo-liberal economics and therefore promotes free markets. Deregulation and free markets policies and environmental protection are usually conflicting aims, although some scholars believe that a market solution can be found. Paterson promotes a privatised market mechanism, arguing for a new paradigm known as 'global environmental governance':

> while such governance is commonly seen in terms of a tragedy of the commons arising out of the anarchy of the inter-state system, it is more fruitful to analyse these dynamics in relating to a conception of global capitalism. While efforts to govern global environmental problems started out as attempts to regulate the side-effects of existing form of capitalism development, they have increasing been organised to channel capitalism in novel directions.[251]

Indeed climate change is a new sort of 'pure public commons'[252] since no state or individual can fashion a solution, although it is clear that that inter-state rivals can cooperate in treaties, accords and protocols.[253] The power of 'Capital'[254] is so pervasive that even international law has been captured.[255] Paterson shows that global governance has been guided by the Washington Consensus and the fetishism of markets today.[256] Now privatisation has gone further, in a 'dynamic change where standards and regulations are obeyed not by governments but in market rules by the market for the market'.[257] Paterson believes that market mechanisms are

> shaping business practice, potentially significantly. Should the variety of schemes to shape investment practice with regard to $CO_2$ emissions – the Carbon Disclosure Project, the Global Reporting Initiative, [United Nations

---

New York and London 1991). Berlin, K. and T. Lang, 'Trade and the Environment', *The Washington Quarterly*, **16** (4, Autumn), pp. 35–51.

251 Paterson, M., 'Global governance for sustainable capitalism? The political economy of global environment governance', in W.N. Adger and A. Jordan (eds), *Governing Sustainability,* (Cambridge University Press, Cambridge 2009), p. 99.

252 UN World Commission on Environment and Development (Brundtland Commission) *Our Common Future*, A/42/427, www.un-documents.net/wced-ocf.htm, 1983 accessed on 19/07/2013.

253 Brown, K., 'Human development and environmental governance: a reality check', in Adger and Jordan (2009). Hulme (2009).

254 Beck (2005).

255 Ibid., and see Grear (2010).

256 Paterson (2009), p 107.

257 Paterson cites instances such as the International Organisation for Standardization's 14000 and the Forest Stewardship Councils (ibid., p. 109).

> Environment Programme] UNEP's Financial Industries Initiative, and so on – succeed in generating a norm which treats $CO_2$-intensive firms as financial liabilities, then substantial change in investment in renewable energy can be expected … But, on the other hand, privatisation not only entails firms attempting to self-regulate to organise and legitimate their growth, but environmental NGOs to fill the void left by declining regulation by states, through developing schemes to put pressures on firms to change practices.[258]

We will see whether these market solutions will work and change the complacency around the climate change debate and ameliorate carbon emissions, and whether corporate governance can be part of this movement. However, there are already a proliferation of carbon trading markets[259] but many commentators believe that financial emission markets are only a way of making money rather than ameliorating the problem of climate change.

> Alongside the development of proposals for emissions trading schemes at global and national level was a positive explosion of activity by financial markets actors … What explains this explosion of activity is that, while emissions trading can be understood in terms of economic efficiency, it very definitely operates through the creation of new markets in which firms can develop economic strategies and secondary markets. In fact, the future markets in this instance existed significantly before the real markets … Emissions trading as a project has been, and continues to be, propelled by realisation by powerful financial actors that here was a new commodity to be sold, new profits to be made.[260]

Similar projects are criticised in the same way, including the Joint Implementation and the Clean Development Mechanism.[261] Corporate governance mechanisms could affect the implementation of sustainable business; so far there are lamentably few effective strategies.[262]

This introduction has sketched some of the issues involving corporate governance in a global context. Now the national background will be

---

[258] Ibid., pp. 109–10.

[259] Including the European trading market, Australian, BP, etc.; see Pulver, S., 'Making sense of Corporate environmentalism: an Environmental contestation approach to analyzing the causes and consequences of the climate change policy in the oil industry', (2007) *Organisation and Environment*, **20**, pp. 1–40.

[260] Paterson (2009), pp. 111–12.

[261] Ibid.

[262] Sands, *Principles of International Environmental Law* (Cambridge University Press, Cambridge 2009); for an European perspective, see Sjafjell (2009), especially pp. 227–8.

considered. Although the sovereignty of states has been severely compromised recently, national governments have some power to act in regulating companies. Although there are growing international regulations to restrict emissions, national corporate governance should also be part of the picture if the planet is to be saved. This would entail embedding environmental policies into corporate governance, which would probably mean that the neo-liberal model of corporate governance would have to be significantly amended.

# 2. The reasons for convergence and divergence

Chapter 2 considers the differences in national and regional corporate governance which stem from the historical, philosophic and economic nature of particular societies. The first section of the chapter grapples with a definition of corporate governance which is by no means settled. The next section considers EU corporate governance and why harmonisation of company law and corporate governance has been extremely difficult and slow, suggesting that there is not an enormous appetite for convergence in corporate governance in the EU. Next, the chapter will focus on the intractable problems of property rights and ownership, showing the divisions which are inherent in these concepts in different jurisdictions. Property rights can be rigid or loose depending on the norms in particular society. The rhetoric used in discussing property rights often ignores aspects of property rights, such as the importance of always keeping in mind the insight that property rights are, in essence, rights against other people. This means that all property rights govern power relations between people. This is crucial for corporate governance because in the neo-liberal ideology, companies are the property of the shareholders: shareholders 'own' the company, or in the nexus of contract parlance, shareholders own 'the capital'. In this section of the chapter, this discourse of 'ownership' is rejected, allowing a wider conception of corporate governance. We consider a number of theoretical foundations of corporate governance. Here we are delving deeper into corporate governance theories. Two important theories explain tensions in the paramount contractual model. First, the agency theory shows why there is a conflict of interests between shareholders and the managements of a company. Second, the economic theory of a 'nexus of contracts' of company tries to demonstrate why the shareholders are dominant in a company's affairs, and why the company is inevitably more successful than it would be if regulators interfered with its business. A contrary conception of companies is the stakeholder theory which is a broad church elevating some stakeholders, but the arguments as to which one should be included are intractable. Finally, the chapter considers financing companies, and argues that there are two kinds of structure, an inside system and an outside system. The inside system is one where a public listed corporation's shares is distributed among a rather limited number of actors. The outside system is where firms are financed directly by the securities market while they are controlled by a limited number of managers. Chapters 3, 4 and 5 will revisit all of the arguments in Chapters 1 and 2, showing where the detailed company structures are influenced by the theories.

## NATIONAL CORPORATE GOVERNANCE

National corporate governance 'reflects public policy choices'.[1] Each country has passed a set of laws that shape the structure of its firms in a way that reflects the dominant ideological and political principles prevailing in its society. Those regulations provide for the internal structure of a company, which reflects the shaping of power between different actors within the company and brings under the regulatory umbrella the shareholders, the directors and the managers but also the employees and the creditors. Therefore, the regulation in question defines the compromises between sometimes competing forces and makes clear social choices, tipping the balance towards one direction or another, clearly reflecting wider cultural and societal trends. Corporate governance involves not only the creation of wealth which is by itself an issue of paramount importance for any society, but it also affects the issue of its distribution, touching upon one of the most sensitive, controversial and therefore deeply fundamental issues at the core of public debate.

The relevant legislation profoundly influences the priorities of firms, the nature of the employment relationship, the relations with the creditors and the suppliers, and the ability of bodies such as pension or insurance funds whose presence and function has a certain importance in the societal context to shape their own portfolios, holding sometimes rather sizeable parts of the shareholding of companies.

Taking into account the significance of the issues along with the actors involved in corporate governance, it is easy to comprehend why the latter so often provokes conflict and heated debates. 'The business enterprise has been one of the most prominent units of analysis for understanding

---

[1] Gourevitch, P.A. and J. Shinn, *Political Power and Control: The New Global Politics of Corporate Governance* (Princeton University Press, New Jersey 2005), p. 3.

modern economic growth';[2] therefore, anything that would determine its architecture along with the balances of a wealth-creating system while effectively dictating its distribution among societal factors, would stand at the core of a debate that would attract a wide range of actors from employees to banks, from directors to shareholders and also from the community itself to top managers: they all play an important role in generating wealth and insist on their respective precedence over other competing interests and the claims of others. The legislative choices made on the part of different jurisdictions as in all cases reflect the parameters of the relevant social debates, encompass their political outcomes and attempt to reconcile competing interests and expectations. The employees whose claims the political elite in a democratic regime always tends to pay attention to, would aim at receiving satisfactory wages, guaranteeing an acceptable quality of life even at the expense of profitability. The managers would mainly seek managerial autonomy, while the shareholders would focus on the profitability of the firm and their assurance as 'providers of capital that their investment will not be misused'.[3] The community in general might concentrate on a totally different agenda, including for example the protection of the environment or the social responsibility of the company. In this way, corporate governance will genuinely mirror the main political choices and the balance of power between the aforementioned actors in a given society.

The way companies are run, their list of priorities and the philosophical rationale that underlies their operation are fundamentally shaped by the prevailing societal values, but at the same time they do leave their distinctive imprint on society. Companies as a wealth creation mechanism or a social institution are providers of employment; they shape if not determine the relationship between the society and the economic model that it has chosen to adopt. Therefore, companies and consequently their governance and regulation are the outcomes of the social consensus reached in a given jurisdiction, but at the same time they act as factors which deeply influence it. The corporation might be

> one of the most successful socioeconomic institutions of modern society … with key features such as the separate legal personality, limited liability, shared ownership by investors, a board structure and transferable shares being

---

[2] Franco, A. and A. Colli, *Business History, Complexities and Comparisons* (Routledge, London 2011), p. 10.

[3] Thankom, C. and A. Copinath, *Corporate Governance and Development, Reform, Financial Systems and Legal Frameworks* (Edward Elgar, Cheltenham 2009), p. xiii.

> salient in firms around the world but the authority and power structure (ie the governance) of a firm can be organised in a number of ways.[4]

The latter appears to be influenced mainly by national values and standards, having somehow defied the power of globalisation; that is not to say that national corporate governance systems and regulations have not experienced external influences, but that their main features at least in Europe and the USA remain distinctively national. This is one reason why the OECD Principles of Corporate Governance and their Guidelines for Multinational Enterprises cannot be easily combined.

Although we will consider the debate about the possibility of significant convergence of corporate governance, it is clear that in the detail of national laws there is much divergence between the countries, often because of cultural differences. The diversity of corporate governance systems can also be attributed to the different set of legal systems in place[5] or the political limitations placed upon financial institutions.[6] The term 'corporate governance' has attracted the attention of numerous academics, practitioners, institutions and committees who have attempted to define it in a precise manner. The definition of a term that has so many and sometimes equally significant components as explained above, has naturally been a challenging task. The 'ownership' structure is a key feature that determines the nature of a corporate governance system. Later we analyse the factors that distinguish corporate governance in the USA from the system in continental Europe and the three jurisdictions that form the focus of this book. Other important influences on a corporate governance system include the regulation of the financial and capital markets, labour law, bankruptcy laws and the banking system. That is partly the reason why introducing a reform of corporate governance is such a complicated, sensitive and highly politicised issue for many parties; apart from the reform of the strictly defined relevant legislation, it involves a change in labour law or tax law and in financial regulation. 'Changing the law ordinarily requires a political consensus

---

[4] Barker, R.M., *Corporate Governance, Competition and Political Parties, Explaining Corporate Governance Change in Europe* (Oxford University Press, Oxford 2010), p. 3.

[5] Coffee, Jr, J.C. 'The Future of History: The Prospects for Global Convergence in Corporate Governance and its Implications' (1999) 93 *NWU Law Review* 641.

[6] Roe, M.J., 'A Political Theory of American Corporate Finance' (1991) 91 *Columbia Law Review* 10; Dignam, A. and M. Galanis, *The Globalization of Corporate Governance* (Ashgate, Farnham 2009).

making agreement among political and corporate elites'[7] on the one hand, and a range of stakeholders such as employees. Taking into account the stakes involved, this is a highly challenging task. Too many parties have too much to lose and therefore they are eager to negotiate hard. Inevitably the winner will be the powerful agent and therefore the law reflects the elite's concept of a fair corporate governance paradigm.[8]

## Corporate Governance: a Definition?

Corporate governance may have been debated to a great extent and by many parties but its precise definition remains an issue that has been left largely unresolved. It has emerged as one of the most important topics within the wider framework of corporate law; it has been thoroughly discussed within the framework of globalisation, as numerous writers have attempted to evaluate whether national corporate governance systems will converge as markets become increasingly interrelated, the links between companies become closer at international level and the legal standards of the West are now effectively being adopted by a variety of nations across the globe. Despite its recently acquired academic prominence and the number of articles and publications it has attracted, its definition remains distinctively diverse. As it is a concept encompassing many socially crucial components described above, it is perceived and interpreted differently by the various parties involved, either at academic or practitioner level. Furthermore, as it involves a diverse set of disciplines from law and economics to sociology, psychology and cultural studies, it is viewed and analysed from a different spectrum with the scientific interests of the researcher in question as a departing point. An interdisciplinary approach would be necessary to fully comprehend corporate governance with its diverse aspects and angles. Therefore, we are provided with an abundance of definitions, all aiming to explain the nature, character and foundations of corporate governance. The lack of a precise commonly accepted definition of the concept in question betrays on the one hand the rather controversial nature of the issue in question, while on the other hand it reveals the magnitude of the challenge accompanying every effort to reconcile the divergent opinions.

The fundamental question of what ought to be the legitimate objectives[9] of the corporation lie behind the divergence and define the debate,

---

7 Jeffrey, C., N. Gordon, M.J. Roe, *Convergence and Persistence in Corporate Governance* (Cambridge University Press, Cambridge 2004), p. 3.

8 Stiglitz, J., *The Price of Inequality* (Allen Lane, London 2012), pp. 66–7.

9 Keay, A., *The Corporate Objective* (Edward Elgar, Cheltenham 2011).

especially between the two sides of the Atlantic. The definitions provided by lawyers, economists and social scientists are usually broad enough to cover both the internal aspects of corporate governance and its external influences; therefore corporate governance has been defined as 'the institutions that influence how business corporations allocate resources and returns',[10] 'the organisations and rules that affect expectations about the exercise of control of resources in firms'[11] and 'the institutional framework in which the integrity of the transaction is decided'.[12] More narrowly, the Australian Royal Commission has defined it as

> referring generally to the legal and organisational framework within which, and the principles and processes by which, corporations are governed. It refers in particular to the powers, accountability and relationships of those who participate in the direction and control of the company. Chief among these participants are the board of directors, and management. There are aspects of the corporate governance regime that have an impact on the relationship between shareholders and the company.[13]

More specifically, corporate governance is 'the framework of rules, relationships, systems and processes within and by which authority is exercised and controlled in corporations'.[14] The Cadbury Code defines it as 'either the action of governing or the method of governing and it is in the latter sense it is used with reference to companies'.[15] It has also been defined as 'the structures, process, cultures and systems that engender the successful operation of the organisation'.[16] Cannon was successful in defining it as 'the sum of those activities that make up the internal regulation of the business in compliance with the regulations placed on the firm by legislation, ownership and control. It incorporates the

---

[10] Norton, J.J. and J. Rickford, *Corporate Governance Post-Enron, Comparative and International Perspectives* (British Institute of International and Comparative Law, London 2005), p. 435.

[11] Ibid.

[12] Williamson, O.E., *The Mechanisms of Governance* (Oxford University Press, Oxford 1996), p. 11.

[13] Royal Commission, *Directors' Duties and Other Obligations under the Corporations Act, Background Paper* 11, November 2001, p. 27.

[14] Department of Treasury, *Report of the HIH Royal Commission*, vol I, 2003.

[15] Cadbury, A., *Corporate Governance and Chairmanship* (Oxford University Press, Oxford 2002), p. 1.

[16] Keasey, K., M. Wright, 'Issues in Corporate Accountability and Governance' (1993) *Accounting and Business Research* 291.

trusteeship of assets, their management and their deployment'.[17] The shareholders usually find themselves included within the definition of corporate governance as the latter is widely viewed as the set of institutions which 'protects the suppliers of capital to the company, particularly the suppliers of equity capital, the shareholders, who have only residual protection after all other claimants have been satisfied … only effective corporate governance can ensure that the interests of the shareholders are protected'.[18] Similarly, Parkinson defines it as 'the process of supervision and control intended to ensure that the company's management acts in accordance with the interests of the shareholders'.[19] Shleifer and Vishny define it as 'the ways in which suppliers of finance to corporations assure themselves of getting a return on their investments'.[20]

In 1999, the OECD defined corporate governance as 'a system by which business corporations are directed and controlled'.[21] Interestingly enough, five years later the same organisation provided a wider definition which took into account elements of the ongoing debate of whether the aims and the structure of the corporation should include a wider range of actors and stakeholders rather than the strictly defined group of shareholders. The essence and parameters of this debate is to be thoroughly presented at later stage. Thus, in 2004 with its new revised guidelines, the OECD defined corporate governance as 'a set of relationships between a company's management, its board, its shareholders and other stakeholders … good corporate governance should provide proper incentives for the board and the management to pursue objectives that are in the interests of the company and its shareholders and should facilitate effective monitoring'.[22] This definition certainly avoids adopting a stakeholder-centred approach[23] on the part of the organisation, but it reflects the debates between different prominent jurisdictions on the

---

[17] Cannon, T., *Corporate Responsibility, A Textbook on Business Ethics, Governance, Environment: Roles and Responsibilities* (Pitman, London 1994).

[18] Owen, G., T. Kirchmaier and J. Grant, *Corporate Governance in the US and Europe, Where are we now?* (Palgrave Macmillan, New York 2005), p. 2.

[19] Parkinson, J.E., *Corporate Power and Responsibility* (Clarendon Press, Oxford 1993).

[20] Shleifer, A. and R.W. Vishny, 'A Survey of Corporate Governance' (1997) *Journal of Finance* 737.

[21] OECD, *Principles of Corporate Governance* (OECD, Paris 1999).

[22] OECD, *Principles of Corporate Governance* (OECD, Paris 2004).

[23] See Chapter 1 on the differences between the OECD Principles of Corporate Governance (2004) and the OECD Guidelines for Multinational Enterprises (2011).

issue, such as the USA on the one hand and Germany on the other, which will be debated later.

The nature of corporate governance as a field encompassing multiple components of divergent nature but of great significance for the society is reflected in the definition provided by Cadbury in 2000. Corporate governance is found to be 'concerned with holding the balance between economic and social goals and between individual and communal goals', therefore further underlining its importance in the general societal context and its key role in establishing a social equilibrium so highly desired in the framework of a contemporary free market democracy.

## EU CORPORATE GOVERNANCE CONVERGENCE?

Corporate governance re-emerged as a heated topic of debate at international level within the framework of globalisation. The sometimes irresistible trends of globalisation have inevitably forced some of the aspects of corporate governance into convergence, especially after the financial deregulation of the 1990s and the increasing emergence of stock markets as a source of finance. This book argues that despite some harmonisation of laws, practices and institutional functions that has indeed taken place, corporate governance systems remain distinctively national, especially in the West. It is astonishing to note that even at EU level, the harmonisation between national corporate governance models has been minimal in comparison with the overall effect that EU-generated legislative initiatives has traditionally had on areas of policy such as the internal market and competition law, let alone monetary union with the introduction of a common currency. The EU managed to harmonise its competition law policy across member states and to introduce institutions at pan-European level to deal with challenges to it. It managed to harmonise at an indeed impressive and widely unexpected level its internal market with a set of over-reaching rules which placed significant limits to national member states' sovereignty, only to promote the creation of a large scale single market where the rules are set by the Court of Justice of the EU and the European Council along with the European Parliament in the form of directives and regulations. The EU created a single market based on the free movement of goods, people and capital accompanied by the freedom of establishment and the freedom to provide services; the latter still has a long way to go. The consolidation of a project of such a massive scale was based on the mutual pulling of national sovereignty as well as on converging policies at an unprecedented number of issues, ranging from removing customs duties and all charges to allowing European citizens and businesses to establish themselves and provide services across the territory of the EU.[24]

Thus, harmonisation of laws and convergence are inherent in the functional identity and the sense of purpose of the EU as a whole; it is built on a notion of consensus and mutual concessions so as to achieve common ground which will provide the necessary space for agreement. It is therefore astonishing that even in this institutional and functional context, corporate governance emerges as perhaps one of the very few areas that resisted the forces of harmonisation at EU level.[25] This does not mean that corporate governance as a field is averse to any form of convergence; it means that despite the favourable legislative and institutional environment that significantly encourages harmonisation, corporate governance retained its national identity against the tide. The EU negotiated the Fifth Directive[26] for several years, only for it to remain a draft due to the massive differences in the role that employees could assume at the board level. Even the relatively recent agreement on the creation of a 'European Company Statute'[27] that would give birth to a truly European Company is in fact a compromise; the European parties to the debate basically agreed that they disagree. Instead of a common European Company whose institutional structure and constitutional arrangements would be unified across the EU, whose member states had already consented to the removal of most barriers to internal trade, the EU had to accept the fact that a common EU corporate governance model could not accommodate the significant divergence among its member states.

The participation of the employees and other stakeholders at the board level assumed a central position in the relevant debates and became the crucial parameter that eventually undermined the consensus. The EU approved a directive on employee participation,[28] which by definition grants to the member states the necessary discretion when introducing its provisions into their internal national legal orders. Taking into account that the otherwise 'European' company now includes corporate forms

---

[24] Even though there has been significant expansion, see J. Dine, M. Koutsias and M. Blecher, *Company Law in the New Europe: The EU Acquis, Comparative Methodology and Model Law* (Edward Elgar, Cheltenham 2007).

[25] Ibid.

[26] OJ (C 240) 2.

[27] Regulation on the Statute for a European Company (SE) EC 2157/2001.

[28] Directive 2001/86/EC supplementing the Statute for a European Company with regard to the involvement of employees.

based on either a single or a dual board model, the scope for discretion was indeed enormous. The status of employees within the company is reflective of a deeply rooted debate that involves the role of stakeholders and the very definition of the membership of the company along with its list of aims. The institutional structure of the company is not a technicality related to the theoretical interests of academics or lawyers, but it is the field which genuinely embodies the dominant ideological and in that sense philosophical ideals which are prevailing in a certain society. This book argues that corporate governance entails an architecture which is the outcome of historical, political and economic developments which shaped the society within which it evolved. It is deeply reflective of the experiences and strengths of the society and the economy within which it is gradually shaped, and it embodies to a great extent its dominant ideological climate. Each 'country's company law has developed according to the societies' own way and consequently companies incorporated under different national laws often have less in common than one would be inclined to think',[29] because 'the centre of gravity of legal development lies not in legislation nor in juristic science nor in judicial decision but in society itself'.[30] The rationale behind its resistance to globalisation and harmonisation therefore lays with its deep roots within the individual national identities, which define the system on the basis of which companies are governed, along with the agenda they ought to pursue and their precise membership; this justifies why we have to deal with 'widely varying conceptions of "company" in different societies'.[31] Corporate governance is not a matter of technical regulation as it mirrors the ideological beliefs prevailing in a certain society, therefore a shift in its structure would be the outcome of a shift in beliefs.

> Central to endogenous institutional changes are therefore the dynamics of self-enforcing beliefs and the associated behaviour. An institutional change is a change in beliefs, and it occurs when the associated behaviour is no longer self-enforcing, leading individuals to act in a manner that does not reproduce the associated belief.[32]

---

[29] Mahmut, Y., 'Shareholding and Board Structures of German and UK Companies' (2001) 22 *Company Lawyer*, 2, p. 47.

[30] Ehrlich, E., *Fundamental Principles of Sociology of Law* (Harvard University Press, Cambridge MA 1936), p. 14.

[31] Dean, J., 'Directors' Duties in Response to Hostile Takeover Bids' (2003) 14 *International Company and Commercial Law Review*, 12, p. 370.

[32] Greif, A. and D. Laitin, 'A Theory of Endogenous Institutional Change' (2004) 98 *American Political Science Review*, November, p. 639.

This explains why company law is not a purely technical form of regulation; it is intrinsically linked with the dominant social trends, notions and beliefs and it forms a part of private law. Legislation in the field of company law

> would be value neutral … the main differences in the shape of the company law of the EU member states often reflect differences in underlying economic conditions and in public policy considerations past and present. The very fact that company law legislation is normally of a prescriptive character is in itself an expression of the public element involved.[33]

It has been argued that corporate governance systems are subject to an irreversible process of convergence, to the degree that we should be talking about 'the end of history for corporate law'.[34] It was argued that 'there is no longer any serious competitor to the view that corporate law should principally strive to increase long-term shareholder value'.[35] These claims are usually founded upon the nature of stock ownership, the increasing importance of capital markets and takeovers. They are also based on the premise that there is a 'dominance of a shareholder-centred ideology and that … the stakeholder model is essentially just a combination of elements found in the older manager-oriented and labour-oriented models … undermining the stakeholder model as a viable alternative to the shareholder-oriented model.'[36] These views support the idea that the pressures arising from globalisation will inevitably bring a convergence of international corporate governance norms into a common model based on absolute shareholder primacy. They are based on the premise that the so-called Anglo-Saxon outsider corporate governance model has been so successful that it is to be transplanted in countries across the world because of the prevalence of the neo-liberal economic model. This book argues that in contrast to this view, member states have managed to resist the pressures of harmonisation flowing not only from globalisation but also from certain international organisations such as the

---

33 Bernitz, U. and W-G. Ringe, *Company Law and Economic Protectionism, New Challenges to European Integration* (Oxford University Press, Oxford 2010), p. 191. See B. Cheffins, *Company Law: Theory, Structure and Operation* (Clarendon, Oxford 1997), arguing the opposite viewpoint.

34 Hansmann, H. and R. Kraakman, 'The End of History for Corporate Law' (2000) *Harvard Law School John M. Olin Center for Law, Economics and Business, Discussion Paper Series*, paper 280 but see a powerful contra-argument by Keay (2011).

35 Hansmann and Kraakman (2000).

36 Ibid. See also Dignam and Galanis (2009).

EU whose very raison d'être has been integration based on harmonisation of legal norms and standards.[37] The debates in relation to convergence have a strong temporal element as they are raised especially at times when one model or other faces challenges that place its structures into question; at that point different corporate governance models that cope better emerge as the inspiration for reform. In the 1990s amidst economic stagnation in Germany, there was a significant debate asking whether the German corporate governance model was the reason behind this stagnation, and whether its model has reached its limit and was in need of profound reform; at that time a booming UK and a growing economy in the USA were offering a clearly attractive model for reform. The eruption of several corporate scandals (with Enron at the forefront) along with the financial crisis of 2008 set aside the illusion about the Anglo–American-perceived perfection and provided the grounds for a new debate about whether Germany with its insider corporate governance model had potentially found the system that can guarantee stability during turbulent times. In fact, aspects of both models have taken some steps towards convergence as the new section 172 of the UK Companies Act 2006 and the greater role that capital markets now play in Germany betray. But that has not changed the fundamental character of the systems in question; it did not affect the core characteristics of the models in question such as their institutional structure or even their clear orientation towards a purely shareholder or stakeholder model. The UK retained its view of the shareholders as the exclusive members of the company and the holders of a property right over the corporation, while Germany maintained its distinctive co-determination system which recognises an effectively managerial role to stakeholders. In effect, national governments 'have a choice to respond to the challenges of globalisation in different ways and that cultural, institutional and other national differences constrain any push to convergence'.[38] For example, 'decades of successful operation of co-determination means it has worked its way into the German psyche and become a virtual habit'[39] to the degree that the country cannot give it away; the pressing harmonising forces of globalisation and the calls for the superiority of the shareholder-orientated model were effectively resisted.

---

[37] Dine, Koutsias and Blecher (2007).

[38] Weiss, M., 'Convergence and/or Divergence in Labour Law Systems?: A European Perspective' (2007) 28 *Comparative Labour Law and Policy Journal*, p. 486.

[39] Richards, A. 'Mitbestimmung: The Future of Co-determination in a Hostile World' (2007) 15 *Debatte*, p. 346.

The resilience of national systems of corporate governance to globalisation even at the EU level provided the grounds for the 'observation there exist various models of capitalism each of which corresponds to local conditions where interacting institutions complement each other'.[40] This book focuses on the analysis of three jurisdictions namely the USA, the UK and Germany, and it aims at refuting the view that corporate governance has indeed converged into a single model across the aforementioned prominent jurisdictions; while not rejecting the view that aspects of the governance of corporations in the countries in question have indeed came closer to a common set of principles, it supports the view that the resilience of corporate governance to harmonisation is a proof of its deeply rooted relationship with national cultural, political and economic norms. Corporate governance is reflective of the dominant ideology of a certain society and expressive of its principal societal consensus.

## OWNERSHIP AND CONTROL

### Who owns the Corporation?

The inability to agree on a commonly accepted definition of corporate governance betrays the fundamental questions that emerge when debating corporate governance: 'who should control the corporation?' and 'for the pursuit of what goals and whose interests?'[41] The replies provided to these questions by various jurisdictions have sometimes been diametrically different, due to different prevailing values, divergent national lists of priorities and divergent societal structures. Naturally, if all these factors vary, replies to the aforementioned questions would significantly vary too. The fact that corporate governance has somehow and to a great extent resisted the forces of globalisation and harmonisation of laws that are common features of an era of increased economic interdependence, proves that its parameters and foundations are deeply rooted in the individual history and the traditions of a society, rendering the corporate governance model distinctively national in its approach and nature. That is not to say that there has been no influence between countries in the international arena, or that the relevant legislative standards of what we

---

[40] Komo, D. and C. Villiers, 'Are Trends in European Company Law threatening Industrial Democracy?' (2009) *European Law Review*, p. 179.

[41] For an excellent review of this topic see Keay (2011), and also the concluding section of this book.

call 'the West' have not spread to the markets and the emerging economies of the East or the South, but rather that the deep links between the models of corporate governance and the prevailing societal values have rendered the approach towards this issue much less universal than one would expect when analysing the operation of corporations with activities across many geographical and product markets.

The natural answer to the first question would be 'the owners of the corporation should be in a position to control it'. And while this reply sounds rather clear and uncontroversial, the rationale behind it reveals a very different and much more complicated reality. The questions in relation to the owners of the corporation have been haunting law, economics and political science for many years with academics, practitioners and social scientists divided as to the nature of the owners of what has emerged as a massively important social institution – the corporation. The recent emergence of the CSR doctrines, the thorough analysis of the German model which includes stakeholders within the company context, the debates within the EU itself accompanying the creation of a European Company with a commonly agreed structure and the ever-alluring American model of corporate governance have dominated the relevant debates, and have been used by both sides of the arguments as a proof or a counter-proof of their convictions. The replies to these questions are so fundamentally important that they simply define the nature of the corporate governance chosen by any given nation, and they constitute the sometimes very delicate yet essentially significant line that distinguishes two corporate governance models from each other. The analysis that follows will highlight the differences between the most prominent corporate governance models and will illuminate the reasons behind their emergence in certain jurisdictions; it will be rather obvious that especially in the main Western jurisdictions that already count centuries of legal and institutional traditions, the models of corporate governance adopted genuinely reflect the prevailing national values and the balance shaped between different societal actors. They are the natural outcome of the historical developments taking place in a certain country which shaped its dominant perceptions, its list of valued principles and in many ways its distinctive cultural identity; in very specific ways corporate governance appears to be a by-product of the same mechanisms that shape both its prevailing legal and societal values and its institutional framework.

The debate over the ownership and the control of the company emerged in a more lively and substantial way in the USA. There the issue presented no particular controversy as the shareholders are considered the exclusive owners of the company;[42] they invest their capital in the corporation by purchasing shares expecting a return of their investment. But as companies grew larger, the shareholding became increasingly more dispersed and owner control started to wane significantly. If control is defined as 'any process in which any person or group of persons … determines i.e. intentionally affects what another person or group or organisation will do',[43] then the waning of the links between shareholders and management betrays a loss of such a control. With the initial natural owners[44] of the company gradually losing control of an entity that continued to grow in size and operations with 'economic actions that had increasing social consequences … the giant widely held corporation came increasingly under the implicit control of its managers, and the concept of social responsibility … arose to provide a basis of legitimacy for their actions'.[45] The Berle and Means[46] seminal article stirred up the debate and brought the issue within the spotlight of the academic community in a rather spectacular way, fuelling a line of articles supporting or rejecting their view. The authors of the article analysed the new landscape in corporate America with the emergence of large corporations and an ever-widening shareholder basis. Their argument amounted to the actual realisation that ownership and control in corporate America have been effectively separated. The shareholders or otherwise the owners of the company[47] no longer possess the means or employ the ability to control what they supposedly own – the corporation. They conclude that shareholding has become so disperse and widespread that the increasing number of shareholders or otherwise the owners can no longer exercise control of what they own, which is the corporation itself. The latter is effectively governed by a rather limited number of managers who take all decisions for what they perceive as the best interest of the company and of course its owners – the shareholders. They did notice

---

[42] Eisenberg, A.M., 'The Conception that the Corporation is a Nexus of Contracts and the Dual Nature of the Firm' (1999) 24 *Journal of Corporation Law* 819, pp. 825–6.

[43] Tannenbaum, A.S., *Control in Organisations* (McGraw Hill, New York 1962).

[44] Hart, O., 'An Economist's Perspective on the Theory of the Firm' (1989) 89 *Columbia Law Review* 1757, p. 1765.

[45] Mintzberg, H., 'Who should Control the Corporation?' (1984) *California Management Review* XXVII, p. 90.

[46] Berle, A. and C. Gardiner Means, *The Modern Corporation & Private Property*, 10th edn (Harcourt, Brace & World Inc., New York 2009).

[47] Hessen, R., 'A New Concept of Corporations: A Contractual and Private Property Model' (1979) 30 *Hastings Law Journal* 1327, p. 1330.

however that the distance between the managers on the one hand and the number of shareholders on the other was becoming wider as time passed by, and the corporations kept expanding while in need of further investment. And in many occasions the managers were more eager to use their decision-making abilities to serve what could have been viewed by an external observer as personal interests instead of the interests of the corporation as a whole and its owners. The article brought to academic attention a development that was to become a common feature of at least what we call the 'Anglo–American corporate model' if we presume for the purposes of the analysis that due to certain similarities (to be thoroughly analysed later) the two countries can fall under the same umbrella; their respective models may be similar but by no means identical. In simple words, disperse shareholding was increasingly contributing to the separation of ownership of the corporation with its control.

The article in question was not however the first piece of work that focused on the analysis of this issue. Some 156 years earlier, Adam Smith wrote in his monumental book, *The Wealth of Nations*:

> Being the managers rather of other people's money than of their own, it cannot well be expected that they should watch over it with the same anxious vigilance with which the partners in a private copartnery frequently watch over their own. Like the stewards of a rich man, they are apt to consider attention to small matters as not for their master's honour and very easily give themselves a dispensation from it.[48]

This highlights one of the most important themes of company law: 'for four hundred years company law has tried to solve the core problem of corporate governance, the separation of ownership and control'.[49] The question emerging rather instinctively would be what sort of ownership is this that it does not entail the ability to control what is perceived as owned? The widely accepted and vigorously supported view that the shareholders are the exclusive owners of the corporation could present some aspects that would require further clarification. The decision-making capacity at corporate level is entrusted to the hands of the managers who take the decisions in relation to important aspects of

---

[48] Smith, A., *An Inquiry into the Nature and Causes of the Wealth of Nations* [1776] (Penguin, London 1999), Book V, Chapter 1, p. 26.

[49] Hopt, K.J. and P.C. Leyens, 'Board Models in Europe – Recent Developments of Internal Corporate Governance Structures in Germany, the United Kingdom, France and Italy' (2004) *European Company and Financial Law Review*, p. 136.

corporate activity; however they cannot found any claim of ownership on the entity they effectively govern. The legal science is deeply precise, including an abundance of legal terminology with clearly defined concepts. Therefore, the owner of an object or property is in a position to control its possession and define its use. The owner of property can allow or prohibit the access to it, and can exercise the full rights of ownership on his possession.

> The sole right possessed by the owner of an asset is his ability to exclude others from the use of that asset. That is, the owner of a machine can decide who can and who cannot work on that machine, the owner of a building can decide who can and who cannot enter the building, the owner of an insurance company's client list can decide who has and who does not have access to the list, and so forth.[50]

No property right is absolute, as Parkinson points out: 'Ownership rights are not absolute[51] (ownership of a knife does not entitle the owner to stab people with it). That shareholders might own companies does not mean that they may insist that directors attempt to maximise profits in any way at all.'[52]

The chapter now analyses two different approaches to property rights to elucidate one of the most intractable problems in corporate governance.

## Different Perspectives on Property Rights

Hutton has analysed very different attitudes which may be discerned in the USA and Europe.[53] His thesis is that the attitude to the ownership of property in the US has been informed by a number of factors. One of these is the existence of the experience of the settlers who arrived at 'a wilderness pregnant with riches', and had 'risked all crossing the Atlantic and who, as fervent Protestants, believed they had a direct relationship with God'. They believed that they were serving God's purpose by taking possession of the land and using it for their own individual purpose.[54]

---

[50] Hart, O. and J. Moore, 'Property Rights and the Nature of the Firm' (1990) 98 *The Journal of Political Economy* 1119, No. 6, December, p. 1121.

[51] For a detailed analysis refuting the justifications for unlimited property rights see J. Harris, *Property and Justice* (Clarendon, Oxford 1996).

[52] Parkinson, J., 'The Socially Responsible Company' in M. Addo (ed), *Human Rights Standards and the Responsibility of Transnational Corporations* (Kluwer, The Hague 1999).

[53] Hutton, W., *The World We're In* (Little, Brown, London 2002).

[54] Ibid., pp. 52–3.

Hutton shows how the writings of John Locke encouraged the view that property both claimed by and created from the land belonged 'exclusively and completely' to the settler and, moreover that the 'purpose of society and Government' was to 'further the enjoyment of property, and political power was only legitimate if it served this end'.[55] Two passages cited by Hutton seem particularly apt:

> The only way whereby any one divests himself of his Natural Liberty and puts on the bonds of Civil Society is by agreeing with other Men to join and unite into a Community, for their comfortable, safe and peaceable living one amongst another, in a secure Enjoyment of their Properties, and a greater Security against any that are not of it.[56]

An instructive viewpoint comes from competition law, which for many years has been struggling to identify the boundary between enjoyment of a right to property and an abusive use of the power that the right to property brings with it. Secondly:

> Every man has a property in his own person. There is no body has any right to it but himself. The labour of his body, and the work of his hands we may say are properly his. Whatsoever then he removes out of the state that nature has provided, and left it in, he hath mixed his labour with and joined to it something that is his own, and thereby makes his property.[57]

The War of Independence and the writing of the constitution did nothing to dispel this mindset, the justification for revolution being the interference by King George III with the settlers' rights to enjoy their property freely.[58] 'Any notion that property rights were a concession granted by the state in the name of the common interest – the European tradition … had been dispelled by the revolution.'[59]

The understanding of property rights then is founded in nature and religion, giving at once a mystical and religious significance to ownership. If a settler prospered, it was evidence of a healthy relationship with God. The availability of vast stretches of land made any egalitarian notions realisable without the concept of redistribution becoming a problem, so that redistribution of property became contrary both to nature

---

[55] Ibid.

[56] Locke, J., *Two Treatises of Government*, P. Laslett (ed) (Cambridge University Press, Cambridge 1988), p. 331.

[57] Ibid., p. 288.

[58] Hutton, p. 56.

[59] Ibid, pp. 58–9.

and religion. The role of the central government was thus reduced to the protection of individual property. The constitution prevented states from doing anything that might impair obligations embodied in contracts. Once the right to own property and to contract had been granted to corporations as well as individuals,[60] and companies holding shares in other companies were equated with individual shareholders, the stage was set for the giant groups of companies that we see today. Further, the resistance to redistribution enshrined in the Fifth Amendment is fertile ground for those seeking to resist regulation on the basis that it is a 'confiscation of property'. The Fifth Amendment prevents the government from depriving an individual of 'life, liberty and property without due process; nor shall property be taken for public use without just compensation'. Thus, although there was a long period between the 1930s and 1970 when property rights were regulated, the fundamental understanding of individual liberty as inextricably intertwined with ownership of property made it very much easier for the ultra-conservatives to build their anti-regulatory policies and have them widely accepted.

> For the constitution remains explicit. Without powerful popular support and a clear sense of national crisis – as over slavery in the 1860s or unemployment in the 1930s – the American constitutional conception is that government at federal and state level is the custodian of private property rights; and the Supreme Court sees its task as policing that injunction.[61]

The old settler cast of mind provided fertile ground for Nozick's arguments that taxation to finance any minimum income for the poor as a form of forced labour and all forms of redistributive justice as coercive.[62] It also provided fertile soil for the concept that corporations are nothing but a 'nexus of contracts'[63] with the obvious result that government should not interfere in that contract.

What, then, of the 'European' conception of property ownership? Of course, it is not possible to reflect subtle and complex differences

---

60 *Dartmouth College v Woodward* (1819) 17 US 518.

61 Hutton (2002), p. 60.

62 Nozick, R., *Anarchy, State and Utopia* (Harvard University Press, Cambridge MA 1973); Hutton (2002), p. 68.

63 Posner, R., *Economic Analysis of Law*, 4th edn (Little, Brown, Boston 1992); Easterbrook F. and D. Fischel, *The Economic Structure of Corporate Law* (Harvard University Press, Cambridge MA 1991); Cheffins (1997); Dine, J., *The Governance of Corporate Groups* (Cambridge University Press, Cambridge 2000) and see later in this chapter.

between understandings of property across Europe. However, it may be possible to detect a general difference of view. Hutton cites Article 14 of the post-war German constitution as capturing some of the flavour of the difference:

> property is not seen in Europe as an absolute right, as it is by US conservatives. Rather, it is a privilege that confers reciprocal obligations – a notion captured by article 14 of the post-war German constitution, which specifies that 'property imposes duties. Its use should also serve the public weal.' Those who own and hold property are members of society, and society has a public dimension to which necessarily they must contribute as the quid pro quo for the privilege of exercising property rights.[64]

This conception of property ownership is coupled with a 'profound commitment to the notion that all citizens should have an equal right to participate in economic and social life, and that the state is more than a safety net of last resort: it is the fundamental vehicle for the delivery of this equality'.[65] To some extent, this attitude was driven by the different experiences vis à vis land ownership when notions of equality became important. In Europe, any attempt at equality meant redistribution, but in the US,

> When John Adams argued in 1776 that the acquisition of land should be made easy for every member of society in order to achieve equality and liberty, he could disregard European concerns with how the state had to intervene to construct a just society: a continent lay before him waiting to be claimed.[66]

The European state thus had a real and vital role to play in constructing a fair society, a far cry from a minimalist role in protecting individual property rights.

The rhetoric used in discussing property rights often ignores the fact that property rights are essentially rights against other people, which means that property rights govern power relations between people. If property rights are seen as a person having rights over a thing, this ignores the fact that the rights actually lie against other persons, a right to exclude, etc. The role that property rights play in wealth distribution is ignored because the person-to-person relationship is clouded by the person-to-thing discussion. Thus,

---

[64] Hutton (2002), pp. 50–1.
[65] Ibid., p. 51.
[66] Ibid., p. 61.

> A theorist who supposes that ownership interests in objects may be justified, say, by a natural-rights argument, but then ignores questions of wealth-distribution, tells only half the story. The same is true, in the opposite direction of one who advocates a certain distribution of 'resources' but who neglects the question whether person-thing ownership relations are to form part of a property-institutional design.[67]

It is because rights over things can never be absolute, but rather made up of a web of rights and responsibilities operating interpersonally that the debate resonates with issues of wealth distribution and power relations. If property ownership meant that I have absolute dominion over three beans and the right to use them as I wished and you have similar rights over five beans, the property distribution debates would exist but they would be a mere matter of counting. Do I deserve more beans than you? Because the reality of property relations is that I may exclude some (but not others) from use of an item, and I may use that item only in non-harmful ways, the discussion of rights and duties becomes infinitely more complex and balanced. It is important, then, to understand what the bundle of rights called property rights actually consists of.

Harris argues that the Hohfeldian 'bundle of rights' concept which emphasises rights against other persons, rather than rights over things, can best be expressed on an 'ownership' spectrum which enables an individual to have more or less exclusivity over the use of the property, and more or less power to use it in designated ways. The concept of ownership is seen therefore as firmly rooted in social expectations which have come to be embedded in legal rules. These include '(1) trespassory rules; (2) property-limitation rules; (3) expropriation rules; (4) appropriation rules. (There may be as well property-duty rules and property-privilege rules)'.[68] This understanding means that attempts to infuse more weight into a particular side of the balance of interests by claiming it is a 'property' right is mere rhetoric, designed to appeal to the conceptions underlying a particular society's view of the standing of 'property'. Of considerable interest in this context is the examination by Harris of 'expansive' definitions of property. In particular, an expansive use of 'property rights' by economists can be discerned. This is property right as including 'any right – whether Hohfeldian claim-right, privilege, power or immunity – concerning the use of a resource, where "resource" means

---

67 Harris (1996), p. 141.

68 Ibid.

all bodily and mental capacities of the rightholder. In other words, all rights are property rights'.[69]

This expansion of the property rights conception is, according to Harris, based on the conflation of owning and ownership. For Harris,

> it is one thing to say that a person is vested with ('owns') either a right or a bundle of rights; it is another to say that what he is vested with is that particular set of open ended privileges and powers over a resource which counts as an ownership interest.[70]

'Conventional' property refers to 'cashable rights' such as bank accounts, shares, etc., 'because expropriation and appropriation rules apply to them – they pass into a bankrupt's estate and they can be inherited ... Cashable rights are the subject of real markets'.[71] Such an understanding would exclude 'social rights' such as the right to use public spaces, which some have claimed as property rights. While Harris is not in principle opposed to this extended use of property, he nevertheless does not see it as an aid to clarity:

> By all means let rights of all kinds be analysed in these terms. Calling all rights 'property rights' is, however, anything but an aid to clarity for the enterprises at hand since both the analyst and the reader must constantly remind themselves that they are not talking about 'property' as ordinarily understood.[72]

More importantly, perhaps is the insight that the use of 'property rights' is a rhetoric which will resonate with the reader according to the 'meaning' of property in a particular society:

> The plausibility of rhetorical expedients of this sort is difficult to assess. They depend on the way you suppose 'property' will ring in the ears of an addressee and on his willingness to fall in line with the terminological shift. Imagine the following dialogue:
>
> Egalitarian: 'For reasons of A, B and C, I maintain that everyone ought to have an enforceable right to work.'
>
> Conservative: 'For reasons of X, Y and Z, I disagree with you.'
>
> Egalitarian: 'But you believe that property ought to be protected, don't you?'

---

69 Ibid., p. 146.
70 Ibid., p. 147.
71 Ibid., p. 149.
72 Ibid.

Conservative: 'I do.'

Egalitarian: 'Well the right to work is property.'

Conservative response 1: 'No it isn't.'

Conservative response 2: 'Why didn't you say that before? Of course, I now change my view to yours.'[73]

It can be seen that this discourse is intended to have the opposite effect from the attempts to understand companies by representing shareholder rights as property ownership rights. In the former case the right to work is put forward as a 'property right' which can only be interfered with care and probably with compensation following. This is likely to have the effect of a redistribution of wealth to poorer communities. In the case of shareholders, since making a property claim about shareholder rights is an attempt to make them the focus for the company's efforts and those of the directors, giving us the structure which insists that directors should act in the service of shareholders and presumes this service to be profit maximisation,[74] the effect is likely to be reversed. In particular, strengthening the shareholders' rights excludes from consideration the interests of employees (and others on whom the company has an impact) and assumes that shareholders may profit at the expense of employees. This enhanced protection by representation of these rights as property rights is likely to have the effect of redistribution of wealth from employees to wealthy shareholders.

We need, therefore to examine very closely the results which might be achieved by the use of any expanded property rhetoric. As Harris notes 'The concept-expanding arguments ... concede, at least arguendo, that property as conventionally understood really deserves prestige and that the rights contended for have an importance which is merely parallel to conventional proprietary interests ... [the arguments] make too much of property'.[75]

In order to reach a proper understanding of what companies should be doing and of better governance, it is extremely important to explode the 'shareholder-owner' myth, see the company as a free-standing structure and create mechanisms to reflect the company's responsibilities towards

---

[73] Ibid., p. 160.

[74] Making a 'property claim' about intellectual property will have the same regressive effect.

[75] Harris (1996), p. 161.

those over whom it has power by reason of the exercise of its property rights by its managers.[76]

The identification of a property right does not in any way, as Harris points out, identify its parameters; it merely appeals to the importance of 'property'. The 'property concept' tells us nothing about the limitations to be imposed. Any recognition of property rights involve (1) a bestowal of the right on one or more persons; (2) a corresponding limitation of the rights of others; (3) limitations on the use of the right by its owner. Where the balance should be struck cannot be deduced from the 'nature' of the rights but needs to be considered as a distributional issue of social justice. If I make and patent a crossbow, and that gives me 'natural' rights in it, this does not mean I may use those rights to injure or bully others.

## Spectrum of Responsibilities: More Power, More Responsibility

Focus on property rights tends to divert attention away from the duties and responsibilities that are associated with them. The exercise of ownership over anything brings with it both moral and legal responsibilities. If I own a poisonous snake, I have both a legal and moral responsibility not to allow it to roam freely around a crowded shopping area. Just as rights over things give me rights against others (other people may not steal my snake) they also give me responsibilities to others (I may not injure them by failing to confine my snake). Great attention has been paid to the 'spectrum' of rights which property ownership brings, but how is the spectrum of responsibilities structured? Again, it is important to bear in mind that the responsibilities are to other persons, just as the rights are rights against other persons. The spectrum of ownership rights might be seen as a sliding scale, giving rights which vary from the nearly absolute – I am holding in my hand a bun which I am about to eat, thus exercising my absolute right to prevent you eating it – to a contingent right to inherit an incorporeal hereditament which will take a gaggle of lawyers to unravel and gives me very limited power over others. The spectrum of responsibilities may also resemble a sliding scale, with the heaviest responsibilities being placed on owners whose property rights give them the greatest power over other people. Thus the ownership of the snake brings with it the possibility of exercising lethal power over others, and consequent heavy responsibility. When ownership of inanimate items is the issue, there clearly is a similar responsibility not

---

[76] Although, as Paddy Ireland notes, this will be a difficult process; Ireland, P, 'Property and Contract in Contemporary Corporate Theory' (2004) *Legal Studies* 451.

to use the item to harm another, such as a knife to stab another person. What about 'neutral' items which have no immediately obvious potential for harm? In those cases the scarcity and necessity factors must come into play and, where items are both scarce and necessary for human dignified existence, ownership of the power to exclude others must bear a concomitant responsibility not to wield that power unfairly.

The inequality of power has been a continuous theme throughout the book, and the following section argues that wherever great power is being exercised over others by virtue of property rights, the consequent responsibilities are greater, the greater the degree of inequality. Unfair use of such power may be regulated by well-known concepts borrowed from competition law.

## Concepts of Ownership: Useful or a Mirage?

Harris argues that the concept of 'ownership' retains value as embedded within it are a bundle of expectations and understandings about the 'just' distribution of property. Ross has argued that ownership concepts are meaningless because they can be omitted from legal language with no loss.[77] This enables a moving on; a mere description of property rights as they stand cannot solve any controversial question. Ross argues that the concept of ownership is meaningless by describing an imaginary island community where people believe in an imaginary form of contamination which they call 'tu-tu'. If you eat the chief's food you become tu-tu. If you become tu-tu, you have to undergo a purification ceremony. Ross argues that the rule could be rewritten: 'if you eat the chief's food, you must undergo a purification ceremony'.[78] In the same way, property rules could be rewritten, leaving out the concept of ownership: if X purchases goods he becomes owner; if he is owner he can sue to prevent interference with the item. In the same way as tu-tu, ownership could be taken out of this description; if X purchases the goods, he can sue to prevent interference with them. However, Harris argues that the concept of ownership has embedded in it the balance of interests that must be taken into account when judges decide a difficult and novel case lying on the borderline between different bundles of ownership rights. Discussing United Steel Workers' case[79] where the Court ruled that a corporation was, as owner of the plant, free to demolish it and not obliged to sell it to the union even at a fair market price, Harris argues that

77 Ross, A., 'tu-tu' (1957) 70 *Harvard Law Review* 625.
78 Ibid., cited in Harris (1996), p. 131.
79 *United Steel Workers v United States Steel Corporation* 631 F 2d (1980).

> An apologist for the court's ruling would argue as follows. There are sound reasons for conferring open-ended use-privileges and control powers over industrial plants on individuals and groups – for example, the inherent property-freedom argument and the market instrumental argument … Those property-specific justice reasons support liberty to act in a self-seeking way. When the judges invoked ownership they were keying into those reasons. They warrant the conclusion that the corporation could act for the benefit of the shareholders without regard to the effect of their decisions on others.[80]

In other words, the concept of ownership stands apart from the mere description of the bundle of rights and contains within it the notion of the arguments concerning the just allocation of those rights. This can be used to solve novel disputes about boundaries of rights.

On the other hand, it could equally be argued that the use of 'ownership or property rights' rhetoric may inhibit finding the solution to the distributional issues involved in a novel court decision, by concealing its distributional effect by the very use of 'property rights rhetoric' (an argument that Harris himself espouses and illustrates with his dialogue between 'conservative' and 'egalitarian' (above)).

The inherent distributional implications contained within any concept of property ownership causes Harris to wrestle with that intractable question of the 'just' distribution of property. This may be a red herring as Harris himself points out that the major importance of unequal distributions of property is the domination-potential. In a brief but compelling analysis, Wilkinson shows how important inequality is. In *Mind the Gap*,[81] he demonstrates that 'inequality kills' and 'income inequality affects health independently of average living standards, of the proportion of the population in absolute poverty, of expenditure on medical care, and of the prevalence of smoking'.[82] Further, inequality brings in its wake a significant increase in violence and social dislocation. It may well be that the extreme inequality of distribution causes unrest in society not only because of simple envy of material possessions but because of a system which perpetuates privilege and seeks to exclude the powerless from having a voice. Thus, an education system which continually perpetrates the rule of the monied classes may engender

---

[80] Harris (1996) p. 137.

[81] Wilkinson, R., *Mind the Gap: Hierarchies, Health and Human Evolution* (Wiedenfeld and Nicolson, London 2000) and see Wilkinson R. and K. Pickett, *The Spirit Level: Why Equality is Better for Everyone* (Penguin, London 2009 and 2010). Stiglitz (2012).

[82] Wilkinson (2000), p. 11.

despair and exclusion in the remainder of the population.[83] Similarly, a world that refuses to permit the poorest to develop or have a say in the way in which the planet's affairs are run will have the same effect. This (Sen) is now accepted as one of the prime indicators of poverty. Thus, justice may not require a mathematical 'slicing of the cake' to ensure equality of resources beyond provision of basic needs, but it may well require checks on the use of power brought by access to material things. This must be particularly so where the goods are scarce and essential to human existence.

## Property and Power

It can be seen, therefore, that problems are often caused not by the concept of property ownership itself but the potential which property ownership has to create unequal power relations. Thus, 'to concede a property relationship between one person and a thing, at any point along the property spectrum, is to negate the liberty of the rest of mankind to use the thing without the licence of the "owner"'.[84] The concept of property as power follows inexorably from the Hohfeldian/Honore/Harris understanding of property rights not as rights over things, but as rights against persons. Inevitably, the property as power effect is exacerbated where there is huge inequality of property ownership:

> Theorists who deplore great inequality in wealth-holdings and recommend measures to alleviate it often have in mind, not the social-psychological argument against wealth disparities … but rather inequality's resultant domination-potential. It is not disparity in bank balances that matters. It is the influence over the lives of others which large property-holdings afford.[85]

So property ownership brings with it power, and the greater the inequality of property ownership, the greater the domination-potential. This is particularly true where the supply of particular goods is in scarce supply.

> If the supply of objects like clothing, furniture and books is drastically restricted, those few who own them could dominate their fellows by the ego-centric exercise of their ownership power to control use. On the other hand, where such chattels are widely available, the use-channelling and

---

83 Wilkinson (2000).
84 Harris (1996), p. 264.
85 Ibid., p. 265.

> use-policing functions of ownership interests … as compared with costly and intrusive regimes of communal use, clearly outweigh such dangers of domination.[86]

If property is understood as governing power relationships, it is even more important in a company context to look at the management who have the real power to deploy the assets of the company. A system of corporate governance is a way to restrain powerful managers.

Paddy Ireland has made it clear that companies fit with difficulty into the property rights discourse.[87] This is because the traditional take on companies is that they are 'the property of the shareholders' or in the 'nexus of contracts' or 'agency' theory of the company, in what amounts to the same thing: that the shareholders own not 'the company' but 'the capital', the company itself having been spirited out of existence.[88] Ireland also shows that there is considerable convergence between the property rights of creditors and those of shareholders; each can be seen as essentially 'outsiders' having contractual rights against the company, rather than 'insiders' with membership rights. The remaining 'insider' rights of shareholders are relics of the time when joint stock companies were run by members, and of an even earlier time when lending for interest was banned but partnership for profit was not. An investment as a 'sleeping partner' was a convenient way to circumvent this rule. What are the relics? One is the rule that the residue of capital on a winding-up belongs to shareholders. The other is that they should have a significant role in the way the company is run. In contrast to that, the shareholders have a claim of control but in practise the exercise of control is an exercise in futility. 'The dictionary definition of ownership emphasises physical possession … it is a right which has no analogue in the case of an intangible asset or collection of assets.'[89] In the company context, the shareholder does not own specific assets of the corporation but rather a proportional slice of the entirety of assets reflected in his stock certificate. 'Ownership of capital should not be confused with ownership of the firm.'[90] 'Property, power and entitlement can be seen as the three central

---

[86] Ibid.

[87] Ireland, P., 'Company Law and the Myth of Shareholder Ownership' (1999) *MLR* 62. See also J. Hill, 'Visions and Revisions of the Shareholder' (2000) *American Journal of Comparative Law* 39.

[88] Ireland (1999).

[89] John, K. and A. Silberston, 'Corporate Governance' (2005) *National Institute Economic Review*, August, p. 87.

[90] Fama, E., 'Agency Problems and the Theory of the Firm' (1980) 88 *Journal of Political Economy* 288.

aspects of a share … a share is an item of intangible property. It is itself a "bundle of rights" giving the shareholder neither the ownership of the company's assets nor ownership of the company as a "thing".'[91] In contrast to the traditional legal theory of property rights, the shareholders are not in a position to exercise the traditional rights inherent in the concept of property; no shareholder is permitted to 'use a listed company's assets for his own purpose or restrict management's access to corporate resources'.[92] The concrete definition of the rights of proprietary nature stemming from the ownership of shares is indeed problematic, considering that the shareholders do not have a right to receive a fixed dividend nor to have their capital returned to them at a specified date. The difficulty in defining the exact scope of the proprietary rights stemming from stockholding is reflective of the challenges in defining shareholding in a traditional 'property right' sense. The corporate concept slices the bundle of rights inherent in property to various pieces; the stockholder 'gets the right to receive some of the fruits of the use of property, a fractional residual right in corporate property, and a very limited right of control. The rights to possess, use, and control the property go to the managers of the corporation'.[93] Thus, only the right to transfer the interest which has also been the overriding aim in the securities markets is 'unequivocally exercised by the stockholder'.[94] According to the court, 'a sole shareholder has no independent right which is violated by trespass upon or conversion of the corporation's property';[95] an astonishing ruling that demonstrates the difficulty of using traditional notions of property in the corporate context.

Therefore, once the link between ownership and control is smashed or at least severely damaged, the status of the shareholders as the sole proprietors of the company with interests that monopolise the company's agenda becomes distinctively less convincing. If the tenant in a rented flat wishes to renovate the property, he will need to ask for the consent of the owner who has to authorise the works and provide the funds for it. In

[91] Worthington, S., 'Shares and Shareholders: Property, Power and Entitlement: Part 1' (2001) 22 *Company Lawyer* 9, p. 258.

[92] Caspar, R., 'Stakeholder Orientation versus shareholder value: a matter of contractual failures' (2004) *European Journal of Law and Economics*, p. 82.

[93] Votaw in M.M. Blair, *Ownership and Control* (The Brookings Institution, Washington 1995), p. 224.

[94] Monks, R.A.G. and N. Minow, *Corporate Governance*, 4th edn (John Wiley & Sons Ltd, Chichester 2010), p. 108.

[95] *W. Clay Jackson Enterprises Inc v Greyhound Leasing and Financial Corporation*, 463 F. supp. 666, D.P.R. 1979, 670.

the company context however the decisions are taken by a small, usually highly specialised number of private individuals, the managers, while the ones perceived as the owners of the corporation will probably lack the information that certain decisions are being taken on their very own behalf. The number of shareholders of a big corporation can exceed the population of a rather sizeable urban conglomeration, and can nowadays amount to millions of individuals; therefore, their consent to decision-making at all times and in their entirety would be practically impossible but also highly undesirable as it would entail the dissemination of detailed information to millions of people, who would probably not possess the knowledge necessary to decide on issues crucial for the company's profitability or existence. Furthermore, this process would demand enormous amount of time and effort, rendering its application simply unthinkable. While interviewed about shareholders exercising their right to vote, one institutional investor noted that

> there is a weakness in the present system of corporate governance in that responsibility for ownership rests with people who don't want it and are not seeking it. We are investing in shares because they give us a good return and it is coincidental really that they bring with them this responsibility. I am not saying we don't want this responsibility. I am saying it is difficult to handle that sort of thing.[96]

That means that democracy as we know it at national level cannot be applied in the company context as the engagement of a vast number of shareholders, at least in large corporations, remains a complicated issue. Tocqueville's central hypothesis was that 'democracy constitutes the sole model of acceptable governance in modern society and it will eventually prevail in all spheres of organised activity';[97] corporations might prove even Tocqueville wrong, at least in the sense of democracy as we know it at the public domain. However, an additional conclusion is the rather unique nature of ownership in this context. If the owner cannot control what he or she owns, then it is not ownership in the traditional sense of the term as we know and experience it in the non-corporate world. Therefore, it can be validly claimed that the fervently supported exclusive ownership rights of the shareholders present certain particularities that render the whole issue more controversial or less clear than initially

[96] Solomon, J., *Corporate Governance and Accountability*, 2nd edn (John Wiley & Sons Ltd, Chichester 2009), p. 19.

[97] Gomez, P-Y and H. Korine, 'Democracy and the Evolution of Corporate Governance' (2005) 13 *Corporate Governance* 6, p. 742. For an excellent review of the reading on the theories of corporate governance see Keay (2011).

envisaged. The legal world might have to accept either that in the corporate context a new sense of ownership has to be constructed, or that shareholders do have a claim towards the company as they are undoubtedly and inexorably linked to it through their shares, but the particular nature of this relationship along with the far-reaching effects of corporate action at social level might require the consideration of other factors when designing the company policies and drafting its aims and targets.

## THE THEORETICAL FOUNDATIONS OF CORPORATE GOVERNANCE

Behind the debates on corporate governance lie its theoretical underpinnings. Several theories have been constructed and elaborated by academics and social scientists in their attempt to shed light on the precise nature of corporate governance, its origins, its structural parameters and the sources of the legitimacy of the aims it pursues along with the internal actors that social science deems as the components of such a system. The theories in question tend to investigate the sources and the historical evolution of corporate governance while aiming to interpret the rationale behind its structure, orientation and components. There is an abundance of articles relating to the various theories that have accompanied the analysis of the theoretical background of corporate governance. They have been vigorously argued by their creators, providing the grounds for a new round of debate among academics or members of the business community whose views coincide with one or other of the relevant theories. The exchange of views and ideas has further contributed to the better understanding not only of corporate governance per se but also of the social phenomenon that is the company. However, the existence of numerous theories in relation to the fundamental aspects of corporate governance, such as its origins and legitimate aims and actors along with the different sets of interpretation of its main features and characteristics, reveals not only the existence of a very interesting set of literature but also the magnitude of controversy always accompanying the issue in question. Different academics and practitioners have elaborated divergent platforms of interpretation of the same legal and social phenomenon: corporate governance. Social scientists, lawyers and economists have all interpreted and thoroughly analysed corporate governance from their point of view on the basis of their educational and professional background and interests, and provided the readers with sometimes conflicting views in relation to the fundamentals of such a phenomenon. This book will focus mainly on four theories that underpin corporate governance today: the agency theory, with its closely linked 'nexus of contracts' theory, the concession theory along with the similar stakeholder theory.

## The Agency Theory

The agency theory[98] is set in the context of the separation of ownership and control that has been analysed previously. The analysis of Berle and Means[99] stands at the very core of this theory. The rapid evolution of the corporation from the joint stock company into the public company of the last century with a shareholding held by millions had led to what has been described above as the separation of ownership from control; the shareholders are deemed as the owners of the company but facing the problem of controlling what they are deemed to own. A separate management is actually running the company and taking all crucial decisions with the shareholders 'best suited to discipline directors'[100] when conducting their duties but failing to effectively monitor their activities and challenge the legitimacy of their decisions. The theory focuses on the components of the relationship, namely the shareholders and the managers, and identifies an agency relationship; the shareholders are the principals who delegate duties to the other party to the relationship, the managers. The problems arising are mainly centred on the managers and their increasing autonomy brought by the waning of links between themselves and their principals. The agents are supposed to represent the principals and pursue their interests, but in practice the relationship has proven more problematic as the increasingly independent and insufficiently monitored agents availed themselves of the opportunity to promote their own agenda instead of serving the interests of the principals. The information asymmetry stands at the centre of this relationship. The principals lack the access to the same level of information about the ongoing decision-making in the corporate context. Therefore, the agents profit from their access to better information in relation to the company's affairs, and more specifically the everyday

---

[98] Jensen, M. and W. Meckling, 'Theory of the Firm: Managerial Behaviour, Agency Costs and Ownership Structure', (1976) 3 *Journal of Financial Economics* 305; Fama (1980); Fama and Jensen, 'Separation of Ownership and Control' (1983) 26 *Journal of Law and Economics* 301.

[99] Berle and Means (2009).

[100] Matheson, J. and B. Olson, 'Corporate Law and the Longterm Shareholder Model of Corporate Governance' (1992) 76 *Minnesota Law Review* 1313, p. 1328.

administration of the corporation. As the links between principals and the company become looser due to an increasing number of shareholders with a very limited portion of the shares that do not justify higher ambitions in terms of involvement in the company's management, the accompanying lack of information about the decisions taken and the discussions made at the top table leave the principals at an absolutely disadvantageous position, especially against their agents.

In such a context, the efforts are directed towards aligning the interests of the agents with those of their principals. This effort involves initiatives that would achieve a highly desirable coincidence between the interests of the two groups so that the agents would have little space to pursue different agendas. This brings to the spotlight the necessity of introducing those 'institutional arrangements that would provide some checks and balances to make sure they do not abuse their power. The costs resulting from managers misusing their position as well as the costs of monitoring and disciplining them to try to prevent abuse have been called agency costs'.[101] The latter have to be added to the previously incurred 'residual loss' which is the reduction in shareholder value brought about by managerial behaviour that fails to fully incorporate shareholder interest in managerial decisions. The granting of benefits or bonuses to managers might lead to such residual losses. Also, different perceptions of risk can lead to further losses for the shareholders as the management might opt for a different list of options on the basis of a different risk evaluation. Assuming a risk to pursue shareholder interests might not seem a particularly appealing choice for the managers who would alternatively incline towards another option that would involve less risk but would also be less beneficial for their principals. In contrast to that, the managers might be willing to assume extra risk to pursue their individual rights, sometimes leading to further residual losses for the shareholders. This is usually referred to as the problem of 'risk sharing'[102] which involves different agendas, diverse perceptions of risk and to a diverging set of interests. The agency theory offers shareholders 'a pre-eminent position in the firm legitimised not by the idea that they are the firm's owners but instead its residual risk takers'.[103] However, at this level much criticism can be raised. Any society aiming to create a dynamic economy that would contribute to the maximisation of wealth would opt for the

---

101 Blair (1995).

102 Shankman, N.A., 'Reframing the debate between agency and stakeholder theories of the firm' (1999) 19 *Journal of Business Ethics* 319.

103 Clarke, T., *Theories of Corporate Governance, The Philosophical Foundations of Corporate Governance* (Routledge, New York 2008), p. 5.

creation of an environment that would foster or at least encourage the taking of risks on the part of the entrepreneurs; however as explained above, the 'entrepreneur is no longer the shareholder who whether an individual or a fund manager simply manages a portfolio of assets but the executive managers'.[104] Therefore, the society as a whole 'plays the role of the insurer for the risks taken … the insurance is free, the risk is largely determined by the behaviour of the injured party and the insurer is granted no specific role in the internal control of the risk. What private insurer would accept such conditions?'[105] The incoherence detected at this point raises certain questions in relation to the safeguards against such risks. The shareholder primacy is founded upon the principle that it is the shareholders who assume the risks of their investment and therefore they should enjoy a status that would provide them with the appropriate guarantees. As analysed above however, despite the intentions and initial developments due to the current structure of large public companies, the managers have assumed the role initially carried by the shareholders. Those risks can have social costs and an adverse impact, either on the local community or in the case of large corporations on the society as a whole. And yet society is usually confined to the timid role of the observer despite having a direct interest in intervening with the form of regulation. Therefore, the insurer provides indeed a free insurance on the basis of the hypothesis that the risk-bearer will behave as expected, despite the lack of institutional guarantees since the insurer cannot participate in the internal control of the risk. These are indeed conditions that no private insurer would ever adhere to. Another reason why the separation of ownership and control has led to a 'characterisation of shareholder interests in strict economic terms was probably because such a structure was originally the most effective way to measure the performance of and hence hold accountable professional directors and managers who essentially have unfettered control over the day to day affairs of the company'.[106] However, the absolute shareholder supremacy (with its evolution into a managerial supremacy in many cases) has functioned in a similar framework in jurisdictions where the shareholders stand at the core of the corporate structure, such as the USA.

---

[104] Clerc, C., 'Questioning the Legitimacy of Shareholder Power' in J.P. Touffut, *Does Company Ownership Matter?* (Edward Elgar, Cheltenham 2009), p. 94.

[105] Ibid.

[106] McConvill, J., 'The Separation of Ownership and Control under a happiness based theory of the corporation' (2005) 26 *Company Lawyer* 2, p. 39.

The shareholders who have entrusted the running of the company to managers might find themselves in a situation where not only are their interests not served in the best possible way, but due to managerial pursuance of self-interest they incur both residual and subsequently agency costs. Costs can include time-consuming efforts or meetings to acquire the information necessary for a more effective monitoring of the managerial group. 'It is generally impossible for the principle or the agent at zero cost to ensure that the agent will make optimal decisions from the principal's viewpoint.'[107] Executive pay can also be regarded as

> an agency cost in itself in that it provides a potentially fruitful and opaque device for self-dealing by conflicted managers … a conflicted board may use the pay-setting process to influence pay and extract rents in the form of pay in excess of that which would be optimal for shareholders given weaknesses in the design of pay contracts and in their supporting governance structures.[108]

In addition to that, the equity-based 'incentive contract may as post Enron scholarship argues deepen conflicts of interest between shareholders and management by generating perverse management incentives to manipulate financial disclosure particularly earnings and distort share prices which can lead to catastrophic corporate failures'.[109] In this context the alignment of managerial and shareholder interests can be pursued with the appointment of independent non-executive directors on the board and with the scrapping of bonuses in the form of extra money or free holidays for example, with the simultaneous introduction of stock options so that the agents will have an additional personal interest to construct a policy that will guarantee profitability and therefore an increase in the value of the shares. In the USA and UK, takeovers have been extensively used as a form of disciplinary mechanism against the managers that would be instantly removed in case of an acquisition, which usually brings with it a whole new set of management. Therefore, the threat of a takeover should function as an incentive to shape a strategy effective enough to foster the profitability of the company. Because 'of the expense of the external mechanisms to the principal's

---

107 Jensen and Meckling (1976), p. 308.

108 Ferrarini, G. and N. Moloney, 'Executive Remuneration in the EU: The Context of Reform' (2005) *European Corporate Governance Institute, Law Working Paper*, paper 32, p. 3.

109 Ibid.

utility, internal mechanisms are generally preferred'.[110] Behind these suggestions lies the problem that they attempt to conceal: the fact that in big public corporations, managers would actually require specially designed incentives so as to perform what should have been their otherwise obvious basic duty; the duty to act in the best interests of the company which in any case includes the shareholders rather than their own. However, the fact that special policies have to be designed and external mechanisms of control have to be put in place to guarantee that managers are motivated enough to perform the basic duty inherent in their role is indicative of the flaws existing in the current framework. As analysed below, much literature focuses on whether the shareholders should be the sole actors whose interests should be taken into account, or whether other stakeholders should be able to be included in managerial calculations as insiders within the company. What appears evident however is that even in the jurisdictions where the shareholders enjoy absolute exclusivity as the only owners of the company (with the principal example of the USA where the agency theory flourished and was reflected in the corporate structure and practice), they find it difficult to compel the management to focus on what is admittedly the fundamental aspect of their role; acting in the best interests of the company, which in the USA among other jurisdictions is basically interpreted as acting in the best interests of the shareholders. Promoting a whole list of incentives to convince the actors who are anyway supposed to act as the agents of the shareholders to adhere to the basic parameters of their role, reveals the magnitude of the challenge faced at this level. If shareholders are the exclusive owners of the company and the management is merely the agent of the shareholders aiming at safeguarding their interest and guaranteeing a return of their investment, then the lack of motivation on the part of the managers to perform this role reveals in a spectacular manner a fundamental flaw lying at the very heart of this model. A variety of scandals, with Enron as an example, reveals the practical repercussions of this relationship, which in many occasions appears to be deeply dysfunctional.

## The Company as a 'Nexus of Contracts'

The theoretical conception integrally linked with the agency theory is the so-called 'nexus of contracts' theory. Theorists have looked at this theory

---

[110] Clarke (2008), p. 119. Walsh, J.P. and J.K. Steward, 'On the efficiency of the internal and external corporate control mechanisms' (1990) 15 *Journal of Management Review* 421.

either independently or in conjunction with the agency theory. According to this theory, the company is simply a nexus of contracts renegotiated by the individuals involved in it, with the principal aim of maximising their own utility[111] and the market value of the company through 'allocative, productive and dynamic efficiency'.[112] The theory's main principle is the fact that companies as other organisations are 'simply legal fictions which serve as a nexus of contracting relationships among individuals';[113] they consist of many 'different kinds of relations that are worked out by those voluntarily associating in a company'[114] and they form 'the substance of the corporate fiduciary duty'.[115] More specifically, the private firm is 'characterised by the existence of divisible residual claims on the assets and cash flows of the organisation which can generally be sold without permission of the other contracting individuals';[116] hence shareholders have 'the greatest stake in the outcome of the company'[117] and therefore the greatest interest in 'the right of control above any other stakeholders'.[118] The natural outcome of this theoretical construction is the fact that since the company is a 'collection of private contractual relationships',[119] it is devoid of any social responsibility and should be left remote from any regulatory interference which would place limitations upon the right to use the free enterprise tool as shaped exclusively by its signatory parties. The economic analysis embarks on the perspective that the company has 'traditionally been thought of more as a voluntary association between shareholders than as a creation of the

---

111 Alchian, A. and H. Demsetz, 'Production, Information Costs and Economic Organisation' (1972) 62 *American Economic Review* 777 and see Cheffins (1997).

112 Mayer, C., 'Corporate Governance, Competition and Performance' (1997) 24 *Journal of Law and Society*, pp. 152 and 155.

113 Jensen and Meckling (1976), p. 310.

114 Easterbrook and Fischel, 'The Corporate Contract' (1989) 89 *Columbia Law Review* 1416, p. 1426.

115 Smith, T., 'The Efficient Norm for Corporate Law: A Neotraditional Interpretation of Fiduciary Duty' (1999) 98 *Michigan Law Review* 214, p. 217.

116 Jensen and Meckling (1976), p. 311.

117 Macey, R.J., 'Fiduciary Duties as Residual Claims: Obligation to Non-shareholder Constituencies from a Theory of the Firm Perspective' (1999) 84 *Cornell Law Review*, p. 1267.

118 Van der Weide, M.E., 'Against Fiduciary Duties to Corporate Stakeholders' (1996) 21 *Delaware Journal of Corporate Law*, p. 57.

119 Fama (1980), p. 290.

state'.[120] Neo-classical economists including Coase have viewed companies as method of 'reducing the costs of a complex market consisting of a series bargains among parties',[121] rendering unnecessary further regulation, especially on the part of the state. The focus is therefore clearly placed on contract as the 'mechanism which brings about exchange',[122] and the company is viewed as possessing a central position in 'the contractual arrangements of all other inputs'.[123] However, even if a purely contractual basis for the company is utterly accepted, it can be hardly viewed as independent from its regulatory background. The governance of corporations is effectuated not only

> through contracts, law and norms but also through the complex set of relationships that exist among these three sources of corporate governance. Contracts are written under the 'shadow of the state' … thus rules, norms and statutes inform the content of contracts that affect corporate law and corporate governance because they dictate the background factors that the parties take into account when they negotiate.[124]

This theory focuses on deregulation by the state, but the construct of contract also has dubious roots especially aligned with the Kaldor–Hicks efficiency doctrine.[125]

Neglecting the regulatory, normative and societal background of the contractual arrangement will not therefore insulate the company from external influences and interventions. The latter are indeed inherent even in the contractual agreement which binds its members. Under this theory,

> company law should have as its sole objective the maximisation of shareholder value. To this end it must set default rules that maximise the efficiency

---

[120] Cheffins (1997), p. 41.

[121] Belcher, A., 'The Boundaries of the Firm: the Theories of Coase, Knight and Weitzman' (1997) 17 *Legal Studies*, 22.

[122] Alchian, A. and H. Demsetz, 'Production, Information Costs, and Economic Organisation' (1972) 62 *American Economic Review*, 777.

[123] Ibid.

[124] Macey, *Corporate Governance, Promises Kept, Promises Broken* (Princeton University Press, Princeton NJ 2008), p. 31.

[125] Ogus, A., *Regulation: Legal Form and Economic Theory* (Clarendon Press, Oxford 1994): Suppose that the policymaker had to choose between (A) a policy that increased society's wealth by $1 million and benefited the poor more than the rich, and (B) a policy that increased its wealth by $2 million, the bulk of which devolved on the rich? Many would argue for (A) on the grounds of fairness but (B) would be considered to be superior in Kaldor–Hicks terms (p. 25).

> of negotiating the nexus of contracts. In this way transaction costs can be reduced, as negotiations do not need to take place in every single transaction … the emphasis is on investors' choices.[126]

The corporation in this framework is to be understood as 'the product of a series of organisational innovations that have had the purpose and effect of economising on transaction costs'.[127]

This theory places a focus on the network of contractual relations existing within a company, but it does not take into consideration and therefore analyse the different nature of the contracts involved. There are actors such as the employees and suppliers who sign contracts with the company, setting the specific legal framework within which they are going to supply either their personal labour or specifically defined products and services to the legal person that is the company. At the other tip of the balance stand the shareholders whose relationship in the company present certain particularities, at least from a legal point of view. On the one hand they have a recognised 'residual claim' bearing the risk of somehow having the return of their investment being jeopardised while being the final actor to receive money from the company in the form of dividends, and after the remaining actors have been satisfied on the basis of their contract. The existence of this residual claim in conjunction with their character as the capital providers justifies their supremacy within the company context. The precedence of the claims of the other actors against the company betrays the contractual nature of their relationship with the company which guarantees returns for their labour, services or products supplied. The shareholders do not fit this model as comfortably as the other aforementioned actors; their relationship cannot be characterised as a contractual one from a purely legal point of view.

Despite that, their supremacy within the UK corporate governance model for example cannot be easily challenged. The Company Law Review Steering Group recognised the absolute dominance of shareholders in the company context requiring directors to 'manage the business on their behalf … the ultimate objective of the companies is to

---

126 Lee, J., 'Shareholders' Derivative Claims under the Companies Act 2006: Market Mechanisms or Asymmetric paternalism?' (2007) 18 *International Company and Commercial Law Review* 11, p. 379.

127 Williamson, 'The Modern Corporation: Origins, Evolution, Attributes' (1981) 19 *Journal of Economic Literature* 1537.

generate maximum wealth for shareholders'.[128] In the UK, the Companies Act 2006 in section 33 provides for the company's articles of association to bind the company and its members to the same extent, as if there were covenants on the part of the company and of each member to observe those provisions. In *Wood v Odessa Waterworks* (1889)[129] Stirling J said: 'The articles of association constitute a contract not merely between the shareholders and the company, but between each individual shareholder and every other.' Despite the fact that at first glance the provision appears to be clear enough to define the relationship between the shareholders on the one hand and the company on the other as contractual, the reality can be slightly less clear. The articles of association might be a contract that binds the company with the shareholders and provides the basis for the regulation of the relations among them as well, but this is no ordinary contract. According to the same Act in section 21, the company can amend the articles with a special resolution demanding a majority of 75 per cent of the members present and voting. This means that in contrast to other contracts, the one standing at the centre of the nexus is not one that requires the unanimity of its signatory parties to reform but can be done on the basis of a reinforced majority of the members who are present and voting. In *Allen*[130] another requirement was added when Lindley MR said: 'the power must be exercised, not only in the manner required by law, but also *bona fide* for the benefit of the company as a whole, and it must not be exceeded'. Therefore, uniquely in order to change the content of the contract, we do not need unanimity but a majority of 75 per cent along with the obligation to act bona fide for the benefit of the company; a requirement that the courts have interpreted in a rather strict manner in any case. Furthermore, as a matter of additional importance the issue who can enforce this contract becomes an exercise in obscurity. The obvious reply to this question would simply be the signatory parties, namely the company and the shareholders. However, both the reality and the legal interpretation of the 'contract' have rendered this reply simply incorrect. While any other contract including the respective of the employees and the suppliers would be automatically enforceable on the basis of its distinctive provisions to the company on one hand and the employees on the other, the shareholders would need the assistance of a

[128] Department of Trade and Industry, The Company Law Review Steering Group, *Modern Company Law for a Competitive Economy: the Strategic Framework* (1999), pp. 34–7.

[129] *Wood v Odessa Waterworks* (1889) 42 Ch D 636.

[130] *Allen v Gold Reefs of West Africa Ltd* [1900] 1 Ch 656.

corporate lawyer to inform them whether they are in fact in a position where they can enforce rights stemming from the 'contract' or not.

The courts have not been very helpful in providing us with a clear interpretation of the concepts in question. In *London Sack*[131] Scott LJ said that the contract, which was created between the members under the predecessor to section 33, did not constitute a contract between them 'about rights of action created entirely outside the company relationship such as trading transactions between members'. Great confusion was also created when despite what was initially thought, shareholder *could not* actually enforce the 'contract' when they were wearing an additional hat. So, even when they are also shareholders, directors of the company or its solicitors might find it difficult to enforce rights stemming from the 'contract'. In such case they are considered 'outsiders' and the courts refuse to grant them the rights provided for by the document that is otherwise taken to be a contract. In *Eley*,[132] the court held that the articles were a matter between the shareholders among themselves or the shareholders and the directors. They did not create any contract between a solicitor and the company. This was so even though the solicitor had become a member of the company some time after the articles had been signed.

This means that there is a subtlety in the definition of an 'outsider' in these circumstances. He is a person unable to enforce the articles or be affected by the contract in the articles. When the person seeking to enforce the articles has effectively two relationships with the company, he may be both an 'outsider' in the sense discussed in *Eley*, but at the same time a shareholder of the company. In this case he might find it difficult to enforce the articles. In *Hickman*,[133] Astbury J cited a number of cases and went on to say:

> An outsider to whom rights purport to be given by the articles in his capacity as outsider, whether he is or subsequently becomes a member, cannot sue on those articles treating them as contracts between himself and the company to enforce those rights. Those rights are not part of the general regulations of the company applicable alike to all shareholders and can only exist by virtue of some contract between such person and the company, and the subsequent allotment of shares to an outsider in whose favour such an article is inserted does not enable him to sue the company on such article to enforce rights which are … not part of the general rights of the corporations as such.

---

131 *London Sack and Bag v Dixon* [1943] 2 All ER 763.
132 *Eley v Positive Government Security Life Association* (1876) 1 Ex D 88.
133 *Hickman v Kent and Romney Marsh Sheepbreeders* [1915] 1 Ch 881.

Therefore, shareholders of this kind would need an additional contract to enforce those rights. To add further confusion, the court ruled in *Salmon*[134] that Salmon who was a managing director was able to enforce his right of veto by way of the contract in the articles. Here the court effectively supported that every shareholder has the right to enforce the articles of the company; a shareholder who also holds a position as an outsider (such as managing director, solicitor, etc.) can, wearing his shareholder hat, enforce the contract in the articles, even if the direct result of that enforcement is of benefit to him wearing his outsider hat. This analysis proves that the consideration of the relationship between the company and the shareholders as contractual could prove to be a challenging issue, accompanied by complicated questions that still need to be resolved. The nature of the contract binding the company with its shareholders presents certain particularities which render its inclusion in this nexus of contracts problematic for lawyers, to say the least.

Subsequently, the position of the shareholders in this contractual equation will also need further legal clarification. In *O'Neil*[135] the company was defined as 'an association of persons for an economic purpose … the terms of the association are contained in the articles of association'. Therefore, the company has an economic purpose 'agreed to by those persons constituting its composite members'.[136] Buying shares, one can therefore become a party to this agreement respecting the purpose of the association, agreeing to its terms and accepting its limitations but also taking advantage of the right to participate in the majority required to alter the terms of the agreement. This is integral in the notion of membership, but whether a contractual nature can be granted to those rights and obligations is an issue that would require more solid legal justification. In this framework the employees, the suppliers or the creditors appear to have a clear contractual relationship with the company while the shareholders have a recognised residual claim in the sense that they have invested money in the company, assuming the risk of seeing no return of their investment. They are the last actor in the list to receive money from the company, usually in the form of dividends in case of profitability and after the employees have been paid on the basis of their employment contract. In fact, a shareholder appointed to directorship will not be entitled to receive a salary if this is not provided for by a separate employment contract; in *Re George*

---

134 *Quin & Axtens Ltd v Salmon* [1909] AC 442.

135 *O'Neil and another v Phillips* (1999) UKHL 24, [1999] 1 WLR 1092.

136 Bolodeoku, O.I., 'Economic Theories of the Corporation and Corporate Governance: a Critique' (2002) *Journal of Business Law*, p. 418.

*Newman*[137] it was clarified that appointment to a directorship does not entitle one to be paid, even if he does in fact work for the company. Fama claims that 'as residual claimants the shareholders guarantee the performance of their contracts by putting up wealth ex ante with this front money used to purchase capital and technology that the corporation uses for its productive activities'.[138] Therefore, the shareholders bear the residual risk but own the capital of the company and the technology therein, but not the company itself which retains its independence as a separate legal person. This statement 'is a first step towards the understanding that control over a firm's decisions is not necessarily the province of its shareholders',[139] as the 'ownership of the residual claim on the corporation's assets and earnings … is not the same as ownership of the corporation itself'.[140]

## The Stakeholder Theory

In contrast to the previous two theories which focus primarily on the shareholders, the stakeholder theory[141] extends its array of attention to all the actors that it considers as stakeholders.[142] The latter is defined as 'those groups without whose support the organisation could cease to exist'.[143] That would include both the internal stakeholders, namely the employees, but also the shareholders and the external stakeholders which are the suppliers, the creditors, the customers but also the community in proximity too. In this sense corporate governance is 'the process by which corporations are made responsive to the rights and wishes of stakeholders'.[144] The roots of this theory can be traced to the realisation that the corporations have evolved into vast entities whose activities and

---

137 *Re George Newman and Co.* [1895] 1 Ch 674.

138 Fama (1980).

139 Ibid.

140 Bainbridge, M.S., *The New Corporate Governance in Theory and Practice* (Oxford University Press, Oxford 2008), p. 32.

141 Donaldson T. and L. Preston, 'The Stakeholder Theory of the Corporation: Concepts, Evidence, Implications' (1995) 20 *Academy of Management Review* 65.

142 Clarkson, M., 'A Stakeholder Framework for Analysing and Evaluating Corporate Social Performance' (1995) 20 *Academy of Management Review* 92, p. 112.

143 Freeman, R.E., *Strategic Management: A Stakeholder Approach* (Pitman, Boston 1984), p. 31.

144 Demb, A. and F.F. Neubauer, 'The Corporate Board: Confronting the Paradoxes' (1992) 25 *Long Range Planning* 3, p. 9.

policies have an enormously far-reaching effect on the livelihoods of many in close proximity to them or even loosely associated with them. Corporate strategies can have a profound effect on the environment, the development of local communities especially in impoverished areas, the employees whose life is utterly dependent on their links with the company and on the suppliers whose production is defined by the nature and the volume of orders. If the creditors are added on this list too, taking into account that they provide the debt capital to the company and therefore constitute crucial factors integrally linked with corporate activity especially at a critical moment for the company's life, then it becomes evident that this theory attempts to embrace all the actors both internal and external that share a sufficient link with the company's activities and whose livelihoods or professional and other development are dependent on the nature of the corporate decision-making. In defining the stakeholder theory, Clarkson stated that

> the firm is a system of stakeholders operating within the larger system of the host society that provides the necessary legal and market infrastructure for the firm's activities. The purpose of the firm is to create wealth or value for its stakeholders by converting their stakes into goods and services.[145]

Blair supports the idea that

> the goal of directors and management should be to maximise total wealth creation by the firm. The key to achieving this is to enhance the voice of and provide ownership like incentives to those participants in the firm who contribute or control critical specialised inputs (firm specific human capital) and to align the interests of these critical stakeholders with the interests of the outside passive shareholders.[146]

The emphasis is now shifted from the shareholders to the stakeholders, although the former are included within the definition of the latter. This shift is 'premised on the theory that groups in addition to shareholders have claims on a company's assets and earnings because those groups contribute to a company's capital'.[147] The agency theory advocated the granting of incentives for managers to align their interests with the respective of the shareholders. The shareholders stood at the absolute

---

[145] Clarkson in S. Turnbull, 'Corporate Governance: Its Scope, Concerns and Theories' (1997) 5 *Corporate Governance: An International Review*, p. 190.

[146] Blair (1995).

[147] Karmel, S.R., 'Implications of the Stakeholder Model' (1993) 61 *George Washington Law Review*, pp. 1156 and 1171.

core of that theoretical construction and their interests were viewed as coinciding with the interests of the company. The nexus of contracts theory recognised a form of shareholder supremacy based on their residual claims along with their ownership of the capital and production, despite avoiding to approve the suggestion that the shareholders are in fact the owners of the company. The stakeholder theory suggests granting incentives to stakeholders this time so that their interests will be found, if not identical, then at least very similar to those of the shareholders so that the ultimate aim which is the maximisation of wealth for the company is more effectively attained. In supporting this, the theory actually emphasises the importance that the actors viewed as stakeholders have for the company and its profitability. The company is viewed as a profit-making mechanism but this time its constituents are not viewed as irrelevant actors who co-exist alongside the shareholders while failing to form a part of the corporate strategy, but as active contributors to the enhancing of the company's profits through the recognition that their high skilled labour, or supplies or their reliability and availability in times of insolvency, constitute necessary components of the strategy aiming at corporate profitability. Therefore, if the company is to avail itself of the opportunity to take better advantage of the aforementioned skills and services, it should also be prepared to include those actors as essential elements of its decision-making, taking into account their interests and special considerations. 'Business is about putting together a deal so that suppliers, customers, employees, communities, managers and shareholders all win continuously over time. In short at some level stakeholder interests have to be joint … or else there will be exit and a new collaboration formed.'[148]

The shareholders as providers of capital remain in a central position, but now more actors are coming under the spotlight to fulfil a multiplicity of aims. The stakeholder theory is 'less of a formal unified theory and more of a broad research tradition incorporating philosophy, ethics, political theory, economics, law and organisational social science'.[149] The tools employed by the theory to bring those actors under the umbrella of the corporate decision-making by elevating their interests as components of the interest of the company, are as analysed above, twofold; firstly, the argument that the inclusion of the stakeholders' interest into the company strategy will align their aspirations with those of the shareholders and

---

[148] Freeman, E.R., A. Wicks and B. Parmar, 'Stakeholder Theory and the Corporate Objective Revisited' (2004) 15 *Organisation Science* 364, p. 365.

[149] Solomon (2009), p. 23.

therefore contribute significantly to the maximisation of profit, principally for their interest; and secondly, that companies have 'in their function as an employer a critical role in interpreting and applying government policy in many sectors and they can exert leverage when dealing with the communities in which they operate often leading to concessions and other benefits'.[150] Therefore, there is clearly a public policy element in corporate functions, even if this is due to the implantation of government policies in crucial sectors.

This realisation gives birth to a moral argument, emphasising the obligations that the corporation as an entity has towards on the one hand its constituents, widely defined to include the stakeholders too, and on the other hand towards the community in the framework of which not only it operates but also it acts as the channel of implementation of governmental policies or the environment. The existence of the corporation 'as an entity separate from the individuals who compose it meant that it could be conceived as a person imbued with a sense of social responsibility'.[151] Inherent in this theory is therefore an element of morality or 'conscience'. According to Berle,[152] this could lead to the corporation unfolding a list of priorities that would include an additional list of targets aside profit maximisation. Conscience was not viewed by Berle as a theoretical construction as the ultimate aim was for conscience to be built into its institutions so that it gives rise to rights and obligations. Conscience would also render certain expressions of corporate power as contrary to the values of the community as a whole.[153]

Criticism of this theory can be founded on the basis that a management with such a multi-purpose agenda will not focus on what should be the primary focus of the company in any case, which is its profitability, but instead on achieving the necessary balances between sometimes conflicting interests undermining the company's fortunes. The arguments of moral character always sound slightly unconvincing to lawyers anyway, who prefer solutions and proposals with a concrete legal basis and justification especially when there are alternative routes towards achieving some of the aforementioned aims; for example, the protection of environment can be achieved simply by the adherence and safeguarding

---

[150] Keay (2011), p. 4.

[151] Dodd, M., 'For Whom are Corporate Managers Trustees?' (1932) 45 *Harvard Law Review*, p. 1161.

[152] Berle, *The Twentieth Century Capitalist Revolution* (Macmillan, London 1955), p. 89.

[153] Berle, *Power Without Property* (Harcourt, Brace & World Inc., New York 1959), p. 90.

of the existing environmental legislation and its standards. Whether such legislation will be in place though in developing countries where for example large MNCs are active through their subsidiaries is another issue, which despite its importance is not going to be analysed at this point. In this framework, initiatives such as the efforts to promote corporate responsibility were viewed as a noble yet non-legally binding exercise that at the very end was adopted by many companies, sometimes in the framework of their public relations strategy despite the positive effects that they brought on the local communities. In any case, introducing a voluntary code aiming at creating an ethical corporation and assuming that 'the prevailing social ethic will always work to correct failures in other governance mechanisms'[154] is anything but an effective way to deal with the problem in question.

## The Concession Theory

The concession theory views the existence and the operation of the firm as a concession granted by the state. Under this theory 'incorporation is seen as a privilege'.[155] Behind this statement is the fact that the corporate tool as we know it today has been created by the state, which granted to it limited liability along with a separate corporate personality and perpetual succession. And it is precisely this legal fiction granted by the state that made the modern phenomenon of the corporation one of man's greatest and most successful creations. That does not by any means imply that the corporation exists to serve state interests; on the contrary, the principal characteristic of the company as a wealth creation mechanism is not being put into doubt, but the role of the state as a legitimate source of company regulation is emphasised. Therefore, from its very basis the concession theory comes into direct conflict with the nexus of contracts theory as it challenges the nature of the firm as a purely private affair exclusively determined by the will of its private members, but defines the corporation as an entity which exists and operates on the basis of the regulation produced by the state and the privileges that the latter has granted to the corporate form. Therefore, in contrast to the nexus of contracts theory, the concession theory views state interference in the company in the form of regulation setting certain standards as wholly legitimate. Private bodies are those founded by individuals among

---

[154] Thomsen, S., 'Business Ethics as Corporate Governance' (2001) *European Journal of Law and Politics*, p. 158.

[155] Macmillan Patfield, F., *Perspectives on Company Law* (Kluwer Law International, London, The Hague 1995), vol 1, p. 8; Dine (2000).

themselves; however, the company is not one of those bodies as it owes its existence to state regulation and its enormous success to the privilege granted again from it. In addition to that, the company is viewed as an 'economic institution which has a social service as well as a profit making function'.[156] Therefore, 'corporations owe an obligation to society to act in a socially responsible manner even if such actions are legally not mandated'.[157] Part 'of this moral obligation derives from the fact that the society originally equipped most businesses with the benefit of limited liability which is a pre-condition for the existence of the corporation in the first place'.[158]

The doctrine of ultra vires serves as a clear indication of the public character of the companies. Nowadays, it has been significantly reduced if not removed by common EU regulation, but its existence for decades revealed the public character of the companies at the first steps of their existence until very recently. Since the company is a fictional entity created by the state which granted to it the privileges that sustained its spectacular growth, then it was found necessary to keep it outside its objects as prescribed by the memorandum. In *Ashbury*[159] the English courts held that if a company did an act which was outside the scope of the objects as described in the memorandum, that act would be wholly without legal effect (void). This so-called doctrine of ultra vires was similar to the law concerning public bodies. The latter are unable to act outside the statutory powers given to them, and it was then felt that the same should be true of companies. The reason that public bodies should be restricted to the powers given to them by Parliament is in order to safeguard democracy. If a public body takes to itself more power than the elected representatives of the people have chosen to give it, it is setting itself up as more important than the electorate. Similar considerations do not apply when companies are considered; however, the existence of the ultra vires doctrine in the UK until recently betrayed the early public body roots of the corporation.

Moreover, the 'limited liability corporation is the greatest single discovery of modern times. Even steam and electricity are less important

156 Dodd (1932), p. 1148.

157 Grossman, H.A., 'Refining the Role of the Corporation' (2005) 10 *Deakin Law Review* 572, p. 575.

158 Schwarz, F., 'The German Co-determination System: a model for introducing corporate social responsibility requirements into Australian Law? Part 1' (2008) 23 *Journal of International Banking Law and Regulation*, 3, p. 127.

159 *Ashbury Railway Carriage and Iron Co.* (1875) LR 7 HL 653.

than the limited liability company'.[160] Why so important? Because limited liability means that if the company becomes unable to pay its debts, the members of that company will not have to contribute towards paying the company's debts out of their own private funds: they are liable to pay only the amount they have paid, or have promised to pay, for their shares. This means that contributors to the funds of businesses which are ran on this limited liability basis may be easier to find. Limited liability therefore makes investment in big projects and ambitious corporations less risky for potential investors. It is the principle that fuelled the great development that the world experienced from the Industrial Revolution and onwards, as it motivated millions of people to invest their personal resources and fund significant projects such as the railways; without those large amounts of capital landmark, technological advances would have been difficult to materialise.

Limited liability should be viewed in conjunction with the legal fiction of corporate personality. The case of *Salomon*[161] is by no means the first case to depend on the separate legal personality of a company, but it is the most widely discussed in this context. In the House of Lords, Lord MacNaughten stated:

> The company is at law a different person altogether from [those forming the company]: and, though it may be that after incorporation the business is precisely the same as it was before, and the same persons are managers, and the same hands receive the profits, the company is not in law the agent of the subscribers or trustee for them. Nor are the subscribers as members liable, in any shape or form, except to the extent and in the manner provided by the Act … If the view of the learned judge were sound, it would follow that no common law partnership could register as a company limited by shares without remaining subject to unlimited liability.

The idea is that the company is an entity separate from the people actually involved in it. This fictional 'legal person' owns the property of the business, owes the debt to business creditors and is in full position to become a party in legal relations; it can sue and be sued on its own, it can become a party to a contract and very significantly it retains its identity and business despite radical changes in the composition, number or identity of its founders and at times membership.

The company does not therefore owe its paramount success to the agreements between the private individuals that comprise it but rather to

---

160 Butler, N.M. in T. Orhnial, *Limited Liability and the Corporation* (Law Society of Canada, London 1982), p. 42.

161 *Salomon v Salomon* [1897] AC 22.

those extremely important privileges granted to it in the form of concession by the state. History would have been written in a very different way and humanity would have evolved in a manner not easy to predict at this point if the company ceased to exist, together with the departure of its founders or members, or if the potential shareholders were aware of the possibility that a shareholding could result in their personal bankruptcy if their business endeavours did not evolve as initially hoped and realistically planned. Although history cannot be written on the basis of the "what if" questions, it can be suggested with a great degree of certainty that the corporate phenomenon would not have been included in human history as one of its greatest success stories having fuelled impressive growth, development and innovation if the state was not so generous in its concessions to the legal fiction that is the company on the one hand, and consequently and indirectly but at the same time very substantially to the private individuals who have participated in corporate projects on the other hand. Therefore, companies cannot be viewed exclusively as a nexus of contracts and relations formed by private individuals independent of any state regulation and devoid of any form of minimal obligations towards the state; the latter is legitimised in regulating the relevant field and ensuring that the company as an institution social and political in nature would adhere to certain rules set by it. That again by no means signals the transformation of the company into an arm of the state or into an entity whose operation would resemble the respective of a public body, as that would constitute a totally undesired interference with its principal aim in any case: to generate wealth. It simply means that the maximisation of wealth should take into consideration factors other than the strictly defined shareholder interests to include other stakeholders with significant roles, both within the company context and in the wider sense.

## CATEGORISING CORPORATE GOVERNANCE

The structure of corporate ownership, which is inherently linked with the means employed by a company to finance itself, can determine the nature and the character of a corporate governance system. Companies with a dispersed shareholding attract investment from the securities' markets and usually from a large number of private or institutional investors. On the other hand, companies with a more concentrated shareholder basis attract financing from a limited number of actors, usually including other corporations, private individuals (in many cases, wealthy families who were usually involved in the founding of such companies), banks and more recently bodies such as pension or insurance funds. Literature favours the use of the terms 'insider' and 'outsider' when referring to the two systems that involve a divergent structure of corporate ownership. As explained below, the 'insider' corporate governance systems are those marked by a more concentrated shareholding basis, with the most prominent examples the systems in place in Germany, Japan and to a certain degree other continental European countries; those economies are marked as 'co-ordinated market economies'.[162] Conversely, the 'outsider' model of corporate governance, genuinely represented by the so-called Anglo–American model of corporate structure and organisation, is founded on a more dispersed shareholding among other characteristics and central features; namely the 'liberal market economies'.[163] Outsider systems emphasise 'competitive market exchange where actors structure their interaction through arm's length bargaining and formal contracts funded by significant capital markets'.[164] On the other hand, the insider systems facilitate 'non market exchange with relational or incomplete contracting, network monitoring based on the exchange of private information inside networks and more reliance on collaborative as opposed to competitive relationships to build the competencies of the firm'.[165] Financing in this case is provided by a closely coordinated network of banks, the state and major private actors such as the founding families or other corporations.

LLSV (R. LaPorta,, F. Lopez de Silanes, A. Shleifer and R. Vishny) examined the legal systems of different countries to determine which one provides the best institutional setting for the alignment of the managerial with the shareholder interests, and the greatest form of protection for shareholders. According to their opinion, common law systems namely in the USA and the UK afford a greater level of protection to shareholders, therefore justifying in their view the largely dispersed shareholding which stands at the centre of the outsider model.[166] Obviously, the USA

---

162 Hall, A.P. and D. Soskice, *Varieties of Capitalism, The Institutional Foundations of Comparative Advantage* (Oxford University Press, Oxford 2001).

163 Ibid.

164 Dignam and Galanis, 'Corporate Governance and the Importance of Macroeconomic Context' (2008) 28 *Oxford Journal of Legal Studies* 2, p. 215.

165 Roe, 'Political Preconditions to Separating Ownership from Corporate Control' (2000) 53 *Stanford Law Review* 539.

166 LaPorta, R., F. Lopez de Silanes, A. Shleifer and R. Vishny, 'Legal Determinants of External Finance' (1997) 52 *Journal of Finance* 1131.
LaPorta, Lopez de Silanes, Shleifer and Vishny, 'Law and Finance' (1998) 106 *Journal of Political Economy*, 1113.

and to some extent the UK can be seen as the most prominent representatives of such a model. The two sets of jurisdictions form the focus of this book; the USA and the UK on the one hand and Germany along with other continental European countries on the other hand such as France, which employ a similar albeit not identical model with that of Germany. The reason behind the choice of the aforementioned jurisdictions lies with their early development into a very influential set of legal orders for the greatest part of the world. Nations around the world have observed, analysed and indeed to some degree adopted policies or institutions that had already flourished in the two sides of the Atlantic, aiming at achieving the same or at least a comparable degree of social stability, legal clarity and economic development as the previously mentioned nations. The latter have traditionally and historically developed distinctive legal orders based on a set of rules that have fostered their individual development, solidified their positions as some of the world's most developed nations and served as a source of inspiration for many others. Moreover, the USA emerged as the world's leading economic power based on its distinctive legal system which includes its corporate governance model, while the European countries in question with Germany at the forefront managed to emerge as one of the world's leading economic poles with the creation of the EU, which created its own distinct legal system on the basis of the already existing legal traditions of its member states. 'Company law vehicles should be the result of legislative processes that are initiated for the most part to create mechanisms designed to reduce agency costs and satisfy the contracting interests of business parties such as investors, firm founders and joint venture partners.'[167] Therefore, the analysis of the arrangements shaped within the framework of the aforementioned prominent jurisdictions will be essential for the understanding of contemporary corporate governance debates. The two sides, namely the Anglo–American as it is very generally phrased – albeit with significant differences between the USA and the UK – and the continental European one with Germany at the forefront – again without implying that there is a single model of corporate governance in continental Europe – are the two distinctive models of corporate governance that have been the most influential internationally and the most interesting from the academic point of view.

---

[167] McCahery, A.J. and P.M.E. Vermeulen, *Corporate Governance of Non-Listed Companies* (Oxford University Press, Oxford 2010), p. 100.

## The Insider System of Corporate Governance

In an insider system of corporate governance, publicly listed corporations' shareholding is distributed among a rather limited number of actors; the latter usually include the government itself, other corporations, the founding family or families of the company in question, banks and recently pension and insurance funds. The term 'insider' also betrays the main source of finance which lies within the company and its existing shareholders; in this context the role of banks as providers of capital is indeed instrumental, as it justifies their role within the company's administration in countries such as Germany. The increasing role of the stock markets as capital providers left its imprint on insider corporate governance systems as well, but not to such a degree as to signal a fundamental change of their core characteristics until now. These companies are marked by the close relationships developed between its shareholders, greatly facilitated by their rather limited number or at least of the major participants among them. The exact composition of the shareholding presents a certain degree of divergence among companies, due to national historical or political circumstances among countries in general. For example, countries such as France have privatised parts of their former public sector, having made the conscious choice to keep large parts of the shareholding in government's hands so as to preserve for the French state an important supervisory or sometimes active role in managing the economic sectors for the nation's prosperity. Therefore, the government withholds for itself the ability to design corporate policy, appoint members of the board or compete in the free market with other corporations. France especially has pursued this policy in many different ways, including the creation of 'national champions' that with the help of the steady hand of the French government in combination with the financing of the private sector can effectively compete with foreign companies in sectors perceived as crucial for the French economy such as industry and energy. On the other hand, in Germany the banks have emerged as an important part of the national economy, holding important chunks of many landmark German corporations. The success of the aforementioned model, especially in the cases of Germany and Japan which in the 1980s brought growth and development and guaranteed social stability and prosperity, has prompted much analysis of its distinctive characteristics, encouraging proposals for its further spread to other jurisdictions, while the economic downturn of the 1990s in Germany, attributed to a variety of other reasons such as the costs of unification, has provided grounds for criticism and proposals to move towards a more Anglo–American-orientated model.

As a natural outcome of the concentrated shareholding, ownership and control appear to be closely linked, in sharp contrast to the USA and the UK. In many occasions the individuals involved in the ownership of the company are also involved in its control, significantly reducing the agency problem. There is no difficulty in aligning the interests of the managers with those of the shareholders as the identity of the latter might indeed coincide with that of the former; even if it does not, the limited number of actors involved in the company and the important and simultaneously comparable size of their shareholding entails the building of a consensus in relation to the basic aims of the company and necessitates a certain degree of coordination of individual actions reflected in the decision-making. As a direct result, takeovers, particularly in a hostile form, are rare. The concentration of shares in a few hands and the existence of a controlling shareholder, the blockholder, significantly reduce such a possibility.

> Institutions are jointly understood rules of the game. They may be either formal institutions (laws) or informal institutions (norms). Institutions, whether formal or informal, generate empirical regularities in behaviour – this is what makes them analytically interesting. In the case of contemporary capitalism, a central behavioural attribute of coordinated financial systems is the degree to which they promote the holding of large blocks of shares among companies as a means of blunting short-term market pressures on company managers.[168]

The existence of definable shareholders who are closely linked with the control of the company, eager to achieve a great degree of consensus in relation with the company's objectives and future plans, has led to a great degree of stability. Since consensus stands at the core of the system, an increasing variety of actors is called up to consent to the company's objectives and operations; these are principally the shareholders, the employees along with the network of suppliers and the creditors. Therefore, a stakeholder approach is adopted and a great variety of social actors are called to contribute responsibly to the smooth operation of the company, acquiring a stake in it and a 'social dividend' from its successful operation. These are companies whose operation is founded on reaching an agreement among its main constituents over its aims and targets, and therefore internal conflicts are largely avoided. This leads to an enhanced ability to operate on the basis of a consensus regarding the long-term policies and objectives of the corporation in question. Stability

---

[168] Culpepper, D.P., 'Institutional Change in Contemporary Capitalism, Coordinated Financial Systems since 1990' (2005) 57 *World Politics*, p. 175.

and consensus emerge as the two foundations upon which planning on a much longer basis can be formed. Companies operating on this basis are usually in a position to draft their agendas of priorities and select their markets or shape their targets for the long term, involving long-term commitments between its constituent actors; the existence of a few major players makes feasible such planning. This advantage has enabled long-term planning in sectors of economic activity where it appears to be of determining importance, like industry and manufacturing. The ability and international prominence of the German, Japanese and to a certain extent French industries in these exact sectors is closely linked with this corporate governance model that facilitates stability in the corporate operation and long-term planning. As mentioned, corporate governance systems are by-products of historical developments, political decisions and economic characteristics, therefore the employment of such a model by countries who have internationally acclaimed industrial sectors and are the world leaders in commodities such as automobiles, domestic electric devices and high quality consumer goods (which demand constant funding, long-term planning and an internal consensus to guarantee the smooth operation of industrial relations and a close cooperation among all actors involved) was not just incidental. These countries consciously designed the corporate governance model that best fitted their industrial capacities and strengths, which are at the forefront of their distinctive national economic model. Naturally, companies governed by systems that are based on a limited network of interconnected actors specialising on the basis of long-term planning on specific sectors would be less vulnerable to external pressures, either by globalisation itself or by an economic crisis such as that of 2008. With labour relations that are marked by an enhanced degree of stability and a clear focus served by concrete set of policies agreed on the basis of consensus, the companies in question are less prone to the external shocks to which counterparts in the USA or the UK are more vulnerable.

On the other hand, this model might present a different set of challenges for legislators. The concentration of shareholding and consequently power to the hands of a few actors does solidify their position within the company, leaving minority shareholders in a rather compromising position as they lack a significant portion of the shares that could safeguard their position within the company, guaranteeing access to information and allowing an effective degree of monitoring the more powerful majority shareholders who are fully entrenched within the company and its structures. When the company's operations are determined by so few equally powerful actors, there is a certain lack of transparency in relation to the decisions taken at the top, at least in relation to the minority shareholders who might end up rather isolated and relatively powerless in a company thus structured. Such an institutional framework can give birth to misappropriation of company's assets on the part of the majority shareholders, with the minority shareholders being in fact incapable of monitoring the company's affairs and everyday function as they lack the necessary information that could potentially assist them to detect such unlawful forms of behaviour.

Taking into account the nature and individual characteristics of the powerful actors within such a company, a conflict of interests at the top level of administration or simply the pursuance of multiple agendas can indeed impair corporate interest. For example, a founding family that continues to constitute an important if waning actor within the company, would be interested in promoting the plans or decisions that could potentially help it to regain some control over the company, rather than pursuing what is genuinely recognised as the interest of the company. This is even more evident in the case of the government when other parameters come into play; for example, public opinion leaning towards nationalisation at a certain historical moment or favouring a certain option over another, such as greater governmental control instead of further privatisation, based on political or sometimes populist calculations, rather than economic analysis with the interest of the company as the main focus. Politicians can be prone to this kind of behaviour, especially in the period preceding a national election. Similarly, banks or other corporations could concentrate more on their individual interests rather than the strictly and objectively defined interests of the company in question. Those factors, in conjunction with the rather feeble levels of minority shareholder protection which usually form a distinctive feature of insider systems, can lead to a potential abuse of power by majority shareholders, significantly impairing the minority shareholders' interests. The Asian crisis of 1997 was claimed to be partly attributable to the excesses of majority shareholder power being uncontrolled by rather toothless minority shareholders, who were simply incapable of firstly detecting the expropriation of their wealth by majority shareholders on time, rendering their reaction ineffective as the results of the crisis vividly demonstrated.

Also, since this model of corporate governance employs a stakeholder approach, it is admittedly more difficult to adjust swiftly to emerging challenges or rapidly changing situations. In order for decisions to be made, a wider consensus among the variety of its constituents is necessary. In times of crisis, different actors will present different agendas with divergent interests, fears and aspirations, rendering a quick response difficult to achieve as a considerably greater effort will be required to reconcile the widely conflicting agendas of the entirety of its actors in a short time. However, the general view in both academia and practice is that this model with all its deficiencies and problems has functioned comparatively well in the nations that traditionally employed it, namely Germany and to some degree Austria, the Netherlands and others.

**The Outsider System of Corporate Governance**

Most prominent representatives of this model are the USA and to some extent the UK. The term 'outsider' refers to the sources of finance and the structure of corporate governance of the relevant corporations. Most firms are financed directly by the securities' market, while they are controlled by a limited number of managers who may operate relatively uncontrolled on the part of the shareholders; despite being perceived as the exclusive owners of the corporation, shareholders fail to establish close links with the managers of their 'property' and maintain rather loose links with the company. This is the typical situation where the separation of ownership and control takes place in a large corporation with an ever-extending number of shareholders financed by the stock market; the shareholders and their interests are at the top of the company's agenda but the managers of the company can appear to pursue interests that are not aligned with those of the shareholders but with their own individual ones. The lack of effective control on the part of potentially millions of shareholders that lack any link with the corporation greatly facilitates this pattern of behaviour. Scandalous conduct of the company's affairs on the part of the managers, such as the misappropriation of company property, can lead to the devaluation of the company which will make it more attractive to a hostile takeover bid; the disperse shareholding integral in the outsider corporate governance model and the lack of a blockholder significantly enhances the chances of a successful hostile takeover bid, and in this case the latter functions as a mechanism of disciplinary nature against the managers. The agency problem in this situation is particularly aggravated, namely the lack of monitoring of the agent (the manager) on the part of the principal (the shareholder).

However, this model guarantees greater flexibility in decision-making since the actors involved in it are significantly fewer than those in a company operating on the basis of the insider model. There may be a plethora of shareholders, but the direction of the company is almost exclusively left in the hands of the managers who can therefore decide on corporate matters with particular speed. The great dispersion of shares and the vast variety of shareholders renders any consensus on the operations of the company unfeasible, so the managers can take swift and over-reaching decisions without much compromising efforts and certainly without the need to engage into lengthy negotiations with other actors – principally the shareholders – since the influence of the latter is rather insignificant. Therefore, important decisions can be taken quickly, taking full advantage of a potentially favourable timing or the conditions of the market at a given moment. Even decisions as important as the restructuring of the company that could entail making redundant thousands of employees can be taken impressively quickly. The managers of the companies in question can therefore adjust must quicker to the demands of the market, and take advantages of the opportunities therein.

This inherent ability could however shift the focus to short-term profitability,[169] potentially undermining elaborate long-term business planning that might not serve the short-term corporate interests but guarantees to greater long-term profitability. With the shareholders in a loose relation with the administration of the company but mainly seeking a return of their investment in the form of dividends and therefore rendering short-term profitability as the most desirable aim, the management is often highly tempted to set aside long-term planning and considerations so as to serve short-term objectives centred around the maximisation of profit in the interest of these private shareholders. Apart from potentially undermining the company's interests in the long term, these practices render more difficult the efforts to found industries that require long-term planning for their successful operation such as manufacturing. This system of corporate governance appears to be more suitable for the type of economic activity that demands swift decision-making, a certain degree of risk-taking, the ability to rapidly re-allocate labour and capital, and flexibility and adaptability to the rapidly changing conditions and needs of the market such as the highly fluid financial services markets. This model responds more quickly to external challenges or pressures precisely due to its ability to restructure itself through the rapid re-allocation of labour and capital. The fact that the world's two leading financial centres are situated in London and New York, the two metropolises whose countries function as flagships of the outsider model, is not coincidental but a direct result of the historical development that produced a certain economic model operating on the basis of the open markets, enhanced fluidity and dispersed ownership.

---

[169] Wallman, S., 'The Proper Interpretation of Corporate Constituency Statutes and Formulation of Director Duties' (1991) 21 *Stetson Law Review* 163, pp. 176–7.

# 3. The United States of America

## THE FORMATION AND EVOLUTION OF CORPORATE GOVERNANCE IN THE USA

The corporation is not an organisation which developed independently of the society that gave birth to it. The company and its governance are not issues of a purely legal or legalistic nature but they constitute complex social phenomena which genuinely reflect the values prevailing in the society within the framework of which they evolved. Different countries have shaped different forms of corporate governance which embody their historical experiences, the balance of power between divergent and sometimes conflicting actors and certainly their prevailing societal and cultural values. The ideological character of the individual systems of corporate governance usually derives from the same ideological roots and set of principles that define that society as a whole. Corporate governance and the corporation itself are not social or legal phenomena that can possibly be viewed and analysed as if they shared no links with the cultural, societal and legal environment within which they effectively developed through time. Law in general tends to reflect the basic list of values and principles that form the priorities of a given society at a certain historical moment. Law as a historical phenomenon has evolved together with the societies that it was meant to serve. Similarly, no societal institutions, either public or private in nature, can be viewed in isolation of the nation that constructed them, the interests and the needs they were founded to serve and of course the set of values that they were designed to adhere to. Therefore, it is only natural that different nations have created distinctive models of corporate governance which reflect their national culture, history and shared experiences. Hall and Soskice believe that the institutions of a,

> nation's political economy are inextricably bound up with its history in two respects. On the one hand, they are created by actions, statutory or otherwise, that establish formal institutions and their operating procedures. On the other, repeated historical experience builds up a set of common expectations that allows the actors to coordinate effectively with each other … to remain viable

> the shared understandings associated with them must be reaffirmed periodically by appropriate historical experience.[1]

Mahoney believes that 'a country's legal system reflects … a set of prior choices about the role of the state and the private sector in responding to change'.[2] We have seen the importance of property rights in the USA stemming from their puritan ethics, and the hatred of government, importance of property and the central tenet of freedom in the USA is a crucial part of the crucible which formed its corporate governance.[3]

## CHARACTERISTICS OF THE LEGAL SYSTEM IN THE USA

### The Role of Shareholders

A review of significant developments in corporate regulation and an examination of the basic characteristics of the USA legal system and culture can provide the reader with a clearer perspective of the nature of the American model of corporate governance, the changes it went through, its distinctive roots and its sources of influence. The character and the aims of the American corporate governance model are fully compatible with the cultural influences that surrounded its enactment by the relevant federal or state laws, regulations and judicial decisions. The role of the shareholders within this model is not only of paramount importance but appears to be its landmark characteristic. Nowadays, their prominence is embodied in the so-called 'business judgement rule' that was spelled out by the Delaware Supreme Court in 1985.[4] According to the ruling, 'under Delaware law, the business judgement rule is the offspring of the fundamental principle … that the business and affairs of the Delaware corporation are managed by or under its board of directors … directors are charged with an unyielding fiduciary duty to the

---

[1] Hall, A.P. and D. Soskice, *Varieties of Capitalism, The Institutional Foundations of Comparative Advantage* (Oxford University Press, Oxford 2001), p. 13.

[2] Mahoney, G.P., 'The Common Law and Economic Growth: Hayek Might be Right' (2001) XXX *Journal of Legal Studies*, p. 504.

[3] Hutton, W., *The World We're In* (Little, Brown, London 2002), and see the concluding chapter of this book. Talbot, L., *Progressive Corporate Governance for the 21st Century* (Routledge, London 2013), especially Chapter 3.

[4] *Smith v Van Gorkom,* 488 A.2d 858, 872 (1985).

corporation *and* its shareholders'.[5] This part of the ruling reveals firstly the dominant theme in the American corporate governance debate which is the relation between the managers on the one hand and the shareholders on the other, and secondly the emphasis on the importance that is ascribed to the latter. On the other side of the Atlantic, irrespective of the differences between the individual legal orders and the respective national literature on the issue in the UK, Germany or France, the main theme in the corporate governance framework is not the relation between the board and the shareholders; the dominance of the debate in question in the American context betrays the agony of aligning the interests of the managers and shareholders so as to serve the latter's interests more effectively. In Europe the main debate refers to the so-called stakeholders and the degree to which their inclusion within the corporate interests and policies is legitimate or not. The divergence in the subject of the debate is indicative of the wide and sometimes opposing views held between the two significant jurisdictions.

Furthermore, the Delaware law where the majority of the sizeable public corporation are seated, defines the fiduciary duty of the directors as owed to the company *and* the shareholders. While this can be implicit in respective European legislative pieces (including the UK which appears to be closer to the American standards than any other big and traditional European jurisdiction), the general rule is that in Europe the directors owe the duties to the company as a whole; that is irrespective of the fact that, for example in the UK, it implies exclusively the shareholders unless the courts judge that the Companies Act 2006 and the new section 172 (to be analysed later in this book) have brought significant changes in this area. In simple words, it can be stated from the very beginning of the analysis of the USA legislative landscape that the establishment of shareholders as the prevailing corporate group seems to go almost unchallenged. As an indication of that, according to *Dodge v Form Motor Co* (1919), 'a business corporation is organised and carried on primarily for the profit of the stockholders. The powers of the directors are to be employed for that end'.[6]

## The Dominance of 'Liberty': US versus European Perceptions

In the US the dominant principle at the top of the country's legislative· agenda has traditionally been 'liberty', to the pursuance of which the

---

5 Our italics.
6 *Dodge v Form Motor Co* 204 Mich. 459, 170 N.W. 668 (1919).

Americans have shaped their legal system. Of course as with all legal concepts, liberty has also been shaped in accordance with the history of the US in a way that reflects its distinctive cultural pattern. While in Europe 'liberty' means freedom against everyone that can infringe it, in the US it is more narrowly defined as freedom against the state. 'The American legal tradition eschews a powerful state role in society and draws on a deep seated philosophy of limited government. Even in the wake of increases in government regulation following the New Deal and Progressive Eras, US law making rhetoric remained hostile towards the regulation of industry.'[7] This type of attitude flows from 'the unique origination of the US as a group of colonies of individuals who fled the tyranny of a controlling government'.[8] This reveals different starting points and understandings of what counts as a just society. While Europeans seem to rely on the state to regulate an ambit of their activities even in the private economic sphere, Americans feel that the latter will be best protected if the state refrains from interfering in such an area. Europeans appear to pursue different political and social ideals founded on the necessity of state interference even in private economic activities, especially in the form of regulation. On the other hand, Americans pursue freedom as an expression of their ability to develop their activities unobstructed by government interference. The conflict reflects unmistakable differences in sensibilities about what ought to be kept out of the state's reach on the two sides of the Atlantic, with the two different cultures of liberty. It is also due to 'cultural norms with Anglo-Saxons and Americans in particular, being more prone to cognitive closure and individualism which are associated with a greater acceptance or even desire to have a maximands consisting of a variable such as shareholder wealth'.[9] It is also an issue of the societal composition, as France and Germany for example are relatively homogeneous in the sense that their history was based from an early stage on the notion of the nation state with common cultural and moral values. US society on the other hand was from the very beginning 'extremely heterogeneous … and pluralistic,

---

[7] Kesan, P.J., 'Cyber Working or Cyber Shirking?: A First Principles Examination of Electronic Privacy in the Workplace' (2002) 54 *Florida Law Review*.

[8] Gladstone, J., 'The impact of e-commerce on the laws of nations. The US privacy balance and the European Privacy Directive: Reflections on the United States privacy policy' (2000) 7 *Willamette Journal of International Law and Dispute Resolution*.

[9] Licht, N.A., 'The Maximands of Corporate Governance: A Theory of Values and Cognitive Style' (2004) 29 *Delaware Journal of Corporate Law* 649.

it is difficult for its population to agree on core values'[10] as their backgrounds were so diverse. Zetzsche adds a religious aspect to the debate about corporate governance by assigning that 'Catholic and Lutheran ethical values were historically more conducive to a stakeholder oriented corporate governance system than Calvinist and Anglican ones'.[11]

European societies have therefore traditionally imposed legitimate limits to economic practices in fulfilment of other superior social aims. For example, the creation of an extensive social state in Europe was founded on similar principles. If judged from a purely economic point of view, it has been proved economically inefficient as it led to the financing of certain costly social policies (such as a collection of social and unemployment benefits or universal health care) which sometimes do not attract the enthusiastic applaud of business world. This is the reason that the social state in the European form was never introduced and implemented in the US. However, the governments of most European countries, which are included in the list of the world's most developed nations, have found it imperative to fund such policies in order to limit existing social differences, achieve a certain degree of wealth redistribution and assist the parts of the society in greatest need; a list of aims that would probably been found difficult to compromise with the American notion of 'liberty'. Therefore, at least in continental Europe, the role of the government in the European economy and society is overwhelming as the state does fund 'extensive social security systems intended to reduce social inequality',[12] while it maintains a central role in health and education; it has also institutionalised a multi-level monitoring of market activities with the introduction of bodies such as the Competition or the Data Protection Authority, aimed at ensuring that markets and private actors adhere to the respective state regulation.

Thus, while Europe relies more on state regulation, the US purports to rely more on market mechanisms. The difference lies in the role of the government in private life. Such a stance shares strong and deep roots in the collective American national identity, culture and historical experience. 'In child rearing Americans concentrate on teaching the child to be

---

[10] Eberle, J.E., 'Human Dignity, Privacy and Personality in German and American Constitutional Law' (1997) *Utah Law Review* 963.

[11] Zetzsche, A.D., 'An Ethical Theory of Corporate Governance Theory' (2007) *CBC Working Paper*, No. 0006.

[12] Yohei, S., 'Monitoring E-mail of Employees in the Private Sector: A Comparison between Western Europe and the United States' (2005) 4 *Washington University Global Studies Law Review*, p. 251.

himself and self-dependent preparing him for his individual struggle in life.'[13] When the United States acquired their independence they drafted their constitution with a clear list of priorities.

> First was the concept of individualism ... second was the principle of limited government with its corollaries ... the moral primacy of the private over the public sphere of society ... third was the central importance of private property and its linkage with the individual's exercise of liberty ... to free citizens from ... control ... exercised over subjects by kings ... in the European society.[14]

The liberty to live without state intervention even in the form of state regulation is an integral part of American identity. If this principle is combined with that of individualism, which entrusts the individual citizens with a variety of rights and the responsibility to conduct their life with minimal interference or even assistance from the state, the reasons behind the American reluctance to adopt the European state-centred approach becomes more evident, as in 'the American society the individual is king'.[15] Furthermore, the primacy of private property, which is to be interpreted as conducting private activities without being subject to persistent regulation by a superior authority, irrespective of whether this is the king or a government, stands at the core of American political beliefs. Hence, it can be easily concluded that 'traditionally Americans have been less likely than Europeans to turn to the government to regulate private enterprise, instead relying on the market or new technologies to address public concerns about commercial activities'.[16] In this cultural and historical context, it is evident why the shareholders traditionally possessed the central role in the American corporate world; the context also explains the federal government's lack of enthusiasm to create a regulatory framework that would include a variety of stakeholders. The shareholders are possessors of the sacrosanct US legal order right of property that legitimises their supremacy within the corporation. Furthermore, when state regulation is not necessary, the private sphere should be left free of any interference for private citizens to exercise their liberty. The principles standing at the core of the US culture, namely liberty, individualism and private property along with the limited role for

---

[13] Westin, A.F., *Privacy and Freedom* (Atheneum, New York 1967), p. 11.

[14] Ibid.

[15] Chew, D.H. and S.L. Gillan, *Corporate Governance at the Crossroads: A Book of Readings* (McGraw-Hill Irwin, New York 2005), p. 42.

[16] Fromholz, M.J., 'Foreign Law: Data Privacy: The European Union Data Privacy Directive' (2000) 15 *Berkeley Technology Law Journal*.

the state that they entail, render any approach close to the continental European model impossible.

## THE PROFOUND MISTRUST OF POWER IN THE USA

America 'was born with a profound mistrust of power'.[17] As early as in the 1930s, the establishment of the Bank of the United States became an expression of the mistrust against power; the bank was granted certain privileges which included its exception from taxation and protection from competition. In return for these principles, the government could appoint just one-fifth of the bank's directors. Initially, companies were chartered by state laws but gradually this requirement was watered down until it was effectively removed, paving the way for a truly private character in enterprise even at the very initial stage of authorisation.

The era following the end of the Civil War left its distinctive imprint on the evolution of corporate governance. The end of the war brought a new round of development with the funding of new projects and the drafting of new plans. The construction of a rail network that would cross through the enormous newly founded country assumed a central position within this framework. The Americans were one of the nations that naturally looked at the development of their infrastructure and transportation networks as the first step to achieve greater trade links, improved growth rates and consequently additional wealth. The existence of an abundance of raw materials, space and labour underlined the growth potential of the nation and provided the grounds for its future development into the world's biggest economy. In '1830 there was only 23 miles of railroad track in the USA, by 1840 it had reached 3,000 miles and had outpaced rail building in Britain'.[18] The 'combination of state generosity and traditional private debt funding exhausted the existing market capacity and the public equity market sprang up to serve the enormous funding needs of the rail company'.[19]

---

[17] Monks, A.G.R. and N. Minow, *Corporate Governance*, 4th edn (John Wiley & Sons Ltd, Chichester 2010), p. 101.

[18] Licht, W., *Working for the Railroad* (Princeton University Press, Princeton NJ 1983), p. 10.

[19] Dignam, A. and M. Galanis, *The Globalization of Corporate Governance* (Ashgate, Farnham 2009), p. 191 although there were significant abuses; see D. Brown, *Hear that Lonesome Whistle Blow* (Henry Holt and Company LLC, New York 2001).

The country experienced the introduction of new technologies that further enabled commercial transactions and opened new avenues for trade. The telegraph and later the telephone further stimulated the need for additional investment and innovation.

Despite this favourable and rather unprecedented environment, the central feature of the economy at that point was the concentration of business and powers in the hands of a few trusts which created a monopolistic situation at the market. Price-fixing and collusive agreements were some of the practices employed by the monopolies at that point, leading to market distortions, artificially high prices and a widespread public discontent towards this form of capitalism and its side effects. This was the societal framework within which the Sherman Act was passed by Congress in 1890. The Act was the first federal statute that placed limitations upon trusts, monopolies and cartels constituting the first antitrust legislation at federal level. Two following Acts, namely the Clayton Antitrust Act 1914 and the Robinson Patman Act 1936, amended the Sherman Act by extending its provisions to cover additional activities such as tying arrangements and unfair pricing. Therefore, even at this point the USA experienced the creation of sizeable business poles concentrating great amounts of power, capital and labour in their ambit. The Sherman Act '[by] prohibiting cartels of small family firms hastened the growth of big business in the USA'.[20] In sharp contrast, family businesses in the UK or Germany were allowed to merge into integrated holding companies to safeguard their continuity and their profitability. Such companies remained essentially 'federations that employed neither middle nor top managers to coordinate flows of goods or to allocate resources'.[21] Such federations were now illegal in the USA. The large corporations facilitated by the Sherman Act were in a position to fund large projects with their increasing fluidity, and although facing certain restriction by federal legislation in relation to price-fixing and concerted practices, they were still expanding in terms of size and number.

Yet tremendous changes were indeed taking place at all levels of American economy. The advances brought by the new technology entailed a reshaping of business structures in order to meet its demands. In the nineteenth century, production was mostly based on the quality of labour and the available craft, but the technological progress that paved the way for mass production shifted the focus from labour to its

---

[20] Chandler, D.A. Jr, 'The Managerial Revolution in the American Business' in T. Clarke, *Theories of Corporate Governance, The Philosophical Foundations of Corporate Governance* (Routledge, London 2008), p. 43.

[21] Ibid.

management. Before the mass production systems became a reality for American business, the industry naturally depended more heavily on the available labour, its engagement with the methods of productions, its personal skills and relations with other workers whose cooperation was a necessary precondition for the smooth operation of the production chain. That was particularly evident in industries such as the metal industry, which again provided the necessary material for other sectors of the economy to subsequently flourish. The central position assumed by workers in the production chain guaranteed a certain degree of control on the actual production itself, since the latter was inexorably linked with labour and their personal capacity to assume initiatives while coordinating their craft with both the rest of their colleagues and with the other factors at different levels of the production chain. The introduction of mass production methods brought fundamental changes to the parameters and the foundations of this equation. The mass production of automobiles and other industrial goods heavily depended on the technological means involved rather than the labour in question. The latter were on many occasions confined to performing previously defined activities rather than being called upon to exercise their individual initiative. This naturally *shifted* the power from labour to managers; the former being the actors who were called upon in predetermined tasks to run the methods of mass production while the latter acting as the individuals who set the whole system in place, distributed the labour to its tasks, provided the company with a business strategy involving the allocation of the corporate resources and the investments needed to maximise production with the further limitation on the role of labour that this would entail, and generally performed all duties that would fall within what someone would simply call 'running the company'. The waning of labour control on the production process and the subsequent emergence of the management as a factor of crucial importance for the well-being and the profitability of the company reshaped the existing balance of power within the company and provided the grounds for the managerial control that was to become a distinctive feature of the US corporate governance system in the twentieth century. Ford, in many ways the flagship of American industry acting as the trademark of corporate America, was a pioneering company in implementing new strategies that took full advantage of the available technological means while having 'no use for experience … wanting machine tool operators who have nothing to unlearn, who have no theories of correct surface speeds for metal finishing and will simply do what they are told to do over and over again from bell time to bell time'.[22] Ford and corporate America passed from the era of increased labour role to the era of managerial prominence. A central feature of the new era was the 'highly stratified educational system that effectively separated out future managers from future workers … thus a deep social gulf was created between managers as "insiders" and workers as "outsiders" in the employment relations of US industrial enterprises'[23] that defined American corporate governance up to this day.

The shift in the nature and scope of company law had begun to take place even before this significant development. Up to the middle of the nineteenth century, corporations were granted their charters by the state legislatures after the examination of their aims and targets that were somewhat connected with what was perceived as a service of some social value and with a certain impact on the community; therefore companies were providing their services in the field of utilities, transportation or financial services. As technological advances expanded the scope of economic activity to encompass sectors such as manufacturing, transportation and industry, it was evident that a wider range of private actors could become involved in the economy generating growth and therefore creating wealth for the society as whole. The right of incorporation was vested 'in the states as one of their sovereign powers, a right so strictly adhered to that the railroads for example found it necessary to incorporate in each state where they operated'.[24] The cumbersome procedure of examining on a case-by-case basis the charters of each company had to be dropped and replaced by a more flexible procedure that would allow the swift foundation of new businesses, especially in the areas created by the rapid and unprecedented technological development. There was a generally accepted need to take advantage of the new technologies, accumulate the necessary know-how to achieve further advances, provide the funds for new investments that would further enhance the existing technological means and introduce the reforms necessary to sustain the newly acquired economic dynamism. The corporate tool was perceived and indeed proved to be the most effective means of achieving the aforementioned goals. The US dealt with these needs by enabling the

---

[22] Arnold, H. and F. Faurote, *Ford Methods and the Ford Shops* (The Engineering Managing Company, New York 1919), p. 41.

[23] O'Sullivan, M.A., *Contests for Corporate Control, Corporate Governance and Economic Performance in the USA and Germany* (Oxford University Press, Oxford 2001), p. 74.

[24] Lorsch, W.J. and E. Maclver, 'Pawns or Potentates: The Reality of America's Corporate Boards' in Clarke (2008), p. 110.

creation of new companies and by removing the obligation to grant individual charters to the companies in question. From the middle of the nineteenth century, legislation was enacted so as to facilitate the incorporation of business enterprises.[25] The shift from the individual case-by-case permission to incorporate, to the general legislation that allowed incorporation to all enterprises fulfilling certain conditions, was of great significance since it underlined and clearly revealed the deeper and essential change in the nature of the corporation in the US law from a private entity with clear public elements in its structure and orientation which was active in areas presenting some social value, into a purely private enterprise able to use the corporate form for all activities considered lawful in a democratic society. This triggered the separation between the state on the one hand and private enterprise on the other, along with the legitimisation of the view that the state is irrelevant to private business activities which should be left intact from its intervention; a view that remains predominant in the US law and theory up to today, genuinely reflecting the prevailing cultural values in the country. The 'enactment of general incorporation statutes obscured the public's contribution and dissolved the image of a corporation as a venture both public and private'.[26] In this context, doctrines such as the doctrine of ultra vires that rendered void any contract signed by the company with a subject that fell outside its defined scope of activities, was gradually set aside, giving the 'corporate directors and managers the *carte blanche* to do virtually whatever they wanted … until its gradual demise'.[27]

These tectonic changes at the heart of company law signalled the emergence of corporations as private bodies attracting only a minimum of state intervention, and the waning of the state role at this level remains a central feature of the US legislation up to today. In this historical context, US corporations experienced a steady and gradual extension of their capacity to act while obtaining on the one hand their independence from the state and on the other additional privileges that further aligned their legal status with the respective of natural persons. The Fourteenth Amendment of the American Constitution enacted in 1868 demonstrates this development; it prohibited the state to deprive a person of life, liberty

---

[25] Hurst, J.W., *The Legitimacy of the Business Corporation in the Law of the United States, 1780–1970* (University Press of Virginia, Charlottesville 1970).

[26] Kaufman, A., L. Zacharias and M. Karson, *Managers v Owners: The Struggle for Corporate Control in American Democracy* (Oxford University Press, New York 1995), p. 17.

[27] Horwitz, M., *The Transformation of American Law, 1780–1860* (Harvard University Press, Cambridge MA 1977), p. 78.

or property without due process of law. Despite the initial intention to use the Amendment so as to protect the rights of citizens with emphasis on the former slaves, the Supreme Court in its *Sante Fe* decision of 1886[28] 'extended its reach considerably in determining that corporations were persons within the meaning of the Fourteenth Amendment'.[29] Therefore, the property of the corporations enjoyed the same constitutional guarantees with the respective of natural persons. The significance of this ruling stems from the fact that now when the states were attempting to 'regulate corporate activities they could be challenged on the grounds that they violated the property rights of the corporations'.[30] Taking into account the central position of property rights both in the US jurisdiction and in the general American psyche and culture, their perceived violation in the form of state regulation was met with great disbelief if not open hostility. Americans interpreted their freedom to pursue economic activities without state intervention or at least with a minimal form of state regulation as a crucial part of their constitutionally protected list of rights. The attempts to introduce limitations upon corporate activities was deemed as an undesirable and ultimately unlawful limitation upon their property rights now constitutionally recognised. In this sense, the US corporate form genuinely reflects the dominant principles and prevailing values in American society. In addition, as the law evolved towards the direction of relaxing the limitations placed upon corporate activity while extending the array of right and privileges granted to them, it not only enabled the activities of these enterprises but also 'contributed to the ongoing shift in the balance of corporate control by legitimising the exercise of that control by the "active insiders"'.[31] The USA 'doesn't have a centralised "czar" whose job it is to regulate corporate governance'.[32] The competition among states to have companies domiciled in their jurisdictions also played a role in shaping the internal structure of the company by extending the control of the active insiders; the further liberalisation of company law was the main consequence of such a competition. 'State based regulation tends to come through contractual enabling – the corporate charter can be built in almost any way that the participants

---

[28] *Santa Clara County v Southern Pacific Railroad Company*, 118 U.S. 394 (1886).

[29] O'Sullivan (2001), p. 81.

[30] Friedman, L., *A History of American Law* (Simon and Schuster, New York 1973), p. 455.

[31] Hurst (1970), p. 70.

[32] Roe, J.M., 'The Inevitable Instability of American Corporate Governance' (2005) 1 *The Corporate Governance Law Review* 1, p. 10.

prefer – and judge enforced fiduciary duties. Regulatory commissions are largely absent in making state corporate law'.[33] In this context, liberalisation meant that directors would not be held 'to the same tight standard as trustees, the so called prudent man rule. Instead directors were expected to exercise the duty of loyalty and the duty of care, and their conduct was judged according to the business judgement rule'.[34] The state of Delaware has emerged the absolute winner in this context, attracting a variety of companies due to its liberal legislative framework setting the pattern for the regulation of companies in other states too. Company law is traditionally viewed in the USA as a matter of regulation at state level, therefore there is no federal company law statute in contrast to the UK for instance. That does not mean that certain corporate issues are not regulated at federal level such as the Sarbanes–Oxley Act 2002 proved.

## The 1920s Speculation Boom: Berle and Means

This period of development was followed by the 1920s, a crucial time from an economic and historical point. This decade was marked by an unprecedented speculative boom which led millions of Americans to buy shares in the stock market; sometimes after borrowing significant amounts of money Americans were able to finance their way in the heart of the then still booming American capitalism. Brokers were eager to lend money particularly to small investors which sometimes exceeded two-thirds of the face value of the stocks they were to buy. The loans were increasing to unsustainable levels, the market crashed and panic spread to investors of all backgrounds and sizes. In the aftermath of the stock market crash of 1929 and the following Great Depression, Congress passed the Securities Act 1933 which aimed at providing the investors with substantial information concerning securities offered for public sale and prohibiting fraud in the sale of securities to the public. This Act was followed by the Securities Exchange Act 1934, regulating the secondary trading of securities left out of the 1933 Act. The Securities and Exchange Commission (SEC), a federal body created by the Securities Exchange Act of 1934, was established as the agency responsible to monitor the application of the relevant legislation. It should be noted that this was also the climate which influenced Berle and Means to publish their article on the modern corporation and private

---

[33] Ibid., p. 11.

[34] Lorsch and MacIver in Clarke (2008), p. 110.

property, that analysed issues of ownership and control. It was in the atmosphere of corporate enlargement marked by large public corporations, with millions of shareholders who were realistically unable to exercise any kind of control over or monitoring of the management of their company. The authors described the ongoing phenomenon of large public corporations rapidly acquiring such a dispersed shareholding that the previously concrete links between ownership and control were effectively smashed, critically affecting all levels of corporate activity. The American corporation was on a course of change from the family-established and ran businesses of the past to the large public companies with the enormous widely diffused shareholder basis of the present, and the American economy was transforming into an economy that fitted the outsider model (as analysed in Chapter 2). This shift at the core of the American corporation posed new dilemmas to legislators and new grounds for debate for the academics. Questions in relation to the balance of power within the corporation were brought from the background to the centre of the relevant debates that are ongoing up to this day. David Halberstam argued that at that point:

> ordinary citizens believed that buying stock – owing part of a giant company – was a real possibility in their lives. By purchasing stocks they became participants in American capitalism … junior partners of Henry Ford II … the Ford family had been joined by some 300,000 new co-owners of their company … It also marked the beginning of a historic shift in American capitalism, a major increase in the influence of Wall Street in companies like Ford. The Street was a partner now and the family had to respond to its norms … Before the war only a small number of Americans held stocks and they were to a large degree of the same class as the owners of the old line companies. The market was a kind of gentlemen's club, virtually off limits to the rest of the society.[35]

This was 'the high-water mark of the old system … now the New York Stock Exchange vowed to make every American a stockholder',[36] appeared to play a significant role that triggered the further dispersion of shares to a wider number of actors, further consolidating a model of dispersed shareholders' basis. At this point the USA diverged even from the UK in the sense that the latter experienced a dispersion of shares at a comparatively large scale, although in the UK institutional shareholders did have a considerably more discernible presence. According to Roe, the

---

[35] Halberstaum, D., *The Reckoning* (William Morrow, New York 1986), p. 227.

[36] Monks and Minow (2010), p. 103.

reason for the development and 'retention of fragmented ownership in the USA was that politicians and the electorate did not want the Wall Street institutions to have the power to control large corporations'.[37] This therefore 'led to legal constraints which prohibited or raised the costs of banks and other institutions holding large blocks of shares'.[38] The prohibition of bank ownership of equity promoted by the Glass–Steagall Act 1933 was indicative of an ideological and political climate that viewed the absence of institutional investors as a prerequisite of corporate democratisation. The prevailing attitude at that point in the USA would contrast spectacularly with the dominant mentality in corporate Germany, where the cross-holdings and cross-ownerships between the banking sector and German corporations marked the emergence of a corporate landscape that was marked by such close links between business and banks that borderlined cartelisation. In any case Roe suggested that the early structures of American corporations created a 'path dependency';[39] on the basis of the latter this very initial ownership structure had a significant influence on legal rules which also determined subsequent structures. The law can contribute on the maintenance of a dispersed shareholding basis by introducing high standards of minority shareholder protection. Coffee argued[40] that the latter enjoy such a high level of protection that they lack the incentive to advance their position within the company assuming additional risks. The advanced level of legal protection they enjoy functions as a motivation to sustain their current status and hence perpetuates the fragmented shareholding of the corporation in question.

## The New Era of Managerial Capitalism: The Neo-liberal Corporate Governance Paradigm

The radical shift in the shareholder basis of the previously family-run corporations led to a new era of managerial capitalism which flourished well through the post-war period and into the 1950s and 1960s. An

---

[37] See Roe, 'A Political Theory of American Corporate Finance' (1991) 91 *Columbia Law Review* 10.

[38] Lowry, J. and A. Reisberg, *Pettet's Company Law: Company Law and Corporate Finance* (Pearson, Harlow 2012), p. 66.

[39] Roe, 'Chaos and Evolution in Law and Economics' (1996) 109 *Harvard Law Review* 641.

[40] Coffee, J., 'The Future as History: The Prospects for Global Convergence in Corporate Governance and Its Implications' (1999) 93 *Northwestern University Law Review* 654.

ever-increasing number of shareholders came to have less control over the managers at all levels of decision-making, further consolidating the weakening of links between ownership and control. The enormous number of stockholders, along with their lack of skills or knowledge on corporate issues in an increasingly complicated corporate landscape, led to a booming of managerial capitalism and a blurring of the image of the shareholders as the absolute prevailing force within the company. Statutes and regulation might have put their interests at the top of the agenda, but the managers were sitting at the top table with interests and agenda that could and in many cases did diverge significantly from those of the shareholders. Despite a self-proclaimed faith to shareholder primacy, US companies have indeed been 'subject to "director primacy" in their operations'.[41]

The 1970s are still viewed as a difficult and rather painful period for the world economy, and the USA was not an exception. The oil crisis and the economic cost of the Vietnam War, along with internal turmoil caused by the consecutive scandals peaking with the Watergate Scandal and the subsequent resignation of President Nixon, led to the outgoing President Carter to talk about 'the crisis of confidence'[42] now marking the Americans and their economy. Within this framework the regulatory initiatives of the Nixon administration were found ineffective and provided the grounds for 'the reactive growth of the anti-regulation, deregulation movement in the late 1970s in which Chicago economists played a key role which provided the leitmotif of the early Reagan years',[43] although as we have seen, this culture started very early in the Enlightenment period. During the 1970s, 'the oversight duties of the boards of directors and the behaviour of management in conducting business operations increasingly were the subjects of legislative action, court decisions and SEC investigations'.[44] In its 1972 Penn Central Report, the SEC noted that 'the directors were generally accustomed to playing an inactive role in company affairs, permitted management to operate without any effective review or control and remained uninformed

---

41 Bainbridge, S., 'Director Primacy in Corporate Takeovers: Preliminary Reflections' (2002) 55 *Stanford Law Review* 791, p. 798.

42 Dore, R., W. Lazonick and O'Sullivan, 'Varieties of Capitalism in the Twentieth Century' (1999) 15 *Oxford Review of Economic Policy* 4, p. 113.

43 Ibid.

44 Norton, J.J. and J. Rickford, 'Corporate Governance Post-Enron, Comparative and International Perspectives' (2005) *British Institute of International and Comparative Law* p. 236.

throughout the period of important developments and activities'.[45] The report might provide an insight of the situation in the specific company under enquiry but it also provides the basic parameters of a situation which was widespread among US corporations.

The 1980s was a period of reform for the USA with a neo-liberal stigma. The economic revolution taking place on the other side of the Atlantic and more specifically in the UK was much more extensive and consequently rather more impressive, but the Reagan administration left its clear imprint on the American economy, further fostering 'the ideology of shareholder value, the dominant belief that the business enterprise was making its best social contribution ... if it was to run to maximise shareholder value'.[46] Shareholder activism became a widely pursued aim in the ranks of stockholders, fuelling the granting of devices to align the managerial interests with the respective of shareholders. Along with the bonuses that boomed during that period, the managers were offered stock options as further incentive to place the company's profitability and therefore the shareholders' interest at the very top of their considerations instead of their personal agenda.

## Dynamism of the Economy and the Seeds of Convergence of Corporate Governance

Despite its troubles in dealing with fierce competition from Japanese manufacturers or to a lesser extent German exporters, the dynamism of the American economy led to the exportation of its corporate governance model to other nations. There was a noticeable shift in business patterns, allowing capital and assets previously kept within the business to be released to the capital markets in the form of bonuses and gifts directly to the managers. When called upon to account for such decisions, managers insisted that all their actions were aiming at increasing shareholder value. This emerged in the USA as the test that defines the legitimacy of the managerial decision or strategy in question. The bonuses and other incentives granted to managers to keep them focused on the pursuance of shareholder interests are directly linked to the maximisation of shareholder value and wealth. The top priority in the agenda are the interests of the shareholders, and if the latter are satisfied in the form of increased dividends then the managers are justified in running the decision-making mechanism as they do, including granting themselves generous packages

---

[45] Ibid., p. 237.

[46] Dore, Lazonick and O'Sullivan (1999), p. 114.

of privileges in the form of bonuses or other gifts. As the majority of the shareholders have minimal links with the company, the only indication that the company is well run and effectively governed is whether or not dividends are going to be distributed to them.

## The Power of the Institutional Investors: Shareholders as Outsiders

> [By the] early 1990s however it had become apparent that US equity shareholdings were increasingly concentrated among large institutional investors, that is, public and private pension funds, mutual funds, insurance companies and banks. This sparked strong academic interest in the potential of these large investors to serve as quasi-regulators and true monitors of corporations and their boards. Much of this attention focused on the role of public pension funds because of the long term investment perspective of their fund beneficiaries and the belief that these funds had fewer conflicts of interest as compared to other institutional investors. This early optimism ultimately gave way in the face of considerable evidence to institutional investor passivity, short-termism, complex and indeed conflicting interests, and the limited impact of investor activism on corporate behaviour.[47]

Coffee argues that

> the logistical demands required of any institutional shareholder that seeks to manage actively a large portfolio of companies through collective decision making by multiple institutions are simply unacceptably costly. As a result institutional investors implicitly recognise a liquidity/control trade-off that leads them to avoid active involvement in managerial decision making except under special circumstances … have led most institutional investors to prefer liquidity to control.[48]

However, this concentration of ownership increases the 'likelihood that management will attend to shareholders concerns and lowers collective action barriers to active investment strategies'.[49]

---

[47] Harper Ho, E., 'Virginia, Enlightened Shareholder Value: Corporate Governance Beyond the Shareholder-Stakeholder Divide' (2010) 36 *Journal of Corporation Law* 1, page 64.

[48] Coffee, C.J. Jr, 'Dispersed Ownership: the Theories, the Evidence, and the enduring Tension Between "Lumpers" and "Splitters"' (2010) *Columbia Law and Economics Working Paper* No.363, European Corporate Governance Institute, *Law Working Paper* No. 144, p. 11.

[49] Black, S.B., 'Shareholder Passivity Reexamined' (1990) 89 *Michigan Law Review* 520, p. 570.

In this context, the main trend in the USA regarding individual shareholder attitudes is for the majority of the shareholders not to avail themselves of the opportunity to keep themselves informed of the developments within the company including its long-term targets, its priority agenda and its decision-making, hence the emergence of the creation of shareholder value as an almost exclusive test that determines the quality of the managerial control in question. Despite the primacy that the interests of the shareholders enjoy in the US system of corporate governance and also in corporate law and theory in general, the shareholders are in fact outsiders to the decision-making process in the publicly traded corporation. The fact that this unique form of ownership does not entail control, co-decision or even active participation in the decision-making process regarding the corporate strategy and the allocation of its resources, leaves the shareholders with one form of checks on the managerial powers: the maximisation of the value of their investment. As long as the shareholders enjoy an increase in the value of their investment, the majority are content enough to let the managers perform what they consider as the most appropriate strategy for the company. The maximisation of shareholder wealth as reflected by the price of the shares in the stock market functions consequently as the legitimising factor of managerial practices and decisions that include the managers' benefits and bonuses, as it effectively provides them with the assurance that the shareholders will not seek any interference with the running of the company. This alignment of the interests of the 'strategic managers of the US corporations with the demands of the stock market is now typically regarded as a defining feature of the market oriented US system of corporate governance'.[50]

## The US Corporate Governance Profile: The Importance of Self-regulation versus Sarbanes–Oxley

As we have seen above, the USA corporate governance model and structure are dictated at the state level rather than at the federal government level. Alongside state regulation there is a complex collection of best government practices issued by a variety of bodies. The traditional distaste of Americans for federal regulation as a form of government intervention has brought in the frontline not only the state legislatures but also a number of self-regulation initiatives which are a rather popular way to tackle policy issues in the USA. They combine the

[50] O'Sullivan (2001), p. 70.

flexibility that Americans consider necessary in the corporate context with the involvement of exclusively private actors who decide among themselves for themselves; the system is therefore lacking the undesired intervention from the government. The historical ambivalence of Americans towards the state differentiates them with the respective attitude on the other side of the Atlantic; Europeans tend to appeal to the state to have their rights protected either against the state itself or usually against powerful private actors, with the corporation assuming the top place in the catalogue. As analysed earlier, different historical experiences fuel different perceptions about fundamental social values which later dictate the nature of the law adopted by a particular nation. And American history has proved that the citizens of the country value liberty as a value of paramount importance; but in the American vocabulary, 'liberty' has a slightly different yet defining content, as liberty against the state rather than against a body that could potentially infringe it, as in Europe. Therefore, self-regulation initiatives and codes of voluntary practices enjoy great prominence in the US context, despite the lack of binding character, or more precisely because of that. Bodies such as the National Association of Corporate Directors, the American Bar Association and the Council of Institutional Investors among many others have issued codes of practices including best corporate government practices.

The spectacular exception that proves the rule is the Sarbanes–Oxley Act 2002 (SOX) which was passed by Congress, dictating mandatory legislative solutions at federal level due to the political pressure created by a wave of massive corporate scandals which culminated with the notorious Enron scandal. The public reaction towards the Enron scandal was so overwhelming that Congress reacted swiftly by passing what is considered as the most radical intervention to company law at top government level. The Bush administration went against the tide and introduced a piece of legislation that would fulfil the definition of what the Americans would call 'big government' with a certain taste of distaste. The SOX Act applies primarily to companies that are subject to the Securities Exchange Act 1934 as amended, and constitutes the most radical shake-up of the current governance system since the securities laws of the 1930s that led to the establishment of the SEC. The SOX Act aims at combating fraud at corporate level, something that in the light of the Enron scandal seems to be a rather legitimate aim. Its section 404 sets a requirement to include in the annual report an

> attestation by an outside auditor to the effectiveness of the firm's internal controls over financial reporting … the CEO and the chief financial officer certify the accuracy of the firm's periodic reports and the effectiveness of its

> internal controls, a requirement that the firm maintain an audit committee composed exclusively of independent directors, and a ban on the outside auditor from providing certain non audit services to the firm.[51]

The SEC was granted additional resources and authority to enforce the relevant legislation while longer prison sentences were introduced for certain forms of white collar crime, and the directors guilty of fraud were now faced with increased criminal penalties along with their disqualification. The CEOs were made more accountable for the issuing of financial statements while auditor independence was further consolidated with the role of the auditor committee significantly enhanced. More specifically, the CEOs were now required to certify that quarterly and annual reports are fully compliant with the existing securities legislation and that they reflect a fair picture of the finances of the company.

It should be noted at this point that the corporate governance of public companies in the USA can be regulated at different levels and by different sources; apart from the aforementioned distinction between federal and state regulation that also flows from the very institutional setting of the country, the listing rules of the three largest equity exchange markets in the USA act as an additional source of regulation for listed companies. The New York Stock Exchange (NYSE) for example, also reformed at that time, requires its listed companies to have three independent committees for audit, compensation and nominating. The NASDAQ on the other hand requires its listed companies to have one independent committee; namely the audit one. The other two in exceptional circumstances can employ one non-independent member. It should be noted that the SOX Act applies to all companies irrespective of origin with a US listing regardless of whether or not its provisions are compatible with their law of origin. The relevant conflict between the SOX Act and the respective legislative standards of other jurisdictions has led foreign companies to opt for their withdrawal from the NYSE. Despite the fact that private companies were mostly unaffected by the passing of the SOX Act, it had a significant indirect effect on their functions and operations as the states passed legislation to align their company laws with the standards set by the SOX Act. Therefore, the accounting practices of state company laws were also affected, with the standards applying now evidently enhanced.

---

[51] Kamar, E., P. Karaca-Mandic and E. Talley, 'Going private decisions and the Sarbanes– Oxley Act of 2002: a cross country analysis' (2009) 25 *Journal of Law, Economics and Organisation* 1, p. 108.

## THE STRUCTURE OF BOARDS IN THE USA AND THE LACK OF EMPLOYEE PARTICIPATION

One of the fundamental institutions in the corporate structure is the board. The US boards continued a tradition that began with the English joint stock companies. Both in the UK and in its colonies, the group of people who actually ran the company would meet on a regular basis.

> Fine furniture was expensive in those days and few people in trade had chairs or tables to contain the group. So the men sat on stools around a long board placed across two sawhorses. The group was named 'the board' after the makeshift table they worked at. And the leader of the group, who did not have to seat on a stool, by reason of his prestigious perch, was named the 'chair-man'.[52]

Nowadays, the boards are assigned with significant duties and functions of critical importance for the company. Among others they have the power to hire or fire the CEO, to fix the compensation of an executive member, to distribute dividends, declare bankruptcy, oversee the conduct of the corporation's business, and review the financial objectives, auditing principles and the strategy plans for the corporation, 'all with an eye towards maximising shareholder value'.[53] Despite the abundance of responsibilities entrusted[54] to the board to oversee and somehow supervise the running of the company and to respond to irregularities when necessary, practically it is not ultimately involved in the actual running of business. Its basic duty is to safeguard the interests of shareholders by effectively monitoring the running of the company on the part of the management. In *re Caremark International Inc. Derivative Litigation*[55] the Delaware Court of Chancery marked that 'only a sustained or systematic failure of the board to exercise oversight – such as an utter failure to attempt to assure a reasonable information and reporting system exists – will establish the lack of good faith that is a necessary condition to liability'. It is evident from the above-mentioned analysis that the employees of the company do not form a part of the company and

---

52 Monks and Minow (2010), p. 226.

53 Keasey, K., S. Thompson and M. Wright, *Corporate Governance, Accountability, Enterprise and International Comparisons* (John Wiley and Sons Ltd, Chichester 2005), p. 252.

54 For an international perspective see the OECD's *Principles of Corporate Governance,* 2004.

55 *Re Caremark International Inc. Derivative Litigation* 698 A 2d 959 (Del. Ch. 1996).

therefore of the board's considerations. In the US, corporate governance 'is defined independently of possible relations to workers'.[56] Company law is distinguished from the structure of labour relations, with absolute dominance of shareholders and managers in the American model of corporate governance. This comes into conflict with the respective attitudes in other jurisdictions, such as the Germany system which guarantees a certain institutional role to the labour employed but to a minor extent also to the UK when according to the new Companies Act 2006 there is a reference to the employees' interest in the relevant section on directors' duties; now the latter have to take the interests of the employees into account when performing the decision-making, among other factors. The standard in the US in relation to labour appears to be lower even than in the UK.

## The Agency Problem: Flexibility versus Accountability to Shareholders

In theory the board serves as the link between those who invest in the company and own it, and those who actually control it. The board comprises of the people who stand between these two groups and attempt to balance their sometimes conflicting interests; the small number of managers who run the company and the vast number of shareholders, who in theory at least own it but in practice have a minimum influence on its decision-making. Therefore, the tasks of the board are rather delicate as they have to act as the mitigating factor between two actors whose aspirations are very likely to conflict. The board has to function as the bridge between sometimes divergent agendas, always taking into account the nature of the actors involved and the practical needs of the company. A company is a complex entity that functions in conditions of intense competition in one or more national or product markets. The managers should be allowed to run the company uninhibited from constant interference on the part of shareholders, who nowadays may outnumber the population of a small European country. Decisions should be able to be taken swiftly, responding to the challenges and the ever-changing conditions in the market rather than adhering to the requirements of a procedure so cumbersome that would eventually lead to corporate failure. Flexibility and subsequently adaptability in the constantly evolving business landscape are two of the factors that are deemed necessary for corporate survival and success. On the other hand,

---

56 Blair, M.M. and J.M. Roe *Employees and Corporate Governance* (Brookings Institution Press, Washington 1999), p. 93.

there is the very real need to safeguard the interests of the shareholders, whose number might render their say in the management unrealistic but who still have the right to demand that their assets are not going to be mismanaged. If the need of the management to react promptly to market challenges is recognised, so is the right of the shareholders to demand that their investment is managed with the appropriate care, as incompetence or fraud are not rare occurrences at corporate level. Therefore, the role of the board as the body which provides the necessary checks and institutional balances is rather important; it has to provide the necessary discretion to managers to run the company effectively while satisfying the need to hold them accountable in case of breach of duty or fraud. And taking into account the scandals that have marked the beginning of the twenty-first century from Enron to World Com and others, it can be legitimately argued that the boards have not met the requirements of their institutional role with the desired success. Although the management is at least in theory under the intense scrutiny of the board, in practice the latter is usually involved in a more lax overview of the operation of the company. Peter Drucker, a management guru, notes: 'whenever an institution malfunctions as consistently as boards of directors have in nearly every major fiasco of the last 40 or 50 years it is futile to blame men. It is the institution that malfunctions'.[57]

## The Duty of Care, the Duty of Loyalty and the Business Judgement Rule: The Role of the Courts

The fragmentation of the relevant US law into 50 pieces due to the fact that these issues are regulated at state level does not allow us to talk about a single company law statutes as in most European countries. However, it is true that the regulation of this issue from state to state presents more similarities rather than any substantial divergence, especially in terms of the principles laying in their foundations or the aims pursued. In general one can find a fiduciary duty that directors in the US public companies would have to adhere to comprising two parameters; the *duty of care* and the *duty of loyalty*. The former is the duty to act in good faith and with due diligence when taking a decision, always on the basis of the interests of the company itself and of its owners instead of their own. The latter includes the right to avoid the conflict of personal with the corporate interests and entails loyalty to the company's shareholders. In both cases directors must 'discharge their duties in good faith;

[57] Monks and Minow (2010), p. 236.

with the care an ordinarily prudent person in like position would exercise under similar circumstances; and in a manner he reasonably believes to be in the best interests of the corporation'.[58] The duty of loyalty was very much shaped by the *Guth v Loft*[59] case of 1939. In that case the court shaped the framework within which the duty of loyalty was to be applied, along with the requirements for its implementation. The court stated that

> corporate officers and directors are not permitted to use their position of trust and confidence to further their private interests. While technically not trustees, they stand in a fiduciary relation to the corporation and its stockholders. A public policy, existing through the years, and derived from a profound knowledge of human characteristics and motives, has established a rule that demands of a corporate officer or director, peremptorily and inexorably, the most scrupulous observance of his duty, not only affirmatively to protect the interest of the corporation committed to his charge, but also to refrain from doing anything that would work injury to the corporation, or to deprive it of profit or advantage which his skill and ability might properly bring to it, or to enable it to make in the reasonable and lawful exercise of its powers. The rule that requires an undivided and unselfish loyalty to the corporation demands that there shall be no conflict between duty and self-interest.

The ruling of the court emphasised the fiduciary relationship that binds the directors with the company and the shareholders; it stated in a rather emphatic manner that the fiduciary relationship in question entails a duty not to bring oneself in a situation where personal interests can conflict with the duty owed to company and the shareholders. Therefore, the court appeared to have produced an absolute rule that prohibits any conflict of interests save perhaps from exceptional circumstances. However, the reality was quite different; the court in fact formulated requirements, the fulfilment of which can actually justify the decision of a director to take advantage of a business opportunity that emerges during his office on his own account. The court clearly stated that

> if there is presented to a corporate officer or director a business opportunity which the corporation is financially able to undertake, which is, from its nature, in the line of the corporation's business and is of practical advantage to it, is one in which the corporation has an interest or a reasonable expectancy, and, by embracing the opportunity, the self-interest of the officer or director will be brought into conflict with that of his corporation, the law will not permit him to seize the opportunity for himself.

---

[58] Pinto, R.A. and G. Visentini, *The Legal Basis of Corporate Governance in Publicly Held Corporations* (Kluwer Law International, London 1998), p. 266.
[59] *Guth v Loft, Inc*, 5A 2d 503 (Delaware 1939).

Therefore, the law will prevent him from taking advantage of a business opportunity when the following three requirements are met: the corporation has the financial capacity to pursue this business opportunity, the latter falls within its line of business and it has an interest or a reasonable expectation to embrace it. From the wording of the ruling, it can be deduced that if the three requirements are not met then the director could take advantage of a business opportunity that emerged during his term without being in peril to be found in a breach of his duty of loyalty to the company. The test which was shaped by this case lays down a concrete three-stage test that can determine the liability of a director in case of pursuing business opportunities on his own account during his course of office. The test in question emerged as the norm employed in similar situations and was later incorporated into statute. Section 144 of the Delaware General Corporation Law states that

> no contract or transaction between a corporation and one or more of its directors or officers, or between a corporation and any other corporation, partnership, association, or other organization in which one or more of its directors or officers, are directors or officers, or have a financial interest, shall be void or voidable solely for this reason.

The duty of loyalty as constructed by the USA jurisprudence provides a much greater scope of discretion to directors who would like to avail themselves of business opportunities which appear during their term of office than the respective interpretation by the UK courts. Section 175 of the Companies Act 2006 provides for the UK version of the duty of loyalty which is more specifically entitled as the 'duty to avoid conflict of interests'. The section in question has to be read in conjunction with section 170 of the same Act, which clarifies that a person who ceases to be a director continues to be subject to the duty in section 175 as regards the exploitation of any property, information or opportunity of which he became aware at a time when he was a director. Therefore, in the UK the director is not only obliged to refrain from taking advantage of business opportunities during his office, but also even after his removal or resignation from that post if he became aware of such an opportunity while being a director. In fact the statutory position in question constitutes the incorporation into the Act of principles that had already been clearly shaped by the courts. In *Bhullar v Bhullar*[60] the court stated that the director in question

---

60 *Bhullar v Bhullar* [2003] EWCA Civ 424.

was found in breach of duty even if the company could not or would not benefit from the opportunity in question. The latter was found as irrelevant. The issue was that the director had obtained access to information that was very useful from a commercial point of view. He was under a fiduciary duty to communicate it to the company. Whether the company would have acquired the property is irrelevant. What matters is that information relevant to the company was not passed to it by the director in question who was consequently found to be in breach of his duty towards the company and therefore liable to account for his profits.

The two rulings embody the diametrically different positions assumed by the courts of the respective jurisdictions, and underline in a revealing manner the divergence in the approach taken.

The 'business judgement' doctrine will find its application at this point too; if the directors can show that they have taken a decision on the basis of their twofold aforementioned duties, then normally judges will not be inclined to investigate the rationale behind it further. With the exceptions of directors having acted in cases of self-dealing or gross negligence, the courts will prefer not to interfere irrespective of whether the decision in question had proven to be a successful one or not. In a sense the business judgement rule 'reflects an inherent tension between two competing values: the need to preserve the board of directors' decision making discretion and the need to hold the board accountable for its decisions'.[61] Directors when taking decisions will not be second-guessed by the courts. In *Smith v Van Gorkom*[62] the Delaware Supreme Court decided that the 'business judgement rule' is 'a presumption that in making a business decision, the directors of a corporation acted on an informed basis, in good faith and in the honest belief that the action taken was in the best interests of the company'. Hence, the party challenging a board decision as uninformed must rebut the presumption that its business judgement was an informed one. In *Re Walt Disney Co. Derivative Litigation*[63] the court explained that a duty of loyalty claim is implicated 'when a fiduciary either appears on both sides of a transaction or receives a personal benefit not shared by all shareholders'. The court also found that acting in good faith is central to the fiduciary duties such as the duty of due care. The court set the threshold for bad faith by stating that

---

[61] Bainbridge, *The New Corporate Governance, In Theory and Practice* (Oxford University Press, Oxford 2010), p. 197.

[62] *Smith v Van Gorkom* 488 A.2d 858 (Delaware Supreme Court, 1985).

[63] *Re Walt Disney Co. Derivative Litigation* 907 A.2d 693 (Del. Ch. 2005).

> a failure to act in good faith [may be found] … where the fiduciary intentionally acts with a purpose other than that of advancing the best interests of the company, where the fiduciary acts with the intent to violate applicable positive law, or where the fiduciary intentionally fails to act in the face of a known duty to act, demonstrating a conscious disregard for his duties.

Therefore, in duty of loyalty cases there is a higher degree of judicial involvement since the burden of proof now belongs to the directors, in contrast to the duty of care cases when it belongs to the plaintiffs, and the decision in question is scrutinised against a standard of fairness. This is important for executive remuneration, as challenging negligent decisions setting remuneration on the basis of good faith as a part of the fiduciary duty of loyalty could be quite difficult. Directorial decisions which are merely inattentive will not be found as mounting to the levels of bad faith necessary to overcome the business judgement rule and therefore render a more thorough judicial scrutiny of the decision imperative.[64] This betrays the general lack of will on the part of the courts to intervene actively in cases of executive remuneration; the latter is viewed more as a matter which falls within the internal affairs and decision-making procedures of the company, save for situations which involved either crude abuse of shareholders' interests or fraud.

## The Unitary Board: Executives and Non-executives

> [Two features of the] corporate form underlies corporate governance. The first is investor ownership which given the breadth of contemporary capital markets implies that ultimate control over the firm often lies partly or entirely in the hands of shareholders far removed from the firm's day to day operations. The second is delegated management … thus a canonical feature of the corporation is a multi member board selected largely or entirely by shareholders.[65]

The boards of US companies are unitary in structure. Along with the majority of nations worldwide, the US has avoided the adoption of the dual-board structure, in contrast to Germany which remains the most prominent example of such a corporate governance system. Inherent in function of the unitary board is the inclusion of both executive and

---

[64] Randall, S.T. and W. Harwell, 'Executive Compensation in the Courts: Board Capture, Optimal Contracting, and Officers' Fiduciary Duties' (2011) 95 *Minnesota Law Review* 846, p. 878.

[65] Kraakman, R. et al, *The Anatomy of Corporate Law, A Comparative and Functional Approach* (Oxford University Press, Oxford 2009), p. 56.

monitoring roles; the former assumed by the executive directors and the latter by the non-executive directors. The executive directors are responsible for the everyday running of the company. Their duties include the planning of the company strategies and the representation of the company to third parties, therefore they occupy a position at the centre of the company's administrative structures. The non-executive directors on the other hand are entrusted with the supervision of the executive ones. Their role does not entail interference in the everyday running of the company or constant presence in meetings and involvement in the decision-making process within the company. Their role involves an advisory element, as usually the individuals who are appointed to these posts can demonstrate a career, a professional record and qualifications that would justify their supervisory duties. Their presence aims to create safeguards against misuse of power on the part of executive directors.

The corporate scandals that rocked the USA at the beginning of this century demonstrated the flaws of such an aspiration. Dealing with such shortcomings is an increasingly challenging task since scandals tend to derive from the nature of the American corporate governance system which ascribes a heavily important role to managers. The supervisees are actually very powerful in the US corporate context, with extensive duties and a firmly consolidated position within the company. The largely diffuse shareholding as explained above has ultimately secured for the managers an enhanced role in the running of the company. The non-executive directors are supposed to 'represent the interests of the shareholders when these are in conflict with the managers … they are the first line of defence for the protection of shareholders' interests'.[66] The problem lies in the fact that even the precise definition of the interests of the shareholders might prove more challenging than initially thought. The rationale behind this difficulty is the lack of homogeneity in the body of shareholders, who in the case of large public companies can number millions of individuals, from entrepreneurs aiming at enlarging their investment portfolio and availing themselves of new business opportunities to citizens that purchased a very small number of shares hoping to resell them as soon as their price further increases. In addition to that, a great number of shareholders simply are not interested in their stock possessions, and return to them years later when they are faced with a need of liquidity. The image is further complicated by the fact that nowadays the shareholders do not just include individuals, whether

[66] Owen, G., T. Kirchmaier and J. Grant, *Corporate Governance in the US and Europe, Where are we now?* (Palgrave Macmillan, New York 2005), p. 12.

businessmen or everyday citizens, but also large corporations which acquire a stake at another corporation, pension funds, investment funds such as mutual funds, hedge funds or sovereign wealth funds. The variety of the actors involved in shareholding guarantees the divergence of interest among them and renders its function as a collective body with a single list of interests virtually impossible. Pension funds are normally orientated towards investing in companies which at least appear to have sound finances and seek to increase their investment in the medium to long term. On the other hand, hedge funds are usually seeking to take advantage of short-term business opportunities often engaging in short selling, aiming at quick profit. Therefore, the non-executive directors would have to interpret the wishes, aims and interests of a body that is not as unified and homogeneous as it initially appears.

Executive directors are also under the duty to run the corporate affairs in the best interest of the company and its shareholders, therefore they arguably face the same challenge to read behind the lines and discern the thin parameters that define the shareholder interest. However, the very structure of the corporation in the US and other countries leaves them better equipped to deal with this challenge. Executive directors are required to dedicate their professional life to the company; they run its everyday affairs and they are heavily involved in the decision-making process. Along with experience comes familiarity with the different actors comprising the company. This by no means entails knowing the millions of people that could potentially be involved in the stockholding of the company, but at least the basic players within this context. Therefore, the executive directors achieve a clearer image of the company geography than the non-executive ones, whose role does not entail their everyday presence and involvement in the company life and decision-making. Dedicating a limited amount of time to the increasingly complex company's affairs and limiting their involvement in the management to the minimum level deprives non-executive directors of the ability to become acquainted with every parameter of the corporate reality and consequently to monitor the executive directors in the most effective possible way, rendering ineffective this form of internal management control.

The same could be argued for the independent directors as outsiders or not affiliated with the company. These are individuals who should enjoy no link whatsoever with the company, and their appointment to the board serves the need to maintain an additional layer of supervision by people who have no personal interest or involvement in the company's affairs and therefore could objectively judge whether the management is adequately fulfilling its role or there are inadequacies that should be addressed or punished. A reform of the NYSE in 1978 that required every listed company to have an audit committee comprising a majority of outside directors significantly influenced the stance adopted by US corporations on the matter, radically enhancing the importance of independent directors and their levels of participation in the boards. New rules adopted by the NYSE after the Enron scandal and in the wake of the SOX Act require all listed companies to have a majority of independent directors and to have all of the main committees composed exclusively of independent outside directors; however, their exposure to liability in the light of their enhanced presence after the latest reforms has made their recruitment much more challenging than in the past. In the USA, 'protection of shareholder interests was a clear priority and part of the legislative intent of the post-Enron reform; enhancement of shareholder participation and power was not … post-Enron legislation in the USA also paid relatively little attention to the issue of executive remuneration'.[67] The Delaware courts had been more active in dealing with this matter and setting some standards that were to be followed when dealing with executive remuneration. In the *Kerbs*[68] case, the court stated that

> this court cannot conclude on the basis of the record here made that the amounts paid or which it may reasonably be anticipated will be paid under this plan bear no reasonable relation to the value of the services rendered … the court cannot but note with concern the growing tendency to assume that a corporation cannot obtain or keep qualified officials unless such persons are given large 'incentives' over and above substantial salaries. These 'incentives' are often given without sufficient regard for general stockholder interest.[69]

The court has therefore set the basic parameters in accordance to which executive remuneration should be formed: it should have a reasonable relation to the value of the services rendered and it should give sufficient regard to the shareholders' interests. However, despite the fact that the judgment in question set a standard against which executive remuneration is to be shaped, in reality it has been applied in such a flexible manner to

---

67 Hill, G.J., 'Then and Now: Professor Berle and the Unpredictable Shareholder' (2010) 33 *Seattle University Law Review* 4, 1005, p. 1016.

68 *Kerbs v California Eastern Airways, Inc.*, 91 A.2d 62 (1952).

69 See the ruling at http://de.findacase.com/research/wfrmDocViewer.aspx/xq/fac.19510928_0001.DE.htm/qx.

the degree that 'the business judgement rule protects almost any compensation decision made by a disinterested committee of the board'.[70]

## Lack of Protection of Shareholders in the USA and the Power of CEOs

Despite that shift towards a greater protection of shareholders' interests, the level of protection granted to shareholders in the UK is indeed more enhanced than in the USA in a 'range of corporate matters such as amending the corporate constitution, convening meetings, and the appointment and removal of directors'.[71] Shareholder protection in the USA corporate context remains lax in comparative terms[72] and it is 'highly unusual in the extent to which it disenfranchises shareholders from both explicit and implicit influence'.[73] Although shareholder protection has been a 'mantra of USA corporate law, shareholder empowerment has not. Yet, empowerment is an important aspect of investor protection ... closely correlated with investor activism ... which is of growing importance in a range of corporate governance areas such as executive compensation'.[74] In this context the enhancement of the role of independent directors offers an additional layer of objectivity on the basis of which a potential abuse is going to be detected and dealt with sooner rather than later; these are people with no agenda, no individual interests at stake, no links with the other actors involved and therefore in no need to make compromises or keep a balance with potentially conflicting interests. Their presence is also important in boards comprising in many occasions the insiders supposedly under monitoring, and where it is not uncommon that the CEO is also the chairman. While in the UK these positions are normally separated, in the US the merger of the two roles into one was widespread practice among corporations, especially before the SOX Act. This development further enhances the already powerful

---

[70] Yablon, C.M., 'Overcompensating: The Company Lawyer and Executive Pay' (1992) 92 *Columbia Law Review* 1867, p. 1904.

[71] Hill (2010), p. 1017.

[72] Hill, 'Subverting Shareholder Rights: Lessons from News Corporation's Migration to Delaware' (2010) 63 *Vanderbilt Law Review* 1.

[73] Gelter, M., 'The Dark Side of Shareholder Influence: Managerial Autonomy and Stakeholder Orientation in Comparative Corporate Governance' (2009) 50 *Harvard International Law Journal* 129, p. 134.

[74] Hill, 'The Rising Tension Between Shareholder and Director Power in the Common Law World' (2010) European Corporate Governance Institute, *Law Working Paper* No.152, Vanderbilt University School of Law, Law and Economics *Research Paper* No.10–11 and University of Sydney Faculty of Law, *Research Paper* nos.10–34, p. 4.

position of the CEO, granting him the additional capacity to shape the agenda of the board meeting and to determine its frequency.

The central position that the CEO enjoys in the US corporate context as the person yielding absolute, almost monarchical, power within the corporation further betrays the notion of individualism lying at the foundations not only of the American political and legal culture in general but also of the American corporate structure in particular. This can be contrasted with an evident notion of communitarianism that forms the core of corporate culture in continental Europe where the management of companies' fortunes are deemed to be more the subject of teamwork and presence. The existence of independent directors could potentially add an additional layer of protection to the power of the CEO, providing the shareholders with extra safeguards to their investment. It should be emphasised at this point that it was the absolute dominance that the CEOs exercised on the board that emerged as the distinctive feature of the corporate scandals of this century. The level of control on the board was so extensive that it was soon 'extended over the professional people retained by the corporation to do its audits and perform other services such as lawyers, investment bankers, financial analysts etc'.[75] The CEO had influence over directors' remuneration, contributing to the excesses of that time as the 'pervasive role of managerial power can explain much of the contemporary landscape of executive compensation including practices and patterns that have long troubled financial economists … CEOs have often used their power over corporate resources to reward individual directors who were particularly cooperative'.[76] Therefore, the latter did not fulfil their duties to the standard required, with a greatly adverse effect on the smooth operation of the corporations involved.

The independent directors also provide a welcome notion of externality to a board whose members might have been voted in by the shareholders but on the basis of a list of nominees handed to them by the managers; this process, remarkably resembling the elections in a one-party state, is significantly reducing the number of internal independent voices as the individuals chosen by the managers will usually enjoy some kind of links with them, either of personal or ideological nature. However, as with non-executive directors, due exactly to their lack of connection with the company in question the independent directors may not desire the level

---

75 Gitlow, L.A., *Corruption in Corporate America*, 2nd edn (University Press of America Inc, New York 2007), p. 12.

76 Kieff, F.S. and A.T. Paredes, *Perspectives on Corporate Governance* (Cambridge University Press, Cambridge 2010), pp. 118 and 126.

of involvement that is necessary for their supervision to be effective. As they have no personal stakes involved, they might show limited motivation to deal with complex issues that would require an increasing part of their precious personal time. Therefore, the very advantages of having an independent or outsider director on the board might evolve into the disadvantages that would handicap his willingness to exercise his role to its full capacity, undermining from the very beginning the effectiveness of his presence. Taking into account that one of the key responsibilities of the board is the determination and fixing of executive pay, the lack of satisfactory supervision, especially in the light of the recent corporate scandals, emerges as an issue of vital importance for the smooth running of the company. Since corporate practices moved from granting salaries to directors to offering them stock options, aiming at aligning their interests with those of the shareholders or bonuses to increase further their incentive to achieve the desired results, an increased supervision is necessary if the excesses of the past are to be avoided in the future. Despite the shortcomings in the performance of their tasks, it has been argued that due to the nature of their role, the inclusion of independent directors at board level has indeed enhanced

> the fidelity of managers to shareholder objectives, as opposed to managerial interests or stakeholder interests … the reliability of the firm's public disclosure which makes stock market prices a more reliable signal for capital allocation and for the monitoring of managers at other firms as well as their own … a 'visible hand' namely the independent board is needed to balance the tendency of markers to overshoot.[77]

Therefore, their role is increasingly important, especially as the tendency to have fewer insider directors and more outsider-independent directors on boards in the US continues.

---

[77] Gordon, N.J., 'The Rise of Independent Directors in the United States, 1950–2005: Of Shareholder Value and Stock Market Prices' (2007) 59 *Stanford Law Review* 1465, p. 1469.

# 4. The United Kingdom

## COMPANY LAW IN HISTORICAL PERSPECTIVE

The development of the social phenomenon that is the company in the UK presents many interesting aspects and is of particular significance. The UK possesses a unique position in the framework of the analysis of the relevant subject matter for a variety of reasons. Firstly, the UK is one of the very few jurisdictions internationally that evolved continuously over centuries, providing the legal world with an abundance of legal principles, norms and regulations that reflect the realities of the historical moment in which they were adopted. As analysed previously in this book, it is impossible to view and assess a piece of legislation independent of the social environment that gave birth to it.[1] In this sense the UK with its centuries' old legal tradition provides us with a clear picture of the legal and social evolution that shaped the corporation and led to the legislative framework and the predominant principles in company law, at least as we know and experience them today. Furthermore, the UK managed to create an empire that at its peak expanded in all continents, therefore resulting in an unprecedented large-scale extension of legal norms and standards. Therefore, the UK legislative standards were adopted by several nations around the world which shared any sort of links with their former colonial power. The country's legal order is based on common law, a mixture of judicial precedence and statutes that proved to be particularly influential for other nations around the world. Within this framework the UK corporate form and along with it UK company law emerged as the pattern to be adopted by a variety of legal orders such as the USA and Australia. Of course as analysed above, the company is the outcome of the internal developments that shape the societal structure of a nation as a whole, therefore the countries in question developed a corporate form with a corporate governance system that despite its evident similarities with their UK counterpart do present their own distinctive characteristics and features.

[1] Talbot, L., *Progressive Corporate Governance for the 21st Century* (Routledge, London and New York 2013), especially Chapter 2.

Corporate governance and law in the UK is interesting for another reason: the concept of the company in the UK legal order experienced a rather dramatic shift from the beginning of the nineteenth century to the mid-nineteenth century, and up until today. The UK was a champion of a more conservative and distinctively more restrictive form of corporate organisation based on two pillars: on the one hand, on the liability of the businessmen involved for the debts that their company had created since its founding, and on the other the cultivation of strong links between management and ownership. Gradually the UK changed from the phase of heavy and clearly restrictive regulation of companies into a norm that we observe today, marked by a significantly more liberal approach that recognises the company as a body with a separate legal personality based on the fundamental principle of limited liability. Furthermore, the UK was no exception to the trend of the gradual breaking of links between ownership and control which as analysed in Chapters 2 and 3 has evolved as the principal feature of the USA company law. However, different historical developments have fuelled a divergence between the UK on the one hand and continental Europe on the other, bringing the UK to the rather exceptional position of presenting greater similarities in terms of corporate law with the USA rather than with its partners across the English Channel. The rationale behind this proximity not only stems from the colonial links shared with the former but also from historical trends in the UK that provided the grounds for a model of corporate governance that would significantly differ from the rest of Europe.

## The Power of the Guilds

Going back almost a thousand years, the Romans might have included in their territory a great part of today's Britain within their empire, leaving an impressive legacy of castles, roads, ideas and expressions that have influenced their successors to an enormous extent; however, the roots of the British corporate model would be chiefly inspired by the Anglo-Saxon legal thinking. England at that time was an agricultural society; 'trades ancillary to agriculture and village life were practiced locally by individual traders and their families. The bulk of medieval trade and industry was professionalized and largely confined to communal towns'.[2] Internal trade in the form of exchanges within or between local communities amounted for the greatest part of commercial activities.

---

[2] Postan, M.M., *The Medieval Economy and Society* (Weidenfeld & Nicolson, London 1972; Pelican, London 1975).

In the twelfth and thirteenth centuries, the 'development of the Flemish commercial society led to the export of the English wool and the growth of foreign trade across the shores'.[3] In the commercial towns both the manufacturers and the merchants 'traded under the aegis of the craft guilds'.[4] Guilds were organisations that controlled the local market which operated as a monopoly. The guilds would set the regulatory requirements to enter the market, the conditions that local craftsmen had to fulfil or the standards for the production of local goods. One can detect the roots of Britain's tendency to self-regulate in exactly these functions. In today's terms, the guilds would have been widely perceived as something between a cartel and a very powerful trade union with rather extensive regulatory capacity, whose function would certainly be prohibited today, both in the UK but also in the rest of the EU as it would definitely come into conflict with the bulk of the existing legislation.

Despite its conflict with modern legislative standards, guilds provided the framework within which the English society of that time conducted trade. The guilds were based on the notion of equality as they aimed at securing a certain share of the market to each member roughly on equal terms. Any initiative on the part of a member of a community to enhance its position in the market, for example by introducing an innovative method of marketing or production, would be seen as an effort to expand one's member share in the expense of another and therefore it would be discouraged. In England at that time, this form of conducting business was the rule rather than the exception. In fact a few guilds were incorporated by the Crown; among those was the Company of Merchant Adventurers which also maintained a monopoly in their field and set the standards to which its members had to adhere. Today this would have been enough to bring the guilds within the scope of application of competition law, with the relevant authorities imposing enormous fines to punish such behaviour that would undermine the fundamental parameters of an open economy where free competition under the existing rules should guarantee its smooth operation. However, in England at that time, 'private profit and competition set brother against brother and was considered an evil'.[5] It is a

---

3 Tricker, R.I., *The Evolution of the Company, Corporate Governance: Practices, Procedures and Powers in British Companies and their Boards of Directors* (Gower, Aldershot 1984), p. 26.

4 Ibid.

5 Ibid.

> sin … precisely that effort to achieve a continuous and unlimited increase in material wealth which modern societies applaud as meritorious … the essence of the argument was that payment may properly be demanded by the craftsmen who made the goods or by the merchants who transport them … the unpardonable sin is that of speculator or middleman who snatches private gain by the exploitation of public necessities.[6]

Interestingly, and quite in contrast with today's landscape, continental European businesses were emerging as pioneers of trade based on corporate forms aiming clearly at profitability. Merchants in Holland, northern Italy and Germany were gradually uniting to form ventures and other financial units that would resemble the corporate form similar to that employed nowadays in Europe. England was again rather exceptional in its strict adherence to monopolies, strict regulation of standards and procedures and an overt distaste for personal profit.

In Chapter 1, we charted the influence of religion on capitalism and how the profit motive was suppressed not only because of the power of the church but also by Kings who wished to make sure that they were supreme. As Europe was clearly evolving towards the direction of creating its first sizeable business units, England experienced the formation of large enterprises too; however, due to the regulatory environment that placed strict restrictions on free trade and the predominant cultural context within which profitability was not perceived as social value of great virtue, the enterprises in question could not trade uninhibited with external trading partners but almost exclusively with Kings. Therefore, 'the beginnings of English commercial capitalism were nipped in the bud and the place of capitalists was taken by regulated companies which for all the commercial and financial power they collectively represented, were still redolent with the medieval spirit of regulation and monopoly'.[7]

## The Beginning of Enterprise, Individualism and Property Rights: The Foundation of the EU's Difficulties in Corporate Governance

Those early characteristics of the medieval agricultural society clearly marked the attitude of the nation towards the company, but also towards the main features of the economic structure of that period. A society comprising a variety of local communities whose prosperity was heavily

---

[6] Tawney, R.H., *Religion and the Rise of Capitalism* (Transaction Publishers, New Brunswick, NJ 1998; originally published by Harcourt, Brace & Company Inc., New York 1926).

[7] Postan, *The English Farmers of the Customs 1343–1352* (Transnational Royal Historical Society, 1959), fifth series, vol IX.

dependent on agriculture was naturally inclined to follow policies deemed as protective of its members engaged in agricultural activities rather than trade. The latter was mainly limited to the agricultural products exchanged within or among the local communities. Furthermore, despite the Roman presence in England, the links of the country with continental Europe remained relatively loose, due to distance among other factors. Despite the structures and distinctive characteristics of the English society of that time, the truth is that the seeds of the entrepreneurial spirit that marked the English businessmen of the following centuries and the main cultural and ideological concepts that provided the grounds for a more liberal approach towards the economy and trade already existed both in the English legal tradition and in English literature. England's constitutional structure:

> including the role of the judiciary took its modern shape as a result of the conflicts between Parliament and the Crown in the seventeenth century. During that period the common law became strongly associated with the idea of economic freedom and more generally the subject's liberty from arbitrary action by the Crown.[8]

The philosophical foundations of such a debate can be traced before that. Magna Carta, a landmark development in the evolution of English constitutional law and traditions, included a variety of rights with a special emphasis evidently attributed to the rights of the individual; the inclusion of the right to property in the list of rights of fundamental importance and the importance ascribed to personal ownership, provided England with the theoretical basis on which its future corporate law was to be determinedly influenced. Therefore, English law was keen from an early stage to cover with its protections aspects of the private life of individuals against intrusions from everyone including the King, and has a rich tradition[9] in the protection of personal autonomy, an attitude that reached its peak as early as in 1604, when in 'Semayne's case it was stated that the house of everyone is to him as his castle and fortress'.[10]

---

[8] Mahoney, P.G., 'The Common Law and Economic Growth: Hayek might be right' (2001) XXX *Journal of Legal Studies*, June, p. 508.

[9] See: Lord Gordon Slynn, 'The Development of Human Rights in the United Kingdom' (2005) 28 *Fordham International Law Journal* 477.

[10] Singh, R., 'Privacy and the Media after the Human Rights Act' (1998) 6 *European Human Rights Law Review*, p. 712.

Magna Carta placed 'individual liberties above all others except communal rights, a concept adopted by British common law in the thirteenth century'.[11] In 1361

> [the] English Justices of the Peace Act provided for the arrest of peeping toms and eavesdroppers. From the beginning the intent to protect an individual from the government was clear: the poorest man may in his cottage bid defiance to all force of the Crown. It may be frail; its roof may shake; the wind may blow through it; the storms may enter; the rain may enter; but the King of England cannot enter.[12]

This position highlights vividly not only the prominent position that individual liberties assumed in the English legal order from a very early point of history but also the concept underlining those liberties: the right to personal property. The King of England could not enter the property of an Englishman due to the fact that it constituted a part of his property and hence enjoyed the protection of the law, even against the high royal authority. It is precisely these concepts of strong individuality and adherence to the notion of personal property that shaped the future regime in company law in a distinctively English way. The status enjoyed by personal liberty and property in the English legal order distinguished the country from its continental European neighbours and led historians to claim that 'England in the thirteenth century was a far more sophisticated market than Marx recognised'.[13]

Despite the monopolistic nature of the market in England at that time, the ideological and cultural grounds that fuelled the creation of a different corporate model based on individualism and property rights was evident from an early phase of the country's history. In addition, the English people showed a preference for regulating their own affairs with limited state interference; even when guilds were at the peak of their power the restrictive illiberal regulation did not flow from the state but from the guilds themselves. The regulations that perpetuated the existence of monopolies at that time were introduced by the guilds and not by the state, betraying yet another expression of individualism that seeks to limit the role of the state in what is perceived as personal affairs. The attitude on the other side of the Channel took state regulation as the

---

[11] Bale, B.R., 'Informed Lending Decision v Privacy Interests in Great Britain' (1997) 10 *Transnational Lawyer* 77.

[12] Cardonsky, B.L., 'Towards a Meaningful Right to Privacy in the United Kingdom' (2002) 20 *Boston University International Law Journal*, p. 396.

[13] Macfarlane, A., *The Origins of English Individualism* (Basil Blackwell, Oxford 1978), p. 201.

norm, setting the standards for almost all fields of human activities on the basis of both the Roman and the Napoleonic legal traditions, further underlining the increasing divergence between the cultural, ideological and subsequently legislative traditions. 'Personal freedom became universal at an early date in our country … self help and self government were for long centuries taught to the English in the school of town life … there were no rights without duties.'[14] Therefore,

> when Jefferson wrote we 'hold those truths to be sacred and undeniable: that all men are created equal and independent, that from that equal creation they demand rights inherent and inalienable' he was putting into words a view of the individual and society which had its roots in thirteenth century England or earlier.[15]

Individuality, property rights and self-regulation enjoy deep roots in English history, having left their clear imprint on all aspects of regulation; company law could not be an exception to that rule, and nor could corporate governance. Every nation constructs the structure of its companies in a manner reflective of its dominant ideological principles and beliefs; it was only natural that English companies would be based on the very same principles that shaped the predominant ideological identity of the nation. This realisation sheds light on the conflicts taking place much later within the EU in relation to the creation of a common European corporate form. The EU found it easier to agree on constitutional texts, provide for the free movement of people and goods, launch common policies in almost all areas apart from company law; corporate governance remains integrally linked to the national cultures and ideologies to a degree that rendered an agreement unfeasible.

## The Era of Free Markets

'[Although] the precedents for an individualistic approach to business and a self-regulatory attitude to corporate governance are to be found in medieval England it was the sixteenth and seventeenth centuries which saw the great flowering of trade and commerce.'[16] 'Elizabethan England represented a new commercial age',[17] with the opening of new trade routes, the launching of new ideas, new methods of communication and

---

[14] Trevelyan, G.M., *English Social History* (Penguin, London 1944).

[15] Macfarlane (1978), p. 202.

[16] Tricker (1984), p. 29.

[17] Wright, L.B., *Middle Class Culture in Elizabethan England* (University of North Carolina Press, Chapel Hill 1935).

subsequently new trade opportunities. The new avenues paved by these developments greatly affected the aspirations of the English society. The agricultural character of the society at that time gradually gave way to trade-orientated classes who could now see their future prosperity in the opening of markets and increased links with other nations, which they now viewed as potential trading partners. The restrictively regulated and inward-looking English economy would look far beyond its borders to exploit a whole new set of trade opportunities. Fragmented small local communities would gradually evolve into towns and cities as urbanisation changed the social landscape, not only in England but also in the greatest part of continental Europe. The guilds and their monopolistic and restrictive practices suddenly seemed the relics of an era with radically different needs and characteristics, and new forms of corporate organisation that would enable trade to thrive were at the forefront of social expectations. In this context as 'traffic and trade become the life blood of the country'[18] the argument that 'trading in companies is most agreeable to the English nature'[19] gains increasing ground in the societal context. Despite the desire for a radical shift in corporate forms away from the guild model to an entity that would greatly facilitate trade, companies in the form we know them today would be created at later stage; at that point the Crown incorporated landmark companies such as the East India Company, the Muscovy Company, the Virginia Company and the North West Passage Company. 'Chartered companies represented a combined effort by governments and merchants to grab the riches of the new world opened up by Columbus, Magellan and Vasco de Gama … they were the lucky recipients of royal charters that gave them exclusive rights to trade with this or that bit of the world.'[20]

## The Importance of Partnerships and the Bubble Act 1720

By the early eighteenth century, small partnerships were the preferred tool to conduct business and trade in England. The owners of the partnerships were also providing the funding for the enterprise. Rapid technological developments paved new avenues for mass scale production for the standards of that historical period and necessitated an increased funding for the expansion of the existing enterprises if they

---

[18] Hill, C., *Intellectual Origins of the English Revolution* (Panther, Oxford University Press, Oxford 1972), p. 359.

[19] Bacon, F. in Hill (1972), p. 446.

[20] Micklethwait, J. and A. Wooldridge, *The Company* (Phoenix, London 2005), p. 25.

were to embrace the novel methods and remain in the market. These developments brought with them the unincorporated company, a form of partnership where some members would run the company and others, usually land-owners or successful traders, would provide the capital. Of course, in case of insolvency all members of the company were liable for the accumulated debt. And while all the circumstances would justify an acceleration of the process of evolution to the incorporated form of company we know today, the widespread speculation taking place on the part of various individuals who encouraged investment in companies such as the South Sea Company with little hope of return, brought a reaction by the state in the form of the Bubble Act of 1720. The directors of the South Sea Company promised potential investors 'fabulous profits and mountains of gold and silver … investors flocked to buy the company's stock, which rose dramatically by sixfold in one year and then quickly plummeted as shareholders realising that the company was worthless, panicked and sold'.[21] This statute, criminal in nature, aimed at protecting potential investors by significantly discouraging the creation of large-scale unincorporated companies with easily transferable shares; it effectively prohibited the creation of joint stock companies without a Royal Charter or private Act of Parliament. Companies with a member liability up to a fixed amount could be founded only after a charter issued by the Crown or a specific Parliamentary Act. The rationale behind the Bubble Act cannot only be traced to the will to limit speculation but also to deep-rooted perceptions of the then financial establishment which felt threatened by the introduction of limited liability and the ability to incorporate without Royal Charter. The ability to incorporate without royal assent on the basis of general criteria would encourage the entrance of new players in the market, which would threaten the dominance of the existing ones. Moreover, limited liability would encourage investment on the part of numerous investors, further reinforcing the market position of the newcomers but also threatening to lead to shared control in the already existing players. The Act embodied an approach towards companies that significantly departs from the corporate model that the UK championed from the nineteenth century and onwards, up to today.

## The Foundation of Financial Services in the UK

Despite the restrictions imposed by the Bubble Act, developments in England were signalling a change of approach. The country was already

---

21 Bakan, J., *The Corporation* (Constable, London 2005), p. 7.

emerging as a leader in finance with three acts paving the way for what became the flagship of the English economy: the Payment of Bills Act of 1698, the Promissory Notes Act of 1704 and the Payment to Bearer Act in 1765 provided the foundations on which England's prominence in the financial industry would be built. The development of an industry which entailed the uninhibited transfer of funds, the swift allocation of resources and labour while of course requiring an abundance of capital was about to shift towards a more liberal legislative framework than that introduced by the Bubble Act. An ever-increasing need for capital, a rapidly emerging financial industry, the opening of new markets internationally through colonisation and the new technological advances called for a legislative response that would facilitate investment, fuelling growth and further development. In addition to that there was a

> need of infrastructural undertakings such as railways and canals to delay paying returns to investors until the line or the canal was completed. This was something that had not been obvious to the early incorporators of such undertakings, who had put many of them into liquidation as a consequence of their practice to pay dividends out of capital during the construction phase of the canal or railway.[22]

In a sense, 'what motivated the promoters of utilities to utilise the corporate form was not the size of the capital but the prolonged period over which it would have to be amortised'.[23]

## Corporate Personality, the Joint Stock Company Act 1844 and Limited Liability

The nineteenth century marked a decisive turn in the evolution of company law in England and subsequently in the UK. The century began with the repeal of the Bubble Act in 1825. The Act had been repeatedly and widely circumvented, while its sclerotic provisions failed to grasp the intensity of the developments taking place at all fronts during that period, thereby impeding growth and discouraging investment. In the same year, the Crown had somehow delegated the responsibility to grant charters to companies to the Board of Trade, who chartered companies which were now able to sue and to be sued. The granting of corporate personality to companies was a landmark development in the history of the country as it

---

[22] McQueen, R., *A Social History of Company Law, Great Britain and the Australian Colonies 1854–1929* (Ashgate, Farnham 2009), p. 27.

[23] Hirst, P.Q., *Law and Ideology* (Macmillan, London 1979).

was the first of two steps – with the other being the granting of limited liability that came soon after – that shaped the business world in a dramatic way. Companies were gradually but steadily acquiring the same rights as private individuals with their legal personality entailing the same bundle of rights enjoyed by a natural person. Companies could sign contracts, assume legal obligations, be a party to a trial and a contract and therefore perform all activities and assume all duties necessary in the increasingly complex economic reality. In addition, companies would gradually be viewed as entities wholly independent from the people behind them, either founders or other investors. The fate of the human capital which founded, ran and supported the operation of the company would gradually be viewed as sharing no links with the existence of the legal person; the presence of the latter could be perpetuated, involving different generations of individuals.

In 1844 the passing of the Joint Stock Company Act contained the roots of today's company law regime and corporate governance structure. The Act required the registration of unincorporated companies, calling directors to conduct and manage the company's affairs while appointing a chairman to preside at the meetings of the members. The fundamentals of the corporate governance structures were effectively laid, with the role ascribed to directors taking shape. A general system of corporate registration and the obligation of registered companies to provide annual financial information to the public were two of the most important features of this legislation. They came as a response to the problems created by the implementation of the Bubble Act, which had boosted favouritism in the granting of royal charters for registration. As the Industrial Revolution was taking place, bringing along rapid and radical changes to all aspects of economic life and activities, it became evident that if England was to profit fully from the technological advances taking place in its territory, it had to legislate corporate structures that would facilitate large-scale investment. At the same time, it had to deal with the increasingly important challenge of dealing with cases of financial mismanagement that had already appeared in the business world, hence the obligation to reveal financial information publicly on an annual basis. Admittedly, the existence of unlimited liability that rendered private investment in companies and hence in ongoing industrial projects a decision of high risk was correctly perceived as the main obstacle to the realisation of the enormous potential of the new economy. In 1854 the Royal Commission on the reform of mercantile law stated that 'the law of partnership which renders every person who … [is] liable to the whole of the debts is unsatisfactory and should be amended to permit such persons to contribute to the capital of such concerns … without incurring liability beyond a limited amount'.[24] The Limited Liability Act of 1855 was passed in such an atmosphere, granting for the first time the privilege of limited liability to the members of joint stock companies that comprised more than 25 members; the companies assumed the responsibility to include the word 'limited' in their name; this principle was however denied to general partners.[25] Despite the granting of the privilege to a limited number of companies, this development certainly marked the end of an era marked by restrictive company forms, and the beginning of a new one where companies would acquire a position at the very forefront of economic development bearing the same rights as private individuals. Furthermore, at times when a great volume of capital was needed, the lack of limited liability discouraged the holders of big capital to invest in companies; with unlimited liability, the greater the wealth, the bigger the risk to be assumed in case of investment. If wealthy investors were to take the decision to sponsor ongoing projects, they had to receive the assurance that their entire fortune was not placed in jeopardy; the assurance they sought came with the form of limited liability.

Viewed from this angle, the granting of limited liability to companies constituted an event of massive historical that significantly contributed to the shaping of the world as we know it today. The introduction of limited liability legislation in England has been characterised as 'a blow for democratic commercial liberty against Tory financial oligarchy'.[26] In this sense the concept of liberty encompassed both the 'freedom from regulation by the state and the impartial grant by the state of corporate status to all comers rather than it being a privilege granted to a few'.[27] However, the granting of limited liability to companies did not receive a universal welcome. Lord Brougham told the House of Lords in 1838 that limited liability was 'contrary to the whole genius and spirit of English law … it would relax that care and vigilance which every partner ought to keep over his association and give a license to every species of fraud'.[28] Similarly the Circular to Bankers in 1840 stated that limited

---

[24] Royal Commission on the Reform of Mercantile Law, Report, 1854.

[25] Section 9 of the Partnership Act 1890.

[26] *The Times*, December 1955, cited in Lord Cohen of Walmer, *One Hundred Years of Limited Liability in England* (Hebrew University, Jerusalem 1957).

[27] McQueen (2009), p. 21.

[28] Parkinson, J. and A. Gamble, *The Political Economy of the Company* (Hart Publishing, Oxford 2000), p. 31.

liability may 'introduce in the place of patient labour and moderate expectations ambitious hopes and the habit of gambling in shares'.[29]

## The Joint Stock Companies Act 1856 and Company Law Act 1862: The Foundation of the Modern Company – Shareholder Primacy and Employees as Externalities

Parliament passed the Joint Stock Companies Act in 1856, which formed a consolidating statute that would leave its distinctive imprint on the whole edifice of British company law in the decades to come. The vice president of the Board of Trade would explain that it is not as important

> to urge the adoption of limited liability … (but to) argue in favour of human liberty that people may be permitted to deal how and with whom they choose without the officious interference of the state … every man has a right to choose for himself between the two principles, and it is ill advised legislation which steps in between him and the exercise of that right.[30]

This statement made at the passing of the bill reveals the parameters of its philosophical and ideological background, that also formed the theoretical basis upon which modern British company law is founded. The granting of the privilege of limited liability to company by the state in practice minimised the risk taken by potential shareholders; it provided solid safeguards to the latter that the extent of their involvement in a given project or company is a purely personal decision. Their liability for debts that might incur would only amount up to the exact value of their investment. Therefore, the shareholders were confident enough to place their money in a company since this pre-fixed amount would serve as the limit to their potential liability. Limited liability absorbs the greatest part of the risk inherent in an investment, allowing the shareholders to plan their future in the safe knowledge that they can deal comfortably even with the worst-case scenario of a corporate insolvency. The granting of limited liability was founded on the basis of the respect of personal liberty; it was noted above that the respect of individual liberties stands at the very core of the English constitutional principles. The English legal order had rallied to the creation of a framework where individual liberties would assume the top position in the agenda. Therefore, individual liberties could be pursued most effectively if the state ceased to interfere in certain segments of human activities. English company law would be

---

29 Circular to Bankers, February 1840, cited in ibid., p. 31.
30 HC Deb. 1 February 1856, v.140, Col.131.

based on those two pillars; on safeguarding a more individualistic approach towards corporate realities that emphasises the role played by the shareholders, who should be able to enjoy a bundle of protection that would squeeze the risk out of their entrepreneurial endeavours, and on limiting the state in a role that would not jeopardise this individualistic approach. This approach would effectively require the state to avoid regulatory interventions that would challenge the notion of shareholder supremacy within the corporate structure, as that would amount to a restriction on personal liberties. Furthermore, this approach would render the shareholders the only members of the company, leaving other actors such as employees as pure externalities to the corporate formation.

The notion of personal property from which the state had to refrain from intervening was a principle so evident even in Magna Carta that it dictated the philosophical foundations of the British company law, leaving its clear and distinctive imprint in the future development of company legislation. In any case the legislative interventions 'between 1844 and 1856 created a new legal framework transforming incorporation from a closely guarded privilege into a freely available right'.[31] The rapidly evolving technological and economic environment fuelled by colonisation and the Industrial Revolution, along with the malfunctions brought by the Bubble Act, shifted the balance towards a much less interventionist approach on the part of the state with a liberalisation in the number of companies achieving incorporation. England moved from restrictive interventionism embodied in the text of the Bubble Act in 1720 to the granting of valuable privileges to companies such as a separate legal personality and limited liability, while limiting the legislative intervention of the state when necessary.

The passing of the Companies Act in 1862 came as a natural development, consolidating previous legislative developments and regulating for the ability of at least seven individuals to subscribe their names to a memorandum of association and form an incorporated company with or without limited liability. That underlying principle of incorporation has survived unchanged up to today. This Act provided the legal basis for the landmark decision of *Salomon*[32] that firmly established the new corporate formation by stating that,

---

[31] Taylor, J., *Creating Capitalism: Joint Stock Enterprise in British Politics and Culture 1800–1870* (The Boydell Press for the Royal Historical Society, Woodbridge, Suffolk 2006), p. 135.

[32] *Salomon v A. Salomon & Co Ltd* [1897] AC 22.

> the company is at law a different person altogether from [those forming the company]: and … the company is not in law the agent of the subscribers or trustee for them. Nor are the subscribers as members liable, in any shape or form, except to the extent and in the manner provided by the Act.

An important effect of the evolution from partnership to company was the fierce adherence of the British judiciary and legal order to the principle of separate corporate personality. This attitude primarily reflected on the reluctance of the British courts to pierce the veil unless a set of strictly defined requirement were not met or unless the statute so required.[33]

The separation between the company as an independent legal fiction on the one hand and the shareholders as the perceived owners on the other was gradually but steadily and decisively taking shape. In terms of ownership and managerial control, the company started to distance itself from its founders and the human reality behind it. A new era was just about to begin in which the 'early nineteenth century companies drew from the normative legal values of the partnership based on contract and agency law, the law of the companies could lay claim to contractual notions of choice, equality and consensus'.[34] Successive Companies Acts passing in 1900 and 1907 did not change the parameters of corporate governance as laid down during the nineteenth century. Parliament opted not to require 'directors to exercise reasonable care and prudence due largely to concerns that respectable individuals would decline to serve as directors'.[35] Apparently, prominent individuals would not consider the prudent running of a company as part of a respectable lifestyle.

## The Great Depression: Some Accountability for Directors

The Great Depression of the 1920s and its links with corporate excesses, especially in the US as analysed in Chapter 3, emphasised the imperative need to introduce controls that would promote accountability in the corporate context. Previous legislative attempts towards this direction were marked by failure. The Directors' Liability Act 1890 aimed at introducing stricter reporting requirements, making directors liable in case of loss suffered by a subscriber to a prospectus when it contained false statements. The legislation

---

33 Sections 212–14 of the Insolvency Act 1986.

34 Talbot, *Critical Company Law* (Routledge, London 2008), p. 11.

35 Cheffins, B.R., *Corporate Ownership and Control, British Business Transformed* (Oxford University Press, Oxford 2008), p. 195.

> was characteristically English in its timidity. It had many loopholes. It also did not impose liability for untrue statements made other than in the prospectus and it sought only to impose civil liability on malefactors. It was a regulatory measure which was still underpinned by the laissez-faire attitude that most matters relating to companies were best left to those involved to sort out themselves ... it was a paper tiger.[36]

Similarly, the Companies Act 1948 introduced the ability of the shareholders to remove a director with a simple majority. In practice the director (who was often the majority shareholder) could vote against his removal with or without the support of potential internal allies, and avoid his removal in an otherwise perfectly legitimate way. In the meantime and as corporations would emerge as a powerful actor in the economic and societal field, the abuse of power on the part of directors attracted the attention of the courts which in many cases were eager to raise the bar and establish the requirement that would determine an increased sense of accountability for the people sitting at the top corporate table. Standards were raised that would determine the liability of a director for a breach of duty of care and skill. In *The Marquis of Bute's Case*,[37] the Marquis of Bute became president of the Cardiff Savings Bank when he was six months old, having inherited the office from his father. He attended only one board meeting of the bank in 38 years. However, he was held not liable for irregularities which occurred in the lending operations of the bank because it was held that he could not be considered liable as he knew nothing about what was going on. Therefore, at the beginning the standard employed for determining whether or not a director was breaching his duty of care and skill was simply that of knowledge; if the director was not aware of the irregularities taking place within the company then he was simply not responsible or liable for them, despite failing to attend any meetings in a period of 38 years. This simply constituted the employment of the laxest possible standard, effectively permitting any form of abuse of the duty of care and skill with the comfortable knowledge on the part of the director that his personal conduct would most certainly go unpunished. Similarly, in *Dovey v Cory*[38] the director was able to escape liability for malpractice which had occurred, on the grounds that he had relied on information given to him by the chairman and general manager of the company. The standard applied here seems to be somewhat stricter than that in *The Marquis of*

[36] McQueen (2009), p. 251.
[37] *The Marquis of Bute's Case* [1892] 2 Ch 100.
[38] *Dovey v Cory* [1901] AC 477.

*Bute's Case*, since the court held that the reliance on the chairman and general manager was reasonable, and the director had not been negligent. The standard in this case was one of negligence, that is, the director must have acted as a reasonable man. If a reasonable man would have been suspicious of the information that was given and would have investigated further, a director who failed to do so could well have been liable for the loss caused by the irregularity. This is a higher standard than that employed in the *Marquis* case, but it admittedly fails to provide the necessary safeguards against directorial abuse.

The courts' unwillingness to interfere even in gross cases of breach of directors' duties clearly revealed the lack of will on the part of the British courts to interfere in the internal life of a company and the internal affairs of the individuals who comprise it. The company was seen as contract whose exclusive parties are the shareholders, and they should be the ones who bear the responsibility of the decision-making, and not the courts. The latter should respect the individual freedom of the shareholders to shape the corporate affairs on the basis of their agreement: their contract. The contractual theory that lies at the very foundations of the British company law defines its nature as a private affair and subsequently dictates not only the extent of any potential interference on the part of the state actors, but also shapes decisively the corporate structure, keeping only for the shareholders the privileged status of the member of the company while leaving out other actors also involved in its everyday running, such as the employees.

The *Re City Equitable Fire Insurance*[39] case marked the shift in the position of the courts towards a purely subjective standard based on three parameters. The court ruled firstly that a director need not exhibit in the performance of his duties a greater degree of skill than may reasonably be expected from a person of his knowledge and experience. Secondly, a director is not bound to give continuous attention to the affairs of his company. His duties are of an intermittent nature to be performed at periodical board meetings and at meetings of any committee of the board on which he happens to be placed. He is not, however, bound to attend all such meetings, though he ought to attend whenever in the circumstances he is reasonably able to do so. And finally in respect of all duties that, having regard to the exigencies of business and the articles of association, may properly be left to some other official, a director is, in the absence of grounds for suspicion, justified in trusting that official to perform such duties honestly. The duty described by the court in this decision remains

---

39 *Re City Equitable Fire Insurance* [1925] Ch 407.

purely subjective, using as a basis for a judgment the individual capacities of the specific person in question holding the post of the director in a given company. Although this is generally accepted as a rising of the standards employed, the truth is that the change was anything but radical. The baby of *Marquis* would most probably pass the test of *Re City Equitable Fire Insurance* as it is exactly the type of conduct that any reasonable person would expect from a six-month-old baby, whose knowledge and experience are by definition non-existent, as apparently are the demands of the court from a director in such cases.

## Accession to the EU

These excesses on the part of directors brought further regulation, which was also introduced as a part of the status of the UK as a member of the EU. The *acquis communautaire*,[40] namely the whole body of EU legislation and judicial decision, had to be incorporated into the British legal order, changing to a certain extent some of the features of the existing company law landscape. The Insolvency Act 1986 was passed in this context, strengthening the protection of creditors in case of insolvency and adding an additional layer of protection against the abuse of directorial duties. The passing of the Directors' Disqualification Act 1986 revealed the albeit moderate intention of the Government and Parliament to introduce an enhanced protection of shareholders in the corporate context. In this context, in *Re D'Jan of London Ltd*[41] Hoffmann LJ stated that the common law duty of care owed by directors was accurately stated in section 214 of the Insolvency Act 1986, requiring a director to demonstrate on the course of his duties firstly the general knowledge, skill and experience that may reasonably be expected of a person carrying out the functions carried out by the director in relation to the company, and secondly the general knowledge, skill and experience that the director has, as it was the case in *Re City Equitable Fire Insurance*. Therefore, the inclusion of an objective criterion that would determine the liability of a director in cases of a breach of the duty of care and skill would significantly enhance the level of protection, bringing more directors within its ambit of application; from now on at least six-month-old babies would find it very difficult to justify corporate abuse.

---

[40] Dine, J., M. Blecher and M. Koutsias, *Company Law in the New Europe: The EU Acquis, Comparative Methodology and Model Law* (Edward Elgar, Cheltenham 2007).

[41] *Re D'Jan of London Ltd* [1993] BCC 646.

The passing of the very significant Companies Act 1985 further solidified an enhanced form of minority shareholder protection while securing the status of the shareholders as the sole members of the company. Despite the enhanced level of protection, the courts appeared again particularly unwilling to interfere in the conduct of the internal affairs of the company and to implement a literal application of the letter of the statute; the ability to raise derivative actions or to sue for the fact that the company's affairs have been conducted in a manner prejudicial for a member's interests were clearly provided for by the statute, but were very ineffectively implemented by the courts, who were eager to place significant limits upon their scope of application with the introduction of a variety of requirements (analysed later in this chapter).

## Tensions between EU Company Law and UK Corporate Governance

This divergence between statute and case law was also due to the unease with which the UK dealt with its obligations as a member of the European Community at that point and admittedly up to now, especially in the field of corporate regulation. The fundamental principles of liberty, self-regulation and individualism, along with the importance ascribed to property rights stemming at the core of the British company law edifice, came into conflict with the more communitarian approaches adopted at the other side of the English Channel. The differences between the two parties in the 1980s were very much reflected in the debates between then UK Prime Minister Margaret Thatcher on the one hand, pioneering the rapid liberalisation of the economy that was anyway taking place in the UK at the time, and then French President François Mitterand who was nationalising crucial sectors of economy in France and championing a different economic model. The battle for the soul of the EC betrayed a conflict between different ideologies, models and philosophical approaches. The Conservative Government in Britain at that time embarked on a highly ambitious privatisation programme, offering shares of companies under state control to the general public; the Government in Britain therefore intentionally promoted a widely diffused ownership structure of public companies. It was not only privatisation which contributed to large-scale change in the shareholder basis of UK corporations; 'what really made a difference to corporate governance in the UK was the transition to widespread ownership of corporations by asset management firms: insurance companies, pension funds, and the unit trusts and investment trusts that provided individual investors with a way to diversify their portfolio through collective investing'.[42] Dispersed ownership in the UK took place much later than in the USA and probably fully unfolded after 1970;[43] interestingly enough, it developed differently, following the emergence of institutional investors while in the USA institutional investors appeared at later stage after ownership had initially been dispersed to millions of individual shareholders. The divergence in historical trends and experiences underlines the notion that although literature uses the term 'outsider' model or the 'Anglo-Saxon' model of corporate governance for both jurisdictions due to their evident similarities and parameters, which have been analysed throughout this book, they are in fact two distinctive models formed in the framework of different societies. This categorisation does not entail any form of claim that the two countries employ an identical model of corporate governance.

As an example of the reverse trends taking place in Europe at that point, only two years after Margaret Thatcher's rise to power in the UK, in 1981 François Mitterand won a landmark electoral victory which granted France its first Socialist government. With the support of the Communists who for the first time after 1947 participated in a governmental coalition, Mitterand attempted a 'quasi-revolutionary reform of the French society'[44] on a pattern which directly conflicted with the respective in the UK at the very same time. Mitterand and his partners talked about a 'rupture with the past and dumping bourgeois capitalism with all its evil works'.[45] In this context he nationalised 36 private banks, 2 industrial banks and 11 industrial firms[46] in his efforts to create a state industrial and financial sector, just as large chunks of British industry were being transferred to private hands. Thus, 'while most EC member states were successful at containing welfare costs in the 1980s, France's spending on social protection increased by more than 30% between 1980 and 1989, reaching 30% of GDP by the early 1990s'.[47] His economic

---

42 Nordberg, D., *Corporate Governance, Principles and Issues* (Sage Publications, London 2011), p. 80.

43 Cheffins (2008), pp. 12–13.

44 Gillingham, J., *European Integration 1950–2003, Superstate or Market Economy?* (Cambridge University Press, Cambridge 2003), p. 137.

45 Ibid.

46 Ibid., p. 141.

47 Schmidt, V.A., 'The Untold Story: The Impact of European Integration on France in the Mitterand-Chirac Era (1981–1997)', *European Community Studies Association Fifth Biennial International Conference, Seattle, May 1997* (University of Massachusetts Press, MA 1997), p. 8.

policy brought him in direct conflict with the UK, where Thatcher's counter-revolution was taking place.

The rise of Margaret Thatcher, a leader with a clear agenda over the future political direction of her country and of certain beliefs over the EC, had a substantial impact on the outcome of the debate over Europe's future identity. Thatcher did not favour further European integration especially in the light of Mitterand's policies, since she was implementing a totally different programme of economic reforms centred around the main features of liberalisation and deregulation, and was not willing to accept French-inspired dirigisme coming from Brussels with the covering of EC regulations. She favoured enlargement over integration since the former would create a 'looser confederation of independent states'[48] friendlier to free markets and liberalism rather than a firmly anchored and integrated union she feared would be ideologically dominated by dirigisme. Thatcher was considered pro-European only when she saw the EC 'exclusively as an organisation for promoting economic liberalism in the industrial and services sectors'[49] and when 'the Community's position as the world's largest trading bloc enhanced Britain's international role. It was the completion of the single market which was received with most enthusiasm by the UK. The passing of the [Single European Act] SEA had many "characteristics of a mega-package deal"'.[50] Thatcher endorsed it because she was very interested in securing the benefits of the internal market for the UK and ensuring that the EC would follow the lines of a policy closer to her choice of economic liberalisation rather than dirigisme. Her former minister Michael Heseltine accused her of being 'responsible for the biggest transfer of sovereignty in British history'[51] with the signing of the SEA in 1987. In 1991 she claimed that 'had she understood the SEA when she signed it, she would not have done so'.[52] She was however determined to promote a more liberal agenda at the EC level; an agenda which favoured

[48] Baun, M.J., 'The Maastricht Treaty as High Politics: Germany, France and European Integration' (1995–1996) 110 *Political Science Quarterly* 4, Winter, p. 610.

[49] Moravcsik, A., 'Negotiating the Single European Act: National Interests and Conventional Statecraft in the European Community' (1991) 45 *International Organisation* 1, Winter, p. 31.

[50] McAllister, R., *From EC to EU, A Historical and Political Survey* (Routledge, London 1997), p. 183.

[51] Pilkington, C., *Britain in the European Union Today* (Manchester University Press, Manchester 1995), p. 43.

[52] Ibid.

liberalisation and the removal of internal barriers to trade. The reforms she had already initiated in the UK were preparing the country for a future in this direction.

## DIRECTORS IN ENGLISH COMPANIES

### The Company as a Contract

The position of directors within the English company is defined among others by the nature of the agreement on which the operation of the company is based. The articles of association and their position within the context of British company law were analysed in the framework of the nexus of contracts theory in Chapter 2. The articles of association enjoy a central constitutional role in the internal affairs of the company. Section 17 of the Companies Act 2006 explicitly refers to the constitution of the company as the document which comprises the articles of association, along with any special resolution that have altered their provisions in the course of the company's life and operation. More importantly, as explained above, section 33 clarifies that the provisions of the articles bind the company and its members to the same extent as if there were covenants on the part of the company and of each member to observe those provisions. The terminology employed is also of particular importance; the Companies Act does not make a reference to the 'shareholders' at this point nor throughout its entire text. Instead, the preferred term is 'members'. This clearly betrays the predominant faith to shareholder primacy along with the legislative acceptance of the fact that they form the exclusive membership of the company on the basis of their property right. The Act leaves no doubt whatsoever in relation to that. The company is indeed a contract which binds its members, and that means the shareholders irrespective of the potential confusion that can arise when they also wear a directorial hat. Therefore, the foundation of the internal management system on the basis of which the company operates has a clear contractual basis in the UK. The articles form the contract that regulates the relationship between the company and the shareholders on the one hand and the relations between the shareholders among them on the other. The contractual nature of the relationship between the shareholders of the company and the company itself might sound unambiguous and uncontroversial as most of the relations founded on a contractual basis, but the reality is distinctively more complicated as the characteristics of the contract in question are rather atypical.

Firstly, in contrast to other contractual forms that can be altered only after the unanimous agreement of their signatory parties, the articles of association can be reformed on the basis of a more limited majority and more specifically on the basis of a special resolution which requires the agreement of 75 per cent of the members present and voting in the general meeting in question. Section 21 of the Act specifically defines the capacity to engage in the alteration of the contract without the unanimous approval of its signatory parties, betraying the special nature of the articles as an agreement of a contractual nature which gives birth to further distinctive parameters. As this provision grants considerable power to the hands of a majority that especially in a limited liability company might comprise just a few shareholders, the courts have added a requirement to that in *Allen*.[53] Lindley MR said:

> the power conferred by what is now section 21 of the Act must, like all other powers, be exercised subject to those general principles of law and equity which are applicable to all powers conferred on majorities and enabling them to bind minorities. It must be exercised, not only in the manner required by law, but also *bona fide* for the benefit of the company as a whole, and it must not be exceeded. These conditions are always implied, and are seldom, if ever, expressed. But if they are complied with I can discover no ground for judicially putting any other restrictions on the power conferred by the section than those contained in it.

The lack of necessary clarity in relation to what precisely constitutes a reform of the articles on a bona fide basis, accompanied by the reluctance of the courts to apply this rule strictly, has further complicated the issue. Astbury J's judgment seems to determine that two separate criteria must be met: the judgment must be within the ordinary principles of justice and it must be 'for the benefit of the company as a whole'. So far as the latter requirement was concerned, the company seems to have been identified with the shareholders, and the reality of the whole plan seems to have been overlooked, for the judge ignored the plan to provide capital on the grounds that there was no formal link between this and the alteration. He also said that the alteration would benefit the majority and not the company as a whole, thus ignoring the company's separate existence as a commercial entity in need of further funding.

---

53 *Allen v Gold Reefs of West Africa Ltd* [1900] 1 Ch 656.

## The Personal Right

Another distinctive feature of the articles as a contract is the capacity of the shareholders to enforce the rights enshrined therein. Despite the articles clearly regulating the relationship between the company and the shareholders, and among the shareholders as a contractual and constitutional document, the ability of shareholders to enforce rights flowing from their provisions is frequently challenged. The courts have constructed a unique distinction between insiders and outsiders in their capacity to invoke constitutional rights within the corporate framework. It is interesting that the English courts have distinguished the outsiders from the insiders in this case on the basis of whether they hold an additional role and capacity to that of the shareholder. According to the relevant case law, only the members of the company who do not hold any other position of power within the company can take advantage of the right inherent in the provisions of the articles. Therefore, the shareholders exercising the role of the company's directors might find it hard if not impossible to invoke the articles, as they are viewed as outsiders to them. It is astonishing that the shareholders will be considered as outsiders to the articles and therefore they will be deprived of their natural right to enforce the articles, should they carry the hat of the director as well. The principle that the contract which binds the shareholders with the company and among them will not extend its privileges and rights to the members of the company is one of the most interesting features of British company law, spectacularly revealing the special nature of the articles as a contract unique in its characteristics and parameters.

At this point it has to be mentioned that the case law provides us with conflicting principles, as the courts seem to have developed two lines of approach towards the ability of directors to invoke rights enshrined in the constitution. In *Eley*[54] the articles of association contained a clause which stated that the plaintiff should be solicitor to the company and should transact all the legal business. The articles were signed by seven members of the company and duly registered. Later the company employed another solicitor and the plaintiff brought an action for breach of contract. This action did not succeed. The court held that the articles were a matter between the shareholders among themselves or the shareholders and the directors (as representing the company). They did not create any contract between a solicitor and the company. This was so even though the solicitor had become a member of the company

[54] *Eley v Positive Government Security Life Association* (1876) 1 Ex D 88.

sometime after the articles had been signed. The case clearly proved that there is a subtlety in the definition of an 'outsider' in these circumstances. An outsider is unable to enforce the articles or to be affected by the contract in question. When the person seeking to enforce the articles has effectively two relationships with the company, he may be both an 'outsider' in the sense discussed in *Eley*, and a shareholder of the company.

In *Quin & Axtens Ltd v Salmon*[55] the articles of association gave a veto to Joseph Salmon which could prevent the board of directors from validly making certain decisions. Although he was a managing director, he had used his power of veto, enforcing his right of veto by way of the contract in the articles despite the fact that there was only one other shareholder who held a similar right. This case can be reconciled with *Hickman*[56] on the grounds that every shareholder has the right to enforce the articles of the company, and it is irrelevant and coincidental that the article sought to be enforced in a single case stands to benefit the shareholder bringing the action more than others. In other words, a shareholder who also holds a position as outsider (such as managing director, solicitor, etc.) can, wearing his shareholder hat, enforce the contract in the articles, even if the direct result of that enforcement is of benefit to him wearing his outsider hat.

The two lines of rulings demonstrate the difficulties encountered when attempting to treat the articles as a typical contract within the framework of contract law. In contrast, the document regulating the internal affairs of the company and the relationship among its components is distinctive, giving birth to rights and obligations that are consequently unique. Recognition of this principle is instrumental for an understanding of the position of directors within the British company and within the framework of the British company law.

**Definition of Directors in the UK**

Section 250 of the Companies Act 2006 defines a '"director" which includes any person occupying the position of director, by whatever name called'. The definition of director is as wide as possible so as to encompass the notions of shadow and de facto directors. The wording of the Act formulates a definition that not only includes the legitimately appointed de jure director but also the people occupying this position

---

55 *Quin & Axtens Ltd v Salmon* [1909] AC 442.

56 *Hickman v Kent or Romney Marsh Sheep-Breeders' Association* [1915] 1 Ch 881.

without holding a legitimate appointment. In this sense, section 251 defines shadow directors as the people in accordance with whose directions the directors of the company are accustomed to act, with the exception of those who do that in the framework of their professional duty and capacity such as consultants, etc. The definition of shadow director has now been considered by the courts. In *Re Hydrodan*,[57] Millett J made it clear that a shadow director is different from a de facto director, that is, a person acting as a director without valid appointment. He said that there are four steps to establishing that someone is a shadow director. These are: (1) the identity of the appointed and acting directors must be established; (2) it must be established that the alleged shadow director directed those directors as to their actions in relation to the company; (3) it must be established that the directors followed those directions; and (4) it must be established that the directors were accustomed to follow directions from the alleged shadow director. The rationale behind these provisions is the possibility that someone responsible for misfeasance could escape liability where he had not officially been appointed as a director, but was really in charge of the business. The Act aims to enhance the protection granted to minorities against abuse of directors' powers, and within the meaning and the definition of the latter it includes the people acting as directors without being validly appointed.

As far as shadow directors are concerned, section 170(5) states that 'the general duties apply to shadow directors where and to the extent that the corresponding common law rules or equitable principles so apply'. Therefore, the decision lies with the judges, who are to decide on the basis of precedent. In *Ultraframe*,[58] Lewison J held that where the governing majority of the board was accustomed to act at the direction of a person, then that person was capable of being a shadow director. Despite that, the court went on to hold that the characterisation of a person as a shadow director did not automatically impose all the same fiduciary duties on that person as were imposed on de jure and de facto directors. Thus, it is for the judge to examine the particular circumstances and facts which would suggest that the existence of a fiduciary relationship for shadow directors come under the same duties as de jure and de facto ones.

---

[57] *Re Hydrodan (Corby) Ltd* [1994] BCC 161.
[58] *Ultraframe (UK) Ltd v Fielding* [2005] EWHC 1638 (Ch).

There is no respective statutory provision for de facto directors. In *Secretary of State for Trade and Industry v Hall*[59] the court stated that the definition of the de facto director required positive action by an individual which showed that he was acting as if he was a director.

In *Holland*[60] the court invoked the definition of the term 'director' by the Companies Act 2006. The court added that persons who are not directors de jure may nevertheless be treated as directors de facto. It defined a de facto director as a person who assumes to act as a director. He is held out as a director by the company, and claims and purports to be a director, although never actually or validly appointed as such. In order to establish that a person is a de facto director of a company, it is necessary to plead and prove that he undertook functions in relation to the company which could properly be discharged only by a director. It is not sufficient to show that he was concerned in the management of the company's affairs or undertook tasks in relation to its business which can properly be performed by a manager below board level. The court stated that in order for a person to be deemed a de facto director, it is necessary to be a part of a corporate governance structure and assume a position which entails a role capable to bear fiduciary duties.

In this case the court stated that the first mention in the case law of de facto directors appears to have been in *Mangles*,[61] a case involving the formation of a dock company by private Act of Parliament. Sir Lancelot Shadwell V-C said (at p. 535) that the Act assumed that persons by whom a call was made had to be directors de facto, and that all that Parliament meant was that, if the call were made by persons appearing to be directors, it should not be necessary to prove their appointment.

## The Duties of Directors

It is important to note that directors owe their duties to the legal person 'the company', rather than to shareholders or potential shareholders. This is particularly significant where the enforcement of those duties is in question, as the right to sue belongs to the company rather than to individual shareholders (clearly reflected in the measures available to them). Also, at this point a clear distinction can be detected with the respective law in the USA. As explained in Chapter 3, the US courts have

---

[59] *Secretary of State for Trade and Industry v Hall* [2006] EWHC 1995 (Ch); [2009] BCC 190.

[60] *Holland (Respondent) v The Commissioners for Her Majesty's Revenue and Customs (Appellant) and another* [2010] UKSC 51.

[61] *Mangles v Grand Collier Dock Co* (1840) 10 Sim 519.

accepted that the directors in the American corporation owe their duties to the company *and* its shareholders. In the UK it is clear that the duties are owed exclusively and directly to the legal person that is the company. In *Hawkes v Cuddy & Ors*[62] one of the principal questions raised was 'what duties does a nominee director of a company owe to firstly the company and secondly his appointor?' The issue was whether the director of the company owed a duty not only to the legal entity that is the company, but also to his nominator. The court noted that the fact that a director of a company has been nominated to that office by a shareholder does not of itself impose any duty on the director owed to his nominator. The director may owe duties to his nominator if he is an employee or officer of the nominator, or by reason of a formal or informal agreement with his nominator, but such duties do not arise out of his nomination, but out of a separate agreement or office. Such duties cannot however, detract from his duty to the company of which he is a director.[63]

Despite the fact that the two jurisdictions belong to the same family of corporate governance systems albeit with their own distinctive characteristics and features, this point serves as a reminder of the sometimes overtly divergent approach assumed by the respective parties. In the UK, the company is the person competent to raise an action against a director since the duties are owed directly to it. Only in exceptional circumstances can a shareholder act independently but still on behalf of the company, with for example a derivative action. The fact that derivative actions are not encouraged by the court, having to fulfil a variety of conditions set by the law itself and leading to compensation which is not granted to the shareholder who raises the action but to the company itself, reveals the importance of such a principle, along with the practical impact of its enforcement. A crucial question that emerges at this point is, who constituted the company in the British context? The reply to this question is relatively simple, as both the statute and the respective case law and theory are unanimous and clear at this point: the shareholders enjoy the exclusive privilege of membership. They are the only insiders to the company, as opposed to the other actors such as employees or creditors who are considered as externalities. As explained above, creditors are granted a special status when the company is approaching or entering insolvency. Despite the new section 172, which includes a list of actors whose interests have to be taken into account when the directors are

[62] *Hawkes v Cuddy & Ors* [2009] EWCA Civ 291.

[63] See Dine and Koutsias, *Company Law*, 8th edn (Palgrave Macmillan, London 2013).

exercising their duty to promote the success of the company, the reality is that little if any has changed in relation to the composition of the corporation in the UK context.

Section 172 constitutes one of the most crucial and somehow controversial parts of the new Act as it provides that:

> A director of a company must act in the way he considers, in good faith, would be most likely to promote the success of the company for the benefit of its members as a whole and in doing so have regard (amongst other matters) to –
>
> (a) the likely consequences of any decision in the long term,
> (b) the interests of the company's employees,
> (c) the need to foster the company's business relationships with suppliers, customers and others,
> (d) the impact of the company's operations on the community and the environment,
> (e) the desirability of the company maintaining a reputation for high standards of business conduct, and
> (f) the need to act fairly as between members of the company.

The fact that for the first time a variety of actors were included in the section which appears to be the legislative cornerstone of directors' duties in the UK led to discussion of a shift in the relevant landscape, bringing the country closer to a German-style stakeholder model where shareholder primacy is gradually eroded giving birth to a model where all the relevant actors find their place in the governance structure of the British corporation. And despite the initial enthusiastic analysis of this section, the reality is quite different and reveals a rather minimal reform from the previous regime. The UK did not betray its faith to the shareholder primacy model to adopt a more pluralist stakeholder-orientated approach. Quite in contrast to that, section 172, despite its wide ambit and explicit inclusion of actors that did not appear in any respective provision alongside the directors in the past, reconfirmed in a spectacular manner the principle of shareholder primacy and the clear subordination of the interests of other actors to the respective interests of the members, that is, the shareholders.

There should be no doubt that shareholders retain their status as the exclusive 'members of the company'. In addition to that, the duty of directors to have regard to the interests of other stakeholders is still owed to the company and *only* to it. The importance of this statement is twofold; firstly the interests of stakeholders other than the shareholders can be taken into account in so far as they are deemed compatible with the interests of the company. If they happen to conflict with the interests of the company then priority is to be given to the interests of the latter. Secondly, if the duty imposed by section 172 to have regard to other actors' interests is breached, it is again for the company (which means its members and namely the shareholders) to act. Therefore, the only appropriate litigants are still the shareholders and in practice the majority ones; alternatively a minority shareholder raising either a derivative action on behalf of the company or acting in accordance with section 994, and a liquidator acting on behalf of an insolvent company. It is very unlikely that the shareholders will act against the directors for having breached their duty to take into account the interest of the outsiders, especially if the directors have been effective in pursuing the interests of the members of the company. Therefore the new section 172(1) 'poses little threat to directors' intent to maximising profits at the expense of stakeholder relationships, but provides a strong normative element which coupled with other forms of stakeholder pressure and the prevailing business climate will encourage boards to consider an increasing range of interests'.[64]

**Duties of care and skill**

Section 174 of the Companies Act 2006 introduced a new provision which embodies the latest judicial developments. While the starting point of the standard applied to directors was shockingly lax and therefore utterly failing to catch directorial incompetence or managerial lack of skill, the judiciary was finally led to the adoption of a stricter standard against which a director will be found in breach of duty of care and skill just thirty years ago. The initial standard adopted by the courts permitted a vast degree of freedom to directors to demonstrate a level of carelessness that could directly undermine any chance that the company had to succeed. In this framework it was very difficult for shareholders to exercise an effective degree of control on managerial behaviour, especially when dealing with careless directors who were simultaneously holders of the majority of shares. The lack of control combined with the application of a minimum standard of a duty of care and skill created a vicious circle when companies were mismanaged by careless directors or directors with the minimum level of skill; the shareholders were either locked in the company in the case of private companies, or saw the price

[64] Fisher, D., 'The Enlightened Shareholder – leaving Stakeholders in the Dark: Will Section 172(1) of the Companies Act 2006 make directors consider the Impact of their decisions on Third Parties?' (2009) *International Company and Commercial Law Review* 1, p. 10.

of their shareholding being gradually decreased and their investment significantly devaluated in the case of the public one.

In *Dovey v Cory* the director was able to escape liability for malpractice which had occurred, on the grounds that he had relied on information given to him by the chairman and general manager of the company. The standard applied here seems to be somewhat stricter than that in *The Marquis of Bute's Case* since the court held that the reliance on the chairman and general manager was reasonable and that the director had not been negligent. The standard in this case was one of negligence, that is, the director must have acted as a reasonable man. If a reasonable man would have been suspicious of the information that was given and would have investigated further, a director who failed to do so could well have been liable for the loss caused by the irregularity. This may well be a higher standard than that imposed in the previous case where there seems to be no suggestion that a 'reasonable man' test should be used to judge the Marquis's inaction.

*Re City Equitable Fire Insurance* explores these issues fully. That case is still generally regarded as important in this area although the courts have moved away from the subjective standards imposed in *Re City Equitable Fire Insurance* to a more objective standard.

In *Re City Equitable Fire Insurance* the judge set out three important rules, which were affirmed in *Dorchester Finance Co. Ltd v Stebbing*[65] where it was also held that there was no difference in the duties owed by executive and non-executive directors.

(1) A director need not exhibit in the performance of his duties a greater degree of skill than may reasonably be expected from a person of his knowledge and experience.

The standard was not a 'reasonable professional director' standard but referred to the reasonable man with the skill and experience actually possessed by the particular director in question. This had two effects. If someone like the baby Marquis of Bute was appointed to the board of a company, he would presumably be held not liable for irregularities, as a small baby has extremely limited skill and experience. This may be fair from the baby's point of view, but the standard does little to protect the public. However, leaving such extreme examples aside, the standard could have been found capable of working quite well and of having sufficient flexibility to be valuable in different types of companies for judging

65 *Dorchester Finance Co. Ltd v Stebbing* [1989] BCLC 498.

the behaviour of different types of directors. Larger and more complex businesses were more likely to employ highly qualified and experienced directors to run affairs. Under the test in this rule, such people will have a higher standard of skill expected of them. Thus the more complex the operation, the more the interests of those with money at stake will be protected. The test was therefore only seriously inadequate where a very inappropriate appointment has been made, whether the operation is large or small.

(2) A director is not bound to give continuous attention to the affairs of his company. His duties are of an intermittent nature to be performed at periodical board meetings and at meetings of any committee of the board on which he happens to be placed. He is not, however, bound to attend all such meetings, though he ought to attend whenever in the circumstances he is reasonably able to do so.

Similar considerations apply to Rule 2, since the duty is to attend meetings and give attention to company affairs 'whenever in the circumstances [the director] is reasonably able to do so'. In the case of a full-time salaried director of a large company, it is obviously reasonable to expect his working life to be devoted to the affairs of the company. The standard will vary to take into account different types of director so that a non-executive director will not be bound to give the affairs of the company so much of his time as would an executive director.

(3) In respect of all duties that, having regard to the exigencies of business and the articles of association, may properly be left to some other official, a director is, in the absence of grounds for suspicion, justified in trusting that official to perform such duties honestly.

At first sight this seems to benefit a director who absents himself or who fails to keep himself informed on company matters so that he will not be aware of any 'grounds for suspicion' and so can safely leave the running of the company to others. However, if this rule is taken in conjunction with the other two rules, it will be seen that the director is obliged (by Rules 1 and 2) to take proper part in the affairs of the company so that unless his appointment has been manifestly foolish (as in the case of the baby Marquis), the rules will work together to provide a sliding scale of responsibility which will weigh heaviest on those most able to do the job, and whose expectations of reward from the job are probably highest.

In extreme cases, however, the rules will not protect those with money at stake. For many years there had been a call for an objective standard of competence to be imposed so that directors could not do the job if they were dishonest or foolish (or six months old). The DTI Company Law Review Committee accepted that an objective standard had been adopted into the general law by analogy with section 214 of the Insolvency Act 1986. In *Re D'Jan of London Ltd*[66] Hoffmann LJ stated that the common law duty of care owed by directors was accurately stated in this section.

The 2006 Companies Act adopts this approach and creates a standard based on two pillars; an objective and a subjective one. Section 174 reads:

> Duty to exercise reasonable care, skill and diligence
>
> (1) A director of a company must exercise reasonable care, skill and diligence.
> (2) This means the care, skill and diligence that would be exercised by a reasonably diligent person with –
>   (a) the general knowledge, skill and experience that may reasonably be expected of a person carrying out the functions carried out by the director in relation to the company, and
>   (b) the general knowledge, skill and experience that the director has.

This means that there is a base level of reasonable expectation which appears to be related to the type of company in which the director finds himself and so imports some of the flexibility of *Re City Equitable Fire Insurance* but, where the director is particularly experienced, he will not be permitted to perform to a lower standard. An example might be if an executive director of a large plc retires and takes a directorship in a small family firm. He would be expected to perform to a high standard because of his past experience.

The statute strikes a good balance, as imposition of too high a standard might pose the same problems as have been experienced in the USA, where the imposition of huge liabilities on the board of directors for negligence (see *Smith v Van Gorkom*[67]) has led to the adoption by a number of states of legislation permitting the elimination of the liability of directors for various breaches of duty. The imposition of liability for negligence proved too strict in view of the huge sums of money involved and led to a distinct reluctance to join boards as non-executive (outside)

---

66 *Re D'Jan of London Ltd* [1993] BCC 646.

67 *Smith v Van Gorkom* [1985] 488 A.2d 858 (Supreme Court of Delaware 1985).

directors. An example of such a law is Delaware Corporation Law, s. 102(b)(7) which was adopted on 1 July 1986 and reads:

> the certificate of incorporation may also contain any or all of the following matters:
>
> (7) A provision eliminating or limiting the personal liability of a director to the corporation or its stockholders for monetary damages for breach of fiduciary duty as director, provided that such provision shall not eliminate or limit the liability of a director, (i) for any breach of the director's duty of loyalty to the corporation or its stockholders; (ii) for acts or omissions not in good faith or which involve intentional misconduct or knowing violation of the law; (iii) under s. 174 of this title [relating to limitations on distributions to stockholders]; or (iv) for any transaction from which the directors derived an improper personal benefit. No such provision shall eliminate or limit the liability of a director for any act or omission occurring prior to the date when such provision became effective.

In English law the excuse of incompetence is clearly unavailable; however, one aspect of company law that always influences the standard imposed on directors in practice is the means of enforcing the duties that are owed.

## An Outside Corporate Governance System

As in the USA, the British financial system is structured so that the provision of finance to the country's corporations takes place on the basis of either a loan or the purchase of securities, hence the categorisation as an 'outsider' system of corporate governance. In the UK the involvement of those who provide the loans in conducting the company's affairs is limited; therefore their role in the governance of the British corporations is consequently minimal. This contrasts with Germany, where it is common practice for the representatives of the lenders which are usually banks to sit on the board. Despite the rather minimal involvement of lenders in the company's affairs and their limited presence on the respective boards, they do exercise some influence on the actual decision-making through the procedural details of insolvency. In the UK, the loans are usually secured with a fixed charge, either a mortgage or a floating charge over the entirety of the company's assets. The latter crystallises into a fixed charge at the moment when the company defaults on its payments. In such an event the company will enter a period where an administrative receiver appointed by the lender will supervise the selling of the company's assets to the satisfaction of the lenders' claim as the foremost priority. At this point the shareholders will find themselves in the rather exceptional case where their influence on the company's affairs will be minimal, fading into a role of secondary importance to the respective of the creditors in case of insolvency. Therefore, when taking decisions in the framework of their duties the directors will always bear in mind the importance of the company's ability to maintain its solvency and service its debts and obligations. Inability to do so can be fatal or at least seriously detrimental to the interests of shareholders and directors. In this case, the creditors emerge as a significant source of external influence on the decision-making process of the company and assume a rather exceptional relationship with the corporate governance structure of the British company. Despite this, the directors will owe no duty to creditors but exclusively to the company, save for the period when the company is approaching or has already reached the state of insolvency. In *Brady*,[68] Nourse LJ regarded the interests of the company as synonymous with the interests of the creditors where the company was insolvent or 'doubtfully solvent'. Thus, where the company is insolvent the interests of creditors and the interests of the company coincide to a considerable degree. In addition, where a company is approaching insolvency, the interests of the creditors are important where an assessment is made of whether the directors acted in the interests of the company.

## Accountability of Directors

Imposing a certain standard of behaviour in the form of directors' duties is probably the most prominent way of internal control on directors' powers. The corporate governance debate in the UK has actually been centred on the inadequacy of those methods of internal control. British company law may accept the principle of shareholder primacy as one of its pillars and most distinctive features, but the apathy among shareholders is eroding their ability to exercise an effective control on the powers of management. In addition, the clear division between the management on the one hand and the shareholders' meeting on the other means that the former rules the company relatively safeguarded from any interference from the latter. The structure of corporate governance in the UK allows for a great scope of manoeuvre on the part of the management. The widespread shareholding of the British public corporations further undermines any potential collective actions on the part of the shareholders. In this context, institutional shareholders seem to prefer to exercise their role as an investor with the principal aim of seeing a return

---

68 *Brady v Brady* [1989] 1 AC 755.

of their investment with an intention of minimal interference in the company's affairs, rather than pursuing the more active role of a shareholder eager to monitor the management. Minority shareholders are therefore left with the choice to found their claims on either section 994 of the Companies Act 2006 – in case of private companies – when the company is being ran at an 'unfairly prejudicial manner' for their own interests, or to raise a so-called derivative action on the basis of sections 260–3. The two sets of articles have been applied and interpreted by the courts in a way that severely limits the ability of minority shareholders to exercise an effective control on the powers of the management. In the case of section 994, a remedy suitable for private limited companies, the basic aim of the shareholder who resorts to such form of protection is to avail himself of the opportunity that this set of articles offer, which is to release himself from the badly managed company while retrieving his investment. Its analysis is useful since it mirrors the dominant judicial attitude towards statutory provisions in relation to minority shareholder protection.

The exercise of the remedy in question, which is by far the most popular form of minority shareholder protection in the UK, evidently results in the departure of the aggrieved shareholder from the ineffectively managed company rather than a change in the quality, style and methods of management that have led to the company suffering losses. Therefore, the successful invocation of the remedy of section 994 will result in the company getting rid of the protesting shareholder rather than the ineffective director who most likely would have breached the duty he owed to the company therefore providing the grounds for successfully resorting to section 994. The management can benefit from the aggrieved and protesting shareholder's removal from the company, which will effectively remove a potentially menacing thorn from the directors' side. If minority shareholders' remedies are all about assisting the shareholders to deal with cases of a breach of directors' duties which can lead to potentially significant losses, then the remedy in question has not only failed to deliver this aim, but has led to the directors removing an annoying source of complaints from their agenda. The minority shareholder might be able to release himself from the company on the basis of onerous requirements and reinvest elsewhere, but the company he left behind may sustain a failing system of management accompanied with an ineffective set of controls and checks. The practical inability to enforce a strict system of internal checks on the directors' actions even in cases of a breach of duty is a feature integral in the function and application of the British company law. The reading of section 994 independent of the courts' interpretation reveals a legislator who purported to grant this section a much wider scope of application; however its application by the courts as will be examined in this book has severely limited its ambit to an extent that could be found as conflicting with the initial intentions of the legislator.

## The Unfair Prejudice Action

Sections 994–6 of the Companies Act 2006 replaced sections 459–61 of the Companies Act 1985, providing a remedy for a member when 'the company's affairs are being or have been conducted in a manner which is unfairly prejudicial to the interests of its members generally or of some part of its members'. Consideration was given to the meaning of unfair prejudice in *Re Macro*,[69] in which the court held that where conduct was unfairly prejudicial to the financial interests of the company then it would also be unfairly prejudicial to the interests of its members. In assessing the fairness of the conduct, the court had to perform a balancing act in weighing the various interests of different groups within the company. The court did not interfere in questions of commercial management, but where the mismanagement was sufficiently significant and serious to cause loss to the company then it could constitute the basis for finding unfair prejudice. The important case of *Re Saul D Harrison*[70] contains an extensive analysis of the operation of section 459 (section 994 under the 2006 Act) to protect 'legitimate expectations'. Hoffmann LJ said:

> In deciding what is fair or unfair for the purposes of Section 459, it is important to have in mind that fairness is being used in the context of a commercial relationship. The articles of association are just what their name implies: the contractual terms which govern the relationships of the shareholders with the company and each other … Since keeping promises and honouring agreements is probably the most important element of commercial fairness, the starting point on any case under Section 459 will be to ask whether the conduct of which the shareholder complains was in accordance with the articles of association … Although one begins with the articles and the powers of the board, a finding that conduct was not in accordance with the articles does not necessarily mean that it was unfair, still less that the court will exercise its discretion to grant relief. In choosing the term 'unfairly prejudicial', the Jenkins Committee (para. 204) equated it with Lord Cooper's understanding of 'oppression' in *Elder*:[71] 'A visible departure from the

[69] *Re Macro (Ipswich) Ltd* [1994] 2 BCLC 354.
[70] *Re Saul D Harrison & Sons plc* [1995] 1 BCLC 14.
[71] *Elder v Elder and Watson* (1952) SC 49.

standards of fair dealing and a violation of the conditions of fair play on which every shareholder who entrusts his money to a company is entitled to rely.'

These rulings clearly indicate the initial intention of the courts to interpret the concept of unfairness in a particularly broad manner. It was therefore believed, at least at that stage, that the respective ambit of application of what is today section 994 would have been particularly extensive since it would allow minority shareholders to resort to the court on the basis of the remedy of the section in question on every occasion that a directors' behaviour had led to the 'value of shareholding seriously diminishing'. That would have provided an effective tool to every shareholder to monitor the management very closely. The concerns that this approach would simply open the flood gates of litigation, leading to a significantly increased shareholder activism that would have undermined the ability of directors to run the company as they consider suitable on the basis of their personal knowledge and experience and granting the courts with the heavy task of acting as the mediating actor between shareholding and management in an ever-increasing number of companies, have led to a significant change in judicial approach. In *Re A Company*[72] the court ruled that the concept of unfair prejudice is larger than the idea of infringement of legal rights. The court stated that 'the member's interest as a member may include a legitimate expectation that he will continue to be *employed as a director* and his dismissal from the office and exclusion from the management of the company may therefore be unfairly prejudicial to his interests as a member'. The removal of a shareholder from the board can be found to constitute a sufficient reason for invoking section 994, as the removed director can found the legitimate expectation to participate in the management of the company which is one of the two requirements of the section 994 remedy. Having been removed from the board he can claim that he still has legitimate expectations to be a part of it. On the one hand, this could be viewed as an indication of the wide scope of the remedy in question, which can cover conduct unfairly detrimental to a shareholder's interest without simultaneously being an abuse of legal rights. However, in practice the court introduced a limitation on the scope of section 994 as from that point the existence of legitimate expectations to participate in the management served as a necessary prerequisite for the invocation of this section. An additional requirement which is not included in the actual wording of section 994 was added.

---

[72] *Re A Company* [1986] 1 WLR 281.

This principle was further confirmed in *Re Leeds United Holdings plc*[73] where the court clarified that the meaning of 'legitimate expectations' entailed 'an expectation of being allowed to participate in the affairs of the company'. Therefore, a minority shareholder who wishes to invoke section 994 would have to prove that he has a legitimate expectation to be allowed to participate in the management himself. The courts did not provide additional information on whether there is a threshold above which a certain shareholding can justify such expectations. Can any shareholder holding 15 per cent of the shares satisfy this requirement and therefore bring himself closer to the successful invocation of section 994? The truth is that the reply to this question is not clear even now. As a result of this uncertainty in relation to the exact scope and the precise interpretation of section 994, the only shareholders who can clearly and unambiguously fulfil the aforementioned criterion are the ones who have already been participating in the management but they were for some reasons removed from that. A former director who has been voted out of the board can easily resort to the remedy of section 994. This is the case even when the director in question has been removed due to an alleged breach of duty. This is astonishing, as it could clearly come into conflict not only with the intentions of the legislator when drafting this section but also and most importantly with the purpose of minority shareholder protection, which is to safeguard the interests of shareholders from a management that has clearly proved to be inadequate or even in breach of its legal obligations. The introduction of the requirement to have legitimate expectations to participate in the management in order to successfully invoke the remedy of section 994 has discouraged the initial target group of this provision, namely the shareholders, to resort to this section. In addition, such an interpretation on the part of the courts has paved the way for directors who have been removed from the board for reasons that can include even breaches of duties, to resort to section 994 quite comfortably. The departure of the courts from the text of section 994 significantly undermines the system of internal checks and controls to the company's management, leaving a significant vacuum within the corporate structures. In *Morris and others v Hateley and another*,[74] the court held that there was nothing in the articles of association requiring the minority shareholder to sell his shares

---

73 *Re Leeds United Holdings plc* [1997] BCC 131.

74 *Morris & Ors v Hateley & Anor*, Court of Appeal – Civil Division, 18 February 1999, [1999] EWCA Civ 819.

if the majority shareholders did not want him to continue as a shareholder. Accordingly the petition failed to resort to section 994 (section 459 at that time). Therefore, it appears that apart from the legitimate expectations to participate in the management, a legal basis in the form of a provision in the articles of association allowing a shareholder to sell his shares at a fair price constitutes an additional requirement for the application of section 994. This means that in order to resort to section 994, the shareholder will have to prove that there is a provision in the articles of association of the company specifically permitting every member of the company either to expressly resort to section 994 or to have his shares bought at a fair price by the company or another shareholder. The shareholder would therefore have to satisfy both requirements in order to bring him within the position most likely to guarantee the protection granted by section 994. As mentioned above, even if the shareholder manages to pass these hurdles and be successful in his petition, the relief granted will principally enable the management to remove him from the company rather than the company to get rid of the director whose actions has led to its devaluation. Section 994 will lead to section 996, which grants as a principal relief the ability to have one's shares bought at a fair price by another member of the company. What the shareholder would achieve at this stage is the retrieval of his investment at levels higher than the current price significantly reduced due to directors' acts, rather than a shift in the management of the company. Therefore, a shareholder who is successful in exercising the remedy in question will not contribute either to a change in the policies of the company that have led to losses or to the removal of directors who have been found in a potential breach of duty. He will simply manage to release himself from the mismanaged company and potentially invest his capital elsewhere. This constitutes a fundamental flaw inherent in the British system of internal management control and checks, as it deprives the members of the company of a significant tool to control the management effectively and monitor its activities. Directors will feel relatively free from most forms of internal controls and continue with patterns of behaviour that have already proven particularly problematic, both in legal and economic terms.

## The Derivative Action

The system of internal checks on the management suffers from another setback with the judicial and legislative shaping of the other pillar of shareholder control; the so-called derivative action. Sections 260–3 of the Companies Act 2006 redefine the remedy in question, creating a new landscape in the relevant part of the law. The new provisions reflect and incorporate a significant part of the predating case law but introduce certain novelties as well. Time will show how the new provisions have been received and interpreted by the courts. It can be stated from the very beginning though that in contrast to section 994, the relevant provisions are drafted in an overtly less ambitious manner, with a wording that clearly leaves a narrow scope to shareholders to unfold their potential initiatives against the management and what they perceive as a misuse of directors' powers. In this sense, the courts will probably interpret the text in question literally if they adjudicate for a limited ability of shareholders to raise a derivative action altogether. The text also seems to suggest this. The rationale behind the derivative action seems to undermine its potential from the very beginning. The latter is a by-product of the separate corporate personality principle; a principle absolutely fundamental for English company law that has been analysed extensively earlier. It simply entails the ability of the company to act on its own, as it possesses a legal personality which is wholly independent from the human realities behind it. The company is in a position to sign a contract, assume legal obligations, become a party to a trial or to a transaction and sue and be sued on its own. Since the legal person can assume all the initiatives that were previously left exclusively to humans, it is evident that shareholders will be prevented from suing the directors for a breach of duty since the company is in a position to do it on its own (the *Foss v Harbottle*[75] rule). Of course, since this principle is purely theoretical, constructed on the basis that the fictional person can indeed act on its own, the basic question emerges in relation to who can decide on behalf of the company to sue its malfunctioning management. This is the theoretical, institutional and judicial framework within which the derivative action was borne and formulated. The need to create such a remedy became imperative when it was realised that the mechanism on the basis of which the company will decide to sue is seriously flawed.

The company will take such a decision in the general meeting where all shareholders can be present, express their views and most significantly vote, promoting one option over another (*Bamford v Bamford*[76]). However, especially in small and medium-sized family-orientated businesses, it is not rare that the directors will simply be the majority shareholders, or at least people promoted and supported by the latter. They will therefore be vaguely interested to say the least to encourage the company

---

[75] *Foss v Harbottle* (1843) 67 ER 189.
[76] *Bamford v Bamford* [1970] Ch 202.

to raise an action against them. This conflict of interests stands at the core of the system in question, revealing the repercussions of the lack of an effective legislative tool to deal with the challenges emerging from the very nature of the corporation. Therefore, the inability of the company to decide to pursue a claim against its management because the latter can effectively control its decision-making mechanism led to the introduction of a remedy that would, theoretically at least, escape the control of the management and be left exclusively at the hands of the shareholders to pursue further. The derivative action was thus created as a remedy against the antiphasis integral in the corporate system that allowed the concentration of the two conflicting roles – that of the plaintiff and the defendant – to the same people; the majority shareholders if directors. That would have been an absolute invalidation of any system of internal management control. A derivative action simply lets the minorities within the company exercise control on the management if they fulfil a list of requirements set jointly by the statute and the courts. It is called derivative as the plaintiffs do not seek to enforce a right that belongs to them but a right that belongs to the company, and due to the special circumstances the company simply delegates to the minorities. A direct repercussion of this that undermines its appeal as an aspect of internal control is simply the fact that since the right to raise the action belongs naturally to the company, if the plaintiff is successful in his attempt then the money is not going to him but instead to the company. Therefore, the plaintiff gains the moral satisfaction of having successfully confronted the malaise at the top of the corporate structure and perhaps exercised to exist in a company that in the future is likely to enjoy a more effective management. Whether that would constitute a sufficient motivation on the part of the plaintiff to put him through the rather onerous process of raising a derivative action is highly doubted. Not only will he need to satisfy the very strict requirements that are necessary in order to be able to resort to the remedy in question and deal with a breach of directors' duty, but at the end if successful he will enjoy a victory of mostly moral character.

Under section 261, a member of a company must apply to the court for the permission to continue with a derivative action. He will have to prove that there is a prima facie case for the continuation of the act for the court to permit it. In order to determine whether a prima facie case exists (which means that permission for a derivative action can be granted), the court will examine the criteria incorporated in section 263, which puts in a statutory form principles and requirements previously formulated by the courts. Therefore, the Companies Act 2006 is the first legislative tool that provides a detailed set of provisions in relation to the derivative action, clarifying aspects that were previously left vague, especially in relation to the issues that need to be clarified in order to proceed with the action; however, at the same time having incorporated most of the principles already shaped by the judiciary, it fails to introduce something radically new to what we already knew and therefore to fix some of the deficiencies of the previous regime.

According to the Act, the courts will grant a permission to proceed on the basis of four requirements. It is interesting to note that these requirements have to be met not for the derivative action to be successful (something that would naturally entail an examination of the substance of the claim), but for the action to proceed. It is important to emphasise that resorting to the remedy is altogether a particularly challenging attempt, demanding a high level of effort and respectively of legal skill on the part of the plaintiff. The latter will have to prove that the derivative action will be for the benefit of the company as a whole. Similarly, he will need to convince the court that a director acting under his principal duty to promote the success of the company under section 172 would have indeed raised this particular derivative action. While it can be clearly argued that those two requirements are nothing more than the by-products of the separate corporate personality principle that defines the nature of the derivative action altogether, the mounting task to fulfil them sufficiently is evident. It is particularly difficult to prove that raising a derivative action will be for the benefit of the company as a whole, especially if the entirety of the company would clearly include the majority elements that might have formed the management against whom the action is aimed anyway. Also, the reply to whether the raising of a derivative action would be compatible with the potential decision of a fictional director who would have acted in strict compliance to section 172 also poses problems. The aggrieved member will have to prove that a director acting on the basis of his principal duty as that defined by section 172, would have raised the derivative action on the exact circumstances as well. This is a very tough requirement to impose on an aggrieved member of the company, attempting to bring an action against a very real director who might already have violated the aforementioned duty enshrined in this section. These questions impose a heavy burden on the member attempting to raise the action and undermine the effectiveness of a system of internal control on directors. They are highly hypothetical, requiring the member of the company to upgrade his claims to the level of the behaviour of a fictional director acting under his principal duty, or to prove that the company in its entirety would benefit from it. The reply to both questions can be argued one way or another and is likely to be negative, therefore depriving the member of his ability to react to management misbehaviour but also the company of establishing a reliable system of internal checks on a management that has every right to feel increasingly uncontrolled. Is the lack of such a system that encourages directorial abuse for the benefit of the company as a whole? It is understandable that the courts would be unwilling to interfere in the everyday running of the company, creating an atmosphere where the management would feel vulnerable to real or calculated accusations, avoid taking any risk and thus erode business initiative and innovation, but the judicial allergy to a system that guarantees even a minimal level of control on management has spread the wrong message to the top of the company, encouraging patterns of behaviour that deviate significantly from the standards of the Companies Act 2006.

In addition, the member would have to prove that the action complained against has not been ratified or authorised by the company and that he is supported by the majority of the independent from the management shareholders. The third requirement refers to section 239 of the Act, which is one of the few jarring changes introduced by the particularly extensive and unexpectedly thorough Act of 2006. While previously the directors could indeed vote for the ratification of their breach of duty at the relevant meeting (if of course they were members of the company), the Companies Act 2006 has effectively removed this ability. Section 239(7) is clear when establishing that the directors in question cannot vote in the relevant meeting; therefore they cannot vote in support of the ratification of their own personal breach of duty. The provision of the Companies Act 1985, which rather scandalously set to an end any aspiration of raising a derivative action and holding the management liable for breaches of duty, was finally removed, paving the way for a theoretically more advanced level of shareholder protection. The pre-2006 provision killed any attempt to hold directors liable for a breach of duty from the very beginning, simply rendering any system of internal control of management a sham. Including section 239 in the list of requirements for the derivative action to succeed is indeed compatible with the nature of the company as a holder of a legal personality, and consequently with the distinctive characteristics of the derivative action. The final requirement set by the law in order for the aggrieved member to pass the prima facie test and get the go-ahead for his derivative action is to convince the court that his action enjoys the support of the majority of the independent shareholders from the management members. This is an incorporation of the principle previously set by the *Smith v Croft*[77]

---

[77] *Smith v Croft (No 2)* [1988] Ch 114.

case. Previously, the case in question imposed this requirement only to derivative actions aimed against a breach of fiduciary duty; however it appears from the new Act that now this requirement becomes universal, also including breaches of duties of care and skill. Respectively, the requirement to prove personal profit from negligence introduced by *Pavlides v Jensen*[78] is now effectively removed by the 2006 Act. This is a fortunate development as having to prove personal profit from negligence is not only highly challenging for the member who is raising the act but also not the case in most of the relevant complaints when the issue is purely negligence. Despite this positive development, the Act still imposes a tough set of requirements for the member to satisfy; and again these requirements are not attached to the judgment on the action which will be wholly founded on the substance of the claims, but for the procedural question of whether the action can proceed or not.

A novelty of the Act can be found in section 262 which provides for a right to continue as a derivative action a claim raised by the company itself against the directors. At this point we have the situation where it is the company which assumes the initiative to raise such a claim and not the shareholder alone, as an exception to the rule. While this procedure is evidently safer for the minority shareholder, as the costs and efforts of resorting to the court are now assumed by the company, in reality the management might be motivated to undermine the whole process and derail the act from ever being granted permission by the court, by for example failing on purpose to provide the court with the necessary evidence to fulfil the criteria set out by section 263. In this case, section 262(2) provides for the ability of the individual shareholder to apply to the court for permission to continue the claim as a derivative claim, on the grounds that the manner in which the company has continued the claim amounts to an abuse of the court process or because the company has simply failed to prosecute the claim diligently. Although this legislative development appears to enhance the ability of individual shareholders significantly to pursue a claim on their own when the directors abuse the whole process for personal benefit, additional requirements set by the same provision renders it an empty shell. He will need to prove that it is 'appropriate for the member to continue the claim as a derivative claim'; more importantly, he has to be granted a permission to proceed on the *same* basis and in accordance with the *same* procedure as if the act was originally raised as a derivative action. Therefore, the individual member will have to convince the court that it is appropriate for him to

---

78 *Pavlides v Jensen* [1956] Ch 565.

continue with the act on a derivative basis which takes him back to the requirements set in section 263 as analysed above. And if he succeeds with that, he will need to prove yet another tough judicial request, and this is to require a permission to proceed on exactly the same basis as if the act was originally a derivative one. Therefore, his additional input after the intentionally failed attempt to promote the action by the management is literally forbidden, and the action is doomed to fail. The statute introduces a new element of internal control which is dealing with the intentionally failed attempts of the company and the management behind it to bring the directors liable for a breach of duty, but it is the statute itself that imposes such conditions that render its own provision simply impossible to produce any real effect. The ability of the members of the company to introduce effective checks on the management is eroded to the degree that they are left relatively powerless to react to cases of directorial breaches of duty. This leaves the English company law with a significant vacuum at the level of establishing a system of internal control that would force the management to feel the necessary pressure to adhere to the behavioural standards set by the law, paving the way for the emergence of other systems of directorial control of an external character such as a takeover or an acquisition that would eventually entail the removal of the management and its replacement with a new set of directors, reflecting the new balance of power after the advent of the new owner. At this point, the similarities between English company law with that of the USA, albeit with even looser forms of shareholder protection, are evident.

## THE ATTEMPTS TO REFORM AND ADJUST

### The Corporate Governance Codes

The abundance of measures prescribing the parameters of corporate governance is a distinctive feature of the UK and its jurisdiction. The UK employs a wide range of laws and self-regulation techniques that shape aspects of its corporate governance model in a unique fashion. Apart from the Companies Act 2006, which forms the authoritative legislative text regulating the core of the British corporate governance model, the country employs a wide range of measures characterised by a distinctive approach that combines clear elements of both soft self-regulation along with the obligation to explain non-compliance. The British legal order was always eager to accommodate clearly defined self-regulation initiatives especially in relation to business; the latter is very much compatible with the emergence of London as an international financial centre and the subsequent regulatory flexibility that this entails. A common law tradition not always comfortable with a concrete legal text dictating in detail business matters and the existence of a large number of public companies whose main source of financing comes from the stock markets, with a large number of shareholders who are effectively subjected to the constantly changing conditions of the markets, rendered a more flexible approach based on a self-regulation model not only increasingly attractive but also utterly coherent with the British legal order and model of capitalism. In the UK the debate in relation to corporate governance became more intense after the corporate governance failures and scandals that rocked the country in the late 1980s and early 1990s. More specifically, the Maxwell and Polly Peck scandals emphatically revealed what a few academics were supporting at that time; the British corporate governance model did not provide for the checks and safeguards necessary to prevent people in control of the companies from abusing their position of power within the corporation and act in a way which is not only unlawful but also deeply detrimental to the corporations' interests. As explained later, the fact that the misuse of power went unnoticed by the institutions and the actors which were set to function as the elements monitoring directorial behaviour and policies, further highlighted the failures of the system. These scandals had an effect on the British legal order comparable to that of Enron on the American legislator; the emphasis on the need to reform the corporate governance model so as to prevent future failures of the kind that marked Maxwell Communications, was at that point universally accepted.

Despite the realisation on both sides of the Atlantic that corporate governance was indeed in need of reform, the two legal orders provided different answers to the similar question. The USA adopted the Sarbanes–Oxley Act, a prescriptive piece of legislation, while the UK was faithful to its tradition of a softer hand regulating business matters and chose a somehow novel form of regulation. This was an approach named as 'comply or explain' by Sir Derek Higgs, author of the 2003 Higgs Report on the role of the non-executive directors. The distinctive feature of this approach is the fact that the regulations stem from a code of best practice which is of voluntary nature, but the lack of compliance with it should be accompanied by a mandatory explanation of the rationale. According to the Code, companies are obliged to state in their annual reports whether they had complied with the provisions of the Code, and in case of non-compliance they have to clarify the reasons and the particular circumstances that justify it. The nature of these measures which combine a set of voluntary norms accompanied by mandatory justification of non-compliance forms the distinctive and characteristic approach taken in the UK towards corporate governance issues, and defines the very nature of corporate governance in the country as a mixture of hard legislation, voluntary norms and mandatory justification of the reasons for non-compliance. In this sense, the UK constitutes a very interesting case of corporate governance regulation.

The circumstances and events that lead to the adoption of the Code shed light not only on its background but also to the flaws detected at the level of the governance of corporations which fuelled the debate in relation to its effectiveness while paving the way for its reform. The sudden death of newspaper mogul Robert Maxwell in the Canary Islands in November 1990 rocked the corporate world and produced dozens of cover page stories that attracted the attention not only of policy-makers and the business world but also of the public. The reason behind the outcry and the widespread press coverage of the issue was not the casualty and the wealthy and widely recognisable business man it involved, but the story and the scandals that were subsequently revealed. The size of the Mirror Group's debt shocked both the City and the press, while the public was appalled to find out that £440 million were missing from the Group's pension fund. It was revealed that Maxwell was pledging shares in the company pension funds as collateral for further borrowing. The main question raised was the reason behind the inaction and the lack of monitoring and objection on the part of the pension fund trustees. It was clear from the events that preceded his death and the debt of his company that he was able to manipulate his position of power, as there was an absolute lack of any sort of control on his ability to act. Maxwell was able to remove the trades unionists from the pension fund and instead appoint his sons Kevin and Ian, while the management of the fund itself was handed over to the 'Maxwell controlled company Bishopsgate Investment Management Limited'.[79] It was therefore clear that Maxwell had pierced the independence of the pension fund and found a way to bypass if not demolish all layers of control. The trustees of the pension fund lacked therefore not only the capacity but most importantly the will to oppose any measure that was in the perceived best interest of the business man in question, albeit severely detrimental to the interests of the fund itself. The DTI Report on Robert Maxwell concluded in 2001 that 'Mr Robert Maxwell ran his companies and the pension funds as if they were one. He moved assets between them as best

[79] Wearing, R., *Cases in Corporate Governance* (Sage Publications, London 2008), p. 32.

suited his overall interests'.[80] Among the main conclusions of the report were that 'no proper system of corporate governance was put in place', and that 'no proper consideration was given to the way Mr Robert Maxwell had run Mirror Group Newspapers nor to the financial controls in place at the time'. A major problem was that Maxwell was both the chief executive and the chairman of Maxwell Communication Corporation for ten years; such lack of segregation of power enabled him to abuse his combined positions with an ease that surprised most outsiders at the time. In addition, the non-executive directors appointed by Maxwell to his boards did not perform their perceived duties to the appropriate standard, or at least to the degree necessary to detect a behaviour that was not just borderline problematic but overtly scandalous. Contrary to their monitoring role, it could be argued that the existence of prominent non-executive directors on the board granted to the board and consequently to its decisions a certain degree of respectability that would have otherwise been lacking or at least existing to a lesser degree. The outside world could comfortably assume that the decisions of the board of a large corporation which enjoyed the consent of reputable personalities would be for the benefit of its shareholders; any shadow of doubt would have been diluted by the presence of non-executive directors whose judgment and experience would function as a filter that would discourage any unfortunate outcomes, let alone fraud. Furthermore, it was absolutely clear that the audit function in the company fell well below any acceptable professional standard. The auditors did not detect and bring to the public attention any transfer of capital from the pension funds to other business activities, despite the enormity of the amounts involved. This utterly ineffective way of auditing performance was accompanied by the removal of the pension fund trustees and their replacement with individuals under the complete influence (if not control) of Maxwell himself.

The fraudulent activities that resulted in one of the most notorious scandals in the UK exposed in the most colourful way possible the flaws, loopholes and deficiencies of the corporate governance system of the country, at least up to that time. Maxwell manipulated brilliantly the almost absolute lack of controls on his ability to abuse his excessive power within the corporation, and carried out a case of corporate abuse that was profoundly detrimental for his corporations. It was obviously the

---

80 DTI Report, Sir Roger John Laugharne Thomas and Raymond Thomas Turner FCA, 2001, accessed at www.pixunlimited.co.uk/Media/pdf/mirrorgroup.pdf.

corporate governance system in place that failed the corporation, as it allowed an individual without a particularly intense sense of business ethics to manipulate its apparent flaws in his attempt to gain additional control.

Consequently, the DTI insisted in its report that 'making non-executive directors more accountable, separating the offices of chairman and chief executive, and providing extra statutory guidance on the duties of all directors to amplify the general principles that it is proposed be incorporated into the Companies Act' should now become a priority. Therefore, the lack of what the report called a 'proper system' of corporate governance was blamed for the scandalous behaviour and the embezzlement of the pension funds that went unnoticed by the people and the institutions which were supposedly providing the necessary checks and safeguards to the system. The concentration of excessive power in one single person with the simultaneous lack of official institutional controls generated a set of events that lead to high indebtedness, the embezzlement of pension funds, the erosion of confidence to the companies in question and to the markets at large, betraying the importance of shaping a corporate governance regime that would include all those monitoring institutions to discourage if not prevent any abuse of such extent in the future.

## The Cadbury Code

Within this rather toxic context, a committee was set up in order to deal with the challenges posed by the Maxwell scandal. The committee chaired by Adrian Cadbury produced its report in December 1992 and it applied to listed companies from June 1993 and onwards; the report widely referred to as the Cadbury Report included a code of best practice which was essentially the first corporate governance Code in the UK whose principal recommendations were incorporated into the London Stock Exchange Listing Rules. Corporate governance was placed at the heart of the reform and was its main aim, along with the need to 'restore confidence in the market'.[81] The lack of transparency and the concentration of multiple roles and positions in one person were obviously features of a corporate governance model that was doomed to produce even more scandals, as it was inherently flawed. The committee therefore clarified from the very beginning of the report that

[81] Plessis du, J.J., A. Hargovan and M. Bagaric, *Principles of Contemporary Corporate Governance* (Cambridge University Press, Cambridge 2011), p. 159.

> the country's economy depends on the drive and efficiency of its companies. Thus, the effectiveness with which their boards discharge their responsibilities determines Britain's competitive position. They must be free to drive their companies forward but exercise that freedom within a framework of effective accountability. This is the essence of any system of good corporate governance.[82]

The 'comply or explain' approach was explicitly introduced by the committee as the report stated that 'the London Stock Exchange intends to require all listed companies in the UK, as a continuing obligation of listing, to state whether they are complying with the Code and to give reasons for any areas of non compliance'.[83] However, there was no regulator officially charged either with the duty to monitor the compliance with the Code's provisions or with the explanation given; the adherence to the standards set by the Code was left to shareholders to monitor. This point is of great significance if viewed within the context of the English corporate governance system: one of its most distinctive features as explained above is a widely dispersed shareholder basis, a great variety of actors that comprise the body of shareholders with a sometimes utterly different set of interests, aims and aspirations. The agency problem inherent in this system is decisively marked by the lack of coordination at the shareholder level; this impacts enormously on their ability to scrutinise the corporate policies and directorial decisions and to monitor crucial aspects of the corporate agenda. A self-regulatory approach, albeit significant, that throws enormous weight on the shoulders of actors who are not by definition capable of exercising the role ascribed to them, is likely to prove insufficient in its effort to address challenges which are well-rooted within the English corporate governance. As long as the performance of the company is good, shareholders are likely to ignore the early signs of trouble that can erupt only in the medium or long term. It takes an actor with a deep involvement in the details of the corporate management to address the issues underlined by the Code and insist on attaining compliance with the standards introduced by it.

The report upholds the unitary structure of corporate boards, restating its faith to its effectiveness and contribution to the smooth operation of companies as long as the directors do indeed exercise their monitoring

---

[82] Report of the Committee on the Financial Aspects of Corporate Governance, December 1992, 1.1. accessed at www.ecgi.org/codes/documents/cadbury.pdf.

[83] Ibid., 1.3.

roles with a sense of duty. The report underlines the importance of the existence of outsider non-executive directors who are encouraged to bring a broader view to the company's affairs along with a higher level of scrutiny of the management's actions. Under the obvious influence of the Maxwell scandal, the committee clarified that it is in the interest of the shareholders that they elect boards which are not dominated by a single individual. In this context, the report had crucially proposed the separation of the roles of the chairman and chief executive; the aforementioned capacities should not be concentrated in the hands of the same person as that would grant him overwhelming leverage in the board. The report also emphasised the importance of the creation of three committees: the audit, nomination and remuneration committees, each with specific duties to deal with auditing, the appointment of directors and their remuneration respectively. The report did not adopt a straitjacket model for all companies in the UK; on the contrary, it employed a flexible framework that permits companies to apply governance practices in the form that is more appropriate for their size, ownership structure and complexities of the running of their business. This approach is compatible with the flexibility that marks the British legal company law tradition. On the other hand, this flexibility provides the management with a wide scope of discretion in relation to the ways that each company will indeed comply with the Code.

In comparison with legislation, Codes can be characterised by five points. They are 'formally voluntary, issued by experts describing best practice, designed to be applied flexibly, built on the market mechanism for evaluating deviations and for enforcing the Code and finally they are evolutionary in nature'.[84] The voluntary nature of the Code, which was the main point of criticism, betrays a respective lack of will on the part of the elected judiciary or executive to interfere heavily in such a field of activities. This conscious choice is mostly indicative of the philosophical view which is dominant in the UK and accepts that business should be left to flourish relatively unaffected by far-reaching regulatory instruments on the part of the state. In the absence of a process by which rules are introduced by the judiciary itself with concrete sanctions attached for non-compliance, the 'formal voluntariness serves as a principal argument

---

[84] Seidl, D., 'Regulating Organisations through Codes of Corporate Governance', *Centre for Business Research, University of Cambridge, Working Paper Series* (December 2006), p. 3.

for their legitimacy'.[85] In any case, 'without coercion there is no authority in need of legitimacy'.[86]

The Cadbury Report was praised as a step forward towards the reform of corporate governance in the UK. Despite its overwhelming acceptance from the business world which was due mainly to the 'comply and explain' approach that it adopted, criticism was raised especially in relation to directors' remuneration. The setting up of the remuneration committee was not perceived as a decisive step towards achieving a more advanced level of transparency, therefore the need to clarify an area that could produce yet another set of negative headlines became increasingly imperative. The main issue of discontent was not principally related to the size of directors' remuneration, as to the lack of a concrete and visible link between the corporate performance which reflects the skills employed by directors and their degree of success and their remuneration. The sight of managers of ailing companies receiving large salaries and even more impressive bonus packages brought yet another crack in the reputation of corporations, further eroding faith in the ability of the market to regulate. In addition, it was predictably argued that there is no motivation to perform well if the benefits are granted to a director irrespective of the company's financial results. And since we are talking about public companies whose financial standing, annual results and reputation per se contributes enormously to their standing in the stock market, with their image to investors heavily influencing their decisions, the significance of re-regulating this field on the basis of greater transparency was easily understood. In this context, the recommendations made by the Cadbury committee to employ remuneration committees to fix directors' pay failed to provide the necessary safeguards, as the link between performance and remuneration was not placed at the core of the reform and consequently at the top of the list of the committee's duties. On the contrary, the establishment of such a committee was perceived as 'a legitimising device to ratchet up pay';[87] instead of introducing controls on the levels of pay and establishing clear links with performance, the

[85] Brunsson, N. and B. Jacobsson, *A World of Standards* (Oxford University Press, Oxford 2000), pp. 21–39.

[86] Kerwer, D., 'Rules that Many use: Standards and Global Regulation Governance' (2005) 18 *Governance: An International Journal of Policy, Administration, and Institutions* 4, October, p. 620.

[87] Ezzamel, M. and R. Watson, 'Wearing Two Hats: The Conflicting Control and Management Roles of Non Executive Directors' in K. Keasey, S. Thompson and M. Wright, *Corporate Governance: Economic and Financial Issues* (Oxford University Press, Oxford 1997).

stamp of acceptance of the remuneration committee on the directors' pay was perceived as legitimising an otherwise obscurely determined level of salary and benefits.

**The Greenbury Code**

The Greenbury Report[88] was issued in 1995 and was aimed at addressing exactly those issues. The report clarified from the beginning that its raison d'etre were the concerns raised in relation to large pay increases and share options gained in the then recently privatised utility companies. These pay increases were combined by simultaneous pay restraints and redundancies for other staff; this controversial situation was widely publicised due to the attention that the ongoing privatisation schemes were attracting, as they involved the flagships of the British corporate world. The contrast between managers receiving high salaries and staff being made redundant was alarming, and indicative of a situation that needed further attention from the regulators if it was to prevent further controversies. Therefore, the elements of transparency on one hand and director accountability on the other hand were placed at the centre of the report. The response of the Greenbury Report was to enhance significantly the role of non-executive directors in the corporate context, permanently including them within the corporate vocabulary and list of actors. The report proposed that the remuneration committee should exclusively consist of non-executive directors who have no personal financial interest in the company in question and no involvement in its running. Their principal obligation was to provide an annual report to the shareholders, disclosing the level of executive remuneration along with the company's policy on the particular issue, accompanied by details and reasons for directors' contracts exceeding a year. The new Code placed an evident emphasis on the role and presence of independent non-executive directors who would shed light on the contracts and levels of pay of the executive directors. The introduction of independent directors with no personal financial stake in the company was indeed a welcome change, and a step towards the ultimate goal which is complete transparency in relation to directors' remuneration.

However, the link between performance and pay was not sufficiently underlined by the new Code. Although it provided for the disclosure of all components of executive remuneration including share options or

---

[88] Directors' Remuneration, Report of a Study Group chaired by Sir Richard Greenbury, 17 July 1995, accessed at www.ecgi.org/codes/documents/greenbury.pdf.

pension rights along with increased publicity on the actual corporate policy towards fixing the pay, it did not focus on the establishment of a convincing link between performance on the one hand and remuneration on the other. If the effectiveness of an initiative is judged on the basis of whether its subject matter produces new headlines, then the Greenbury Code did not address remuneration with the degree of effectiveness aspired to by its author. The business world, academia, the legislature and an increasingly agitated press would soon bring remuneration within the public spotlight. Despite the dynamism of the 1990s in which a lavishly revamped Labour Government came to power by a landslide victory and brought within the public debate a rhetoric of growth accompanied by a sense of fairness, remuneration issues continually attracted the attention of the public. The optimism of an era marked by rapid growth and a popular government while the notions of 'financial crisis', or 'sovereign debt' were hardly discussed outside academia, diminished the intensity of the corporate governance debate, but the issue of remuneration seemed to act as a magnet for public attention in any case.

## The Hampel Code

The Hampel Report that followed in 1998 produced the Combined Code of the same year, which although reformed, still provides best corporate government practices today for all the UK listed companies. The novelty of the report was the shift of focus from transparency and accountability to the prosperity of the business. The report recognised the centrality of the aforementioned principles and concepts to the corporate governance debate, however it shifted the principal aim of the latter to business success by redefining the priority of the board, and therefore the core around which corporate governance is centred as the success of the company. That does not mean that the previous reports refrained from pursuing exactly that, but their attention was instead shifted due to the scandals of their time to matters of accountability and transparency.

The Hampel Report was founded on the somehow questionable premise that due to the contribution of the preceding Codes, the public companies were now sufficiently accountable so the focus should be shifted to the most important task of the board: the success of the company. From the very beginning, it stated that

> public companies are now among the most accountable organisations in society. They publish trading results and audited accounts; and they are required to disclose much information about their operations, relationships, and remuneration and governance arrangements. We strongly endorse this

> accountability and we recognise the contribution to it made by the Cadbury and Greenbury committees. But the emphasis on accountability has tended to obscure a board's first responsibility – to enhance the prosperity of the business over time.[89]

It is evident that with regard to upholding the right of a variety of stakeholders to hold the directors accountable for issues such as pay, there is a considerable change of wording in the Hampel Report in relation to the previous ones. Despite the formal recognition of the contribution of the previous Codes to corporate governance, the Hampel Report somehow diluted their basic elements and re-established the nature of the corporate governance debate towards a more managerially orientated direction, as the focus of attention seemed to move distinctively towards the managers rather than the shareholders or any outside elements such as the public. The delicate yet discernible shift towards an increasingly managerial approach would also mark the 1998 Combined Code. In this sense the Hampel Report took a step backwards from the previous Codes as it did not address the issues of accountability and transparency of the board with the sense of emergency equivalent to their importance. At a time when the corporate social responsibility doctrine was emerging to prominence, reflecting the view that the corporations should acquire a greater sense of accountability not only towards their insiders but also to the wider public, the Hampel Report receded to a notion of corporate success that is interpreted independently of the reputation of the corporation, its image to the public and the markets, and the ability of its shareholders to exercise a more effective control on the board. The success of the company is directly and closely linked to effective monitoring of its board, therefore the latter cannot be seen as an undesired externality to the former.

The Combined Code of 1998 reflected the basic directions of the committee, while, as its name betrays, providing a combined catalogue of principles and best practices stemming from the entirety of the three Codes. The Combined Code did therefore include most of the preceding provisions and did not diverge from the previous Codes but to a few points. The Cadbury Code for example recommended the existence of an independent element on the board when the roles of the chairman and the chief executive were combined on the same person; the Combined Code went a step further by requiring companies who opt for the concentration of such a degree of power in one person to justify publicly the grounds

[89] Hampel Committee, Final Report, January 1998, accessed at www.ecgi.org/codes/documents/hampel23.pdf.

on which they made this choice and to identify an independent non-executive director in their annual report, irrespective of whether or not the two posts are combined in the same person. The Cadbury Code required the remuneration committee to report to the shareholders; this requirement was transferred by the Combined Code to the board which now had to report to the shareholders instead of the committee. Cadbury previously recommended that boards should include at least three independent non-executive directors; the Combined Code redefined this requirement as equivalent to at least one-third of the board, with the additional requirement that audit committees should comprise at least three independent non-executive directors. The existence of three independent non-executive directors became the minimum standard to be adhered to, while larger boards comprising in excess of nine members should include a bigger number of independent directors to comply with the one-third ratio requirement. The Combined Code also dealt with the issue of internal control in Provisions D.2.1 and D.2.2, which required the directors to report to the shareholders a review of their internal control system. The relevant sections set the general framework within which the effectiveness of the internal control systems should be evaluated.

## The Turnball Code

The Turnball Committee was set up in 1999 in order to address this very issue. It aspired to implement the aims of the relevant part of the Combined Code, and to establish and design a new institutional framework that would deliver the foundation of a formal system of internal control. The approach adopted by the report was identical to the one adopted previously by the aforementioned Codes. The Turnball report was a code of best practices that had no intention of being prescriptive; on the contrary, the aim was to provide a code that could be used as a guide of how different companies operating in diverse industries can set up an internal control system that would respond to their individual needs and the distinctive risks they face. The close coupling of internal control and risk management stands at the core of the report; in this context risks include not only the purely financial ones but also those related to the ongoing business choices and decision. When directors set their agenda with the corporate objectives that need to be fulfilled on a short or longer term basis, they are required to consider the risks inherent in the achievement of those objectives. The rationale behind that is the belief that companies which manage to identify risks at an early stage have the ability to address them more effectively, with a positive impact on the company's performance. The Turnball Code was important in the sense that it addressed an issue that despite its increasing prominence within the framework of the corporate governance debate, had failed to attract a sufficient amount of attention up to that point. Its approach amounted to a framework of principles in the form of a code of best practice that could be adhered to by business, allowing a great sense of flexibility as to the extent of the introduction of the new rules and the internal tools employed for their implementation.

## The Combined Higgs, Tyson and Smith Codes

The corporate scandals of Enron and Parmalat shifted the agenda towards providing those institutional safeguards that would function as a firewall to protect British enterprise from scandals of such magnitude and range. The failure of institutional safeguards in both cases provided the grounds for the new set of reforms in the form of Codes that took place in the UK, paving the way for a revised Combined Code that was eventually adopted in 2003 and replaced the 1998 text. Five years after the first Combined Code, the spectacular collapse of Enron rendered necessary an analysis of its rationale and the subsequent reshaping of the current regulatory framework. The reports of that time focused on what was perceived as one of the most major failures of the system: the inadequacy of the layer of protection that non-executive directors were supposed to provide, and the lack of capacity on the part of the auditors to detect the ongoing abuses and to bring them in the public eye before the situation escalated out of control. The initiatives in the UK took place in parallel with similar initiatives in the USA. However, despite similarity in terms of the themes discussed and the subject matter of the debates per se, the nature of the response was quite different. The USA opted for the adoption of a statutory instrument, the Sarbanes–Oxley Act of 2002, while the UK remained faithful to a more flexible soft-law approach that allows great room for discretion, leaving the necessary scope to companies to adapt the Code to their individual situation, nature and risks without facing the possibility of becoming the subject of a 'one size fits all' approach.

The Higgs, Tyson and Smith Reports of 2003 and the subsequent Combined Code of the same year were the outcomes of that choice. The Higgs report concentrated on the enhancement of the role of the non-executive directors in the direction of further enabling them to monitor the decision-making of the board, with the ultimate aim of establishing the mechanism necessary to prevent Enron-style scandals from taking place. The Code provided for a further increase of the participation of the independent non-executive directors on the board, raising the ratio to half the members of the board; further provisions permitted greater remuneration for them. Interestingly enough, the Code attempted to address the agency problem inherent in the British corporate model by encouraging the cultivation of links between independent non-executive directors and shareholders; the former are advised to become acquainted with the major issues and concerns in the shareholder agenda so as to be in a considerably better position to represent the shareholders and indeed their predominant concerns on the board. That would supposedly help the non-executive directors to align their agendas with the shareholders' interest and therefore mitigate the existing agency problem. Aligning the interests of directors (let alone the independent ones) on the one hand, with shareholders and their interests on the other on the basis of the provisions of a code of best practice is almost unattainable. It was explained earlier that the agency problem is present due to the nature of the corporate governance model adopted by the UK and the USA to different extents, and encouraging the independent directors to listen to the shareholder requests and comprehend their agenda is not going to heal the rift that on many occasions appears between the interests of the two parties involved.

The Tyson Report 'provided another piece of the jigsaw by highlighting how a range of different backgrounds and experiences among board members can enhance board effectiveness and by exploring how a broader range of non-executive directors can be identified and recruited'.[90] The report placed emphasis on the diversity in the backgrounds, skills, and experiences of non-executive directors that enhances board effectiveness by bringing a wider range of perspectives and knowledge to bear on issues of company performance, strategy and risk. According to the report, that can also send a positive and motivating signal to customers, shareholders and employees, and can contribute to a better understanding by the company's leadership of the diverse constituencies that affect its success. Therefore, after the Higgs report that attempted to deal with potential Enron-style situations with the 'soft' alignment of the interests of the increasingly present non-executive directors with the respective agenda of the shareholders and therefore addressing the agency problem, the Tyson report continued the trail from that point and onwards. The efforts to incorporate the shareholder agenda

---

[90] The Tyson Report on the Recruitment and Development of Non-Executive Directors (June 2003), accessed at www.thecapability.uk.com/postboylbs/templates/non-personalised/documents/Tyson_Report_June_2003.pdf.

into the board one were followed by the efforts to bring a greater variety of stakeholders within the corporate decision-making process. That did not by any means constitute any deviation from the widely accepted view that the stakeholders in question were still an externality to the company, but it did attempt to provide their agenda with a pathway that leads to the boardroom. The tool for that was once again the independent directors; companies were now encouraged if not required to appoint non-executive directors of divergent backgrounds to reflect the variety of actors that comprised the group of stakeholders who were subject to the effects of the corporate actions. Therefore, despite the strong adherence to the unitary model of corporate governance or maybe due to it, the Code had no other choice but to create another tool that would enable at least a feeble form of stakeholders' concerns representation on the board. Non-executive directors emerge as the people with the key role of monitoring the decision-making process of the board, maintaining a close link to the shareholders so as to be recipients of their concerns, interests and views and passing to the board the views of a range on stakeholders, depending on their own personal professional or other origin. They are advanced to the role of the link between a management which may be prone to isolation (not only from society but also from the shareholders), and those actors whose representation on the board is now sought. Viewed from this angle, the Codes in question constituted a major effort to heal the agency rift within the company and the often utterly divergent agendas pursued by the company and societal actors or stakeholders.

These reports were accompanied by a third one in the same year, the Smith report of 2003, which focused on the role and the function of the audit committee; another principal aspect of corporate governance which was viewed to fail spectacularly to come up to the expectations for its role in the Enron case. The report addressed the relationship between the external auditors and the company they audit, along with the role and the responsibilities of the audit committees. In any case as the report clarified, 'nothing in the guidance should be interpreted as a departure from the principle of the unitary board'.[91] The guidance contained recommendations about the conduct of the audit committee's relationship with the board, the executive management and internal and external auditors. According to this report, the management is under an obligation to ensure the audit committee is kept properly informed, and should take the initiative in supplying information rather than waiting to be asked.

[91] The Smith Report 2003, at 1.6, accessed at www.fide.org.my/v1/publications/reports/0008_rep_20081211.pdf.

The board should make it clear to all directors and staff that they must cooperate with the audit committee and provide it with any information it requires. In addition, executive board members will have regard to their common law duty to provide all directors, including those on the audit committee, with all the information they need to discharge their responsibilities as directors of the company. The audit committee should review the significant financial reporting issues and judgments made in connection with the preparation of the company's financial statements, interim reports, preliminary announcements and related formal statements. The audit committee should also review the clarity and completeness of disclosures in the financial statements. It should monitor the integrity of the company's internal financial controls.

Despite the welcome shift of attention to auditing, the report did not go as far as to prevent auditing companies from offering other forms of services such as consulting to clients they audit; this is a field where a different approach could have been adopted by introducing legislative regulations to set a certain standard that would have to be adhered by everyone in the business world. The pattern followed was the familiar one of pursuing flexibility, but auditing is a field where more decisive initiatives of legislative nature could have been taken to respond sufficiently to the severe abuses of loosely defined auditing standards that lead to the type of scandals that the Code was attempting to address in the first place.

## The Combined Code of 2008

The history of corporate governance codes in the UK reached another level in 2008 with the adoption of the Combined Code of that year. The 2008 Combined Code was a text that comprised the combined wisdom of the previous ones, having incorporated their basic aspects as analysed above. The 2008 Combined Code was issued by the Financial Reporting Council and aspired to act as the norm for corporate governance practices for listed public companies in the UK. It replaced previous Codes, codifying in a way the previous texts into one; the term 'codifying' shall not give the false impression that the new Code assumed the form of hard law. In contrast to that, the Code remained absolutely consistent with the self-regulatory approach which is still the norm. Despite the evident self-regulatory nature of the 2008 Code, a statement of compliance is now required by the Listing Rules issued by UK Listing Authority; the listed companies are now under the obligation to include a statement of compliance in each of their annual reports. Therefore, despite the nature of the approach which remains bound to self-regulative norms, an element of compulsion can be traced in the obligation of the listed companies to submit a statement of compliance attached to their report on an annual basis.

The Code promotes a more formalised set of principles while attempting to standardise a corporate governance norm. The 'comply or explain' approach which emerged as the cornerstone of the previous Codes and reports remains at the heart of the 2008 Combined Code; it has now emerged as one of the most distinctive features of corporate governance policies in the country. The approach which does allow for a great degree of flexibility can comfortably accommodate both the instinctive inclination to deal with business matters on the basis of self-regulation and also the flexibility evidently desired on the part of business in the UK. The 2008 Combined Code included provisions for directors, remuneration, issues of accountability and shareholders. Interestingly, in its preamble the Code notes that 'good corporate governance should contribute to better company performance by helping a board discharge its duties in the best interests of shareholders'.[92] The vocabulary chosen is significant since it is stated that directors should exercise their duties in the best interests of shareholders rather than the interests of the company. Despite the fact that in the UK context the contractual basis of the company entails the inclusion within the corporate context of shareholders as the sole members of the company, it is still the dominant view in theory and jurisprudence that the duties are to be exercised in the best interests of the company. Therefore, despite the definition of stakeholders as externalities, English courts have still found it imperative to adjudicate in favour of the company rather than the shareholders. In the USA as analysed in Chapter 3, the definition of the duties of directors is broader as they have to be exercised in the best interests of the company and its shareholders. In this context the terminology employed by the Code at its very preamble seems to depart from the norm as defined by the courts.

Although shareholders are encouraged to scrutinise the explanation provided by the company in relation to non-compliance with the Code's provisions, it is noted that 'they should not be evaluated in a mechanistic way and departures from the Code should not be automatically treated as breaches'. The voluntary, self-regulatory approach based on soft law is evidently embodied in this phrase as the Code defines itself as a set of principles which must apply when appropriately based on the individual

---

[92] Financial Reporting Council, The Combined Code on Corporate Governance, 2008, accessed at www.ecgi.org/codes/documents/combined_code_june 2008_en.pdf.

characteristics of the company in question. The Code therefore does not provide for a set of rules which should be universally applicable but they have to be tailor-made on the basis of the individuality of every case. Shareholders are indeed to keep that in mind and to note that departure from the Code should not be automatically treated as a breach. Therefore, the Code requires shareholders who are not only vigilant in their monitoring of the company's affairs which can anyway prove difficult, but also motivated enough to discern the cases which, irrespective of their lack of compliance with the Code, are justified in doing so due to the particular circumstances and conditions prevailing in the relevant company.

The Combined Code of 2008 clearly supports an idea that 'there should be a clear division of responsibilities at the head of the company between the running of the board and the executive responsibility for the running of the company's business'. The separation of the two positions of chairman and chief executive (see below for consideration of the 2010 UK Corporate Governance Code) is now effectively established as one of the cornerstones of UK corporate governance provisions; a sharp contrast with the approach taken in the USA where the two positions are often merged in the same person. The concentration of the two offices in one person is regarded as putting too much power into the hands of a single individual, which can lead to the perilous situation of fettering powers of decision. Corporate scandals such as the Maxwell one which were linked to a great extent to the uncontrolled and insufficiently monitored concentration of power in the hands of a single person who could pierce the (anyway thin) layers of control on his powers, have evidently left their imprint on the national approach towards corporate governance. The separation of the two offices now appears to be a universally accepted feature of the English model.

In relation to executive directors and the board as a whole, the Code proves that it is indeed very flexible. Its provisions are drafted in the most general possible way so as to catch the institutional arrangements of as many companies as possible. The relevant part simply states that 'the board should not be so large as to be unwieldy. The board should be of sufficient size that the balance of skills and experience is appropriate for the requirements of the business and that changes to the board's composition can be managed without undue disruption'. Therefore, the sizes of the board as well as the skills appropriate for a director are left widely open to interpretation and utterly within the discretion of the shareholders. The Code consciously refrains from setting even an indicative standard of either the size of the board or more importantly the qualifications deemed as appropriate or acceptable at minimum level for directors. The inclusion of non-executive directors on the board is emphatically provided for as a means of ensuring an additional layer of monitoring on the unitary board, aiming at raising the accountability of the institution in question. Similarly, the Code states that 'there should be a nomination committee which should lead the process for board appointments and make recommendations to the board. A majority of members of the nomination committee should be independent non-executive directors'. Despite this indeed positive measure the Code remains intentionally vague as to the criteria for appointment which should be 'made on merit and against objective criteria'. The lack of clarity in relation to the requirements that have to be met before appointment does not obscure the importance of requiring a majority of independent and non-executive directors on the nomination committee. The provision, albeit voluntary, is in a position to foster a corporate culture that will offer greater assurances of transparency and accountability as the appointment procedure is now somehow standardised. The inclusion of identifiable actors who can claim a level of independence, although this is to be judged on an individual basis, can certainly enhance transparency. In a corporate world embroiled in suspicion and headlines about directors failing to perform up to the expected standards, designing a procedure which can result in raising levels of accountability can only be welcome.

As far as remuneration is concerned, the Code follows the familiar norm by stating that 'levels of remuneration should be sufficient to attract, retain and motivate directors of the quality required to run the company successfully, but a company should avoid paying more than is necessary for this purpose'.[93] The provision is sufficiently lax to accommodate a wide range of payment arrangements. What is 'necessary' is not defined, and within the context of an open economy and a competitive market the directors' salaries can exceed not only what is necessary but also what is appropriate, especially for companies which are not managed well and are performing accordingly. Although, the Code states that 'a significant proportion of executive directors' remuneration should be structured so as to link rewards to corporate and individual performance', it clearly does not provide for any respective obligation to link payment with performance in an unambiguous manner. The recent debates taking place in relation to executive pay in the UK demonstrate in a rather emphatic manner that this part of the Code remained an empty shell, and

---

[93] See the contrast between this text and the World Bank corporate governance template (p. 12).

its light touch failed to motivate a more sensible policy on executive payment. The lack of any mechanism to evaluate the relationship between remuneration and performance is a serious loophole that allowed a degree of executive excesses that have clearly undermined the effectiveness of the rules in question. The image of executives of insolvent or recently nationalised companies and banks making the headlines due to their continuously impressive salaries proved the inadequacy of the current framework, the insufficiency of the soft-law approach and the lack of any mechanism to support the anyway ineffective voluntary framework. The 2008 Code includes guidelines for performance-related remuneration such as bonuses and share option schemes; 'a typical director's remuneration package includes a variety of components: a fixed salary, benefits in kind, a bonus based on short term performance and an equity based component based on long term performance'.[94] However, this issue is going to be examined under the latest and currently in force 2010 UK Corporate Governance Code, which sets the framework for the issues in question.

## The 2010 UK Corporate Governance Code

The 2010 UK Corporate Governance Code[95] is the next step in the line of reports and Codes that started in 1992 with the Cadbury Code. Despite the evident shift of terminology into a title that sounds more umbrella-like and all-encompassing, the 2010 Code is essentially the next natural step after the 2008 Combined Code. The latter is revamped and slightly reformed to create a document which is now granted a title that reflects the norm of the UK corporate governance system. Despite the initial impression that the UK has now moved towards an even more standardised form of corporate governance regulated by legally binding instruments, the 2010 Code remains faithful to the non-voluntary 'comply and explain' approach. This emerges as one of the most distinctive features of the UK corporate governance as it seems to survive each attempt to reform the consecutive Codes and comfortably finds its place at the core of each one of them. 'Comply and explain' has emerged as the central principle which simply embodies the flexibility inherent in the English approach towards corporate governance issues. Despite the passing of an

---

[94] Padgett, C., *Corporate Governance* (Palgrave Finance, London 2012), p. 101.

[95] 2010 UK Corporate Governance Code, Financial Reporting Council, June 2010, accessed at www.frc.org.uk/documents/pagemanager/corporate_governance/uk%20corp%20gov%20code%20june%202010.pdf.

impressively extensive Companies Act in 2006 which extended to over 1,000 pages, the UK regulatory authorities and business world evidently made the conscious choice to deal with the particularities of corporate governance with soft legislation rather than as a part of the Companies Act 2006. The aim of the Code is to

> create a structure for the internal operation of the company which will minimise the risk of the company being mismanaged and which will also improve the way in which the company makes its senior management decisions. Bound up in all of this is an implied criticism of the ability of traditional company law to achieve effective corporate governance.[96]

As mentioned above, the 2010 Code is the natural next step within the history of the evolution of Codes in the country. It maintains the main characteristics of the previous Codes while introducing minor reforms at certain parts. The Financial Reporting Council concluded that the final version of the Cadbury Code brought into force in 2008 was fit for purpose, but reform was now deemed necessary to attempt to respond to the challenges emerging from the financial crisis of 2008 and onwards which marked the City of London and exposed certain shortcomings of the UK corporate governance system, especially in relation to the board of directors and its effective monitoring along with the issue of directors' remuneration. It is not a coincidence that these issues were included in the 2010 Code as the centrepieces of the limited reform.

One of the central parameters of the 2010 Code is leadership; the Code states that 'every company should be headed by an effective board which is collectively responsible for the long-term success of the company'. The Code therefore makes a partial reference to section 172 of the Companies Act 2006, albeit in a more general manner. The pattern against which the effectiveness of the board is to be measured is once again not defined, although the long-term success of the company seems to be the main criterion. The emphasis here can be placed on the words 'long-term' success of the company; it seems that decisions which bring short-term relief to the company while undermining its long-term potential are now viewed as practices which do not qualify a board as effective. The Code attempts to address one of the shortcomings of the English corporate governance system, which due to the breakdown between ownership and control and the subsequent waning of the monitoring role of the shareholders favours short-term over long-term profit to a certain degree.

---

[96] Hudson, A., *Understanding Company Law* (Routledge, London 2012), p. 178.

The directors were encouraged to act swiftly so as to guarantee the distribution of dividends to shareholders; if the shareholders kept receiving their share of profits from the company they would not be inclined to question the effectiveness of the decision-making at the executive level of the company. They would have the impression that since the company is in a position to distribute dividends it is well-managed, and therefore the need to monitor is not imperative. The need on the part of the directors to achieve short-term profitability could however undermine the shaping of a strategy that might prove less impressive in the short term but more sustainable in the long term with the shareholders bearing its benefits at later stage. At this stage the Code actually goes beyond section 172 which makes a reference only to the 'success of the company' rather than the 'long-term success of the company', and it is indeed a very welcome step of potentially great and certainly symbolic importance. It could have been even more substantially influential if the same wording was included in the text of the Act which is legally binding, rather than forming a part of the Code which despite its importance and prominence remains a voluntary instrument which lacks a legally binding power. Despite that, the shifting of the emphasis from a lack of definition of the 'success of the company' that promotes a short-term interpretation of it to its definition on the basis of its 'long-term' prospects is very much welcome, and it remains to be seen whether it will prove sufficient to foster a change of corporate culture.

The second main parameter of the 2010 Code is effectiveness. To that end the Code states that 'the board and its committees should have the appropriate balance of skills, experience, independence and knowledge of the company to enable them to discharge their respective duties and responsibilities effectively'. The Code adopts almost word-by-word the definition adopted by previous Codes and along with it the same amount of vagueness and lack of clarity over what constitutes an appropriate balance of knowledge, skills and experience. The Code might be absolutely consistent with its preceding texts, but at this stage it falls short of the Companies Act 2006. Section 175 on the duty of care and skill includes a dual test of subjective and objective nature that creates a respectable threshold which can now catch directorial behaviours that fall below the double standard. Of course, the Code is by definition a more flexible tool than the Act, but as analysed above it can indeed set standards which go well beyond the Act; the definition of the effectiveness of the board falls short of that aspiration. It should be noted at this point that the 2010 Code has introduced a requirement of establishing what it calls an appropriate combination of executive and non-executive directors, with particular emphasis on independent non-executive ones. The rationale behind these provisions and the spirit of the text is to prevent any individual or group of individuals from dominating the board's decision-making. Elements of that principle that took full shape with the 2010 Code had appeared even from the first Codes, which attempted to address the shortcomings of a system so overtly exposed by the corporate scandals of the 1990s such as the Maxwell one, highlighting the negative repercussions of the dominance of the board by a single over-powered individual who can benefit from the lack of sufficient checks to the detriment of the company. The introduction of non-executive directors on the unitary board with an enhanced array of capacities is viewed as a measure sufficiently equipped to remedy the abuse of directorial powers. In the light of this principle, the 2010 Code set the bar quite high as it provided that at least half the board (excluding the chairman) should comprise non-executive directors; this requirement would not apply to companies below the FTSE 350 which should have at least two independent non-executive directors on board. Despite those reforms the Code left the independence criteria unchanged.

The Code follows the lines of the previous texts in its other parameters as well but it does introduce many novel elements. The Code now provides that all directors of FTSE 350 companies should be submitted for re-election annually. This applies only to larger listed companies; however in the Preface the Code encourages also the boards of smaller companies to consider their policy on director re-election on an annual basis. This provision aims at fostering a greater degree of shareholder involvement in the company's affairs; that certainly entails greater involvement in the monitoring of the management as well. In a corporate governance system where shareholder participation remains a target worth pursuing, the inclusion of such a provision attempts to address shareholder apathy and to heal the agency problem inherent in the English public company. Greater involvement necessitates an enhanced awareness of the company's affairs which subsequently improves monitoring and therefore accountability. Although this arrangement can indeed enhance the accountability of directors as they will have to be re-elected on regular intervals on the basis of their performance, the assessment of their office on an annual basis is likely to encourage a short-term strategy, undermining the previously defined necessity to pursue the long-term success of the company. The directors will not have the time or the chance to prove the effectiveness of their plans on a long-term basis and may therefore be inclined to opt for short-term success to ensure their re-election. The issue of accountability is absolutely essential for the running of companies but the assessment of the directors' term in office on such a short term may undermine the shaping of a long-term strategy for the company; the latter is essential but it bears benefits which can be reaped at a time when re-election will already have been doomed. This is why every office and the position of directors within the context of English company law is considered fixed on a term that provides the person in question the time necessary to unfold a strategy with a long-term potential; that is necessary at the company level as well.

As far as the board is concerned, it is interesting to note that the 2010 Code introduces for the first time an element of diversity at the board level, and more specifically gender diversity. The Code does not make a significant step to the enhancement of female participation compared to other jurisdictions, especially the Nordic ones which regulated for a gender quota on board, but faithful to its roots that emphasise the need for flexibility and the urge to avoid rigidity the Code provides the companies with the necessary scope to draw their own policies and make their own choices. However, the road has been paved for greater female representation at the board level; and taking into account that the principles introduced by one Code tend to evolve into a more advanced stage into the text of the next version, it is highly likely that the UK might move towards a quota choice in the future. Whether future Codes will move towards this direction cannot be predicted at this stage, and neither can the effectiveness of a quota on the performance of the board.

Looking at board evaluation, the 2010 Code maintains the provisions previously adopted and gathered under a single title in the 2008 Code; however the new Code states that, in addition to an annual internal evaluation of the board, there should be an externally facilitated evaluation at least once every three years. The Code added that the statement verifying whether the external facilitator has any connection with the company should be made available. The 2010 Code also introduced two new elements in relation to the provisions dealing with accountability and more specifically financial and business reporting; a new requirement that companies should disclose their business model in the annual report, and a new principle setting out the board's responsibilities in relation to risk. Hence, companies are now required to explain in their annual report the basis on which the company generates or preserves value over the longer term – the so-called business model – along with the strategy for delivering its objectives. That should be included in the same part of the annual report as the business review; this is consistent with the requirement set by section 417 of Companies Act 2006.

With regard to risk management, the Code attempted to remedy the absence of a provision allocating the management of risk in the 2008 text. Therefore, the 2010 Code states that the board is responsible for determining the nature and extent of the significant risks it is willing to take in achieving its strategic objectives. In assessing risk, the board should maintain sound risk management and internal control systems. The main principle that requires a sound system of internal control has been expanded to cover risk management. The requirement for formal and transparent arrangements for considering how the board should apply the internal control principles now applies to risk management as well; yet another reform introduced by the 2010 Code. The general wording which is adopted at this stage and the novelty of the provision does not permit further analysis, but we can assume that it is likely to lead to a significant increase in the formation of risk committees.

In addition, the Code has enshrined new principles relating to the leadership of the chairman and the effectiveness of the board. It provides that the chairman is responsible for leadership of the board and ensuring its effectiveness; he also has responsibility for training, evaluation and board composition. It should be noted that there is a new provision on the role of the senior independent directors who should provide a sounding board for the chairman and serve as an intermediary for other directors when necessary. Non-executive directors are now required to constructively challenge and help develop proposals on strategy; it is evident that the wording employed by the 2010 Code is much stronger, clearly aiming at achieving a much more active involvement of the non-executive directors in the company. Furthermore, the 2010 Code now introduces the principle that all directors should be able to allocate sufficient time to the company to discharge their responsibilities effectively. While previously an indicative time commitment of 30 to 36 days was set for a non-executive director on a major bank board, the Financial Reporting Council (FRC) concluded that it would not be appropriate to introduce such indicative levels for the directors of non-financial companies, recognising that there may be circumstances where a candidate might not be able or required to commit that amount of time, but could still make a worthwhile contribution. The chairman and other non-executive directors will be required however to devote more time to the discharge of their responsibilities going forward; this is implicit in the general spirit of the relevant provisions.

As far as remuneration is concerned, the Code now includes a new supporting principle according to which performance-related elements of executive director's remuneration should be designed to promote the long-term success of the company. Whether that is consistent with the annual re-election of the directors has yet to be seen. The Code has also been amended to make clear that any pay-outs under incentive schemes should be subject to non-financial performance criteria where appropriate and compatible with the company's risk policies and systems. Companies should give consideration to the use of provisions that permit the company to reclaim variable components in exceptional circumstances of misstatement or misconduct. Remuneration of non-executive directors should now not include any performance-related elements. The issue of executive remuneration in the UK has to be viewed within the general context of the dispersed ownership that constitutes the main feature of corporate UK. As analysed previously, executive remuneration aims at healing the agency problem inherent in the corporation with dispersed shareholding. A remuneration increasingly comprising of equity-based pay and share options has attracted the attention of both the media and academia due to its surprisingly high levels and its loose link to performance. While due to mainly media attention the issue of executive remuneration has been viewed as an essential problem which needs to be dealt with immediately, executive remuneration itself 'is not the problem: it is simply the outcome of a wider failure to address defects in corporate governance in dispersed ownership systems, particularly with respect to board passivity, and a symptom of the intractable conflicts at the heart of the separation of ownership and control'.[97] Therefore, executive remuneration can be viewed not independently as a problem which stands on its own, but rather as the natural outcome of a series of failures inherent in corporate governance systems of dispersed ownership and as a symptom of its aspects such as the shareholder inability to control the management. The drafting of the Code to deal with issues which apparently the law could not resolve serves as a proof of failure.

The issue of executive remuneration has emerged at the centre of one of the most heated debates in the UK in the last 15 years. The financial crisis of 2008 and the ongoing turbulence in international markets due to the prevailing sovereign debt crisis in the EU and the insecurity that it creates, in conjunction with a fragile private sector that undermined the return to previously strong growth, has placed the debates in question within a different context. Executive remuneration catches the public attention throughout the West, but few nations have experienced such a variety of reactions and undergone such soul-searching than the UK. By

[97] Ferrarini, G. and N. Moloney, 'Executive Remuneration and Corporate Governance in the EU: Convergence, Divergence and Reform Perspectives' (2004) 3 *European Company and Financial Law Review*, p. 255.

definition, executive remuneration is higher in countries such as the USA and the UK who as previously analysed employ an outsider system of corporate governance. The agency problem lies at the core of the particular system as the interests of directors and shareholders are gradually diverging to the degree that they may even be brought in direct conflict with each other. The separation between ownership and control within the American or the English corporation is particularly discernible, and its effect on the practical ability of the management to perform its traditional duties to safeguard the interests of the company which in both cases coincides with the interests of the shareholders is palpable. Therefore, in both jurisdictions the issue of executive remuneration entails much more than the need to attract skilled individuals to the post; it simultaneously emerges as the tool that can remedy the agency problem to a sufficient degree. If the performance of the company is indeed good, then the shareholders will reap the benefits of the effective management which enhanced profitability; consequently the directors will deserve not only their salaries but also bonuses. Granting bonuses may function as an incentive for the management to design the policies necessary to safeguard the profitability of the company. Apart from the fact that the very need to grant bonuses to the management as an additional motivating factor which will persuade them to fulfil what is legally and ethically their duty is reflective of a flaw inherent in the system, its disassociation with the actual performance of the company is indicative of shortcomings that could undermine the effectiveness of a governance system. The UK has been embroiled in cases of excessive executive remuneration and bonuses handed with impressive generosity to managers of companies which narrowly escaped insolvency, principally because of their nationalisation. In Germany or France the questions in relation to executive remuneration are also significant, but due to continuing strong links between shareholding and management on the one hand and a greater monitoring of the board by fewer and therefore more powerful shareholders, such excesses have not been detected to the same extent.

## The 2012 UK Corporate Governance Code

The 2012 Code was adopted at the end of the year and introduced just a few changes to the 2010 text. The frequency with which Codes are adopted in the UK and the minimal scope of reforms that each one brings to the already-established corporate governance regime of the country demonstrates on the one hand the adherence of the business and legal world of the country to a flexible, hands-off approach to corporate governance (non-)regulation which is susceptible to constant change and adaptation to the newly emerged trends and needs, and on the other the timidity of their expressed aims which are rendered obsolete or insufficient soon after their adaptation. The 2012 Code is visibly faithful to such an approach. It is a consolidated text which follows the style and approach adopted by the 2010 text, while introducing a limited number of changes. According to its text 'the new Code applies to accounting periods beginning on or after 1 October 2012 and applies to all companies with a premium listing of equity shares regardless of whether they are incorporated in the UK or elsewhere'.[98] The central principles which form the core of the document and which embody its principal philosophy remain intact; namely listed companies are required to report on how they have applied the main principles of the Code, and either to confirm that they have complied with the Code's provisions or to provide an explanation in relation to their failure to do so. Companies reporting on reporting periods beginning before 1 October 2012 should continue to report against the 2010 Code, although they are encouraged to apply the updated set of provisions introduced by the 2012 Code even before the actual deadline.

Interestingly enough, the 2012 Code hints at addressing the principal problem which stands at the very foundation of English company law, the separation of ownership and control, and the agency problem that this has brought to the core of the English corporate governance model. The 2010 Code attempted to address the waning of the links between shareholders and directors. To that end, the 2012 Code recognises in its Preface that 'the impact of shareholders in monitoring the Code could and should be enhanced by better interaction between the boards of listed companies and their shareholders. The UK Stewardship Code, which provides guidance on good practice for investors, should be seen as a companion piece to this Code'.[99] The strengthening of the link between shareholders and the board emerges as the central aim of the consecutive Codes, as its profound significance for the enhancement of the monitoring of the board and therefore for the improvement of accountability and transparency within the public company is recognised and acknowledged, albeit timidly. Perhaps the texts of the 2010 and 2012 Codes which attempt to address this issue in a clearer way (at least at terminological level) may

---

[98] The UK Corporate Governance Code, September 2012, Financial Reporting Council, accessed at www.frc.org.uk/getattachment/a7f0aa3a-57dd-4341-b3e8-ffa99899e154/UK-Corporate-Governance-Code-September-2012.aspx.

[99] Ibid., Preface, Principle 1.

lead to a future reform of the 2006 Companies Act towards that direction, but this is an issue which remains to be seen in the many years to come.

The Preface of the 2012 Code and more specifically the new Principle 7 introduces another interesting feature, which although expressed in a subtle manner paves the way for perhaps a more decisive approach in the future towards other stakeholders and more specifically creditors. The Preface states that

> while in law the company is primarily accountable to its shareholders, and the relationship between the company and its shareholders is also the main focus of the Code, companies are encouraged to recognise the contribution made by other providers of capital and to confirm the board's interest in listening to the views of such providers insofar as these are relevant to the company's overall approach to governance.

English company law had always reserved a special position for creditors at special occasions such as during insolvency, but it was only after the passing of the 2006 Companies Act and more specifically of section 172 that a more inclusive approach was put on the table of negotiations. The 2012 Code adopts a very cautious vocabulary in relation to that, as after re-affirming the adherence to shareholder primacy as a corollary of the English corporate governance model, it states that 'listening to the views of other capital providers insofar as they are relevant to the company's approach to governance' is indeed desirable. It can be supported that we may see further developments at this front, especially if we take into account the step-by-step approach adopted by the country in relation to the shaping of the corporate governance Codes. Firstly, an issue is subtly opened by a given Code, and then the next one takes a step further towards addressing the issues and the concerns in question. It will be very interesting to see how this issue evolves into the texts of the future Codes, which if judged on the basis of the recent history and practise, shall start to be negotiated quite soon.

In the same vein, the 2012 Code introduces new provisions on gender participation, bringing the issue in question further into light with the engagement of the nomination committee. The 2012 Code now states that

> a separate section of the annual report should describe the work of the nomination committee, including the process it has used in relation to board appointments. This section should include a description of the board's policy on diversity, including gender, any measurable objectives that it has set for implementing the policy, and progress on achieving the objectives. An explanation should be given if neither an external search consultancy nor open advertising has been used in the appointment of a chairman or a non-executive director. Where an external search consultancy has been used, it

> should be identified in the annual report and a statement made as to whether it has any other connection with the company.[100]

Therefore, the issue of greater diversity at the level of the board is placed on more measurable dimensions, and the nomination committee is under a loosely defined but stated requirement to provide an explanation of its objectives and the rationale behind a potential failure to achieve them. In the same section, the 2012 Code provides us with further detail on the requirement set to the board already by the 2010 Code to 'undertake a formal and rigorous annual evaluation of its own performance and that of its committees and individual directors'. The new B.6 principle clearly states that the 'evaluation of the board should consider the balance of skills, experience, independence and knowledge of the company on the board, its diversity, including gender, how the board works together as a unit, and other factors relevant to its effectiveness'. It seems that the Code moves towards the adoption of a more inclusive approach when it comes to the evaluation of the performance of the board, which is to be based on the analysis of a bundle of actions and functions that will determine its adequacy in performing its duties. As stated in the framework of the 2010 Code, while the taking of steps towards this direction is a welcome development, the 2012 Code appears to be particularly toothless as the standard it sets falls well below that of the 2006 Companies Act, which sets a particularly high standard against which the breach of duty of care and skill is to be measured. The 2012 Code does not include any standard on the basis of which a potential lack of skills is to be assessed. Nevertheless, even a change of terminology can be significant even on symbolic terms.

The new Provision B.6.2 adds a few changes to the 2010 Code as well. According to it, the 'evaluation of the board of FTSE 350 companies should be externally facilitated at least every three years. The external facilitator should be identified in the annual report and a statement made as to whether they have any other connection with the company'. Therefore, now the annual report should include details upon the external facilitator and a statement highlighting any connection between the company and its external evaluators. In addition, the new Provision C.1 adds the requirement of 'fairness' to the previous text by stating that 'the board should establish arrangements that will enable it to ensure that the information presented is fair, balanced and understandable'. Those principles should be further explained by the directors in their annual reports which should reflect the existence of an element of 'fairness' in the

100 Provision B.2.4 of the 2012 Code.

drafting of reports and accounts. This is viewed as essential for enhancing the quality of financial and business reporting and therefore transparency and accountability within the corporate context.

To that end, the 2012 Code introduces a reformed set of Provisions C.3.2 and C.3.3 which will attempt to consolidate further the notion of accountability by adding to the duties of the audit committee a responsibility to 'report to the board on how it has discharged its responsibilities'. Provision C.3.3 should be read in conjunction with Provision C.1 which as mentioned above inserted the requirement of 'fairness' to the drafting of the reports and accounts. On the basis of the relevant provision of the 2012 Code, the audit committee is now 'where requested by the board, to provide advice on whether the annual report and accounts, taken as a whole, is fair, balanced and understandable and provides the information necessary for shareholders to assess the company's performance, business model and strategy'. Therefore, audit committees are now to provide to shareholders information on how they have carried out their responsibilities, including how they have assessed the effectiveness of the external audit process. On the basis of Provision C.3.7, 'FTSE 350 companies should now put the external audit contract out to tender at least every ten years', with the aim of ensuring a high quality and effective audit, whether from the incumbent auditor or from a different firm. This is yet another novelty introduced by the 2012 Code, always aiming to enhance transparency within the public corporation.

## Director's Remuneration

In the UK, the beginning of the 2008 crisis raised critical questions about the sustainability and the legitimacy of a remuneration model that essentially rewards management which has proven to be so spectacularly ineffective. The country was about to experience the first banking collapse of the century; such an event would have been highly destructive for an economy that was about to enter the phase of recession. The run-up to banks and the subsequent panic that could bring a whole economy to its knees, undermining any prospect of a short-term return to normality forced the then Labour Government under Gordon Brown to bail out the Northern Rock, the Royal Bank of Scotland and Lloyd's TSB. The bail out funds created a significant burden on the public finances of the country at a crucial time when the economy was ailing. Overspending at that point to avert a banking collapse was one of the factors that led to the impressive increase of the central government debt of the country from a low 42.7 per cent of the GDP in 2007, to an impressively higher 61.1 per cent of the GDP in 2008, only to escalate to

75.3 per cent in 2009 and 85.5 per cent in 2010.[101] The public debt therefore climbed almost 50 per cent in only three years! In real figures the debt climbed from $1.23 trillion in 2007 to $2.07 in 2010;[102] an increase of $800 billion in four years; $200 billion on average per year! The evolution of the deficit in the same period was quite spectacular as well, as it went from 2.8 per cent in 2007 to 4.8 per cent in 2008 and then culminated at 10.8 per cent in 2009 only to stabilise at 10.3 per cent in 2010.[103] It was evident that a combination of the international financial crisis that started in Wall Street in 2008 with the sub-prime market bubble and the collapse of Lehman Brothers (the landmark point in the turning of a crisis into a moment of determining importance for the world economy, along with the flirting of the banking sector with disaster), led to the deterioration of the main economic figures in the UK to a degree that a painful programme of spending cuts became imperative under the following Coalition Government. Within this context, and despite the facts that much of the banking sector was indeed technically nationalised and the public was dealing with a series of public spending slashes in a rather stoic manner, the news that the managers of the failed corporations continued to enjoy packages of privileged treatment and lucrative bonuses was not only provocative for a public dealing with the impact of austerity in its everyday life but also a reminder of the failure of a system that forges a hands-off approach to executive remuneration. The invisible hand proved to be too invisible, and the self-regulatory approach that entrusts the responsibility of determining executive pay to the board resulted in failure.

The UK Corporate Governance Code of 2010 as analysed above links remuneration with performance, but it fails to provide for the means to enforce such an association. Therefore, the provision in question albeit correct constitutes more an expression of wishful thinking rather than a policy whose implementation is rendered imperative by the Code. The issue of executive remuneration is not just reflective of the fairness of a corporate governance system that ensures that the board is an effective institution that guarantees the interests of the company, but it is also directly linked to important issues such as the accountability at the top of the company and transparency in relation to its functions. It also acts as

---

[101] See the OECD data accessed at http://stats.oecd.org/Index.aspx?DataSetCode=GOV_DEBT.

[102] See the OECD data accessed at http://stats.oecd.org/Index.aspx?DataSetCode=GOV_DEBT.

[103] See the OECD data accessed at www.oecd-ilibrary.org/economics/country-statistical-profile-united-kingdom_20752288-table-gbr.

an aggregating factor to the agency problem; the management is not only left alone to pursue an agenda that is obviously diverging from the respective of the shareholders and the interests of the company, but it is also rewarded for doing so. And in the case of nationalisation it raises an additional issue of how a government spends public capital which could have been diverted to other directions. In this context, in November 2011 the High Pay Commission found that high pay is 'corrosive' to the UK economy; it called for greater transparency in the setting of executive pay and supported that employees should sit on remuneration committees.[104] The report showed that executive pay rose sharply – the pay of the head of Barclays was up nearly 5,000 per cent in 30 years – while average wages had increased just threefold. The report stated that 'stratospheric increases in pay are damaging the economy – distorting markets, draining talent from key sectors and rewarding failure. There appears to be little truth in the myth that pay must escalate to halt a talent drain in executives'. The Institute of Directors in its statement supported that 'the current pace of increase in executive pay is unsustainable. The legitimacy of UK business in the eyes of wider society is significantly damaged by pay packages that are not clearly linked to company performance'.[105] Quite importantly, the Institute concluded that 'Remuneration committees should explore ways of engaging with employees on remuneration policy. This will be important in increasing the legitimacy of executive remuneration in the eyes of wider society'. This is an important aspect of the issue in question; the granting of bonuses was supposed to heal the divergence of interests between the shareholders and the company with the respective of the management; that is, to fail if the link between performance and pay is smashed. Therefore, the inclusion of employees in the remuneration committee will promote transparency, foster accountability and certainly provide additional checks by individuals whose personal interests do indeed coincide to a maximum degree with the respective of the company. Their personal income depends not only on the company's performance in the wider sense but also in avoiding any type of mismanagement that can result in tangible losses or in the undermining of corporate reputation which impacts on the long-term profitability of the company. Despite their exclusion from the company's definition within the context of an outsider system of corporate governance, their inclusion within the institutional framework that determines

---

[104] See the report accessed at http://highpaycommission.co.uk/wp-content/uploads/2011/11/HPC_final_report_WEB.pdf.

[105] See the statement accessed at http://press.iod.com/2011/11/25/iod-calls-for-action-on-executive-pay/.

the level of executive pay is useful if it is to deal effectively with a flaw that could potentially undermine the company by failing to deal with the agency problem.

It goes without saying that along with the employees, the role of the shareholders should be drastically increased; their stamp of approval on executive remuneration should be rendered a precondition for the determination of executive pay. The lack of shareholder active involvement in the determination of executive pay should be considered an anomaly inherent in a system which claims to be predominantly shareholder-orientated but does in fact lean towards managerial dominance. If the directors are the agents of the shareholders within the context of the contractual theory, then the inability of the former to have a determining say in fixing the salary of the latter is clearly undermining their property right on the corporation. The UK corporate governance model appears to recognise a property right to the shareholders but strips it of aspects of its main functions such as the ability to shape executive remuneration. Failing to involve shareholders at this level twists the shareholder-orientated model of the country into managerial dominance patterns that should have been found incompatible with its main principles. There is no point in declaring adherence to shareholder primacy and to their property right if they cannot be actively involved in fixing executive remuneration.

In fact this was the suggestion promoted by Business Secretary Vince Cable in January 2012; however it still remains a suggestion as it has not been incorporated into concrete legislation. In a country whose system of corporate governance is a genuine expression of the outsider corporate governance model in the framework of which shareholder primacy is sacrosanct, the lack of a role of determining importance granted to shareholders in relation to this issue is in fact astonishing and reveals a contradiction that betrays its flaws. The ability to monitor remuneration even by the inclusion of shareholders is further complicated by the fact that the move from individual to institutional shareholders meant that hedge funds for example are focused on short-term profitability; issues such as directorial remuneration and bonuses among other matters of everyday company function fall outside of their interests.

## The Stewardship Code

The Stewardship Code is centred on the belief that shareholders should be integral to the company's ethical principles. The International Corporate

Governance Network[106] is trying to strengthen the position of investors; the G20 and the EC are building up a set of stewardship principles calling on shareholders to consider long-term interests more in corporate governance.[107] Institutional shareholders are usually envisaged as taking from the company without responsibility. A flurry of Codes and soft-law regulation were promulgated during the financial crisis of 2008 and the responsibility of shareholders was considered more carefully. A number of reports and inquiries pinpointed the apathy of shareholders particularly during the boom years after the recession.[108] The Stewardship Code is intended to bolster shareholders' responsibilities to find out what managers are doing. Surveillance, transparency and voting are key points of the Code, as well as a duty for big institutional shareholders particularly insurance companies, pension funds and fund managers to adhere to a 'stewardship duty towards their company'. The idea is that rather than pocketing the dividends which flowed in from casino gambling, shareholders would consider long-term investment and manage the directors:

> So far, many investors have welcomed this development and more than 140 asset owners, advisory firms and fund managers have signed up to the Code. Market participants and industry groups are also largely supportive of the ideas behind the Code. Its supporters say that the Code will bring the so-called 'ownership' corporation to the top of the agenda, promoting active owner participation.[109]

Scepticism abounds however because short-termism cannot be regulated by soft law, and the culture of the UK is prone to weakness because of institutional investors who must get profit for their own shareholders and eventually the end owner; the pensioners or insurance premium holders. Institutional shareholders owe a duty to their own constituents. The Stewardship Code promotes dialogue between shareholders and management, and communication is suggested. The cost of the Code for shareholders and taxpayers might be great because finding the information from management sources is expensive, however a legislative

---

[106] See their website at www.icgn.org.

[107] European Commission, *Green Paper – Corporate Governance in Financial Institutions Policies and Remuneration Policies,* COM (2010) 284, 2 June 2010; Sullivan, R., 'UK Seen as Model for Stewardship Guidelines', *The Financial Times*, 1 August 2010.

[108] Demetra, A., 'Shareholders and corporate scrutiny: the role of the UK stewardship code' (2012) 9 *European Company and Financial Law Review* 3, pp. 342–79.

[109] Ibid., p. 345.

solution is also difficult involving judicial oversight of fiduciary duties for shareholders or strengthening the regulators' powers.[110] Scepticism is also rife in the media, as often reporters consider that soft law is often a way of deflecting criticism and legislative solutions.[111]

## Shareholders' Activism is not Effective: Other Accountability Mechanisms are Necessary

The UK Government rejected the mandatory inclusion of employees in the remuneration board; along with a vague intention to somehow engage them more actively within this process without reaching full participation and the inability to shape a concrete system of monitoring of executive pay on the part of shareholders, that cannot make anyone too optimistic that something is going to change radically, in the short term at least. A binding shareholder vote if implemented in a legally binding way may indeed engage shareholders into the decision-making process that leads to the shaping of executive pay, but if it is left for the companies to self-regulate themselves again, the results might be as disappointing as in the recent past. Otherwise, the voices which advocated the so-called 'responsible capitalism'[112] and the 'naming and shaming of boardroom pay which is not linked with performance' or the 'forcing of fat cats to justify bonuses'[113] will remain statements viewed within the framework of electoral pledges and political games, failing to change the existing status quo. The composition of the remuneration committee is of absolute importance since if it is dominated by executives who have an interest in setting each other's pay then it is going to function as the moral alibi and in many ways unjustified in the sense of a lack of a concrete link with performance remuneration. A report published in April 2012 by the High

---

110 David Walker recommended a voluntary solution: Walker, D., 'A review of Corporate Governance in UK Banks and other Financial Industries Entities, Final recommendations' (2007) accessed on 28 December 2012 at http://webarchive.nationalarchives.gov.uk/+/http:/www.hm-treasury.gov.uk/d/walker_review_261109.pdf. See P.L. Davies, 'Institutional Investors: A UK View' (1991) 57 *Brooklyn Law Review* 129–39.

111 Pratley, N., 'Kicking Cans, Shaming Tax Avoiders and Licking the Banks into Shape', *The Guardian*, 27 December 2012.

112 Vince Cable, *The Guardian*, 18 September 2011, accessed at www.guardian.co.uk/politics/2011/sep/18/vince-cable-executive-pay-bonuses.

113 Vince Cable, *The Independent*, September 2011, accessed at www.independent.co.uk/news/business/news/cable-ill-force-fat-cats-to-justify-bonuses-2356829.html.

Pay Centre[114] showed that nearly half of remuneration committee members are either serving or former company bosses, therefore rendering the whole monitoring procedure an exercise in futility. The report stated that committees, which set chief executives' pay, succumb to 'group-think' because they are dominated by a 'closed shop' of highly paid current and former directors who benefit personally from rising pay levels.[115] Over 46 per cent of people sitting on pay committees are or have been head company executives; through the common process of benchmarking, current executives may have an indirect financial interest in increasing pay in other companies.[116] 'It takes a very brave remuneration committee to seek to pay its executives below the median,' the report states. 'It is seen as the equivalent of admitting they are mediocre or not up to the job.'[117] A committee which includes shareholders, despite the given indifference of both individual shareholders and institutional ones (especially of those whose interests do not include anything but quick profit such as hedge funds), is a difficult equation which has however to be solved. And this is the point where the participation of non-shareholding actors with a clear interest in the company such as the employees can in fact promote shareholder interests by introducing monitoring of executive pay. This should be coupled with more thorough remuneration sections in the annual reports of the company which will demonstrate the exact amount granted to each executive and its links with performance; the figures should be stated clearly for all shareholders to comprehend and hence access and control. Clarity in the statement of the figures in question will bring transparency. Complicated remuneration sections in the annual reports obscure the capacity of shareholders who are quite passive and reluctant to intervene in management matters to comprehend the data. Cases of shareholder activism[118] expressed at annual meetings may be a rather premature sign that things are about to change towards

---

[114] See the report at www.highpaycentre.org/blog/publication-the-new-closed-shop-whos-deciding-on-pay. According to it, 46 per cent of people sitting on remuneration committees are current or former lead executives; 41 out of 366 remuneration committee members are current lead executives; 33 per cent of FTSE 100 companies have a current lead executive on the remuneration committee; 9 per cent of FTSE 100 companies have a current FTSE 100 lead executive on the remuneration committee.

[115] Full report accessed at http://highpaycentre.org/files/hpc_dp_remco.pdf.

[116] Ibid.

[117] Ibid.

[118] 'Year of Investor Revolt: Are Investors showing their Teeth at Last?' *The Guardian*, 26 April 2012, accessed at www.guardian.co.uk/business/2012/apr/26/investor-revolt-shareholders-showing-teeth-at-last.

the direction of a more active participation on the part of shareholders within the corporate context, but this may also be attributed to high press coverage of the excesses in executive remuneration. Whether or not the recent phenomena are to evolve into a more powerful expression of shareholders' presence can only be judged on the basis of the medium- to long-term analysis. The high profile removal of a knighthood from former Royal Bank of Scotland (RBS) CEO, Fred Goodwin, might have been impressive in media terms as apart from the gesture itself it was a public rebuke quite unusual for British standards, but in order to deal with the issue of executive pay, more permanent and sustainable provisions that will engage in a mandatory manner shareholders and employees should be established. Otherwise, the case of Goodwin, albeit extreme involving a large package granted to a manager of a nationalised bank, will not be exceptional in the future. Under his leadership, the balance sheet of RBS containing its loans and investments grew to £2 trillion, almost equivalent to the British GDP; this was supported by loss-absorbing capital equivalent only to a fiftieth of that. Being too dependent on unreliable wholesale finance after the unfortunate takeover of ABN Amro in 2007, it could no longer borrow from the markets which were severely turbulent after the collapse of Lehman Brothers, and was therefore bailed out by the government. RBS confirmed in 2012 it was paying out '£785m in bonuses despite recording another loss of £2bn last year. As the bank announced the fourth consecutive year of losses since its October 2008 bailout, the state is currently sitting on a £20bn loss on its 82% stake'.[119] RBS received more than £45 billion of capital big emergency loans from the Bank of England, and insurance against losses provided by the Treasury. RBS faced additional losses causing further burden to the national budget; and to add insult to injury, the issuing of the bonus created a media outcry that proved the controversy accompanying executive pay and the need to regulate it properly. A media 'furore surround[ed] the award of a near £1m bonus for chief executive Stephen Hester which he waived, he was still on course to be handed £600,000 in bonuses while close colleagues could be handed up to £11m depending on the share price and their performance'.[120] The bonus pot

[119] *The Guardian*, 23 February 2012, accessed at www.guardian.co.uk/business/2012/feb/23/rbs-commercial-status-2bn-loss.

[120] *The Guardian*, 22 February 2012, accessed at www.guardian.co.uk/business/2012/feb/22/rbs-400m-pound-bonuses-expected-loss.

would have given the lower paid employees of the ailing bank 'approximately £6,000'[121] per capita had it been distributed to them.

The Goodwin affair proves that it was not just a media storm over 'corporate greed' but a failure of a whole system of checks which were supposed to prevent such an overt case of management failure. The focus should have been placed on the omissions that were spectacularly highlighted by the affair. What happened to the remuneration committees? And why did not the non-executive or the independent directors detect any irregularity? This obviously proves that the system put in place by the Codes with a combination of an excessive laissez-faire approach accompanied by a lax system of controls did not work. And if the system of checks failed to catch such an extreme case of management failure then everyday cases of abuse might be even harder to detect. The media glitz will pass, but if legislation is not put in place to introduce mandatory voting of shareholders and employees on the remuneration committee on the executive pay, then the cases of failure will not be so exceptional in the future.

121 *The Guardian*, 23 February 2012, accessed at www.guardian.co.uk/business/2012/feb/23/rbs-commercial-status-2bn-loss.

# 5. Germany

## INTRODUCTION

Germany is a country which occupies a central position within the EU's political and economic context. However, it is neither the obvious significance of the country as the continent's main economic power nor geopolitics that renders a chapter on Germany necessary. It is rather the fact that this country has gradually shaped a system of corporate governance which has proved to be particularly influential for other countries looking to make like-minded reforms. The German system of corporate governance evolved in close conjunction with the developments taking place in the country at economic and (frequently problematic) political level, and it clearly reflects both the main historical trends in the German society and also the main political choices that shaped its society.[1]

The corporate governance system in Germany took its current shape in the post-Second World War period, when successive governments made the conscious choice to construct an inclusive governance system based on consensus between its various constituencies. The German company grants ample room to employee participation, accommodating it within the actual institutional setting of the company; this is embodied in the landmark dual board system that even today remains the most distinctive feature of the German corporate governance model. The corporate landscape in Germany is characterised by a dense network of companies closely related to each other and to the banking system.[2] The banks play

---

[1] See Carr, W., *A History of Germany, 1815–1990* (Bloomsbury Academic, London 1991); Craig, A.G., *Germany, 1866–1945* (Oxford University Press, Oxford 1980); Traynor, J., *Mastering Modern German History, 1864–1990* (Palgrave, London 2007); Kitchen, M., *A History of Modern Germany 1800 to the Present* (Wiley-Blackwell, Oxford 2011); Blackbourn, D., *History of Germany 1780–1918: The Long Nineteenth Century* (Wiley-Blackwell, Oxford 2002).

[2] See Beck, S., F. Klobes and C. Frank, *Surviving Globalisation?: Perspectives for the German Economic Model* (Springer, Dordrecht, The Netherlands 2005).

a pivotal role in corporate governance as they have historically been the provider of capital to German enterprises; their significance is marked with their presence at the level of corporate boards. The establishment of a generous proxy voting system encouraged and facilitated an enhanced presence of the banking sector at the decision-making process and at the board level. Cooperation as a concept is integral to the philosophical foundations of the German economy, the impressive development of which gave birth to a distinctive model of social market economy widely divergent from the respective models adopted in the USA and in the UK, and was in fact dependent on the cooperation between a wide range of companies of divergent size. The famous family-owned businesses of the country named *Mittelstand* were able to create a network with the country's limited liability and public companies, *Gesellschaft mit beschränkter Haftung* (*GmbH*) and *Aktiengesellschaft* (*AG*) respectively, by providing them with the necessary components of their products. Large car industries receive part of their equipment by the *Mittelstand*, which specialise in the unique production of a certain component or part of machinery. The creation of a large network of companies involving the small family-owned *Mittelstand* and extending to the *GmbH* and *AG* has fostered a culture of collaboration and co-efficiencies rather than competition. If the banks with their close links to the companies in question are added to the equation, it becomes apparent that the German economy is largely operating on the basis of a finely orchestrated range of small, medium and large companies which are specialists in their respective field and part of the production chain accustomed to mutual dependency and common synergies. This explains why cartelisation as a phenomenon marked the German economy of the twentieth century, while the notion of competition did not enjoy the prominence in Germany that it enjoyed in the Anglo-Saxon context. The basic parameters of the German economic model are complemented by a widespread system of apprenticeships undertaken by the young labour that is specialised at a very early stage in the technical aspects of production. The orientation and content of apprenticeships are normally in the engineering field, and they aim to train young individuals to fit into that network of expertise at the respective level of production; either by producing a component of the final product at the *Mittelstand* or at one of the factories of a large public *AG* where the product (for example, a car) is one step before entering the phase of marketing and sale. Therefore, a system of coordinated constituencies, each one compatible and consistent with each other, was set in place where companies of all sizes along with the banks which would provide the capital were set to cooperate at all levels of production. The system guaranteed the continuous flow of skilled labour, not only through an advanced education system but also on the basis of the apprenticeships which were designed to provide the German industry with the labour specialised enough to serve the system put in place.

From this brief introduction to elements of the German corporate governance system and more generally to the German economic model, the substantial differences between the former and the economic and societal realities in both the USA and the UK are laid bare. As we explain later in this chapter, Germany placed cooperation and consensus at the centre of its model; it reserved for the aforementioned values the place that competition has assumed within the American and the English context. Due to its historical development that was marked by spectacular conflicts and painful wars,[3] and the lack of a highly centralised authority capable of taking central decisions for the entirety of the nation during a great part of its history (reflected in a decentralised federal system of administration), Germany was much more inclined than the UK to adopt a more inclusive approach, both at the level of its own governance and at the level of corporate governance. The nation usually rallies around coalition governments that involve either like-minded parties or 'grand coalitions' that involve the Christian Democrats with the Social Democrats, the two poles of the political system. Germany seems particularly attached to the notion of cooperation that will involve a major degree of consensus-building. This contrasts with the UK, where national politics appear to be confrontational, with coalitions constituting the exception to the rule rather than the rule itself, and the country usually governed on the basis of a clear mandate handed by the electorate either to the Conservatives or Labour Party to pursue their set of policies marked by their own ideological stamp such as pro-Europe or anti-Europe, pro-NHS reform or anti-NHS reform, pro-market policies or more labour-friendly strategies. A large country with a fragmented constitutional setting at multiple layers and a deeply problematic recent history which left a clear imprint on collective memory and national identity, Germany seems determined to avoid the ghosts of the past and follow a reconciliatory approach that instinctively involves a variety of actors. At corporate level this would involve the stakeholders with the employees as the most obvious examples; the latter are not included in a notional way within the company but they are represented on the supervisory board and therefore

[3] See Tooze, A., *The Wages of Destruction: The Making and Breaking of the Nazi Economy* (Penguin, London, New York 2006); Wiesen, J., *Creating the Nazi Marketplace, Commerce and Consumption in the Third Reich* (Cambridge University Press, Cambridge 2010); Fullbrook, M., *A Concise History of Germany* (Cambridge University Press, Cambridge 1992).

granted a sometimes determining say on the company's affairs. The institutional architecture of the German corporate governance structure also recognises the importance that the banks have historically played in that country as the provider of capital and the main creditor of the companies. Banks are usually represented on the board, and in the past they yielded a great degree of power due to the proxy voting system that allowed their excessive and disproportional representation at the general meeting. The inclusion of a divergent range of actors within the corporate equation was therefore clearly indicative of a social landscape which was wholly different from the respective in the UK.

An additional factor that enabled a more inclusive approach on the part of the German corporation was the fact that companies in the country seemed more inclined to complement each other in the same line of production but at different levels, rather than compete. This substantial point defined the character of German company law as well as its orientation, and betrays the origins of corporate governance deeply rooted within the national legislative tradition and social history, which explain its resistance to the forces of globalisation. It is argued from the beginning of this book that despite harmonisation at some aspects of corporate governance, the latter remains distinctively national as it is defined by parameters that go deeper in history, societal development and economic structure than the current forces of globalisation that have swept other fields of law. In the light of this, the whole theoretical basis of the German corporate governance stands at the other tip of the balance with the English governance model. Germany's system purely expresses an insider system of corporate governance, in contrast to the English outsider model. As analysed earlier, the term 'insider system of corporate governance' indicates the source of financing of the corporation which comes from the 'inside of the company', either in the form of shareholders' contributions or banking loans. This directly contrasts with the significance role that the stock markets hold within the English corporate governance model as the foremost source of funding. While the English public company will resort to the stock market to attract capital and simultaneously render itself wide open to new shareholders, the German company may look to sources of finance that rest closer to itself; its own shareholders and the banks, although there is an increasing importance of stock markets within the German context as well. Frequently, the sources of financing are among its existing shareholders, rendering its financing if not an internal affair then at least a process which is more inclusive in terms of the number of the actors it involves. The company essentially remains under the control of the same actors, or it experiences a state of affairs where the change in its control is not deemed to be radical;

traditional shareholders maintain their positions of power with new ones – normally a banking institution – added to the rather limited list. In any case, the dispersion of shares to the number of individuals or institutions experienced in the UK is relatively uncommon in Germany, at least to the extent detected in the UK. That does not mean that the Frankfurt stock market is irrelevant in the financial considerations of the German corporate world; it is just merely indicative of the natural tendency of German corporations to look for their capital in their 'inside'.

As analysed in Chapter 1, the difference in the source of finance is not a technicality that can be bypassed without any further ramifications on the understanding of the substantial background of the examined corporate governance systems. The rationale behind that is that the divergence in the financing of the corporations provides the grounds for subsequent distinctive approaches in the entire institutional setting of the corporation in question; it is a factor of determining importance that coshapes the discernible parameters on the basis of which the corporation is to be institutionally constructed and hence governed. It is evident that the corporation cannot be viewed independently of the society in the framework of which it gradually takes shape, as it reflects its dominant values, strengths and needs. Hence, as explained in Chapter 2, the German corporate governance system would normally involve a more limited number of shareholders than the respective English system; shareholders with a majority of the shares or an influential portion of the stock holding to be deemed as 'blockholders' normally exist. They are in a position either to appoint the management or exercise a significantly closer control to it. Therefore, the phenomenon of the separation of ownership and control which has so openly marked the American and to a great degree the English corporation has not emerged as one of the trademarks of the German corporation. The latter appears to have a management closely linked to its important shareholders; in addition, the dual board structure ensures that additional actors that may not be included in the list of shareholders (such as the employees and the creditors) assume a monitoring role that adds yet another layer of control placed upon the management. The decision-making of the latter is not only the subject of scrutiny by the owners of the company (something that at least in theory is also the case in the UK), but it emerges as the point of reference for employees and creditors alike. The inclusive institutional setting which finds the supervisory board as its uppermost expression guarantees the existence of strict controls upon the management that the respective English or American directors will experience rather exceptionally. This degree of consensus-building will impact upon the flexibility of the decision-making system and its ability to adapt swiftly to the outbreak of a crisis or a rapid shift in the market conditions. While the manager of the English company will avail himself of the opportunity to lay off workers in order to deal with an unfolding crisis, the manager of the German company will need to engage with a process that will entail a degree of minimum agreement on the part of all the actors represented on the board; the latter will be limited, relatively powerful, with a personal stake at hand and a possibly widely divergent agenda. The shareholders represented on board with a potential block-holding capacity may amount to the founding family which may aim at maintaining some form of determining say over the corporation, the government which may aim at avoiding a corporate restructuring that could impact on its electoral prospects in a politically sensitive time and constituency where the factory is situated, a bank may require prudent policies which can guarantee its investment while avoiding the tarnishing of its reputation, while the employees will simply want to save their jobs. These objectives may coincide towards a commonly set policy in due time but it is more likely that the management will need to employ a great range of skills to reach an agreement in the medium to longer term. The system lacks the flexibility of the English management to respond to a potential market shock; however it has proved if not ideal then at least quite capable of serving the main strengths of the German economy and therefore society which is its industrial might.

The industrial sector constitutes the backbone of the German economy and the landmark sector of its economic model. Despite the external shocks that industry may suffer from say a sudden oil crisis, it is an economic sector that needs long planning, stability and consensus rather than swift decision-making which naturally favours short-term prospects. Therefore, the system in place in Germany appears to be not only compatible with the country's main economic sectors but highly supportive of its strengths. As analysed in Chapter 4, the UK's world-class financial sector requires a system that guarantees swift decision-making, entailing the engagement of a minimum range of actors and can guarantee the rapid reallocation of capital and labour, rather than a procedure which for the needs of the industry in question is rather cumbersome. That is consistent with the approach that views corporate governance through more national rather than globalised lenses, as it considers them as intrinsically linked to national strengths and needs rather than to widely defined globalised trends. That is not to refuse any harmonisation within the field in question as countries are not immune to mutual influences or globalisation for that matter, but the core of the system seems to remain distinctively national.

## CORPORATE GOVERNANCE IN A HISTORICAL PERSPECTIVE

While a 'complete documentation of the history of German company law is not available to date',[4] the main milestones in its evolution can be traced if the relatively recent Germany history is analysed. Although the first embryonic forms of companies emerged as early as in twelfth century with the creation of the first urban centres and the cultivation of trade links between the medieval cities of that time, the current company forms started to take shape much later. Forms of partnerships of limited or unlimited nature did exist in the country for centuries, but production and distribution were mainly controlled by guilds up to the eighteenth century. At the beginning of the nineteenth century, Germany – a collection of 38 sovereign states with a predominantly agrarian economy[5] – was no exception to the rule as guilds and other restrictive practices formed the dominant feature of trading goods and services both in the UK and in continental Europe. Germany however experienced the rapid development of a company form that very much resembles the contemporary large public company later than the UK. The main reason for that may be historical. During the seventeenth and eighteenth centuries the UK experienced unprecedented expansion through colonisation, as explained in Chapter 4. The country expanded its territory to encompass new lands into the five continents; the repercussions of such an expansion of international scale on the global ambitions and the trade aspirations of the country were indeed immense. New markets were opened, new trade ways were explored and new products were discovered as the increasing links between the UK and its colonies established trade in its truly global dimensions. Within that framework, large scale corporations such as the East India Corporation started to take shape. Of course crucial elements of contemporary company law such as limited liability and corporate personality were not yet fully shaped, but the seeds of what would later become known as the public company were effectively laid. This was not only important from a legal point of view, but it was also a greatly significant turning point for the mentality of that time; the guilds and the restrictive practices of that point were found to amount not to protectionism as initially aimed for, but to restrictions to the amazing potential that

---

4 Kübler, F., *Gesellschaftsrecht*, 4th edn (C.F. Müller Juristischer Verlag, Heidelberg 1994).

5 Fohlin, C., *Finance Capitalism and Germany's Rise to Industrial Power* (Cambridge University Press, Cambridge 2007), p. 15.

the new trade routes presented. The existing company tools were proving insufficiently equipped to deal with the magnitude of the new choices offered by colonisation and expansion. The UK was therefore emerging into a fertile land for new ideas, new ideals and incentives for innovation. The need to attract capital was obvious to a country which was faced with a vast array of choices that were obviously in need of exploration. The invitation addressed to the public to buy shares and provide the finance necessary for the exploration of the new markets was rendered necessary by the speed of changes and the magnitude of challenges lying ahead. And while the UK was the subject of such rapid changes, having to readjust its legislative and commercial practices to address the newly emerged challenges effectively, Germany was safely anchored in the continent. Despite the fact that even before unification the country occupied a central position in the continent that was strategically crucial, Germany did not experience a scale of expansion comparable to that of the UK at that point. Therefore, the internationalisation of its trade links and interests became distinctive at a later point than the respective aspirations of the UK. The latter's exposure to international exchanges, new products and ideas along with its already well-rooted and clearly stated faith in property rights and individualism created a new form of dynamism that encouraged the creation of large companies with a far-reaching aim both economically and geographically, and a gradually shaping class of people who were acquiring property rights not only on their domicile but also on corporations. Germany's exposure to a more cosmopolitan approach to trade was considerably more limited at the time, and that was reflected in the evolution of its company law practices and its corporate governance architecture.

## The Importance of Early Infrastructure in Germany on Corporate Governance: The Significance of the Banks

Despite the aforementioned differences with the UK and its respective evolution at that point of history, the German economy was also about to experience the impact of the development of the railroads on both its economy and companies. Railways began to expand mainly in the 1840s as the country embarked on reaping the benefits of a cheap and reliable transportation network that could connect the different states that comprised Germany in its modern form, and hence created a larger unified market. The advances in technology and market accessibility along with the cheaper transportation of goods generated profitability and prompted the founding of an increasing number of companies in the 1850s. 'The newly formed firms were concentrated in mining, insurance and banking as well as in the railroads themselves together absorbing about 92.7% of all capital invested in Prussian joint stock companies during these twenty years.'[6] The need for capital was now much bigger than at any point previously, and that naturally emerged as the catalyst not only for the creation of large scale companies of the public limited liability form but also to novel funding techniques very much related to the shape that corporate governance was to assume in Germany in the following years. The financial institutions at that point were adjusted to accommodate the specific needs of an economy which was agrarian in nature; industrial Germany was only in its embryonic form. The traditional elements of the financial system at the time comprised 'agricultural credit institutions, government securities and short term trading capital for international and interregional trade'.[7] The financial system of that time was orientated towards funding activities of mainly agricultural nature and was strictly regulated by the local governments. Despite its shape and orientation, this tightly constructed network of credit institutions, securities and banks with its provision of a combination of short- and long-term finance would significantly influence the shape of banking techniques to be employed at the later industrialised stage. The network between banks and companies and the interrelation between the two remains a distinctive feature of the German corporate landscape even up to now. At that point,

> through their rigid regulation the governments of Prussia and Saxony in particular minimised outside competition for their note issuing banks. Because of tight government control over banks of issue, the majority of financial intermediaries were private banks. These executed a substantial share of the economy's payments, linked savers with investment opportunities, and helped found new businesses.[8]

The relationship between the Berlin credit banks or 'Great Banks' and German business remained crucial for the country's industrialisation. That could be contrasted with the UK which resorted to the stock market to fund its own industrialisation. In Germany the banks provided to the companies the funding necessary to materialise their strategic planning. As the role of the banks in the corporate context was enhanced and they

---

[6] Riesser, J., *The German Great Banks and their Concentration* (The National Monetary Commission, Government Printing Office, Washington 1911), p. 48.

[7] Tilly, R., 'Germany 1815–1870' in C. Rondo (ed), *Banking in the Early Stages of Industrialisation: A Study in Comparative Economic History* (Oxford University Press, New York 1967), p. 154.

[8] Fohlin (2007), p. 17.

were anchored in a relationship closely linked to each other, they guaranteed a place on the supervisory board which granted them not only a monitoring role of the management but also an active role within the corporate institutional settings. They were therefore instrumental in leading the companies to float their shares to the public to enable the repayment of bank loans. They remained influential as they exercised depository voting rights on behalf of their clients; their role in 'placing new securities and in lending with shares as collateral … ending up voting the shares of companies that used their underwriting services'[9] gave rise to their proxy voting powers. As explained above, German business experienced the separation between ownership in a much more moderate way than the UK, let alone the USA; however the process of separation between ownership and control embarked with the floating of shares to pay back the banks which had provided the initial capital and funding to the company sponsoring their activities and now sitting on the supervisory board. In contrast to the UK and the USA where the dispersion of shares to a larger number of actors entailed the loss of control on the part of the owners, in Germany a crucial element shifted the power back to ownership; the voting rights. Multiple vote shares were shares that carried multiple voting rights with them, and they were quite commonplace at that period.

> In the interwar years this instrument was used extensively and was usually justified as means of fighting dilution of family control … allowing founding families to keep their grip on the company … as the votes per share ranged 20 and 250 times higher than the normal voting right … these privileged shares were given to members of the supervisory board or to banks that committed themselves to vote according to the controlling group.[10]

The power of the future shareholders was therefore extensively restricted, decreasing the effects of the dispersion of shares and along with it the side effects of the separation of ownership and control; Germany did not experience the Berle and Means doctrine in the same way as the USA as it rallied behind multiple vote shares to keep the two notions closely attached to each other.

Today the issuing of such shares is not permitted. The emergence of banks as the primary source of capital within a tightly regulated

---

[9] Morck, K.R., *A History of Corporate Governance Around the World, Family Business Groups to Professional Managers* (The University of Chicago Press, Chicago 2007), p. 14.

[10] Ibid., p. 262.

environment forged their instrumental position within the German corporate edifice and fostered their links with companies; those links were integral enough to exist even up to the modern day. The links developed at an early stage between national banks and national businesses were enhanced by the restrictive legislative framework enacted by the executive; the latter had a clearly protective effect as it safeguarded the national financial institutions from competition. Germany was never profoundly inspired by the notion of free competition in the way and to the extent that this doctrine appeared to be particularly influential within the UK and the USA context.

## Education: Highly Skilled Labour

Another repercussion of the spread of railways and the advances in the field of engineering is that it forged a widely spread technical culture that transcended both the business world and the education system. What distinguished Germany from the UK at that point was that it placed a focus on the acquisition of such skills that would advance the country as a technological pioneer among the world's nations with relevant aspirations. While the UK was reaping the benefits of its impressive industrial revolution by forging an open corporate culture with elements of cosmopolitanism and was reaching the markets of the five continents with its mercantile fleet, Germany drew a slightly different lesson. Apart from the obvious business opportunities that technological developments, easier and cheaper transportation and a greater selection of markets naturally brought, the creation of a system that guaranteed the generation of highly skilled labour and – crucially – management that would guarantee technological innovation and leadership in the long term became central in the country's aspirations. Germany looked behind the exciting picture of the time and sought to create a system that would guarantee the flow of highly specialised individuals with a technical background; this was a precondition for its emergence in the forefront of international technological leadership. Already in 1851,

> the London exhibition of that year showcasing the latest advances in technology, spurred on Germany's emerging entrepreneurs. Within five years one of these new technologies, the Bessemer process, revolutionised the German iron and steel industry … it greatly improved the efficiency of production thus increasing the quantity and quality of steel available for heavy industry.[11]

---

[11] Fohlin (2007), p. 16.

As new technologies revolutionised production methods and changed the nature of the German economy from an agrarian into an industrial one, the country

> put in place the world's most sophisticated system of higher education which would ultimately make the nation a leader in science based chemical and electric industries … to develop and disseminate technical education in the Prussian economy … a number of technical institutes were established and a network of trade schools in the provinces.[12]

The establishment of universities across Europe and the UK was a commonplace practice even at that time, as the value of education in a rapidly changing world was universally acknowledged. What differentiated Germany from other countries and the UK in particular was the absolute focus on technical education. Germany demonstrated an urge which it materialised into a concrete, well-engineered plan to foster a general culture of technical education that would provide the private individuals equipped enough to upgrade the country into technological and industrial excellence. Interestingly enough and as a further point of divergence with the approach adopted in the UK, Germany was determined to acquire not only highly skilled labour but *also* managers with advanced technical skills; that remains up to now a distinctive mark of the German economic model.

The close link between science, industry, labour and management was a crucial and greatly characteristic parameter of the German business world. The network of technical schools and institutions would 'supply the emerging German industrial sector with technically trained managers … industrial enterprises also forged long term research links with these educational establishments often sending their employees to work on joint projects with academics'.[13] The result of such close links between academic institutions, technical establishments, labour and management was the competitive advantage acquired by the country's industry in chemicals, metals, steel and machinery. The central choice on the part of the country's political establishment was not just to educate labour so as to provide business with highly skilled individuals with a specialised technical background; it went beyond that in creating highly skilled managers as well with an insight to technology who would further

[12] O'Sullivan, M.A., *Contests for Corporate Control, Corporate Governance and Economic Performance in the United States and Germany* (Oxford University Press, Oxford 2001), p. 234.

[13] Ibid.

consolidate such a culture in their company. The accumulation of technological knowhow both at the labour and at management level was crucial in the reorientation of the German economy towards industry and its emergence as an international leader in the field in question. The fact that the close links between technical institutions, academia and business were orchestrated by the government is also highly indicative of the institutional and political framework within which business evolved in the country. It is also reflective of the general consentaneous culture that retains a central position in the national psyche; the country planned a long-term strategy that would involve yet another network of actors closely working together to achieve an end. The academic institutions would cooperate closely with business, which would send its employees to participate in technical projects aiming at providing them with the necessary skills to successfully fit into a production chain that became increasingly demanding and specialised. In addition, the managers of a company with recognised aspirations of industrial excellence would have themselves acquired the technical knowledge necessary to engage into the practicalities of the field in question, contributing decisively to corporate success. The concepts of 'cooperation', 'networks', 'close interaction', 'consensus' and 'long-term planning' seem to be monotonously repeated every time an analysis of the German corporate and economic model is considered, to the degree that it is recognised that they are fundamental concepts to this model. A system of apprenticeships that provides young Germans with the necessary technical skills to qualify for a position in the country's industrial sector has generated the flow of specialised labour even up to the modern day. Its success was so instrumental to Germany's competitiveness and export-driven economy that the UK only recently has expressed its ambition of putting in place a similar system for English youth.

## The German Commerce Code of 1861: The Supervisory Board

The German Commerce Code of 1861 'provided the first codification of company law including the public limited company';[14] it also established the two-tier system of corporate governance based on the existence of a management and a separate supervisory board. At that point as well as for the following decades, the supervisory board was staffed by shareholders aiming among others at supervising the managers; it was not

---

14 Schmidt, H., J. Drukarczyk, D. Honold, S. Prigge, A. Schüler, G. Tetens, *Corporate Governance in Germany* (Nomos Verlagsgesellschaft, Baden-Baden 1997), p. 34.

until the 1950s that the employees were granted the right to be extensively represented on that board. The two-tier system remains up to now the most prominent and distinctive of the German corporate governance model. A few decades later in 1926, 'the idea of introducing a US type board system was discussed by the 34th conference of Germany jurists but rejected on the grounds that the dualistic system enabled companies to control powerful chairmen of corporate boards'.[15] Before the uniform Code was accepted by all German states, the '1870 amendments struck down the requirement of a government permit. Government control of public limited companies was also abandoned'.[16] The same requirement was introduced in the UK with the Bubble Act of 1720 which the country considered as the appropriate response to the speculative phenomena that took place before the enactment of the Act. The supervisory board was legislated and established at that point as a mandatory feature of the public company; it would soon emerge as the trademark of the whole German corporate governance edifice. 'During the three years after the 1870 amendments 843 public limited companies were founded.'[17] And while that was an encouraging number which demonstrated that the already existing need to employ such a corporate form for the purposes of trade, the truth behind that figure was less encouraging, as 'in many instances the sole purpose was to defraud investors by merchandising the shares'.[18] The parallels with phenomena that had already taken place in the UK earlier with the South Sea Company case and the ensuing large scale speculation which led to the Bubble Act of 1720 are evident. Germany was experiencing at that point what the UK had experienced even more colourfully more than a century earlier. The legislative response to the similar challenge however was different in Germany. While the UK (as explained in Chapter 3) opted for the adoption of the Bubble Act of 1720 which radically reshaped the legislative landscape of that time by introducing rather severe restrictions to corporations, with the most significant among them the obligation of joint stock companies to acquire a royal charter, Germany removed such a requirement with the amendment of the Commerce Code of 1870. And it did not intend to go down that road again; whether the English experience played any role in the German considerations is not clear. What is clear is the fact that the

---

[15] Mäntysaari, P., *Comparative Corporate Governance, Shareholders as a Rule-maker* (Springer, Berlin, Heidelberg, New York 2005), p. 252.

[16] Schmidt et al. (1997), p. 34.

[17] Wiedermann, H., *Gesellschaftsrecht* (Beck, München 1980), p. 27.

[18] Schubert, W. and P. Hommelhoff, *Hundert Jahre modernes Aktienrecht* (Berlin 1985), pp. 56, 133 and 159.

German legislature would not place companies under the obligation of acquiring government permission – the equivalent of the royal charter – again; German company law had moved away from such a choice which was clearly among the proposed solutions at that time. Instead it opted for introducing a new set of controls that would stop before the obligation to be granted permission, but which would clearly constitute a step towards the direction of creating additional layers of monitoring of the management of the company. The fact that Germany as a jurisdiction detected from an early point the need not to limit the scope of activities of the corporation or the authorisation procedure on the basis of which a company is born, but to achieve a more effective control of its management, betrays the fine yet important line that distinguishes the approaches adopted in the country with the respective in the UK. The UK had a longer experience in speculative and fraudulent phenomena within the corporate context, as it pioneered the creation of public companies to support its international trade aspirations and later the demands of its industrial revolution. However, in the aftermath of the South Sea Company scandal, it chose a very restrictive form of regulation in the shape of the Bubble Act; the shadow of the latter in the development of UK company law was indeed heavy. It introduced excessive regulation which ultimately severely limited business activity to deal with scandals that were merely reflective of the lack of checks on the managerial class of the company. After increasing pressure from the business world and the realisation that overly excessive regulation which places the ability to form a company under the obligation to acquire a royal charter (a procedure which was cumbersome even for the standards of the era in question), the Bubble Act was removed and the UK moved towards the adoption of legislative framework which is remarkably similar in its ideological foundations to the Companies Act 2006.

Germany on the other hand refrained from reintroducing the set of limitations to business and corporate activities that it had previously removed, and contemplated a range of measures which had a wholly different aim; this was not to restrict the creation of companies of that type by enhancing state control on them but to rearrange the affairs within the company itself by introducing a layer of checks and controls on the management of the company. The choice of measures adopted reveals a difference not only in practice and tools employed but also in the objectives pursued and the actual perceptions of the problem in question. The UK dealt with corporate fraud of that time with a big legislative piece which restricted business as a whole; Germany dealt with it by continuing to encourage corporate activities but focusing on placing the management under additional control. The supervisory board, which was recently enacted and a part of the dual board structure that would emerge as one of the landmark features not only of the German corporate governance but also of the country as a whole, was about to assume a very significant role within this framework. The 1884 amendments therefore brought the regulation of the 'founding procedures, the valuation of assets, the maintenance of the statutory capital, and the duties of the board members and of the shareholders' meeting. In particular they strengthened both the control duties and control powers of the supervisory board and instituted director liability'.[19] The focus was gradually but steadily moving towards enforcing a concrete set of directors' duties while promoting the role of the supervisory board and the shareholder meeting in achieving this aim. The country was also slowly moving towards the direction of adopting minimal forms of shareholder and creditor protection while looking at the rights of the workers within the corporate context. And although 'the contractual relations between the company and others were viewed as primarily governed by the market',[20] the road had been paved for the creation of a corporate environment within the context of which a stakeholder-friendly approach would become the norm.

## The Regulation of Small Companies

Smaller businesses had found the provisions of the Code too challenging to fulfil due to their size; their capacity to adjust to its requirements was rather limited. However, there was an urgent need on their part as well to acquire access to limited liability and the privileges that it entailed, especially in relation to containing the risk inherent in an investment. Under the light of pressures to accommodate the needs of a growing number of individuals with an entrepreneurial spirit, the *GmbH* Act of 1892 was passed; it created the private limited liability company.

## Dynamism, Technology, Science and Education: A Cooperative Framework and Cartels

The legislative framework of the country was therefore evolving to adapt to its new business landscape and to accommodate its ambitions. The country was entering the twentieth century with a certain degree of dynamism as an emerging industrial power. Its system of combined clusters of companies, banks and training institutions matched the

---

19 Schmidt et al. (1997) p. 35.
20 Schubert and Hommelhoff (1985), p. 62.

country's aspirations, leading to a breakthrough in technological development and the creation of a generation of highly skilled employees and appropriately qualified management to sustain the ongoing industrial drive. The close interactions between banks and businesses, the links between businesses and training or academic institutions and the federal system of a country which was getting increasingly accustomed to shaping agreements for the common future based on mutual compromise and negotiations after uniting into a single entity in 1871, created a cooperative environment within the framework of which the notion of consensus assumed a central position. The country's rather restrictive legislative framework had a protective effect on the local banking sector and businesses, while as mentioned above Germany did not seem to share the same enthusiasm either for free and unrestricted competition or for an invisible hand with the UK, or the USA for that matter. Within this framework, a particular characteristic

> of the early phase of industrialisation was the operation of cartels but it also featured prominently in the relationship between industry on the one hand and both the state and the financial institutions on the other … German business showed a tendency towards large scale and vertical integration and extensive use of professional managers was made.[21]

At that point Germany seemed to be 'the home of industrial combination as far as Europe is concerned'.[22] By 1905 'over 350 cartels had been created and although they only accounted for twenty five percent of total industrial output their influence was all pervasive in those industries – coal, chemical and steel – where the greatest competitive advantages had been secured'.[23] They were fuelled by the depression of 1901–1903, but having spread from common pricing to regulating output and marketing strategies they basically evolved into a prominent feature of the German industrial landscape and economy. Other countries at the time such as the USA were not immune to such clearly distortive or (in today's terms) illegal practices and techniques but Germany was less motivated to deal with such phenomena than its counterpart on the other side of the Atlantic. While the USA enacted the Sherman Anti-Trust Act in 1890,

---

[21] Wilson, E.J., *British Business History, 1720–1994* (Manchester University Press, Manchester 1995), p. 70.

[22] Carter, G.R., *The Tendency Towards Industrial Combination* (Constable, London 1913), p. 8.

[23] Chandler, A.D. and H. Daems, *Managerial Hierarchies: Comparative Perspectives on the Rise of the Modern Industrial Enterprise* (Harvard University Press, Cambridge MA 1980), p. 88.

which remains one of the most prominent pieces of legislation that signalled a radical shift in the approach against cartelisation, Germany did not present any respective legislative initiative. Cartelisation worked in conjunction with stricter legislation which was more protective of local business, granting to the newly industrialised nation the scope to develop its national industry so as to deal with the challenges of international competition, especially by the USA and the UK. And while such practices were simply a cacophony within the liberalism that was the dominant ideology in the UK, it fell quite comfortably within the German ideology of the time which did not present sensitivities of that nature. Today cartelisation is clearly viewed as a practice which is not only illegal but highly distortive; however in the context of that historical timing it was viewed as 'a positive asset to German economic development particularly as a means of creating greater trading stability in conjunction with the protective umbrella of import duties and the encouragement it gave to marketing through the distribution syndicates which emerged from the 1890s'.[24] Cartelisation entailed an increased form of protectionism which did 'inhibit horizontal merger activity as a means of concentrating production largely because the security afforded by cartels provided little incentive to acquire competitors'.[25]

## Cooperation between the *Mittelstand* and Large Companies

Despite the fact that 'large scale business has played an important role in the economic development of Germany',[26] small and medium-sized family firms continued to form the backbone of the economy, just as they did in the UK. The difference with the UK lies in the fact that those companies otherwise known as *Mittelstand* became increasingly integrated within the business architecture of the country by constructing a range of crucial industrial products such as machinery that were either directly exported to other markets or built into the industrial production of bigger companies and then marketed for either exportation or internal consumption. The pattern that emerged as the *Mittelstand* was the crucial cooperation within the production chain between small, medium and

---

[24] Carter (1913), p. 46. MacGregor, D.H., *Industrial Combination* (George Bell & Sons, Cambridge 1906), pp. 191–216.

[25] Wilson (1995), p. 72.

[26] Daems and H. Van Der Wee, 'The Rise of Managerial Capitalism' in Tilly, *The Growth of Large Scale Enterprise in Germany since the Middle of the Nineteenth Century* (Martinus Nijhoff, Leiden, the Netherlands, Boston 1974), p. 145.

large public firms. Their production was consistently compatible and in many occasion complementary, as smaller companies were and still are producing parts of the machinery or hardware that is later built into a car, a motorcycle, a train or an engine that larger companies would construct and export to the world. Therefore, interestingly enough the notion of cooperation became a distinctive feature that marked the coexistence of firms of various sizes too. Family firms found their way into the absolute core of Germany's production and export activity by integrating their expertise and specialisation into the actual planning of public companies; Germany's exports are to a great extent the impressive result of the cooperation between its large, middle and small firms as well as of the consistency in their production and exportation orientation.

In the UK, despite some synergies, the two types of companies usually play in different leagues that rarely transcend each other. Usually, and of course every rule has its fewer or more abundant exceptions, private limited and public limited companies in the UK appeal to different markets and offer a range of products that can rarely be found in competition with each other as they address divergent needs and range of consumers. This is maybe due to the gradual diminishing of manufacturing as the main activity at national level and the emergence of finance and services as the field where the UK can claim international prominence. Germany on the other hand continues to rely heavily on industry and manufacturing and it is still one of the top exporting nations at international level. Among other factors this is attributed to the fact that its small and large businesses have accumulated the knowhow necessary to coordinate their production into manufactured and industrial goods which are later exported to other markets. 'The very large number of small and medium sized private companies still run by their founders and their families with an extraordinary record of sophistication and export orientation'[27] remains an unusual feature of German business culture.

## Turbulence in the Twentieth Century

The great turbulence of the beginning of the twentieth century naturally had a profound impact on German companies and corporate behavioural patterns as well; the political, economic, societal and military turmoil of that time that led to the eruption of the First World War affected every aspect of public life and activity, and business would not be an exception.

---

27 Hampden, T.C. and F. Trompenaars, *The Seven Cultures of Capitalism: Value Systems for Creating Wealth in the United States, Britain, Japan, Germany, France, Sweden, and the Netherlands* (Doubleday, New York 1993), p. 230.

The tight linkages between the state, the banks and business would not only survive this challenging period of time but they would emerge rather stronger. Business patterns and governance models would therefore avoid reform on a more liberal direction as cartelisation would further entrench itself into the German business world as a response to the critical conditions of that time and the demands of a war. Due to the very special conditions that a world war entails, German business did not only avert any possibility of reform but experienced a further consolidation of the coordinated practices that marked so distinctively the previous years as well. In 1914 Germany experienced supply problems, effectively due to the British blockade which was imposed on that year. Despite the blockade Germany did manage to receive supplies of certain products from 'Sweden [which] kept on delivering substantial quantities of foodstuff, iron ore and wood pulp which became a substitute for cotton in the German powder and explosives industry. Norway provided non ferrous metals, Holland farm produce. During the war imports fell to 40% of the pre-war level'.[28] To deal with this anomalous situation the country established the War Raw Materials Department in the same year. Although they 'controlled raw materials through Germany, fixed maximum prices, allocated raw materials and developed substitutes, the raw materials corporations led by industrialists were responsible for the acquisition, control and distribution of those materials which were particularly important for the war effort'.[29] Industrial companies found themselves not only in close cooperation with each other to build the goods necessary for the war but also with the government. The pattern of industrial relations that had clearly been shaped in the previous century was therefore solidified by the war and the need to rally the country's industrial might behind the war efforts. The industry already accustomed in coordination, cooperation, synergies and tight regulation felt comfortable in an environment that bound companies together among themselves or with the government. That was reflected also in the corporate governance of the companies in question which passed through the war relatively unaffected with a similar mix of board representation on the part of the banks, institutional shareholders, the government and founding family among others. In fact, 'in providing goods for the war economy government and industry worked closely together to an extent

[28] Braun, H.J., *The German Economy in the Twentieth Century, The German Reich and the Federal Republic* (Routledge, London 1990), p. 25.

[29] Ibid., p. 26.

which might justify the use of the term "symbiosis"'.[30] The term is quite indicative of the level of links between private and public sector which is undoubtedly impressive and demonstrates that a more coordinated model of economy involving extensive links between the main private and public actors of the economy is deeply rooted in German history, economy and society. It is only natural that the latter will throw its weight on the shaping and the formation of the model of corporate governance that the country would gradually give birth to. This model could only express the balances shaped within the country and serve Germany's strengths, interests and aspirations effectively. It cannot be viewed devoid of its historical, economic and societal context as it is the outcome of the essentially political developments that have marked the country in the last couple of centuries. This also betrays why Germany is not an exception to the rule which sees countries faithfully adhering to their respective corporate governance models, which being the by-products of a long process of historical developments embody in a genuine way the main principles and values transcending the various elements of the society in question.

That decade would leave its imprint on Germany as its military defeat accompanied by the loss of international markets, the impairment in its infrastructure and the demands on the part of the victors for reparations had a devastating effect on its economy. The Treaty of Versailles which institutionalised the victors' demands with high interest rates suffocated the economy of the defeated nation which was crippled by high inflation, mass unemployment and lack of financing. The external interventions that aimed at guaranteeing the payment of the instalments on time but prevented swift industrial recovery that would place into peril the fragile growth in competing nations, added insult to injury of the defeated country. However, within that grim context, companies which

> had invested in managerial organisations before 1914 entered the Weimar Republic in relatively powerful positions. They had been accorded preferential treatment in the award of contracts by wartime military procurement offices. The large profits realised from those contracts as well as their already substantial accumulated earnings provided them with investment funds or at least the capacity to borrow from abroad at a time when the rest of the industry was financially constrained.[31]

---

[30] Dietmar, P., *Die Deutsche Wirtschaft in der Zweischenkriegszeit* (Steiner, Wiesbaden 1977), p. 78.

[31] Turner, Jr, H., *German Big Business and the Rise of Hitler* (Oxford University Press, Oxford 1985), p. 10.

Those enterprises used their resources to 'take shares in other enterprises thus creating industrial concerns … in which a holding company held long term shareholdings in a number of member firms that maintained their legal identities but combined some of their resources and coordinated certain dimensions of their activities'.[32] This guaranteed that the companies that survived with a certain level of liquidity the ruins of the war would comprise a part of an institutional network that yet again encouraged coordination on a concern basis.

Another central feature of this period was the cross-shareholdings among the different companies which formed the membership of the concern. The cross-participations in the shareholding of the businesses that formed a part of the network not only guaranteed cooperation but also organised synergies and the existence of influential shareholders with a dynamic presence of the boards. The balance of power reflected in this institutional arrangement was reflected both at the level of management and boards; the German post-First World War boards would be homogeneous in the sense that there was an evident element of cross-shareholding.

## The Second World War: Strengthening the Cartels and 'Corporate Democracy'

The period that followed the First World War and led into the Second World War is well documented, as it was without any doubt one of the most important historical periods not only for Germany but for the entire world; the result of the most destructive military confrontation in history was simply devastating, with dozens of millions of lives lost. In addition, millions of people had to endure the pain of having been forcefully displaced or homeless while infrastructure and industry were destroyed at an unprecedented level. In the aftermath of the war, the notion of management as employed by Germany both at national and at corporate level became the focus of increased attention on the part of the Allies, who partially attributed to it the policies that eventually led to both wars. The Nazis had concentrated all powers to their central authority as they managed to create an utterly totalitarian state that controlled most aspects of public life while adopting intrusive techniques to monitor the privacy of the population as well. That lead not only to a crude and widespread abuse of human rights as the latter were firmly redefined after the war, but also to a strong central government which through the concentration

[32] O'Sullivan (2000), p. 238.

of powers and establishment of tight controls over the private and public aspects of social activities managed to intensify the country's efforts to re-militarise itself and re-engage into a war of international dimensions, aspirations and reach. In Nazi Germany the already concentrated industrial sector provided a fertile ground for its further coordination by the Third Reich as it was preparing for war. The preparation for war 'led to strengthening of linkages among companies through the Nazi policy of enforced cartelisation followed by their system of main committees and industrial rings … the Nazis transformed the economy's traditional sectors by forcing many smaller companies to integrate their industrial operations with those of the larger combines'.[33] 'The authoritarian hand of the Nazi state also intervened to shape the skill formation system by integrating the apprenticeship training structures in the *handwerk* sector with industrial needs thus laying the foundation for the modern German system of apprenticeship'.[34] In addition, the National Socialist government left its stamp on corporate governance, and in a quite ironic and profoundly unintentional way it influenced the current state of affairs in Germany's corporate governance model. The National Socialists reformed the corporate governance system in their attempt to consolidate their grip on the country's industrial sector by essentially introducing a fiduciary duty towards stakeholders; and if that sounds as an all-encompassing corporate strategy to embrace the various components of the company and to unite them into the common cause of corporate well-being, it has to be clarified that the agenda was very different. The *Reich* was included within the definition of stakeholders[35] and therefore what today would come under the title 'corporate democracy', at that historical point was definitely anything but that. It banned voting by mail, and forced shareholders who could not vote in person to register their holdings with banks and entrust banks with proxy voting rights. This bestowed the large banks with voting control over much of the German large corporate sector. The *Reich* then took control of the banks.

---

33 Dore, R., W. Lazonick and O'Sullivan, 'Varieties of Capitalism in the Twentieth Century' (1999) 15 *Oxford Review of Economic Policy* 4, p. 107.

34 McKitrick, F., *The Stabilisation of the Mittelstand: Artisans in Germany from National Socialism to the Federal Republic, 1939–1953* (unpublished phd thesis, Columbia University).

35 Morck and L. Steier, *The Global History of Corporate Governance, An introduction* (National Bureau of Economic Research, Cambridge, MA 2005), p. 9, available on www.nber.org/papers/w11062.pdf.

## The Marshall Plan and the Beginning of the EEC

The lessons from the First World War were learned, and the Allies not only refrained from founding a system of reparations similar to the one introduced by the Treaty of Versailles but insisted on putting into place a massive financial and economic aid in the form of the Marshall Plan. The Marshall Plan reshaped Europe and Germany in particular, contributing in a determining manner to its reintroduction into the international markets; 'West Germany's economic and political revival is hardly imagined without the Marshall Plan'.[36] And while that post-First World War political error was rectified and the Allies shifted their position from repayments into aid, their focus was shifted to management. The management of the country was reformed as the Nazis were removed from power, a new Basic Law was enacted with human rights at the forefront of its provisions and (West) Germany was anchored within the European Steel and Coal Community at the beginning and the European Economic Community (EEC) afterwards. Having created an institutional framework that placed its crucial steel industry (for military conflicts) under a common European institutional roof, Germany was steadily leaving behind its lethal past and moving into advanced forms of European integration that would enhance its economic and political ties with the other Western European nations, allaying the fears that the painful experience of the past could be repeated in the future. And while democratisation and Europeanisation in the form of further integration within the EEC was actively pursued by consecutive governments of both Social Democrats and Christian Democrats origin, paving the way for further reform, business was not subjected to reforms of the same intensity.

## Coordination, Protectionism and the Cold War

The system of cartelisation that entailed a high level of coordination, synergies and cross-participations in the shareholding of a variety of companies on the basis of tight links between industry and government, was thought to have also contributed significantly to the two world wars. It enabled Germany to avoid competition from abroad and therefore to shield its national industry from external pressures which could have either liberalised it or impaired its ability to engage in mass production of

---

[36] Abelshauser, W., 'West German Economic Recovery 1945-1951: A Reassessment' (1982) 135 *Three Banks Review*, The Royal Bank of Scotland Group, p. 45.

machinery which was crucial for the wars. It also permitted the country to endure the devastating impact of the wars in its economy and to regain high levels of production in due course. Furthermore, it created a network of tightly linked enterprises that were difficult to penetrate or acquire. The existence of influential shareholders and significant blockholders guaranteed that foreign takeovers and acquisitions were relatively rare within the German corporate context. In simple words, along with the democratisation of the political system of the country, the Allies seemed to be very interested in the democratisation at the level of corporate governance as well and with that the focus was placed on relaxing the intensity of links that bind companies, banks and the government into a common network. That was crucial so as to prevent any future concerted effort to provide industrial support to heavily aggressive military plans or aspirations. However, as Germany was increasingly democratised, gradually setting aside fears that it would re-emerge as the epicentre of yet another world war, and as it was effectively re-establishing itself as an active member of the EEC subject to its jurisdiction and in close cooperation with the other member states, the pressure to pass from coordination into market control was gradually waning. A factor which contributed significantly to that was the Cold War which rapidly changed the priorities of the Allies who viewed Germany with a renewed sense of trust, more as an ally at the forefront of the antagonism with the Soviet Union rather than a country whose model of corporate governance posed a serious challenge to Western security. In this context, despite the radical reshaping of the country's foreign policy and internal institutional and political architecture and constitutional setting, corporate governance would remain, if not intact, at least relatively unreformed.

The German model of corporate governance as it was analysed above would remain distinctively German even after the war and way into the post-war era. In this context many of the major German industrial companies on which the rapid post-war growth was based

> were those that became dominant before World War II and prime vestiges of pre-World War II managerial control – namely inter-company shareholding networks and bank-industry relations (as shareholders, as supervisory board members, and most importantly as trustees for their depositors' shares) – remained strong in the post-war decades … and played a role in insulating German enterprises from market control.[37]

[37] O'Sullivan (2000), p. 240.

In Germany, 'the most important source of financial commitment for the corporate sector in the post war era was the access of the major industrial enterprises to internally generated funds which rendered most of them relatively independent of external sources of finance'.[38] Therefore, the cross-shareholdings, the respective presence at board level and the neatly shaped links between companies would continue uninterrupted throughout the twentieth century.

> In 1960 non-financial enterprises accounted for 35.7% of total assets held in West Germany in the form of shares, making them by far the largest stockholder group[39] … in 1984 non-financial enterprises held 36.1% of shares issued by German enterprises.[40]

> Unlike the US experience there was no sustained movement of populism against financial centralisation and centralised control. Organised cartel-like competition prevailed among business groups; labour was incorporated into the system, given strong protections in job security, in social security, voice on the boards and a strong political party in the national democracy.[41]

## Employee Participation, a Crucial Difference from the Anglo–American Model of Corporate Governance

The organisation of labour into work councils and the establishment of a system of codetermination which embodies the enhanced status of labour within the context of the German corporation, probably constitute the most distinctive features of the German corporate governance system. The turmoil and the previous period of

> conflict led Germany to seek a 'middle way' between unbridled capitalism and strong socialism … labour leaders sought to be represented on the boards partly to convince the Allies not to dismantle Germany's coal and steel industry by asserting that labour would constrain the wartime industrialists via positions on the firm's supervisory boards.[42]

---

[38] Esser, J., 'Bank Power in West Germany Revised' (1990) 13 *West European Politics* 4, p. 17; and Edwards, J. and K. Fischer, *Banks, Finance and Investment in Germany* (Cambridge University Press, Cambridge 1994), p. 228.

[39] Ibid., p. 182.

[40] Ibid., p. 180.

[41] Gourevitch, A.P. and J. Shinn, *Political Power and Corporate Control* (Princeton University Press, Princeton NJ 2005), p. 161.

[42] Roe, J.M., *Political Determinants of Corporate Governance, Political Context, Corporate Impact* (Oxford University Press, Oxford 2006), pp. 29 and 30.

In fact Mark Roe suggests that the 'ultimate reason for the prevalence of social democracy may have been a history of war and turmoil during the first half of the 20th century in the core civil law countries'.[43] The system in question enhances the position of labour within the corporate context in multiple ways. Apart from their supervisory powers granted to labour on the basis of their ability to appoint members of the supervisory board, codetermination 'may serve as a channel transmitting crucial information to employee representatives, which puts employees in the position to act early and improves their bargaining position'.[44] The place reserved for labour within the administrative structure of the German company serves as the red line that utterly separates the US and UK corporate governance model with the German one. Roe has argued that 'shareholder primacy could be inefficient when an industry is concentrated because the shareholders of a monopolist will gain part of the consumer surplus while according to macroeconomic theory another part of it will be completely lost to society'.[45] As analysed extensively in this book, the so-called Anglo-Saxon model with its variations remains instinctively faithful to the principle of shareholder primacy by recognising an almost sacred right of property to the shareholders; the latter are viewed not only as the exclusive owners of the company but importantly enough they also form its exclusive membership. Despite a reform of English company law to encompass a more stakeholder-friendly terminology within the framework of the new section 172 of the Companies Act 2006, the core of the English company law model remains anchored on the basic principle of shareholder primacy, to the degree that any shift to an approach based on a stakeholder-orientated approach remains wishful thinking. In this context as it was explained in Chapters 3 and 4, both the English and the American corporate governance models may have evolved towards a direction that blurs the line between shareholder primacy and managerial domination, but they remained firm on one point: labour remains an externality to the business. Therefore, its presence at board level is not justified as it would not reflect corporate reality. Any attempt to propose even minimal reform at that level met stiff resistance on the part of business and legislature, as a more stakeholder-friendly approach remains

---

43 Roe, 'Legal Origins, Politics, and Modern Stock Markets' (2006) 120 *Harvard Law Review*, p. 462.

44 Gelter, M., 'The Dark Side of Shareholder Influence: Toward A Holdup Theory of Stakeholders in Comparative Corporate Governance' (2008) *Discussion Paper* 17 (Harvard Law School, Cambridge MA), p. 59.

45 Roe, 'The Shareholder Wealth Maximisation Norm and Industrial Organisation' (2001) 149 *University of Pennsylvania Law Review*, p. 2066.

foreign and largely incompatible with the current English or American model. There are other countries in Europe which employ a model of corporate governance which adopts a more inclusive approach towards labour; France or Italy are examples. However, Germany would stand on its own, with a system of employee participation and involvement at top corporate level that amounts to the full incorporation of labour into the administration of the company and along with it a clear stakeholder parameter into corporate governance. In this sense the German model of corporate governance remains unique as it has created an institutional framework that proved to be particularly accommodating of all the network of actors that form the essential elements of the German economic model as a whole. Labour and creditors (mainly banks) have been effectively represented at the level of the supervisory board, creating in effect a company with a dual board system whose composition reflects the complex realities and the network of actors which shaped corporate Germany. The concept of social codetermination 'basically revolves around the idea of works councils (*Betriebsräte*) a system where ordinary workers are actively involved in structuring their day to day environment in personal and social matters'.[46]

It is important to note that the system which has guaranteed an increased level of employee participation and the emergence of labour as one of the actual parameters of corporate governance, has historically evolved on the basis of cross-party support. The enhanced employee participation was upheld by Social Democrats and Christian Democrats alike, guaranteeing the continuous support of the parties which formed the backbone of the governmental coalitions that have ruled the country, especially from the Second World War and onwards. Already 'before the First World War, codetermination was developed by both liberal and Christian theorists as a process necessitated by industrialisation and as an acceptable alternative to revolutionary employee practices'.[47] Cross-party support ensured the continuity of the scheme, as it removed the risk of it evolving into the pet project of one of the parties that would soon be unravelled by the other when it was elected to power. It also contributed to achieving the universality of its acceptance not only by business but crucially by the society at large. It was therefore increasingly viewed as an aspect inherent not only in German corporate governance but also in

---

[46] Grossfeld B. and U. Lehmann, 'Management Structures and Workers' Codetermination in Germany with European Perspectives' (1994) 1 *Corporate Law Development Series*, p. 41.

[47] Raiser, T., 'The Theory of Enterprise Law in the Federal Republic of Germany' (1988) *American Journal of Comparative Law*, p. 117.

German culture. It underlined the more inclusive approach taken by the German business which was purely reflective of the concessionary approach on the basis of which the German corporation is shaped and founded. It also seemed to assume a central position in the institutional culture of a country which traditionally – and even more decisively after the Second World War – placed consent in the core of its political objectives. A large nation organised on a federal basis that maintained certain elements of heterogeneity with a recent troubled past was determined to proceed on the basis of an approach that would link its different components into a consensual effort to achieve growth and prosperity. Within this framework, employee participation found the fertile ideological, political and societal ground to flourish and become part of the national model of corporate governance, emblematic of the new post-war Germany and its 'social economy model'. The latter was rooted in

> Catholic philosophy of social ethics … as well as Protestant ethics … where distribution and the protection of the individual in a community were the focal point … the Church's answer to the problem of the alienation of the worker in the nineteenth century was the strong source for the intellectual basis of the Christian Democratic Party and the Christian Social Union in Bavaria. Together with the traditional orientation of the Social Democrats to workers as their prime voters … [they] produced an orientation in which social elements and collective approaches gained importance.[48]

An economic model which was shaped to a great extent by a tradition of enhanced state intervention in the economy, accompanied by governing parties whose ideological identity was compatible to an inclusive agenda, was a favourable environment for enhanced employee participation in the corporate context.

## The Works Councils Act of 1920 and Codetermination

The Works Councils Act of 1920 was the first important legislative text concerning social codetermination. It was amended in 1922 by the Power of Work Councils to Appoint Members to the Supervisory Board Act, which promoted exactly what its unusually long title signalled; the appointment of members of the supervisory board by the work councils. This was the first important legislative text that involved the appointment of a part of the membership of one of the two boards – the supervisory

---

[48] Siebert, H., *The German Economy, Beyond the Social Market* (Princeton University Press, Princeton NJ 2005), pp. 24–5.

one – by the work councils, which means the employees. It was an initial but very significant step from a legal and symbolic point of view, which paved the way for employee participation at the supervisory board level. The Act survived for twelve years as it was repealed by the Nazis in 1934, and the subject remained largely off the political agenda until the foundation of the Federal Republic of Germany – effectively West Germany – in 1949. The latter brought labour and its main concerns within the public agenda in its effort to break from the past and re-establish the entire bundle of rights removed by Hitler on a more solid and concrete basis. Within this framework labour rights in general and employee participation on boards in particular assumed a central position in the legislative list of priorities. The country was not only smashing its links with the past but it was also struggling to reform its economy and society on a basis that would make a repetition of the previous era simply impossible. With the support of the Allied powers it was embarking on the plan to re-establish itself as a prosperous nation, and for that the development of its industrial capacity served as a necessary precondition. All components of the German society were needed to rally behind that cause. Labour was therefore a crucial element in that equation. In this context the Works Council Constitution Act passed in 1952 (*Betriebsverfassungsgesetz*); a year before, the *Montag-Mitbestimmungsgesetz* Act of 1951 provided for parity employee representation at supervisory level. The Works Council Constitution Act of 1952 largely re-established the links with the pro-war situation concerning the work councils by once again breaking with the Nazi period; the Act in question provided the main legislative framework in which employee participation evolved in the country even up to today. Section 76 established the rule of one-third employee participation on the supervisory board which was reformed in 2004 by the One Third Participation Act (*Drittelbeteiligungsgesetz*). Nowadays the 1952 Act 'no longer contains the provisions regarding one third employee participation at supervisory board level but deals exclusively with matters relating to the works councils … in practical terms the one third participation regime did not change in 2004, it is now only regulated under the One Third Participation Act of 2004'.[49]

Interestingly enough, despite the evident existence of the necessary theoretical, philosophical and legislative background that enabled the development of the relevant schemes on the basis of cross-party support

---

[49] Du Plessis, J.J., B. Großfeld, C. Luttermann, I. Ingo, O. Sandrock and M. Casper, *German Corporate Governance in International and European Context*, 2nd edn (Springer, Heidelberg, Dordrecht, London, New York 2012), p. 153.

from almost the entire political spectrum, the Allies played also a significant role in forging such a regime in the German corporate landscape. As mentioned above, the Allies were determined to avoid the mistakes made after the First World War and therefore avoided the imposition of retaliatory payments that would leave the country on its knees and undermine any future prospective for peace and cooperation. Apart from the large financial aid granted to Germany, there were concerted efforts to democratise corporate Germany. Of course the term assumes its precise content on the basis of the origin of its users. When the USA and the UK talked about the democratisation of the German company, they meant the liberalisation of the regime within which it operated and its openness to market forces. Their plans entailed the abolishment of the networks and the links between industrial units which fuelled the cartelisation of the previous period, insulating the national industry from international competition while ensuring that it could grow uninhibited from global pressures and sustain a military conflict. In this context it is interesting to note that

> the main impetus for supervisory codetermination by employees actually came when the British occupation authorities and German trade unionists were determined to ensure that the German nation should never fall into the dictatorial pattern of the Third Reich. The specific method invented was to make it compulsory for labour and management to work together at the level of the supervisory board (codetermination!) … to ensure that the very strict class distinction that existed in Germany would not emerge again.[50]

The British believed that the incorporation of labour into the administrative structures of the German company would eliminate the possibility of a restive labour creating problems, while it would ensure the administration of the German corporation on a more inclusive basis that would gradually diminish the differences between the different components of the German society. Germany should develop on a peaceful and consensual basis, and the Allies were determined to push for reforms that would guarantee that. It is ironic that the UK at that historical point viewed employee participation as mitigating conflicts stemming from class distinction and as promoting a more inclusive corporation that can evolve on a consensual basis. The UK reacted to the adoption of such a model so fiercely in the following decades that it sank the proposals to create a truly European Company with a single corporate governance model in the framework of the EU later.

---

50 Ibid., p. 155.

Germany had already adopted the dual board structure as early as in 1861 with the Commerce Code. This Code pioneered the establishment of a two-tier structure creating a powerful monitoring institution which was none other than the supervisory board. As noted above, the establishment of the supervisory board at that point of the nineteenth century did not signal an enhanced presence of employees at board level, as the board in question was reserved for shareholders. The structure on the basis of which the German corporation was ran included a notion of increased shareholder control on the management; that was exercised by the supervisory board – an essentially shareholder institution – on the management board. Employee participation on the supervisory board was introduced by the *Montan-Mitbest* Act of 1951 and the *Betriebsverfassungsgesetz* Act of 1952, followed by the 1976 *Mitbestimmungsgesetz* Act. Therefore, despite the fact that the terms 'supervisory board' and 'labour participation' seem to coincide in people's mind and in part of the literature, the truth is that the former did not involve the latter for almost a century. Employee participation was officially introduced to the supervisory board within the political framework of the post-War 1950s after the insistence of the Allies who viewed the creation of a sustainable and inclusive corporate democracy in Germany as a precondition to peace. Of course as explained above, labour involvement was not a foreign concept to German business which was already accustomed to work councils, apprenticeships and closely constructed links with institutions providing technical education, while business was anyway orientated towards a consensual approach in pursuing their affairs. However, an institutionalised involvement in the management of the company was an additional and utterly significant step from a political, economic as well as purely symbolic view which was not initially met with the universality of acceptance that it has assumed today. In fact the whole concept of 'parity employee representation at supervisory level was observed with great scepticism when in 1951 it was forced upon the German population … there was hardly any other statute that had been met with so much rejection and distrust by the legal profession in Germany as the *Montan-MitbestG* of 1951'.[51] The reaction of the management was also one of 'horrified outrage. It predicted that labour representatives would come blundering into management affairs like a herd of bulls in a china shop'.[52] German academia and business viewed it as an intervention

[51] Ibid., p. 164.

[52] Vagts, F.D., 'Reforming the Modern Corporation: Perspectives from the German' (1966) 80 *Harvard Law Review* 23, p. 68.

external to the nature of corporate governance; it was effectively a means to prevent 'revolutionary employee techniques'.[53] In fact, even as codetermination at supervisory level was increasingly accepted by business and academia alike, the reactions did not fade. The 1976 *Mitbestimmungsgesetz* Act was even brought before the Federal Constitutional Court[54] by German companies, who alleged that the Act in question was contrary to certain articles of the Basic Law; more specifically the participation of employees on the supervisory board was supported to be abusing article 14, paragraphs 1 and 2 of the Basic Law on property rights; this referred to the fact that employee participation was viewed as an infringement of the property rights held by shareholders. They were deprived of the full control of the corporation in the case of labour involvement at the top level of the administration of the company. This argument which was brought before the court is very similar to arguments voiced in the UK when debating corporate governance. It is exactly this intrusion within the sphere of the shareholders' property right over the corporation which justifies their exclusive membership and therefore representation at board level that deprives labour codetermination of its legitimate character. Had the court accepted this line of thinking then the German model of corporate governance would have received a rather decisive blow from the inside, and the changes that would have been triggered may have resulted in a model much closer to the English one. However, the Federal Constitutional Court adjudicated differently. The *Mitbestimmungsgesetz* Act of 1976 was 'neither a danger to collective bargaining nor did it prevent the normal functioning of enterprises. Since the final decision within the supervisory board still rested within the shareholder representatives the guarantee of private property was not violated'.[55] Therefore, the Act was found constitutional and along with it the whole model of employee codetermination at the level of supervisory board was found to be compatible with the constitutional rights and traditions of the country. In any case, enough time had passed so as to test the new institution which had already produced a level of stability and a level of cooperation to such a degree that it was becoming a norm that business was increasingly eager to maintain.

---

53 Raiser (1988), p. 120.

54 German Federal Constitutional Court (*BVerfGE*), vol 50, 290, 1979.

55 Weiss, M. and M. Schmidt, *Labour Law and Industrial Relations in Germany* (Kluwer Law International, London 2008), p. 256.

Only three years after that ruling, the Supreme Court in Civil Matters[56] provided yet another ruling which demonstrated that the initial controversy had receded and that matter which was previously controversial was now evolving into an aspect of the legal culture of the country. The court upheld the previous decision of the Federal Constitutional Court and went one step ahead by adjudicating that the 1976 *Mitbestimmungsgesetz* Act had been passed in the public interest. Therefore, when the by-laws of Siemens *AG* were found to violate the Act, this 'was found to be susceptible to constituting a ground to declare the provisions of the By Laws null and void'.[57] The court recognised that this Act

> must be allotted special importance in context of the politics relating to corporations since it represents the result of fundamental decisions reached after years of confrontation … it stretches beyond the interests of the persons immediately affected by it … it does indeed serve the common weal of the community … it aims at the entire national economy.[58]

It is interesting that the court places emphasis on the significance that the Act has assumed within the framework of the 'politics relating to corporations and the fundamental decisions that were related to them'; this statement serves as recognition of the crucial role that the Act has played within the political context explained above. It also signals a shift in the approach on the part of the German legal world towards the Act; as Germany was reaping the benefits of stability and growth, initial reactions were fading and the Act was becoming an integral part of the German society and a landmark of its corporate governance model.

### Wider Stakeholder Participation in the Political Context: Property and the Public Good

The place that the society reserved for a corporate governance model that entailed the institutional recognition of the existence of a variety of actors alongside the shareholders was also reflective of an ideological background that differed to that in the UK to a particularly noticeable extent. The wording of the constitution of Germany – the Basic Law – clearly underlines the philosophical divergence between itself and the UK.

---

56 German Federal Supreme Court in Civil Matters (BGHZ) volume 83, 106, 1982.

57 Du Plessis et al. (2012), p. 166.

58 Ibid.

Article 14(2) of the Basic Law on 'property, inheritance and expropriation' states that 'property entails obligations. Its use shall also serve the public good'.[59] While the constitution clearly recognises a right to property as most constitutional texts in the West do, it sets certain limitations to it. These stem from the mere acceptance that property does indeed entail obligations and most importantly that its use shall also serve the public good. The fact that a public good dimension is added to the right of property is of immense significance. It signals an approach that views public good as integral to the right of property; it also renders the public good and the interests of the society as the constitutional limitations to the right of property. Therefore, despite the latter being recognised and protected at the highest possible level in a given legal order, it is accompanied with a clearly defined limitation: the public good. An essentially private right is constitutionally safeguarded as long as its existence does not undermine what is perceived as the public good. The antithesis of this constitutional arrangement with the respective in the UK is astonishing. From the era of Magna Carta, the UK's rich legal tradition was based on the sacredness of the right to property. The essentially private right to property assumed from an early stage a central position within the legal system of the country. The phrase 'an Englishman's home is his castle' embodies the profoundness of the right in question in the nation's mind; the home is the castle of its owner and no one can enter unless explicitly permitted by the owner. Property is a sacred right which should be safeguarded against interventions. Similarly, at the level of company law as it was explained above, the importance ascribed to property is materialised into the exclusivity of the rights granted to shareholders. The latter owe their privileges which amount to exclusive membership to their status as 'owners' of the company. They hold a property right and therefore, they can exercise a level of influence on the corporation that could be justified by their 'ownership' of the corporation; the latter naturally does not include any other actors aside the owners. Furthermore, since the company is owned by the holders of the property right, it is deemed to be a private affair in which the state should not interfere; the contractual character of the company which is viewed as an agreement between private individuals devoid of any social parameter that renders any state interference in the form of excessive legislation for example unnecessary, is inherent in this model. The contractual nature of this model is fuelled by the centrality of property in

---

[59] Basic Law for the Federal Republic of Germany, Grundgesetz, available at www.iuscomp.org/gla/statutes/GG.htm#14.

the English legal order and defines the character and naturally the membership of the English company. Similarly, a different perception of the same right in Germany signals a different approach and sets the ideological and consequently the legislative context within which the German company has been shaped. Property shall be used in serving the public good; that means that a castle-like approach that renders property unapproachable to the King or the legislator is anything but dominant in Germany. The notion of public good has to be accommodated when regulating property and that at the company law level brings more stakeholders within the broader corporate picture; this helps to mitigate the 'divergence between sectors of society about the purpose of companies'.[60] The grip that shareholders hold on the company is loosened by the inclusion of other actors within the corporate context; employee participation at board level is the embodiment of such a principle. Moreover, the belief that the company has to contribute to what is broadly defined as 'public good' is inherent in the article in question, and reflected by the theoretical background behind the German company: the concession theory.

## The German Concession Model of Companies

We analysed the concession theory in Chapter 2, and here we revise the argument. The concession theory views the company as an expression of a concession granted by the state to the entity that is the corporation; the state granted to it the privileges of legal personality and limited liability, fuelling its emergence as one of the most successful social and legal experiments in human history. Since companies owe their historic success to the concessions granted consciously by the state, they ought to return part of the profit to the society at large. In fact, the *Aktiengesetz* of 1937 contained the rule that

> the two tier system is not designed for the benefit of shareholders only. It is there also to protect the public interest and it is normal to say that members of the management board do not act in the interests of the shareholders only. By law, members of the management board are expected and entitled to carry out their duties for the benefit of shareholders, employees and the society as a whole.[61]

---

[60] Charkam, J., *Keeping Better Company, Corporate Governance Ten Years On*, 2nd edn (Oxford University Press, Oxford 2008), p. 32.

[61] Mäntysaari (2005), p. 253.

Although the current *Aktiengesetz* lacks a similar provision, it still 'applies as a general uncodified principle'[62] supported by the spirit of the Basic Law and the aforementioned provision. In English company law that would have been dealt with on the basis of a clearly self-regulative approach; the corporate social responsibility initiatives are prominent in this context yet not legally binding. In Germany, a notion of social responsibility is inherent in property rights and therefore in company law as well. This signifies a different starting point for the two jurisdictions which betrays a different ideological approach and a divergent constitutional arrangement, which is reflected in a different institutional setting and ultimately a different corporation. This is why corporate governance serves as the exception to the rule that globalisation brings harmonisation of the legal standards at all levels; by embodying principles that remain distinctively rooted in the national history and culture, corporate governance has resisted globalisation, at least to its core that seems to remain national.

## THE INSTITUTIONAL ARCHITECTURE OF THE GERMAN COMPANY

### The *Gesellschaft mit beschränkter Haftung* (*GmbH*)

German company law distinguishes basically between partnerships on the one hand and corporations on the other hand. This section will focus on corporations. The *GmbH* is the most common company form in Germany. Its title translates into 'company with limited liability', and it corresponds to the respective private limited company within the UK context. This corporate form appeared in Germany at the end of the nineteenth century, and the respective developments that had already taken place in the UK. However, in the UK this form, albeit by far the most popular form of incorporation, mainly involves small and medium-sized businesses which on many occasions are family-run. Therefore, in the UK there appears to be a link between the corporate form in question and the size of the company. In Germany, this link appears to be less evident; *GmbH* are not confined to small family businesses as they may hold a payroll which includes more than 500 employees. Thus, the link between size and corporate form in Germany appears to be distinctively less discernible than the respective in the UK. The *GmbH* may be formed

---

62 Ibid.

by one or more natural or legal persons for any purpose deemed lawful. According to paragraph 2(1) of the German Private Limited Liabilities Companies Act (*GmbHG*), the statutes must be executed in a notarised form by its founders for it to be incorporated; the procedure is more formalised than the one complied with by the English limited liability companies. Within the framework of the latter the submission of the memorandum of association and articles – which may be the standard ones – to the Registrar will suffice. The purpose of the *GmbH* will have to be set out clearly (*GmbHG* paragraphs 1 and 3), while in the UK section 31 of the Companies Act 2006 now provides for the ability of the private limited liability companies to operate on the basis of an all-purpose object clause. The institutional structure of the *GmbH* will include the shareholders' meeting and the management board. However, the *Drittelbeteilungsgesetz* 2004 requires *GmbH* with 500–2000 employees to set up a supervisory board as well. The employees are widely represented at the level of the supervisory board as they appoint one-third of its members. If the *GmbH* has a payroll which includes more than 2000 employees then the employees will acquire an even greater say in the administration of the company as their representatives will now occupy half of the supervisory board's seats, on the basis of the *Mitbestimmungsgesetz* 1976. This is a clear demonstration of the system of codetermination on the basis of which German companies are effectively operating. The principle embodies the notion that the larger the company is, the more extensive and therefore influential the involvement of the employees at the top of the governance hierarchy should be. The company must have one or more managing directors (paragraph 6, *GmbHG*). The managing directors are appointed by a shareholder resolution passed with a simple majority of the votes cast (paragraph 46(5) and paragraph 47), unless the articles provide otherwise or a codetermination act requires that the managing directors be appointed by supervisory board (mainly for companies in the steel and coal sector). As far as the directors are concerned, their principal duty is to manage the company with the skill and diligence of a conscientious businessman (paragraph 43(1)). The German law permits the ratification of the breaches of duties of directors on the basis of a resolution as long as they refrain from voting on the resolution in question (paragraph 47(4)). This provision is very similar to the respective section in the Companies Act 2006 in the UK. Section 239(4) explicitly permits the ratification of directors' duties, again on the basis of a resolution. The directors may vote on the resolution in question but their vote cannot be taken into account; this provision constitutes one of the basic reforms initiated by the Act in question to the previous law.

## The *Aktiengesellschaft* (*AG*)

The *AG* is the German public limited liability company. One of its central and most distinctive features is the existence of a two-tier system that functions as the landmark characteristic of the German corporate governance model in general. As explained before, the latter consists of the management board entrusted to run the everyday business of the company and assume all the strategic decisions relating to its policy-making and future plans, while the supervisory board does exactly what its title reveals; it supervises the executive. Therefore, its basic function is purely of controlling nature; it acts as a monitoring mechanism which ensures an enhanced level of transparency and control on the powers of directors. The *Drittelbeteiligungsgesetz* renders the establishment of supervisory boards compulsory in all public companies except from those who employ less than 500 individuals. This is further reflective of the role of size within the German corporate framework; it is not unusual in Germany for public companies to have fewer employees in their payroll than private limited companies. This is rather rare in the UK, where size is a factor of determining importance when choosing the form of incorporation, and the distinction exists between family businesses and small and medium enterprises choosing to incorporate as public limited companies while larger firms in greater need of larger amounts of capital opt for becoming private limited companies. In Germany however this does not appear to be the case. The attractiveness of the relatively less complicated legislative framework applying to *GmbH* rather than to *AG* may make the incorporation with the form of the former more attractive than the latter. In this context, size does not appear to enjoy the same status as the distinguishing factor as it does in the UK.

### The management board

The first of the two boards of the two-tier system is the management board. Every German public company must have a management board according to paragraphs 33, 36(1) and 37(4), *AktG*. The members of the management board are appointed by the supervisory board for renewable periods not exceeding five years. But if the articles do not provide otherwise, companies who share capital exceeding €3 million must have at least two persons on the management board (paragraph 76, *AktG*). The appointment of the members of the management board is subject to two conditions; only natural persons can become members of the management board, and cross-membership on both the management and the supervisory boards is prohibited on the basis of paragraphs 76(3) and 105(1) respectively. The members of the management board are appointed by the supervisory board for a period of five years, according to paragraph 84(1), *AktG*. This can be contrasted with the Companies Act 2006 in the UK which does not set a specific term after the expiration of which the directors of the company should withdraw from the executive. The terms of office are left unregulated, reflecting the liberty of the members of the company to shape those arrangements on the basis of their agreement; in addition to that, the UK Corporate Governance Code provides for the annual re-election of board members. This approach is absolutely consistent with the contractual view of the company as a purely private affair whose parties are in a position to agree among them on how the company is going to be run. The same rule applies to the composition of the boards in the UK companies which is left within the discretion of the shareholders; a change of attitude is detected only in relation to listed companies which are subject to the UK Corporate Governance Code that as analysed in Chapter 4 requires the inclusion of non-executive directors on the board. Despite the 'comply or explain' approach adopted by the Code, it should be noted that this requirement is not set by legislation.

**The supervisory board: appointing and dismissing directors and the consensus model of corporate governance, in contrast with the UK**

In contrast to the *GmbH*, both the appointment of directors and their removal from the board are not made exclusively by the shareholders, but by the supervisory board (paragraph 84, *AktG*). This forms an essential difference between the two corporate forms but it also underlines the substantial divergence between the German public company and the English plc. The supervisory board exercises the functions which form the core of the shareholders' powers in the UK; the ability to appoint and remove directors forms the superior form of shareholder control as it embodies the notion of shareholder supremacy since it is clearly an aspect of their property right. Since they own the company and they are legally established as its exclusive members, they have the natural right to appoint and remove management. This substantial right integral in the notion of shareholder primacy which is dominant in the UK is now transferred to the supervisory board within the context of the German *AG*. Taking into account that the supervisory board is comprised to a considerable degree by employees and other individuals who will be naturally lacking the capacity of the shareholder, this provision basically entrusts property right-style rights to non-shareholders. That is a clear indication of the more inclusive approach adopted by the German company law which is evident at the level of the governance of companies. It reflects a notion of membership which is significantly wider than the respective in the UK since it entails the granting of rights normally assigned to owners to individuals who do not hold stocks of the company. The adoption of such principle by the UK Parliament would have been a jarring change from the current legislative regime; it would mark a shift in legal and corporate culture of such a magnitude that would render its application if not impossible, then at least greatly controversial.

The supervisory board can remove members of the management board on the basis of 'compelling ground' according to paragraph 84(3), *AktG*. The latter has been interpreted and defined so as to include within its scope mainly the following parameters: 'a gross breach of duties, incompetence to execute management functions in an orderly fashion and a vote of no-confidence from the general meeting unless the vote of no-confidence is obviously unfounded'.[63] The necessity to invoke a 'compelling ground' so as to remove a director from the management board could result in placing a limit on the supervisory board's potential intention to remove a member of the management due to pure disapproval of his views. Therefore, the rationale behind the 'compelling ground' is to avoid opening the pathway for numerous calls on the part of the supervisory board to remove directors from the management board, just because there is no common ground between the approaches adopted by both sides. Despite the first reading of the aforementioned principle as a limitation placed upon the supervisory board, the fact that what constitutes 'compelling ground' 'is not a closed one'[64] may indeed lead to a different conclusion. The list of factors which comprise the definition of the 'compelling ground' is not in fact an exhaustive one, which clearly leaves enough flexibility in its interpretation and consequently the discretion to the supervisory board essentially to add additional grounds for removal. And if that can potentially lead to increasing the level of monitoring upon the directorial activities and the decision-making, it could also lead to removal of members of the management board by the supervisory one on the basis of disagreement on aspects of company policies or the future strategic planning of the company. This is an essential tool at the hands of a responsible supervisory board which will genuinely act in the best interests of the company; a different agenda may prevail however and that enormous flexibility may be used to simply get rid of members with views which differ from the respective of the

63 Du Plessis et al. (2012), p. 65.
64 Ibid., p. 66.

supervisory board. The German corporate culture based on an inclusive approach founded upon the careful building of consensus among the various components of the company may help to mitigate the differences and use all the available tools responsibly, but this is a system that in practice may place an excessive burden on the shoulders of the management board and potentially not with the best intentions.

Furthermore, within the UK context, shareholders are free to pursue their own personal interests; it is the directors of the company who are under the duty to promote the success of the company in good faith. The right of shareholders to pursue their own personal interest is also proved by the willingness of the English courts to allow shareholders agreements to come into effect. The latter can dictate the behaviour of shareholders at the general meeting by setting in place an agreement on their concerted voting for or against a certain proposal put forward by the management. Directors find it hard to become parties to such agreements taking into account their aforementioned duty which they owe directly to the company. In Germany it is interesting to note that paragraph 53 of the *AktG* provides that

> shareholders owe a duty of loyalty towards the company and other shareholders … for example a shareholder who is also regarded as a primary insider may not take advantage of that information by acquiring or disposing of securities. If he does so he breaches not only insider rules but also his duty of loyalty.[65]

The duty is based both on the case law of the Federal Court of Justice of Germany and on the German Civil Code.[66] In the *ITT*[67] case a minority shareholder managed to sue a majority one for having breached the duty of loyalty that he owed to the company; the court found him liable, forcing him to compensate the company. This constitutes a sort of treatment that would be reserved for directors in the UK and not shareholders. It is highly indicative of their status as the owners of the company in the UK and their respective status as members of the company among other stakeholders in Germany. The former guarantees absolute primacy within the UK context as the company is being run for the interest of its members, and therefore the shareholders are permitted

---

65 Mäntysaari (2005), p. 379.

66 See section 242 of the German Civil Code on the 'Performance in Good Faith': An obligor has a duty to perform according to the requirements of good faith, taking customary practice into consideration. See: www.gesetze-im-internet.de/englisch_bgb/englisch_bgb.html#p0716.

67 BGHZ 65, 15 ITT.

to pursue their agenda. The German approach entrusts shareholders with the duty to pursue the success of the company including its components. In this framework the pursuing of a personal agenda unrelated to the common corporate good enters a grey area which may be in violation of the *AktG*.

The board has the power to represent the company while any violation of internal procedures will not impact on third parties (paragraphs 78 and 82, *AktG*). These provisions are similar with the respective provisions in the UK. Section 161 of the Companies Act 2006 provides for the protection of third parties in case of violation of internal procedures on in case of a non-fulfilment of a requirement introduced internally by the articles of the company. The underlining notion which justifies the relevant provisions in both jurisdictions is the fact that directors are indeed entrusted to represent the company in its relations with third parties. The latter are not required to become fully aware of the entirety of internal procedures that would impact on the ability of directors to act, and become involved within what may be a labyrinth of internal rules, requirements and procedures. This would have significantly impaired commercial transactions as third parties would be required to essentially monitor internal compliance; this would have a grave effect on their willingness to contract and would therefore produce an overall negative effect on trust between parties and trade in general. Therefore, third parties are protected as their involvement in the internal corporate affairs is ruled out in both jurisdictions.

Paragraph 82 of *AktG* lays down a duty to comply with the articles of association and the guidelines given by the supervisory board and the general meeting within their defined powers. The articles of association are much less extensive and detailed than the respective of an English company. This is reflective of the contractual nature of the English company; the articles express the core of this principle as they form the voluntary agreement on the basis of which the members of the company have agreed to pursue its goals and aims. The move towards the model articles that has emerged into a trend lately does not obscure the fact that the constitutional documents of the average English company are wide and detailed enough to embody their agreement on all aspects of the operation of the company. In Germany, the thorough legislation in the form of company law and labour law statutes do not leave the appropriate discretion for such arrangements at the level of the articles of association which cannot deviate from the law and more specifically in this case from the *AG*. Paragraph 23(5) states that the articles may introduce additional provisions only in cases when the issue in question has not been regulated by statute; taking into account that there is concise legislation on most matters, few things are left to be dealt with at the articles level. The German company unlike 'a purely private association … has features of a social institution which assigns non contractual status rights and obligations to its members independent of their will and exchange value in the market … governance involves both externalisation of private interests onto corporatist associations and internalisation of societal interests within the firm'.[68] The Companies Act 2006 in the UK also serves as the limitation to the scope of the articles, but there is more discretion left to the members as to the scope of the articles' provisions on the basis of the Act.

## The Duties of the Board: The 'Interests of the Company'

The basic duty of the members of the board is to act in the interests and for the benefit of the company in good faith.[69] Directors must serve the interest of the company irrespective of whether they were appointed by the supervisory board or elected by shareholders. Their duties are owed to the company whose interest they ought to pursue. The phrase the 'interests of the company' (*Unternehmensinteresse*) is central to the directors' duties. In the context of a company where different constituents enjoy a certain degree of influence on the decision-making process even indirectly, the notion of the 'interests of the company' provides the aim that needs to be met; at this level the similarity with the approach adopted in the UK is more than evident. The difference lies in the definition of the content of the 'interests of the company'. In Germany the definition will reflect the character of the company itself as a more inclusive legal entity, therefore the 'interests of the company' will include 'at a minimum the interests of the employees, the creditors and the shareholders'.[70] Thus, shareholders and stakeholders will comprise the groups whose interests are within the 'interests of the company' that must be served. This reflects a divergent definition of membership in the corporation which apparently is open not only to shareholders but also to stakeholders, at least as far as their interests are included within the 'interests of the company'. The contrast with the UK but also with the USA approach towards this issue is evident; in the UK the directors owe

---

[68] Gospel, H. and A. Pendleton, *Corporate Governance and Labour Management, An International Comparison* (Oxford University Press, Oxford 2005), p. 86.

[69] See section 242, BGB (German Civil Code).

[70] Cahn, A. and D.C. Donald, *Comparative Company Law* (Cambridge University Press, Cambridge 2010), p. 335.

their duties to the company just as in Germany, but although they must pursue the interests – or the success – of the company, the latter is viewed as coinciding with the interests of its exclusive members, the shareholders. The new section 172 of the Companies Act 2006 has introduced a stakeholder approach that does however find its limits to the shareholders' interest, as the interests of the stakeholders may be taken into account in so far as they do not conflict with the respective of the shareholders. Section 417(5)(b) requires quoted companies to provide an annual report which must include information about the companies' policies in relation to the environment, the employees and the community. That, however, does not change the central position adopted by the UK law in relation to the issues in question.

In the USA context, the relevant case law has established a set of principles that diverge from the respective German attitude even further. As explained in Chapter 3, in the USA the duty of directors to act in the 'best interests of the company' has been interpreted to amount to a 'fiduciary duty to the company and its shareholders';[71] the court clarified that the 'directors of a corporation owe a fiduciary duty to the company *and* its shareholders on matters related to the corporation … this duty extends to the stockholders collectively'.[72] This approach appears to be adopted consistently by the USA courts.

> It is well-settled that directors of a corporation owe a fiduciary duty to the corporation and its stockholders … the affairs of corporations are generally entrusted to the exclusive management and control of the board of directors; and there is an inherent obligation, implied in the acceptance of such trust, that they will use their best efforts to promote the interest of the shareholders.[73]

At this level, as analysed in Chapter 3, USA case law differentiates itself even from the UK jurisprudence, which insists that the directorial duties are owed exclusively to the company irrespective of whether this in fact refers to the interests of the shareholders. However, the approach adopted by the German law and the national courts is in contrast to the principles dominant in the USA context.

---

[71] *Central Iowa Power Co-op v Consumers Energy*, 741 NW 2d 822 (2007). See the case at http://ia.findacase.com/research/wfrmDocViewer.aspx/xq/fac.20070919_0000776.IA.htm/qx.

[72] Ibid.

[73] *Storetrax.com Inc. v Gurland* 915 A 2d 991, 1000 (2007). See the case at http://ia.findacase.com/research/wfrmDocViewer.aspx/xq/fac.20070206_0000032.md.htm/qx.

Paragraph 93(1) of *AktG* adds a duty of care and responsibility, clarifying that 'in conducting business, the members of the management board shall employ the care of a diligent and conscientious manager'. The duty of confidentiality is added by paragraph 93(1) *AktG* and made a criminal offence by paragraph 404(1). Paragraph 93(2) states that 'Members of the management board who violate their duties shall be jointly and severally liable to the company for any resulting damage'. Paragraph 93(3) also includes nine additional situations where a director will find himself in breach of duty if found to fulfil the requirements of the provision in question. In any case, the paragraph clarifies that the burden of proof is breached by the directors in question. At this stage it is important to note that the German law on directors' duties is marked by the adoption of the so-called 'business judgement rule'. The latter is incorporated in *AktG* and more specifically in paragraph 93(1)2; the relevant part of the statutes states that the members of the management board 'shall not be deemed to have violated the aforementioned duty if, at the time of taking the entrepreneurial decision, they had *good reason to assume* that they were acting on the basis of adequate information for the benefit of the company'.[74] The rule in question whose inspiration and in fact title has been drew by Anglo-Saxon jurisdictions[75] acts as the borderline between managerial liability and directorial risk-taking and decision-making. The members of the management board are not going to be held liable for decisions that they took on the basis of their reasonable belief that they were acting on the benefit of the company; that would limit the discretion granted to the supervisory board to raise issues of liability in relation to the managerial decisions. Therefore, the directors can be found liable in cases of breach of duty or when they assumed decisions which a reasonable director would not have taken when acting for the benefit of the company. However, decisions that involve a degree of risk that a director has taken on the basis of his reasonable belief that they would contribute to the well-being of the company are unlikely to be penalised. The test of reasonableness assumes a central position within this context as it shapes the delicate limits above which the directors' decisions will give raise to claims or not. Therefore, on the basis of the text of the statutory rule in question, a director will escape liability if he is in a position to prove that his actions have indeed

---

[74] See the English-language version of the *AktG* at www.nortonrose.com/files/german-stock-corporation-act-2010-english-translation-pdf-59656.pdf.

[75] See the ARAG case, BGHZ 135, 244, 1997.

fulfilled the following four requirements; if he has taken an *entrepreneurial decision* in *good faith* while being *reasonably* in conviction that he was acting for the benefit of the company on the basis of previously acquired *appropriate information*. Similar to that, the German Corporate Governance Code states in section 3.8:

> The Management Board and Supervisory Board comply with the rules of proper corporate management. If they violate the due care and diligence of a prudent and conscientious Managing Director or Supervisory Board member, they are liable to the company for damages. In the case of business decisions an infringement of duty is not present if the member of the Management Board or Supervisory Board could reasonably believe, based on appropriate information that he/she was acting in the best interest of the company (Business Judgement Rule).

This approach is very similar to the respective adopted in the USA, which employs the same doctrine under exactly the same name, as explained in Chapter 3.[76] In the USA, with the exceptions of directors having acted in cases of self-dealing or gross negligence, the courts prefer not to interfere irrespective of whether the decision in question has proved to be a successful one or not. In both jurisdictions the element of risk inherent in the decision-making at managerial level would exempt directors from liability even if their behaviour does not meet best practices if they were acting in good faith. In the USA as explained in Chapter 3, the court stated in *Smith v Van Gorkom*[77] that the 'business judgement rule' is 'a presumption that in making a business decision, the directors of a corporation acted on an informed basis, in good faith and in the honest belief that the action taken was in the best interests of the company'. Hence, in this case in the USA the party challenging a board decision as uninformed must rebut the presumption that its business judgement was an informed one. In Germany however, it is the directors who have to prove that they were acting on the basis of adequate information for the benefit of the company. Therefore, despite the fact that the two doctrines are basically identical, the level of protection granted to directors in Germany is in fact lower than the respective under the same doctrine in the USA.

Paragraph 93(1)2 of *AktG* appears to set in place a system of prescribing the limits to directorial liability which is also similar to that established by the respective section 172 of the Companies Act 2006 in

---

76 See *Re Walt Disney Co. Derivative Litigation* 907 A.2d 693 (Del. Ch. 2005).

77 *Smith v Van Gorkom* 488 A.2d 858 (Delaware Supreme Court, 1985).

the UK, albeit in a clearer and more structured manner. This is also consistent with the character of the German jurisdiction as a civil law one in contrast to the common law traditions of the UK, which despite the existence of an enormous Companies Act, has still left a great deal of scope to the courts to interpret its provisions. As analysed in Chapter 4, section 172(1) states that 'the director must act in the way he considers … to promote the success of the company'. Therefore, the law provides for a principally subjective test so as to determine whether a given director has effectively pursued the success of the company or failed to do so. The good faith test remains the main standard against which his actions will be judged. Were the acts of the director performed in good faith for the benefit of the company as a whole? If the reply to the question is positive, the court is more likely to find a director acting in accordance with his statutory duties. Therefore, directors are bound to act bona fide in what they subjectively consider to be the interests of the company.[78] The court will not attempt to determine whether the decision in question has objectively been the best at a given moment for the company. In the UK the question is not whether, viewed objectively by the court, the particular act or omission was in fact in the interests of the company, but whether the director honestly believed that his act was in the interests of the company. The issue is as to the director's state of mind while a test of reasonableness will clearly be taken into account. There is no universal consensus over the precise magnitude of similarity or divergence in the application of the test in question in the UK and Germany, but the approach adopted by Germany appears to be clearer and structured on a more coherent basis; the post-2006 jurisprudence of the English courts is still evolving.

## The *AktG* Derivative Action

In the context of the directors' duties, the right to raise a derivative action is important. It is astonishing to note that the derivative action was only introduced into German corporate law as the new paragraph 148 of the *AktG* in 2005 by the *Gesetz zur Unternehmensintegrität und Modernisierung des Anfechtungsrechts* (*UMAG*). It was only in 2005 that the German law provided for the existence of a 'real' derivative action; the term 'real' refers to the (currently recognised by law) ability of a minority shareholder to bring an action against the management on his own, requesting the paying of damages to the company (a personal right).

---

[78] *Regentcress v Cohen* [2001] 2 BCLC 80.

In order to qualify for a derivative action, the shareholder wishing to raise it needs to meet the quorum requirement of paragraph 148(1) of *AktG*, which states that only shareholders whose aggregate holdings at the time of filing the petition equal or exceed one per cent of the share capital or amount to at least €100,000 can raise the action.

In addition, the shareholders need to prove that they have acquired the shares before they gained knowledge of the alleged breach of a member of the management or supervisory board, or of the alleged damage to the company. The shareholders shall demonstrate that they in vain filed a petition to the company requesting to institute the necessary legal proceedings itself within an appropriate period of time. The shareholders in question should also present evidence that supports the damage suffered by the company because of the gross breaches of law. Finally, the court has to be convinced that no overriding interests of the company exist which would prevent the assertion of such damages claim. The introduction of derivative actions, although surprisingly delayed, demonstrates the willingness of the legislative to increase shareholder protection by forging a more friendly approach to minority shareholder remedies. Despite the positive nature of this first step towards the adoption of a more minority shareholder-friendly attitude, the obstacles towards the successful resort to the remedy in question still exist and are largely related to the suspicion against minority shareholders' remedies in a jurisdiction which was not accustomed to them. The contrast with the UK which boasts a tradition almost two centuries old of derivative actions – with all the restrictions which accompany it, as explained Chapter 4 – is indeed impressive. Due to the widely dispersed shareholding basis of the English public companies and its adherence to shareholder primacy, the country developed a system of minority shareholder protection which with all its deficiencies and hurdles raised mainly by the judicial interpretation of the relevant statutes in the UK, constructed a regime of minorities' protection that emerged as a pattern for many other jurisdictions. In fact La Porta et al. concluded that strong corporate law protection for shareholders led to dispersed shareholding patterns, while weak shareholder protection led to more concentrated shareholders' patterns.[79] With companies which have a more concentrated shareholding and the main shareholders on the board, Germany found that need less imperative, and it responded to that trend with considerable delay. It will

---

[79] La Porta et al., 'Law and Finance' (1998) 106 *Journal of Political Economy*, pp. 1113–55. Also 'Corporate Ownership Around the World' (1999) 54 *Journal of Finance* pp. 471–517.

take years until a full-scale minority shareholder protection culture is forged in the country, but the introduction of derivative actions, even on the basis of restrictive criteria, only seven years ago was the first evidently important step.

## The Remuneration of Directors

Paragraph 87 of *AktG* is concerned with the 'principles governing the remuneration of directors. The aggregate remuneration of each member is required by that paragraph to bear a reasonable relationship to the duties of the relevant director and the condition of the company but may be reduced by the supervisory board if there is a deterioration in the situation of the company'.[80] Paragraph 88(1) states that directors may not engage in transactions in the same field of activities as the company unless they have received the consent of the supervisory board. This is a form of a duty not to bring oneself in a situation where personal interest conflicts with the duty owed to the company. Furthermore, the management board must report on its activities to the supervisory board so as to enable it to oversee the company's management (paragraph 90, *AktG*).

> If a public company is a listed one, the management and the supervisory boards are required by paragraph 161 AktG to state annually whether they have complied with the recommendations of the Corporate Governance Code and if not what recommendations were not applied; such recommendations do not have a binding effect.[81]

In 2005 the German Parliament approved the Disclosure of Management Board Compensation Act (*VorstOG*) which aimed at forging a culture of greater transparency in relation to the executive pay. One of the central provisions of this Act was to introduce an obligation to disclose each member's compensation individually. Albeit on the basis of exceptions, the Act constituted an important legislative development that contributed to greater accountability in relation to issues of executive pay, as it broke with the previous tradition of revealing the total figure of payments granted to the whole management board rather than the precise amount received by each member individually. The previous regime did not guarantee the existence of the necessary safeguards against excessive payment since the publication of the total amount of compensation

---

[80] Andenas, M. and F. Wooldridge, *European Comparative Company Law* (Cambridge University Press, Cambridge 2009), p. 309.

[81] Ibid., p. 310.

granted to the entire board did not reveal the exact sum received by each member, and therefore any link between performance and payment was impossible to be detected, let alone reasonably upheld. The total amount may have appeared to be large, moderate or indeed small, but in any case there was no information about which criteria were employed so as to determine the specific amount of money handed to each member and consequently the rationale behind its precise determination. The previous legislation which evidently failed to establish a regime of accountability and trust was replaced by the 2005 Act, which was indeed instrumental in paving the way for a greater sense of transparency to be achieved. This is also reflected in the German Corporate Governance Code which in section 4.2.4 states that

> the total compensation of each one of the members of the Management Board is to be disclosed by name, divided into fixed and variable compensation components. The same applies to promises of benefits that are granted to a Management Board member in case of premature or statutory termination of the function of a Management Board member or that have been changed during the financial year. Disclosure may be dispensed with if the General Meeting has passed a resolution to this effect by three-quarters majority.

The 2005 Act was accompanied four years later by the Management Compensation Act of 2009 (*VorstAG*) which consolidated further the shift in the practices accompanying the definition of executive pay. It is important to note that the 2009 Act was incorporated into the *AktG*, and therefore became an integral part of the company law culture of the country. The Act clarified the principal role granted to the supervisory board in the determination of executive pay. The latter is responsible for setting the amount of compensation which is to be granted to the members of the management board. The supervisory board reaches a decision that will define the limits of remuneration on the basis of a dual criterion; personal performance and the economic capacity of the company. This is further incorporated within the scope of paragraph 87(1) *AktG* as well as the Code of Corporate Governance whose provisions are centred around the same principles. Therefore, the German law prescribes a system for the determination of remuneration which has some very specific pillars; firstly the enhanced role handed to the supervisory board which is to determine the exact amount, and secondly the criteria to be employed while doing so. The involvement of the supervisory board in issues of executive compensation is of paramount importance as the power in question is vested into an internal corporate institution which is fully aware of the economic situation of the company. The supervisory board is actively involved with the monitoring procedure of the executive and is in full knowledge of the decisions made, the strategic plan adopted and the agenda of the executive. It is also fully aware of the impact that the decision-making has had on the finances of the company. Therefore, it is in a position to evaluate whether the decision-making of the executive has been instrumental for the success of the company, and whether the economic capacity of the latter justifies the granting of compensation at any level. Furthermore, the granting of remuneration on such a basis acquires an additional layer of legitimacy since it brings with it the stamp of approval of an institution that comprises a set of stakeholders closely linked with the company; the employees and the creditors are therefore expressing their consent to granting compensation to the managers at the agreed level and amount. This signals the consistency of the remuneration with the fulfilled corporate objectives and the achieved profitability. The German Code in section 4.2.2 adheres to such an approach by clarifying that

> Criteria for determining the appropriateness of compensation are both the tasks of the individual member of the Management Board, his personal performance, the economic situation, the performance and outlook of the enterprise as well as the common level of the compensation taking into account the peer companies and the compensation structure in place in other areas of the company.

And in any case the compensation structure must be orientated towards the sustainable growth of the enterprise. That seems to constitute a crucial parameter to be taken into account when elaborating the levels of compensation, as the latter should guarantee the long-term sustainability of the company. It was noted from the beginning of this book that the notion of long-term sustainability as well as long-term planning is inherent within the German corporate governance model. The insider corporate governance model normally involves a less fragmented shareholder basis and an inclusive system of coexistence at top institutional level. This institutional architecture is based on consensus among the various components of the corporation and favours the planning of a long-term strategy for the company. In contrast to that, managers in the UK are more inclined to achieve short-term profitability which will lead to the distribution of dividends to the shareholders, as that will be perceived by the latter as an indication of corporate success that renders a more active involvement on their part unnecessary. In Germany, the notion of long-term sustainability however is crucial, since the shareholders are anyway involved within the management company while actively interacting with the other stakeholders and holding the directors of the company accountable for their decisions. Therefore, the latter are on the one hand in a position to design the long-term planning of the company on a more solid basis while being monitored more closely especially as to their remuneration, which may not be linked with performance and could therefore undermine the long-term sustainability of the company. The criteria applied for determining the executive compensation do not only reflect the existing company reality but they also guarantee a degree of transparency and accountability which, when accompanied by the legitimacy inherent in the approval by the stakeholders, deprives this issue from the controversy that it often attracts in the UK or USA, where such balances are nonexistent. Thus, by the UK or the USA standards, German executives are 'modestly paid. The reasons could include the moderating influence of the German society, the moderating influence of ownership concentration, the moderating influence of employee representatives on the supervisory board, monitoring in general and restrictions in the use of share options in the past'.[82]

As far as the supervisory board is concerned, paragraph 192(2) *AktG* states that share options may not be granted to its members as the latter do not form a part of a management organ, although it does not rule out performance related remuneration. The ruling of the Federal Court of Justice of Germany *(Bundesgerichtshof, BGH*) in *Mobilcom*[83] clearly confirmed that the members of the supervisory board cannot be compensated with share options.

The supervisory board (*Aufsichtsrat*) is always mandatory in the *AG* unless they are not subject to codetermination; these are the companies with fewer than 500 employees. The composition of the supervisory board is basically determined by the codetermination laws applying in each case. 'In Germany shareholders play a limited role in the management of large companies. Shareholders do not elect all members of the supervisory board.'[84] This is a clear indication of a corporate culture where the notion of shareholder primacy does not form its main principle. The number of its members depends on the amount of stated capital as well as the number of employees; it should however consist of at least three members; the articles may increase such a number. The appointment of members by the employees does not only signal the erosion of shareholder primacy as this is known and dominant in the Anglo-Saxon corporate culture, but it also embodies a divergence

---

82 Mäntysaari (2005), p. 302.
83 BGH, 16 February 2004, II ZR 316/02.
84 Mäntysaari (2005), p. 250.

from the principle of independence of board members that is in place, at least in theory, in the aforementioned jurisdictions. While in the UK, the independence of the members of the board is to be safeguarded as the latter have the duty to act in the best interest of the company as a whole, in Germany it is recognised that the members of the board can in fact represent the interests of a certain constituency of the company such as primarily the employees or the creditors (usually the banks). The independence of the management of the company is safeguarded by the fact that membership on both boards is not permitted; therefore the executive role is confined to the management board subject to the monitoring of the supervisory board, the members of which can take into account the interests of their constituencies. Although this arrangement can raise a few eyebrows in terms of the ability of the supervisory board as whole to fulfil its function irrespective of the individual agendas, it has to be noted that it operates within a corporate culture that is founded upon the notion of consensus. The various components of the company are accustomed to coexisting within the corporate shell on the basis of mutual compromise, negotiations and ultimately consensus. The more inclusive approach adopted by the German company and the decades of experience of coexistence at board level has gradually elaborated a notion of collaboration for the benefit of the company. Within the German context this clearly includes the benefit of the shareholders but also the benefit of the stakeholders directly involved in the corporate project. The notion that they all constitute a part of the company builds a different mentality that provides for the ability to reach common ground rather than a confrontational approach based on the crude interpretation of self interest. Therefore, despite the institutionalised ability of members of the supervisory board to pursue a personal – in the sense of constituency-friendly – agenda the existing culture of consent in the best interests of the company is instrumental in decreasing the differences and mitigating the divergence into common ground. Despite that, there is the risk that the members of the board will neglect the overall benefit of the company and will take a narrow view of their individual interest leading to conflicts at board level. In any case, it is not within the ability of the supervisory board to interfere into the everyday running of the company that usually insulates the corporations from similar risks. The Code deals with this issue in section 5.4.2 where it states that

> to permit the Supervisory Board's independent advice and supervision of the Management Board, the Supervisory Board shall include what it considers an adequate number of independent members. A Supervisory Board member is considered independent if he/she has no business or personal relations with

> the company or its Management Board which cause a conflict of interests. Not more than two former members of the Management Board shall be members of the Supervisory Board and Supervisory Board members shall not exercise directorships or similar positions or advisory tasks for important competitors of the enterprise.

Therefore, the German Code includes a provision which is similar to the respective in the UK Code, which refers to the inclusion of so-called independent members in the supervisory board; the latter defined as having no business or relation with the company which can cause a conflict of interests. This requirement appears to be less strict than the respective in the USA and in the UK, where the independent directors are defined as having no relation with the company whatsoever. The German Code appears to promote a slightly different definition which involves individuals that have no relation with the company, which can cause a conflict of interests; therefore any other type of relation with the company or the management board that does not give birth to conflicts of interests can still qualify the individual in question as independent. The institutional checks already in place in the German corporation do not demand the strict definition of independence that the USA and UK counterparts found imperative in their respective national framework.

At this stage it is interesting to note that the members of the supervisory board with the aforementioned status and characteristics as appointed by the constituents of the company or as having a relation with the company (even when not giving rise to conflicts of interests) would probably fall short of the definition of independence within the letter of the Sarbanes–Oxley Act in the USA. The appointment by employees would signify a departure from the notion of independence that would be unacceptable for the USA legislative standards. But then again, the unitary board in the USA, accompanied by a vastly dispersed shareholder basis which renders the monitoring of managers a very difficult task, places a range of challenges on American legislators which differs significantly in its nature from the respective faced by the German legislator, and therefore the Sarbanes–Oxley Act's provisions are the prescript medicine for that 'disease'. Its application within the context of the German corporation would have been difficult and in fact rather pointless as the issues emerging within the latter are significantly different in scope and nature from the respective not only in the other side of the Atlantic, but also in the UK.

## Term of Office for the Supervisory Board

The *AktG* provides for most of the details in relation to the appointment and term of the members of the supervisory board. Their term of office is normally five years unless the articles set a more limited term (paragraph 102, *AktG*). Paragraph 103 lays down the framework for the removal of a member of the supervisory board.

> If a member is elected by the shareholders … they may remove him without cause by three quarters of the shareholders actually voting on a general meeting … persons who appoint members to the supervisory board pursuant to the articles may replace them at any time, and they may be removed by a simple majority … if they no longer satisfy the requirements specified in the articles in relation to the right to appoint … furthermore a court may remove a member of the board.[85]

The fact that shareholders require a three-quarters majority in order to remove a director from the board is indicative of powers which are significantly less extensive than the powers held by shareholders in the English company. In the UK a director can be removed from the board after the passing of an ordinary resolution on the basis of Section 303 of Companies Act 2006. The German law appears to have introduced an increased threshold for the removal of a member of the supervisory board. The members of the board in an English company exercise a role which will be clearly executive, while the ones on the supervisory board of the German public company will have a different set of agenda centred around their monitoring duties; however, the higher threshold which is to be achieved in Germany can be viewed as a limitation upon shareholder power to exercise a set of powers which will stem from a property-right approach towards the company as a whole. Increased transparency in relation to the annual financial statements of the company is achieved with the active involvement of the supervisory board in this process. The management board should submit to the supervisory board the annual balance sheet of the company together with the auditor's report, according to paragraph 170, *AktG*. The financial statements of the company therefore form the focus of the screening procedure that involves the supervisory board. The supervisory board not only provides a report to the general meeting after the examination of the relevant documents according to paragraph 171, *AktG* but it also has to provide its approval on the basis of paragraph 172, *AktG*. The highly important role of its

---

85 Andenas and Wooldridge (2009), p. 312.

members as the institutional guardians of the accountability of the management board and of the transparency of the financial statements of the company renders the provisions applying to the duties of the members of the management board applicable to the membership of the supervisory one as well (paragraph 116, *AktG*).

## THE GERMAN LAW ON COMPANY GROUPS

The German law on company groups is predicated on a concept of linked shareholders ownership as well as control between parents and subsidiaries. The Fourth Directive 78/660/EEC on companies' annual accounts and (Article 1 of) the Seventh Directive 83/349/EEC on consolidated (group) accounts use a group concept which loosely follows German law. The Takeover Directive 2004/25/EC is also similar.[86] Many efforts have been made to define parameters of the 'group' in order to challenge wrongful decisions in any place where the group has significant operations. Due to these difficulties, the EU did not pursue its proposal of a Ninth Directive on Company Groups.[87] The German law *Konzenrecht*[88] applicable only to stock corporations and a partnership limited by shares, although a vigorous body of developing law applies it to other companies. Under this law a distinction is made between contractual and de facto groups of companies. In contractual groups, the creditors of the subsidiary are protected by a legal obligation of the parent towards the subsidiary to make good losses at the end of the year. Shareholders other than the parent company have a right to periodic compensation payments, and must be offered the opportunity of selling their shares to the parent at a reasonable price. They have a right to an annual dividend, which is calculated according to the value of their shares at the same of the formation of the contractual group and the likelihood of the dividends without the formulation of the group. The board of the subsidiary has to give a report on all transactions, measures and omissions during the past year that result from its membership of the group.[89] The conclusion of the contract between members of the group is encouraged by the ability

---

[86] See paragraph 29(2) of the *Wertpapiererwerbs und Übernahmegesetz* (*WpÜg*) of 2001.

[87] The Proposal was strongly influenced by German *Konzenrecht*; see Andenas and Wooldridge (2009).

[88] *Konzenrecht*: paragraphs 15–19 and 291 et seq of the *Atiengesetz* 1965.

[89] Ibid., Paragraph 212.

of the parent company to induce the subsidiary to act against its own interests, thus legitimising the concept of the interests of the group as a whole.

However, the concept has been little used. Hopt observes that most groups have chosen 'cohabitation without marriage'.[90] The *Konzenrecht* enacts an equity group relationship that, based on its capital share or on agreement, the *parent company* has the right to appoint at least 30 per cent of members of the *subsidiary's* board of directors or supervisory board or of the managing directors, or if the parent has at least 30 per cent of votes at the subsidiary's general meeting. However where the group relationship has not been formalised, the court may impose a fiduciary duty on the majority shareholders in a group in favour of minority shareholders in the group or in the group's subsidiaries. This means that there is a mix of contractual formal legal groups and de facto groups, depending on the jurisprudence. The law and courts recognise a concept of 'control'. A controlling enterprise can influence another by direct or indirect means.[91] A company which has a large number of shareholders who vote will be able to control other enterprises and therefore will be likely to direct the subsidiary through continuous instructions. An enterprise the majority of whose shares or votes are held by another enterprise is presumed to be dependent on that enterprise.[92] If a controlling and one or more dependent enterprises are under uniform management, they are treated as a formal contractual group.[93] However 'the concepts of uniform, management and controlling and dependent companies are of an economic nature and perhaps somewhat vague'.[94] For many years, the German Federal Court applied these legal consequences for LLC groups which written German law does not cover. The Federal Court applied joint stock company law on contractual groups accordingly, that is, it recognised the parent's right to exercise control, power and the obligations mentioned above. However, in the meantime, the Federal Court has changed its jurisprudence. The Court now applies an approach based on fiduciary duties.[95] The German jurisprudence is

---

[90] Hopt, K., 'Legal Elements and Policy Decisions in Regulating Groups of Companies' in C. Schmittoff and K. Wooldridge (eds), *Groups of Companies* (Sweet and Maxwell, London 1991).

[91] *Konzenrecht*, paragraph 18(1).

[92] Ibid., paragraph 17(2).

[93] Ibid., paragraph 18(1).

[94] Andenas and Wooldridge (2009), p. 453.

[95] Eroglu, M., *Multinational Enterprises and Tort Liability* (Edward Elgar, Cheltenham 2008), especially p. 189.

equivocal. The concept of 'control' is particularly crucial in this context. We have seen that a controlling enterprise can influence another by direct or indirect means.[96] Although the *Konzenrecht* is mired in technical legalities,[97] it has been copied in a number of jurisdictions[98] and it could be extended by clauses that put in an extraterritoriality element. This was done in Albania, and while Albanian company law cannot revolutionise the world, it could have a role in fostering a culture of accountability in company groups including in MNE, particularly if other jurisdictions legislate to control MNCs along similar models. This concluding part of this chapter[99] will argue that the recent reform of company law in the Balkans[100] shaped on German patterns could be a model for a new set of national laws on company groups.[101]

## The Legislative Provisions

Article 207

Parents and Subsidiaries

> (1) A parent-subsidiary relationship shall be deemed to exist where one company regularly behaves and acts subject to the directions or instructions of another company. That control shall be called control group.
>
> (2) If a company, based on its capital share in another company or based on an agreement with that company, has the right to appoint at least 30 per cent of members of the Board of Administration or Supervisory Board or of the

---

96 *Konzenrecht,* Para 18(1).

97 Hopt, K. (1991).

98 The *Konzenrecht* has been copied in Brazil, Portugal, Slovenia, Croatia, and Taiwan; see Andenas and Wooldridge (2009), pp. 448–9. Albanian Law has an extended extraterritoriality concept: see Law on Entrepreneurs and Companies, No. 9901, 2008.

99 In 2008, I was privileged to be allowed to draft Albanian company law with a colleague, Dr Michael Blecher, of the Deutsche Gesellschaft für Internationale Zusammenarbeit (GIZ: German International Cooperation).

100 The 2008 Reform of Albanian Company Law on Entrepreneurs and Companies, No. 9901.

101 The extraterritoriality issue is included in the Albanian law. If other jurisdictions copy this model it holds out hope for lawyers and activists concerned to hold the power of MNCs accountable to legal standards. The Albanian model suggests that certain provisions of national law might provide an effective route both for constructing the environmental responsibilities of MNCs and for holding them to account for the human rights violations and environmental damage that they cause.

administrators of that company, or if it has at least 30 per cent of votes at the General Meeting, it shall be considered a parent of the other company and the other company as its subsidiary. That control shall be called an equity group.

(3) The parent's rights over the subsidiary as specified in Paragraph 2 of the present Article shall be considered such even where those rights are exercised through another company, controlled by the parent or a third party acting on account of that other company or the parent itself.

(4) The third party shall be presumed to act on account of the parent if it falls under the specifications laid down in Article 13 Paragraph 2 and 3 of the present Law.

Article 208

Legal Consequences of a Parent-Subsidiary Relationship

(1) Where there is a parent-subsidiary relationship as defined in Article 207 Paragraph 1 of the present Law, the parent shall have a duty to compensate the subsidiary for its annual losses.

(2) Partners, members or shareholders of the subsidiary shall at any time have the right to request the parent to buy their shares or securities in the company.

(3) Creditors of the subsidiary shall at any time have the right to require the parent to offer adequate security for their claims owed by the subsidiary.

(4) Creditors of the subsidiary shall include persons who have incurred damage due to a subsidiary's actions wherever the subsidiary is registered.

Article 209

Fiduciary Duties Arising in Equity Group

(1) In a parent-subsidiary relationship as defined by Article 207 Paragraph 2 of the present law, the representations of the parent must take account of the following:

a) any duty of the parent under Articles 14 to 18 of the present Law, or in case of a limited liability company, Articles 98 of the present Law, and in case of a joint stock company, Article 163 of the present Law;
b) the way a decision might affect or benefit the group of companies a whole;
c) interests of the subsidiary company.

(2) A representative of the parent shall be deemed to be in breach of fiduciary duties if the independent board members would not in view of the above-listed have taken that decision.

(3) The representative of the parent shall be obliged to comply with the provisions regulating fiduciary duties to the subsidiary, including the obligation to act in the best interest of the subsidiary.

Article 210

Liability for Breach of Fiduciary Duties

(1) Where a representative of the parent acts in breach of the fiduciary duties under Article 209 of this present Law, the parent in whose name the representative has acted shall be obliged to compensate the damage caused thereby.

(2) In the circumstances set out in Paragraph 1, of the present Article, members of the parent's administration organs shall be jointly and severally liable for the damage caused.

(3) Members of the subsidiary's management organs who act in breach of the fiduciary duties shall be held liable jointly and severally, along with the persons specified under Paragraph 2 of the present Article.

Article 211

Action for Compensation of Damage

(1) If a subsidiary has not, within 90 days of the discovery of the damage referred to in Article 209 Paragraph 1 of the present Law, initiated a necessary procedure to claim compensation for the damage, the subsidiary's claim may be filed:

a) Where the subsidiary is a partnership, by every partner;
b) Where the subsidiary is a limited liability company, by the member representing at least 5 per cent of the total vote in the General Meeting or a smaller amount specified by the statute, and/or any of its creditors. Article 91 Paragraph 6 of the present law shall be the applicable provision in that case;
c) Where the subsidiary is a joint stock company, by the shareholders representing at least 5 per cent of the basic capital or a smaller portion set by the statute, and/or any of its creditors whose claims against the company amount to at least 5 per cent of the basic capital.

(2) A claim under the present Article must be submitted within 3 years from the time the damage becomes evident.

(3) Creditors of the subsidiary shall also include persons who have incurred damage due to a subsidiary's action, wherever the subsidiary is registered.

Article 212

Sell-out Right

If the parent holds 90 per cent or more of the subsidiary's shares, the holders of the remaining shares shall have the right to request the parent to buy those shares at the market price within 6 months of the request.

## The Company Group Dilemma

A key strength of Articles 207 to 212 of the Albanian Law on Entrepreneurs and Companies, No. 9901, 2008 is that it takes into account 40 years of debate within the EU and between its member states, as well as debate at the global level[102] regarding the way in which MNCs/groups should be legally drafted. The philosophical tensions concerning various company models means that drafting legislative provisions concerning groups of companies is imbued with particular difficulty, especially concerning the complex issues of extraterritoriality, the limitations of transplanting laws, the complications of transition economies and the operation of the company veil. This makes the drafting process especially challenging, but embedded in the Albanian legal provisions is, nonetheless, a robust attempt to address the realities (and by corollary the negative effects) of power relations which arise in company groups.[103]

Article 98, for example, obliges administrators to consider their duties 'in good faith and the interest in the best interests of the company as a whole, paying particular attention to the impact of its operation on the environment'.[104] The maximisation of the company's own assets, and the question of compliance with legal expectations, moreover, is conceptualised within the legislation as being not only in the interest of all the investors (shareholders), but also in the interest of creditors, employees and the economic system as a whole. In short, the 'interest of the company' explicitly recognises the social embeddedness of the company

---

[102] UN Commission of Transnational Corporations or 'Group of Eminent Persons', 'The Impact of Multinational Corporations on Development and on International Relations' (UN pub E74 IIA 5), 25 (*OECD Guidelines for Multinationals Principles of Corporate Governance*, 2005).

[103] Gillespie, J.G., *Transplanting Commercial Law Reform* (Ashgate, Farnham 2006); Trubek, D., 'Scholars in Self-Estrangement: Reflections on the Crisis in Law and Development Studies in the United States' (1974) *Wisconsin Law Review* pp. 1062–1102 (with Marc Galanter); Dine, J., *Companies, International Law and Human Rights* (Cambridge University Press, Cambridge 2005).

[104] Limited company provisions, article 163 mirrors the same articles in joint stock companies.

and its broader social parameters. Globalisation, however, presents a challenge to this more holistic national approach. Globalisation means that the coincidence of shareholders', creditors', employees' and 'public' interests in the economic success of the individual company may even be destroyed if the company is integrated into a larger group of companies which may no longer pursue the interest of the individual company – especially if the company is affiliated in a group which has different ethical principles in view. This reality was part of the background challenge for the Albanian drafting process. It is clear that as globalisation has speeded up, ever greater numbers of companies have become affiliated with international companies, while the laws of national parliaments may not have legislated higher standards for companies. While human rights and international law standards have challenged some of the worst outrages as CSR NGOs communicate more effectively, there is obviously the ongoing need to cope with the undesired political, social and economic effects, or 'externalities' which such groups produce. It is essential to subject them to adequate national and international regulatory frameworks. However, as we have seen, there is as yet no international answer to the central problem of the extraterritoriality issue and 'jurisdictional arbitrage'. In part, philosophical and political difficulties explain this failure – certainly in the EU context. The EU has not, as a result, pursued the finalisation of its proposal for a Ninth Directive on Company Groups,[105] and there is no EU legislation on group liabilities. Instead, the EU's legal attitude has become 'pragmatic', addressing single problem areas of corporate groups such as annual accounting in a group and the acquisition of major shareholdings in publicly held companies by takeover bids.[106]

While German law is normally acknowledged as presenting the most sophisticated legislation on group liability, the drafting process of the provisions of the Albanian law was conducted with all the scholarship on

---

[105] The Proposal was strongly influenced by German *Konzenrecht*.

[106] The Directive on takeover bids was finalised in 2003. There is a good account of the EU attempts to draft a Directive concerning Groups (The draft Ninth Directive) in Vanessa Edwards's book, *EC Company Law* (Oxford University Press, Oxford 1999), see particularly pp. 390–1: 'footnote 24 reminds us that the late Professor Gower was a particularly ardent advocate of Commercial legislation on groups, going so far as to state that "to my way of thinking, the one thing that the EC ought to be concentrated on the corporate field is doing something about groups … something has got to done about this, instead of bothering about piddling little things like harmonising rules about the one-member private limiting company!"'.

the limitations of transplanting laws vividly in mind, as well as the central importance of fair trading in the global international market. Article 207, paragraph (1) is, in fact, the most innovative part of the Albanian structure. This explicitly defines the first form of parent-subsidiary relationship, known as a 'control group'. The concept merges the concept of dominance from German law on groups (*Konzenrecht*) and deploys the notion, drawn from other jurisdictions of the 'controlling influence' or 'dominance', in order to determine whether 'a subsidiary is "accustomed to act in accordance with the directions or instructions" of the parent company'. Article 207(1) goes beyond the German approach, however. The Article does not require that such control is based on shareholdings, agreements or based on contract, thus improving on the German concept which has proved too restrictive (it accepts special group regulations only where dominant influence and control are mediated by a shareholding relationship or based on contract).[107] The Albanian approach is more realistic and critical. It accepts that one of the most important factors defining the existence of a significant relationship between companies is the flow of money rather than the share structure, and accordingly deploys a dominance concept without referring to significant ownership and voting powers.[108] The concept is broad enough, moreover, to include relationships such as franchising or other kinds of supply or distribution, outsourcing of certain enterprise functions or quality-assurance systems which 'at the surface' are using the contractual instrument, but which 'in reality' build organisations which may be treated according to group parameters.[109]

While Zerk has argued that there is no reason why an enterprise theory might be constructed on a control basis rather than on an equity basis,[110] she misses a significant point. She argues that

---

[107] TBB Zeitschrift fur Wirtschaftsrecht (1993) 589.

[108] See also Dine, *The Governance of Corporate Groups* (Cambridge University Press, Cambridge 2000), p. 181.

[109] Weitzenboeck, E., *Between contract and partnership: Dynamic networks as collaborative contracts and more* (Oslo University PhD thesis, April 2010); Weitzenboeck, *A Legal Framework for Emerging Business Models: Dynamic Networks as Collaborative Contracts* (Edward Elgar, Cheltenham 2012). The German system excludes profit pooling, partial profit transfer and business leasing contracts; see Andenas and Wooldridge (2009), p. 434.

[110] Zerk, J., *Multinational and Corporate Social Responsibilities: Limitations and Opportunities in International Law* (Cambridge University Press, Cambridge 2006), p. 235.

> [w]hat is crucial in each case is the presence of a 'control' relationship between parent and foreign affiliate (however related) that is sufficient to justify the imposition of liability on the parent in the particular case … to establish 'primary' liability, the plaintiff would need to demonstrate the parent company's familiarity with the risk associated with the relevant activities and close involvement with the day-to-day operation of its foreign affiliate.[111]

The radical change presented by Article 207 is closer to the reality that the enterprise theory needs to encompass: once the group is recognised as an enterprise, the *whole of the group, not just the parent company*, could be sued, whatever its business. Of course, there would be exceptions, but these could be controlled, perhaps using a concept such as the affiliates being on a 'frolic on their own'. In this way, some of the intractable obstacles and difficulties that dogged the ATCA 1789 and any other universal jurisdiction system could be removed. One crucial difference of approach concerns the role of the chain of causation. This would no longer need to be proved between individual companies, but rather there would be a defeasible presumption of liability placed upon each entity in the MNC group. This removes, for example, the related hurdle of proving whether entity had control of the tortious situation, and as Zerk recognises, '[a]lthough there may be contractual disclaimers of liability and indemnities, this should not affect … liability in tort towards a third party'.[112]

The parameters of the definition remain open to interpretive dispute, of course. Control must actually be realised by concrete 'directions or instructions', which are not only carried out in one or a few single cases but require some degree of repetition: the subsidiary must be 'accustomed' to, or used to acting in compliance with them. This particular approach was built on an insolvency provision in the UK[113] merged with a generalisation of the German formal and de facto group rule.[114] Article 207(2) of the Albanian Law on Entrepreneurs and Companies, No. 9901, 2008 mirrors the German equity concept on groups, in effect, which defines the rights of control groups and its constituents.[115]

---

[111] Ibid.

[112] Ibid.

[113] UK Company Law Act 2006, shadow directors 1985. Now subsumed in Company Law Act 2008, section 251.

[114] Paragraph 311 et seq, German Law on Shares (*Aktiengesetz*).

[115] Article 207(2) of the Albanian Company Law mirrors the Fourth Directive 78/660/EEC on companies' annual accounts and (article 1 of) the Seventh Directive 83/349/EEC on consolidated (group) accounts using a group concept which the new Company Law loosely follows in its definition of 'equity groups',

However, viewed in the light of the global context, Article 207(1) and (4) are perhaps the most innovative provisions. Article 207(1) uses the control group concept and stipulates that '[c]reditors of the subsidiary shall include persons who have incurred damage due to a subsidiary's action wherever the subsidiary is registered'. This means that tort victims of an MNC, including subsidiaries or entities, are conceptualised as creditors as a result of their claims. This is indeed a ground-breaking approach, but still requires further regulations in order to consolidate the definitions deployed and particularly to draft tighter definitions concerning 'control'.

Article 208 implements provisions for both control groups and equity groups, and it is notable that the details in the law defining 'equity groups' remains clearer than for 'control groups' (see Articles 209 to 212). The control group legislation still lacks some of the important provisions found in the equity group law, but it is useful that Articles 98 and 163 ('Limited Liability Companies' and 'Joint Stock Companies') are found in both group designs, because *all* of the companies which are found in the enterprise will have fiduciary duties for directors. Articles 98 and 163 of the Albanian law deals with fiduciary duties, which are constructed as being common to all company forms and therefore part of any group. Such fiduciary duties are crucial in the design of company law, since they can be a way to balance the inevitable disadvantages in contractual bargains. (There still remains, however, a potential loophole in the Albanian law, if other entities become part of the group, because the law does not recognise partnerships or contractual arrangements such as franchises.)

Article 209 (2) establishes a breach of duty for a representative of the parent company. The standard is if no independent directors of the subsidiary company could have reached the decision that was made. In that case the representative will be liable. This standard allows the court to consider all the aspects of a business decision, including the long-term advantages of a group decision even if measured against short-term disadvantages – factors likely to influence the decisions of the independent directors of subsidiary companies, who cannot but respect their

article 207 (2). Thresholds are, however, loosely referring to the standards introduced by the Takeover Directive 2004/25/EC and its transposition in some Member States (like Germany): article 207(2) requires for an equity group relationship that, based on its capital share or on agreement, the *parent company* has the right to appoint at least 30 per cent of members of the *subsidiary*'s board of directors or supervisory board or of the managing directors, or if the parent has at least 30 per cent of votes at the subsidiary's general meeting.

company's embeddedness in the group. The consequences for breach of duty of both the parent's and the subsidiary's 'administration' (that is, managing directors, boards of directors or supervisory boards) are provided by Article 210. The right to derivative action is provided by Article 211.

However, more work needs to be done. In particular, the control group provisions need supplementation with provisions from the equity group provisions, including the fiduciary duty to take into account the interests of the company group as a whole and the interests of the subsidiary. Overall, it is apparent that the broader conception of the company envisaged by these provisions of Albanian company law borrows in part from the continental European social market (contentious in the UK), in which the company is a living entity with employees, shareholders, customers and suppliers, and where wider implications for human beings and the environment more naturally form part of the company's normative remit. It is worth reiterating that administrators within Albanian company law are explicitly placed moreover under a duty to perform 'in good faith and in the best interests of the company as a whole, paying particular attention to the impact of its operation on the environment'.[116] It is crucial however that the Albanian model should be further refined. If such laws are to withstand international special interests, particularly the MNCs' lobbies, and any shocks that can be thrown in the path of courts and litigants, it is imperative that drafting should be stringent. This is particularly vital in the light of the broader picture in which democracy stands imperilled by globalisation and in which MNC accountability is weakened by extraterritoriality principles.

Clearly the control of MNC power is a decisively important consideration. National laws present an opportunity for the construction of decisive sanctions and controls. While the proposed model put forward here requires refinement, it is very much to be hoped that the academic legal community will analyse it and refine the possible legislative models, press such reforms upon governments and legislatures and promote the international spread of a network of strong national accountability structures for MNC human rights and environmental liabilities.

---

[116] Articles 98 and 163 of the Albanian Law on Entrepreneurs and Companies, No. 9901, 2008.

## The Status of German Corporate Governance in German Company Law

The introduction of a Code which sets the principles underlining the institutional setting of companies in Germany followed the trend successfully set by the UK in 1992 with the introduction of the Cadbury Code. Despite the fact that corporate governance remains distinctively national in its core characteristics and structural foundations, and is the outcome of a long and ongoing process of historical, political and economic developments accompanied by respective progress at social level, a certain interaction between the most prominent jurisdictions is inevitably observed. The developments taking place in the UK which led to the drafting of the Cadbury Code did indeed attract the attention of the German businesses as well as its legislature and academia. It is interesting to note however that while the introduction of a code which is a form of self-regulation fits very comfortably with the English legal system and legislative traditions as well as its corporate realities, the same cannot be supported with the greatest degree of certainty for Germany as well. In the UK the ideological belief in the 'inherent superiority of self-regulation… and the political imperative to develop and maintain the position of London as a major financial centre meant that political pressure could also be brought to bear against intrusive regulations or regulators'.[117]

The belief in self-regulatory capability of the market is not new 'at least in economic theory. Founded on the efficient market hypothesis, neoclassical economics has provided a theoretical basis for a self-regulatory model of governance by contract rather than mandatory rules drafted by legislature'.[118] Within this context Hayek argued[119] that there is no party whatsoever and that includes the state which can produce efficient regulation for all parties because it lacks all the necessary information. He entrusts this capacity exclusively to the market which can put in place the appropriate mechanisms and rules on the basis of private negotiations between the parties involved. State intervention in

---

117 Sun, W., J. Stewart and D. Pollard, *Corporate Governance and the Global Financial Crisis, International Perspectives* (Cambridge University Press, Cambridge 2011), p. 52.

118 Galanis, M., 'Vicious Spirals in Corporate Governance: Mandatory Rules for Systemic (Re)Balancing?' (2001) 31 *Oxford Journal of Legal Studies* 2, p. 327.

119 Hayek, F., 'The Use of Knowledge in Society' (1948) 35 *American Economic Review*, 519.

this case is not only unnecessary but undesired. While the UK and even more emphatically the USA have a tradition of introducing standards and norms on the basis of voluntary codes and self-regulation, Germany is a jurisdiction which placed hard law at the core of its regulatory arrangements. In this context the introduction of the Code seemed, if not to break with the previously established tradition, at least to emerge as a rather exceptional choice as 'the role of industry self regulation has traditionally been limited as far as the governance of German public limited liability companies is concerned. The governance of AGs is characterised by mandatory legislation'.[120] In this sense the Code initially drafted in 2002 with its final version elaborated in 2010 seems to reveal a new trend in German legislative culture that expresses the need for greater flexibility in relation to some aspects of corporate governance. The German Corporate Governance Code was preceded by the Takeover Code published in 1995 and modelled around the patterns set by the City Code on Takeovers. A relatively new territory for high profile self-regulation initiatives, Germany was naturally looking to the highly experienced UK to acquire the knowhow of drafting and introducing voluntary codes.

The German Corporate Governance Code as analysed above sets standards for the management and supervisory boards of the public limited listed companies of the country. The standards which are adopted from a third country are aborted from the local jurisdiction if the latter fails to adapt them adequately to the national legislative culture; the Code could not have been an exception to that. Furthermore, the introduction of the Code by no means changes the fact that the two most important sources of rules on the management of a German *Aktiengesellschaft* (AG – public limited company) are the *Aktiengesetz* (*AktG*) and labour law. 'The role of contracts is limited.'[121] The centrality of labour law and the mandatory standards it sets plays a substantially influential role within the context of German jurisdiction that in a way counterbalances the force of the Code and acts as the limitations placed upon its text. The Code remains a voluntary text while labour law sets the requirements that have to be complied by companies in their relations with their employees. This is the somehow rigidly set framework within which the German Code has to operate. The respective Code in the UK is mainly orientated towards somehow waning the side effects of absolute shareholder primacy by encouraging the engagement of the company with a range of

[120] Mäntysaari (2005), p. 245.
[121] Ibid., p. 272.

stakeholders, without of course shedding any doubt whatsoever on shareholder dominance within the English corporate context. The German Code places its focus on a different aspect of corporate governance; this is understandable since what constitutes the subject matter of the English Code is already thoroughly regulated by German company and labour law. The German Code deals with aspects of the function of the two boards which constitute the landmarks of German corporate governance: the management and the supervisory boards. The centrality of labour law within this context does not leave a great deal of discretion to the Code so as to introduce or encourage a different set of standards at this level in any case. In this sense both the starting point and the final aim of the German Code seem to diverge significantly from the respective English one. The establishment of a Code is anyway more compatible with the English legal tradition that upholds a more contractual understanding of the company; in this context the company is viewed as a collection of contractual relationships. The nature of the relationships defines the nature of the company as a principally if not wholly private affair. The Code is organised institutionally and structurally on the basis of private agreements; a contractual arrangement. The theoretical background, on the basis of which the English company has been shaped up to this age, is therefore a particularly fertile ground for self-regulation initiatives to flourish. The latter embody by definition the notion of flexibility inherent in privately set relationships, as well as the priority handed to private actors and the industry to regulate themselves; the Codes can comfortably accompany the invisible hand of the market in its attempt to sort its own affairs without the external intervention of the state. In contrast to that, Germany appears to opt for a great degree of legal certainty, achieved mainly in the form of state regulation which deals in detail with most aspects of corporate governance. And when referring to state regulation in relation to corporate governance in the German context, one does not refer exclusively to company law but also and sometimes equally importantly to labour law. In addition to that, Germany never demonstrated an enthusiasm for a company form which grants the exclusivity of membership to shareholders; a more inclusive approach reflecting an utterly different philosophical approach to corporate governance was adopted. Its insider corporate governance model, which extensively analysed in this chapter, is clearly centred around a corporate setting that involved a wider range of actors represented even at board level, eroding significantly a notion of shareholder dominance based on the recognition of an exclusive property right on the corporation. Within this context, the company is not viewed as a purely private affair devoid of any regulatory intervention but more as a private affair which institutionally involves a variety of actors whose balances, checks and governance has to reflect the wider consensus achieved at societal level in relation to the role of corporations in the country. The company adopts a more inclusive approach and encompasses a variety of actors within its structure, therefore rendering an approach reserving exclusivity to shareholders as simply irrelevant; within this context the notion of the company as a wholly private affair to be left intact by state regulation is simply out of line with its substantial parameters. Germany was therefore historically much more inclined to set the main parameters of corporate governance on legislative stone and to provide for the regulatory standards in the form of mandatory laws rather than self-regulation. The Code is an expression of this rule.

In its Foreword, the Code states that it applies only to listed corporations, although it is recommended that non-listed companies respect its provisions. Furthermore, the Code provides the ideological stigma of its drafters in the clearest possible manner by stating that 'the obligation of the Management Board and the Supervisory Board is to ensure the continued existence of the enterprise and its sustainable creation of value in conformity with the principles of the social market economy (interest of the enterprise)'.[122] The social market economy entails a 'complex historical compromise between liberalism and two competing countervailing forces, social democracy and social Catholicism; between traditionalism and two opposed versions of modernism, liberalism and socialism; and of course between capital and labour'.[123] The social market economy which defines the German economic and corporate governance model finds its place at the very beginning of the document, betraying the philosophical framework within which German corporations are regulated. Since the Code is not a legally binding text, it is not mandatory in its application; however non-application of its provisions should be accompanied by the disclosure on the part of the listed companies on an annual basis. The obligation to disclose non-compliance with the Code annually may be summarised into the rule 'comply or disclose'. Interestingly enough, the Foreword explains that the recommendations of the Code are marked in the text by use of the word 'shall'. Companies can deviate from them, but are then obliged to disclose this annually. This enables companies to reflect sector and enterprise-specific

---

[122] German Corporate Governance Code, as amended on 26 May 2010, Government Commission, Foreword.

[123] Streeck, W. and K. Yamamura, *The End of Diversity? Prospects for German and Japanese Capitalism* (Cornell University Press, New York 2003), p. 11.

requirements. Thus, the Code contributes to more flexibility and more self-regulation in the German corporate constitution. Furthermore, the Code contains suggestions which can be deviated from without disclosure; for this the Code uses terms such as 'should' or 'can'. The remaining passages of the Code not marked by these terms contain provisions that enterprises are compelled to observe under applicable law.

At this stage the German Code appears to embark from a different set of objectives with the respective UK one which is based on a clear 'comply or explain' principle. In fact the UK Code was quite a pioneer in introducing such a principle. The German Code clearly opted for a lighter approach which rendered disclosure rather than explanation necessary after failure to observe its provisions. Perhaps, the obligation of German companies to adhere to a wide range of statutory rules gave rise to a lighter approach towards the Code, which was viewed as a step towards achieving a greater degree of flexibility. On the other hand, the UK Code attempted to deal with issues left largely out of the text of the Companies Act 2006, as explained in Chapter 4. Despite the initial divergence in the methods to be employed so as to achieve their respective aims, the two Codes have indeed converged into the adoption of 'comply and explain' principle. Germany moved towards the adoption of 'comply or explain' principally due to EU law. More specifically, Directive 2006/46/EC on the annual accounts of companies added a new article 46a(1)(b) to Directive 78/660/EEC which clearly stated that

> to the extent to which a company, in accordance with national law, departs from a corporate governance code an explanation by the company as to which parts of the corporate governance code it departs from and the reasons for doing so. Where the company has decided not to apply any provisions of a corporate governance code it shall explain its reasons for doing so.[124]

Therefore, the directive introduced the principle of 'comply or explain' into German jurisdiction as well by its incorporation into the German legal order. This is now also incorporated into section 3.10 of the Code which clearly states that

---

[124] Directive 2006/46/EC of the European Parliament and of the Council of 14 June 2006 amending Council Directives 78/660/EEC on the annual accounts of certain types of companies, 83/349/EEC on consolidated accounts, 86/635/EEC on the annual accounts and consolidated accounts of banks and other financial institutions and 91/674/EEC on the annual accounts and consolidated accounts of insurance undertakings (Text with EEA relevance). See: http://eur-lex.europa.eu/LexUriServ/LexUriServ.do?uri=OJ:L:2006:224:0001:01:EN:HTML, accessed on 25 April 2013.

> the Management Board and Supervisory Board shall report each year on the enterprise's Corporate Governance in the Annual Report (Corporate Governance Report). This includes the explanation of possible deviations from the recommendations of this Code. Comments can also be provided on the Code's suggestions. The company shall keep previous declarations of conformity with the Code available for viewing on its website for five years.

At this point a striking difference between the German Code and the UK Code has to be underlined. Despite the voluntary character of the German Code, the declaration of compliance with its provisions appears to enjoy a statutory backing in Germany to a degree that is exceptional if not unique for Codes of voluntary character. Paragraph 161 of *AktG* effectively introduces a legal obligation on all listed companies to make an annual declaration of compliance with the Code's recommendations, which by process they gradually cease to be recommendations and acquire a distinctively more binding character. Paragraph 161(1)(1) of *AktG* clearly states that 'the management board and supervisory board of the listed company shall declare annually that the recommendations of the "Government Commission German Corporate Governance Codex" … has been and will be complied with or which recommendations have not been or will not be applied and why'. Therefore, the two boards are under the legal duty to declare which provisions of the Code they have not applied and the reasons which justify that; furthermore there is also the parameter of presenting their future intention to comply with the Code or the reasoning behind their choice to diverge from its provisions. In effect, this means that the declaration of compliance can lead to

> strict liability of the management board and the supervisory board members whenever the actual corporate governance practices do not correspond with the declared principles … they can be held liable in tort or criminally for misleading and deceptive declarations or blatantly incorrect declarations in the declaration of compliance that needs to be issued annually.[125]

Therefore, paragraph 161 of *AktG* effectively blurs the border between voluntary and binding as it creates a legal obligation to explain non-compliance, vesting the German Code with a binding touch that the UK Code clearly lacks. Despite the fact that the Code is a text which is not produced by the national Parliament and therefore lacks the force of law, its links with paragraph 161, *AktG* should not be underestimated.

Section 2.1.2 of the Code states that 'in principle, each share carries one vote. There are no shares with multiple voting rights, preferential

---

[125] Du Plessis et al. (2012), p. 35.

voting rights (golden shares) or maximum voting rights'. This provision is highly important as it signals the break with the past, when Germany granted the ability of multiple voting rights per share and therefore safeguarded the excessive voting power of many of its companies' creditors; this was one of the defining factors which maintained the influence of the banks on the German boards throughout the previous century, as explained earlier. The Code therefore essentially repeats the previous legislation that enacted the principle 'one share, one voting right'. The latter creates more equality among the shareholders of a company while relaxing the grip that some of them may hold on the corporation.

# 6. Conclusion: The importance of the existence of national systems of corporate governance

Perhaps the most important conclusion of our research is that national corporate governance 'reflects public policy choices'.[1] Each country has passed a set of laws that shape the structure of its firms in a way that reflects the dominant ideological and political principles prevailing in its society. 'At the heart of the ... capitalist system, the free market economy, lies company law'.[2] It is through the medium of companies that wealth is created. More than this, the way in which companies are regulated says a great deal about the values to which each society and the global community gives preference. As we found at the instigation of this investigation, despite some harmonisation of laws, practices and institutional functions, corporate governance systems especially in the West remain distinctively national. During the research it is clear that even at EU level, the harmonisation between the national corporate governance models has been minimal in comparison with the overall effect that the EU-generated legislative initiatives has traditionally had on areas of policy such as the internal market, competition law let alone monetary union with the introduction of a common currency. Resistance to globalisation and harmonisation lies deep in the roots within the individual national identities, which define the system on the basis of which companies are governed, along with the agenda they ought to pursue and their precise purpose.[3] Drafting company law and the norms of corporate governance is a vital part of democracy, particularly because of the

---

1 Gourevitch. P.A. and James Shinn, *Political Power and Control, The New Global Politics of Corporate Governance* (Princeton University Press, Princeton NJ 2005), p. 3.

2 Pettet, B., *Company Law* (Pearson Education, Edinburgh, 2001), p. 3.

3 Dean, J., 'Directors' Duties in Response to Hostile Takeover Bids' (2003) 14 *International Company and Commercial Law Review* 12, p. 370.

imbalance of power in many countries.[4] This highlights one of the most important themes of company law: 'for four hundred years company law has tried to solve the core problem of corporate governance, the separation of ownership and control'.[5] So property ownership brings with it power, and the greater the inequality of property ownership, the greater the potential for domination. This is particularly true where the supply of particular goods in scarce supply.

> If the supply of objects like clothing, furniture and books is drastically restricted, those few who own them could dominate their fellows by the ego-centric exercise of their ownership power to control use. On the other hand, where such chattels are widely available, the use-channelling and use-policing functions of ownership interests … as compared with costly and intrusive regimes of communal use clearly outweigh such dangers of domination.[6]

If property is understood as governing power relationships, it is even more important in a company context to look at the management who have the real power to deploy the assets of the company. Paddy Ireland has made it clear that companies fit with difficulty into the property rights discourse.[7] This is because the traditional 'take' on companies is that they are 'the property of the shareholders' or in the 'nexus of contracts', or 'agency' theory of the company, in what amounts to the same thing: that the shareholders own not 'the company' but 'the capital', the company itself having been spirited out of existence.[8] Ireland also shows in that there is considerable convergence between the property rights of creditors and those of shareholders, each of which can be seen as essentially 'outsiders' having contractual rights against the company, rather than 'insiders' with membership rights. We have seen that ownership of property including companies profoundly changes the way that

---

4 Wilkinson, R. and K. Pickett, *The Spirit Level: Why Equality is Better for Everyone* (Penguin, London 2009 and 2010). Stiglitz, J., *The Price of Inequality* (Allen Lane, Penguin, London 2012).

5 Hopt, J.K. and C.P. Leyens, 'Board Models in Europe – Recent Developments of Internal Corporate Governance Structures in Germany, the United Kingdom, France and Italy' (2004) *European Company and Financial Law Review*, p. 136.

6 Harris, J., *Property and Justice* (Clarendon Press, Oxford 1996), p. 265.

7 Ireland, P., 'Company Law and the Myth of Shareholder Ownership' (1999) *MLR* 62. See also J. Hill, 'Visions and Revisions of the Shareholder' (2000) *American Journal of Comparative Law* 39.

8 Ireland (1999).

individuals think. In the US and the UK, individualism is particularly important. As we found in Chapter 2,

> there is a weakness in the present system of corporate governance in that responsibility for ownership rests with people who don't want it and are not seeking it. We are investing in shares because they give us a good return and it is coincidental really that they bring with them this responsibility. I am not saying we don't want this responsibility. I am saying it is difficult to handle that sort of thing.[9]

That means that democracy as we know it at national level cannot be applied in the company context, as the engagement of a vast number of shareholders, at least in large corporations, remains an issue that is complicated from many aspects to say the least. Tocqueville's central hypothesis was that 'democracy constitutes the sole model of acceptable governance in modern society and it will eventually prevail in all spheres of organised activity';[10] corporations might prove even Tocqueville wrong, at least in the sense of democracy as we know it at the public domain.

However, an additional conclusion is the rather unique nature of ownership in this context. If the owner cannot control what he or she owns, then it is not ownership in the traditional sense of the term as we know it and experience it in the non-corporate world. Therefore, it can be validly claimed that the fervently supported exclusive ownership rights of the shareholders present certain particularities that render the whole issue more controversial or less clear than initially envisaged. The legal world might have to accept that either in the corporate context a new sense of ownership has to be constructed, or that the shareholders do have a claim towards the company as they are undoubtedly and inexorably linked to it through their shares, but the particular nature of this relationship along with the far-reaching effects of corporate action at social level might require the consideration of other factors when designing the company policies and drafting its aims and targets.

The inability to agree on a commonly accepted definition of corporate governance betrays among others the fundamental questions that emerge when debating corporate governance. The two fundamental questions

---

9 Solomon, J., *Corporate Governance and Accountability,* 2nd edn (John Wiley & Sons Ltd, Chichester 2009), p. 19.

10 Gomez, P-Y. and H. Korine, 'Democracy and the Evolution of Corporate Governance' (2005) 13 *Corporate Governance* 6, p. 742. For an excellent review of the reading on the theories of corporate governance, see A. Keay, *The Corporate Objective* (Edward Elgar, Cheltenham 2011).

asked are ‘who should control the corporation?’ and ‘for the pursuit of what goals and whose interests?’[11] As we saw in the Preface, the reply provided to these questions by various jurisdictions has sometimes been diametrically different, due to different prevailing values, divergent national lists of priorities and divergent societal structures: (1) legal based corporate governance scholarship focusing on shareholder rights, agency problems between shareholders and the management on companies and different models of boards;[12] (2) an economic analysis of corporate governance trying to assess the efficiency of different models of company structures;[13] (3) the debate between the shareholder primacy model versus the stakeholder design of company and whether the models are converging;[14] (4) a soft-law focus which involves wider issues including ethical principles in companies, including issues of sustainability, corporate social responsibility. This category includes the concession theory of companies.[15] We have focused on the contractual/shareholder primacy or neo-liberal model of company governance. It is perhaps fitting to reprise the burden of the preface: The shareholder primacy or the neo-liberal model is dangerous for a number of reasons. It is an extreme sort of utilitarianism without significant ethical principles.

- It allows the growth of mega companies backed by powerful international institutions including the IMF, the WB, the OECD and the WTO.
- It changes the balance of power between states, individuals and countries and the mega companies, including the financial sector (‘the markets’) and the international institutions.

---

11 For an excellent review of this topic see Keay (2011).

12 Andenas, M. and F. Wooldridge, *European Comparative Company Law* (Cambridge University Press, Cambridge 2009); Du Plessis, J.J., A. Hargovan and M. Bagaric, *Principles of Contemporary Corporate Governance* (Cambridge University Press, Cambridge 2011).

13 Dignam, A. and M. Galanis, *The Globalization of Corporate Governance* (Ashgate Publishing, Farnham 2009).

14 Hansmann, H. and R. Kraakman, ‘The End of History for Corporate Law’ (2000) *Harvard Law School John M. Olin Center for Law, Economics and Business Discussion Paper Series*, paper 280.

15 For example: Parkinson, J., ‘The Socially Responsible Company’ in M. Addo (ed), *Human Rights Standards and the Responsibility of Transnational Corporations* (Kluwer, The Hague, 1999); Boeger, N., R. Murray and C. Villiers (eds) *Perspectives on Corporate Social Responsibility* (Edward Elgar, Cheltenham 2008); Keay (2011).

- It is disastrous because of the burgeoning inequality between nations and individuals.
- It is profoundly anti-democratic because of the powerful actors.
- It is disastrous for the environment.

This is particularly clear in the Eurozone crisis where taxpayers have had to bail out the big banks. In fact the society as a whole 'plays the role of the insurer for the risks taken … the insurance is free, the risk is largely determined by the behaviour of the injured party and the insurer is granted no specific role in the internal control of the risk. What private insurer would accept such conditions?'[16] In fact the managers have assumed the role initially carried by the shareholders, allowing absolute shareholder supremacy to evolve into managerial supremacy. Those risks can have social costs and an adverse impact either on the local community or in the case of large corporations on the society as a whole, especially where there are MNCs. We have also seen the consequences of spiralling executive pay, because it can be regarded as 'an agency cost in itself in that it provides a potentially fruitful and opaque device for self-dealing by conflicted managers … a conflicted board may use the pay-setting process to influence pay and extract rents in the form of pay in excess of that which would be optimal for shareholders'.[17] We have seen ingenious incentives to convince the actors who are anyway supposed to act as the agents of the shareholders to adhere to the basic parameters of their role; however, if management is merely the agent of the shareholders aiming at safeguarding their interest guaranteeing a return of their investment then the lack of motivation on the part of the latter to perform this role reveals in a spectacular manner a fundamental flaw lying at the very heart of this model.

We have also considered the theory of a company as a nexus of contracts, the idea that the company is a 'collection of private contractual relationships',[18] devoid of any social responsibility, and it should be left alone from any regulatory interference which would place limitations upon the right to use the free enterprise tool as shaped exclusively by its signatory parties. In this conception the company has 'traditionally been

---

[16] Clerc, C., 'Questioning the Legitimacy of Shareholder Power' in J.P. Touffut, *Does Company Ownership Matter?* (Edward Elgar, Cheltenham 2009).

[17] Ferrarini, G. and N. Moloney, 'Executive Remuneration in the EU: The Context of Reform' (2005) 32 *European Corporate Governance Institute, Law Working Paper*, paper 32, p. 3.

[18] Fama, E., 'Agency Problems and the Theory of the Firm' (1980) 99 *Journal of Political Economy*, p. 290.

thought of more as a voluntary association between shareholders than as a creation of the state'.[19] This theory focuses on deregulation by the state (and we have seen, that is a fiction); the construct of contract also has dubious roots, especially aligned with the Kaldor–Hicks efficiency doctrine.[20]

In this book we have focused on the stakeholder theory, using German corporate governance as an example. Stakeholder theories of companies extend to the actors that it considers as stakeholders.[21] For those who espouse stakeholder theories, corporate governance is 'the process by which corporations are made responsive to the rights and wishes of stakeholders'.[22] The roots of this theory can be traced to the realisation that the corporations have evolved into vast entities whose activities and policies have an enormously far-reaching effect on the livelihoods of many in close proximity to them or even loosely associated with them. 'Business is about putting together a deal so that suppliers, customers, employees, communities, managers and shareholders all win continuously over time. In short at some level stakeholder interests have to be joint … or else there will be exit and a new collaboration formed.'[23] The stakeholder theory is 'less of a formal unified theory and more of a broad research tradition incorporating philosophy, ethics, political theory, economics, law and organisational social science'.[24] There is also a moral dimension, the existence of the corporation 'as an entity separate from the individuals who compose [means] … that it could be conceived as a person imbued with a sense of social responsibility'.[25] Inherent in this theory is therefore an element of morality or 'conscience'. The intractable issue is how the priorities can be arranged, and if the managers have duties to the company, this means that there are shifting priorities and multiplicity stakeholders.

---

[19] Cheffins, B., *Company Law: Theory, Structure and Operation* (Clarendon Press, Oxford 1997), p. 41.

[20] Ogus, A., *Regulation: Legal Form and Economic Theory* (Clarendon Press, Oxford 1994).

[21] Clarkson, M., 'A Stakeholder Framework for Analysing and Evaluating Corporate Social Performance' (1995) 20 *Academy of Management Review* 92, p. 112.

[22] Demb, A. and F.F. Neubauer, 'The Corporate Board: Confronting the Paradoxes' (1992) 25 *Long Range Planning* 3, p. 9.

[23] Freeman, E.R., A. Wicks and B. Parmar, 'Stakeholder Theory and the Corporate Objective Revisited' (2004) 15 *Organisation Science* 364, p. 365.

[24] Solomon (2009), p. 23.

[25] Dodd, M., 'For Whom are Corporate Managers Trustees?' (1932) 45 *Harvard Law Review* 1161.

At end of this conclusion we will consider some implications for inequality, democracy and the environment. Although the neo-liberal corporate governance model purports to be a moral system, it is fundamentally flawed. It is based on contract which itself is not neutral for any party who is disadvantaged. We discussed the Faustian pact: utilitarian theories can be good for economic growth but often the instruments that are used are immoral or at least amoral. It seems that without regulation and a concern for the disadvantaged or vulnerable states, the rich are able to exploit property including companies.

The concession theory is also part of German corporate governance. The consensus politics that Germany espouses is at the root of its corporate governance. The concession theory views the existence and the operation of the form as a concession granted by the state. Under this theory, 'incorporation is seen as a privilege'.[26] The corporate tool as we know it today has been created by the state which granted to it limited liability along with a separate corporate personality and perpetual succession. In concession theories, the role of the state as a legitimate source of company regulation is emphasised. This means that concession theory comes into direct conflict with the nexus of contracts theory as it challenges the nature of the firm as a purely private affair exclusively determined by the will of its private members, but defines the corporation as an entity which exists and operates on the basis of the regulation produced by the state and the privileges that the latter has granted to the corporate form.

More divergence of the understanding of corporate governance is found when financing the company is considered. Companies with a dispersed shareholding attract investment from the securities' markets and from a large number of investors, usually private individuals or institutional. On the other hand, companies with a more concentrated shareholder basis attract financing from a limited number of actors, usually including other corporations, private individuals (in many cases, wealthy families who were usually involved in the founding of such companies), banks and more recently bodies such as pension or insurance funds. We have used the terms of 'insider' and 'outsider' when referring to the two systems that involve a divergent structure of corporate ownership.[27] An insider system of corporate governance is the one in place by a country whose publicly listed corporations' shareholding is

---

[26] Macmillan Patfield, F. (ed), *Perspectives on Company Law*, vol 1 (Kluwer Law International, London 1995), p. 8.

[27] Dignam and Galanis, 'Corporate Governance and the Importance of Macroeconomic Context' (2008) 28 *Oxford Journal of Legal Studies* 2, p. 215.

distributed among a rather limited number of actors; the latter usually include the government itself, other corporations, the founding family or families of the company in question, banks and recently pension and insurance funds. In many occasions, the individuals involved in the ownership of the company are also involved in its control, significantly reduced the agency problem. There is no difficulty aligning the interests of the managers with those of the shareholders, as the identity of the latter might indeed coincide with that of the former; even if it does not, the limited number of actors involved in the company and the important and simultaneously comparable size of their shareholding entails the building of a consensus in relation to the basic aims of the company, and necessitates a certain degree of coordination of individual actions reflected in the decision-making. Since consensus stands at the core of the system, an increasing variety of actors is called up to consent to the company's objectives and operations; these are principally the shareholders and the employees along with the network of suppliers and the creditors. Therefore, a stakeholder approach is evidently adopted and a great variety of social actors are called to contribute responsibly to the smooth operation of the company, acquiring a stake in it and a 'social dividend' from its successful operation. However, in an insider company model, there are other challenges including the mix of majority/minority shareholders. Minority shareholders might be isolated and powerless against a strong entrenched majority, especially if the majority shareholders have a powerful consensus in the company.

The outsider model of companies is prominent in the USA and to some extent the UK. The term 'outsider' refers to the sources of finance and the structure of corporate governance of the relevant corporations. Most firms are financed directly by the securities' market, while they are controlled by a limited number of managers who may operate relatively uncontrolled on the part of the shareholders; despite being perceived as the exclusive owners of the corporation, shareholders fail to establish close links with the managers of their 'property' and maintain rather loose links with the company. The agency problem in this situation, namely the lack of monitoring of the agent (the manager) on the part of the principal (the shareholder), is particularly aggravated. This particular company model however guarantees greater flexibility in decision-making since the actors involved in it are significantly less numerous than the respective in the company operating on the basis of the insider model. Managements' discretion allows significant flexibility of market fluctuation, however it also allows them to arrange the business against the wishes of employees and other stakeholders, including the shareholders.[28] It is also focused on profit because the investors are remote from the other stakeholders; this also means that short-term decisions are rife. As we found in Chapter 2, the outside system of corporate governance appears to be more suitable for the type of economic activity that demands swift decision-making, a certain degree of risk-taking along with the ability to rapidly reallocate labour and capital, with a great degree of flexibility and adaptability to the rapidly changing conditions and needs of the market such as the highly fluid financial services markets. This model seems to respond more quickly to external challenges or pressures, precisely due to its ability to restructure itself through the reallocation of labour and capital particularly rapidly. The fact that the world's two leading financial centres are situated in London and New York, the two metropolises whose countries function as the flagship of the outsider model is not coincidental but a direct repercussion of the historical development that shaped a certain economic model operating on the basis of the open markets, enhanced fluidity and dispersed ownership.

Chapter 3 considered three corporate governance models in some detail, beginning with the model in the USA, and here the fundamental point can be encapsulated in the doctrine of shareholder primacy. We said that the role of the shareholders within this model is not only of paramount importance but appears to be its landmark characteristic. Nowadays, their prominence is embodied in the so-called 'business judgement rule' that was spelled out by the Delaware Supreme Court in 1985.[29] According to the ruling, 'under Delaware law, the business judgement rule is the offspring of the fundamental principle ... that the business and affairs of the Delaware corporation are managed by or under its board of directors ... directors are charged with an unyielding fiduciary duty to the corporation and its shareholders'.[30] In Europe there is more emphasis on the company, and directors owe their duties to the company, often including stakeholders (including society). European societies have therefore traditionally imposed legitimate limits to economic practices in fulfilment of other superior social aims. There is an inherent tension between the American notion of 'liberty' and the strong public interest ethic. The book charts the ascendancy of managers to

---

[28] Wallman, S., 'The Proper Interpretation of Corporate Constituency Statutes and Formulation of Director Duties' (1991) 21 *Stetson Law Review* 163, pp. 176–7.

[29] *Smith v Van Gorkom,* 488 A.2d 858, 872 (Delaware Supreme Court, 1985).

[30] Ibid.

extent that the US corporate governance is now a culture of 'director primacy' rather than a 'shareholder primacy' system.[31] We show that as long as shareholders enjoy an increase in the value of their investment, they are content enough to let the managers perform what they consider as the most appropriate strategy for the company. The maximisation of shareholder wealth as reflected by the price of the shares in the stock market functions consequently as the legitimising factor of managerial practices and decisions, that do include the managers' benefits and bonuses as it effectively provides them with the assurance that the shareholders will not seek any interference with the running of the company. Employees are not part of the company and are not involved with corporate governance. In the US, corporate governance 'is defined independently of possible relations to workers'.[32] Company law is distinguished from the structure of labour relations. The power of management is not absolute; the Enron scandal reformed the importance of independent directors and their grip on some committees including the audit committee. However, shareholder protection in the USA corporate context remains lax in comparative terms[33] and it is 'highly unusual in the extent to which it disenfranchises shareholders from both explicit and implicit influence'.[34]

In the US the grip of management is further enhanced by the power of the CEO. In the UK the office is usually split into two positions: the independent director takes a position as chairman and takes a long-term view of the companies' prospects, while the CEO acts as the supervisor of the executives. However, in the USA the two positions are often merged, allowing the CEO enormous power. This is another cultural difference between Europe and the USA coming from the influence of individualism. The scandals that erupted in the early twenty-first century were heavily influenced by the power of the CEO, and even accountants,

---

[31] Bainbridge, S., 'Director Primacy in Corporate Takeovers: Preliminary Reflections' (2002) 55 *Stanford Law Review* 791, p. 798.

[32] Blair, M.M. and J.M. Roe, *Employees and Corporate Governance*, (The Brookings Institution, Washington 1999), p. 93.

[33] Hill, 'Subverting Shareholder Rights: Lessons from News Corporation's Migration to Delaware' (2010) 63 *Vanderbilt Law Review* 1.

[34] Gelter, M., 'The Dark Side of Shareholder Influence: Managerial Autonomy and Stakeholder Orientation in Comparative Corporate Governance' (2009) 50 *Harvard International Law Journal* 129, p. 134.

auditors and lawyers were implicated because of the pervasive dominance of them.[35] The debate about independent directors is ongoing. One argument that has been put forward is that the independent directors will not be able to supervise the company effectively because of its distance between the details of the business. As we presented in Chapter 3, some scholars argue that

> the fidelity of managers to shareholder objectives, as opposed to managerial interests or stakeholder interests … the reliability of the firm's public disclosure which makes stock market prices a more reliable signal for capital allocation and for the monitoring of managers at other firms as well as their own … a 'visible hand' namely the independent board is needed to balance the tendency of markers to overshoot.[36]

The UK corporate governance system is also in flux. We considered the historical roots of company law, and showed that many other nations' corporate governance were heavily influenced by the British Empire. Later we showed that individualism is endemic in the early history of England. 'Personal freedom became universal at an early date in our country … self help and self government were for long centuries taught to the English in the school of town life … there were no rights without duties'.[37] Therefore, individuality, property rights and self-regulation enjoy deep roots in English history, having left their clear imprint on all aspects of regulation; company law could not be an exception to that rule and naturally nor could corporate governance. The landmark Joint Stock Companies Act 1844 contains the roots of today's company law regime and corporate governance structure. Importantly a general system of corporate registration and the obligation of registered companies to provide annual financial information to the public were also two of the most important features of this legislation. This Act was followed by the Limited Liability Act of 1855, granting for the first time the privilege of limited liability to the members of joint stock companies that comprised more than 25 members; the former assumed the responsibility to include the word 'limited' in their name; this principle was however denied to

---

[35] Gitlow, L.A., *Corruption in Corporate America*, 2nd edn (University Press of America Inc, New York 2007), p. 12.

[36] Jeffrey, G.N., 'The Rise of Independent Directors in the United States, 1950–2005: Of Shareholder Value and Stock Market Prices' (2007) 59 *Stanford Law Review* 1465, p. 1469.

[37] Trevelyan, G.M., *English Social History* (Penguin, London 1944).

general partners.[38] The laissez-faire philosophy was by that time dominant. The Joint Stock Companies Act of 1856 was a key turning point: it formed a consolidating statute that would leave its distinctive imprint on the whole edifice of British company law in the decades to come. The key quote that we used in Chapter 4 citing the vice president of the Board of Trade is a telling revelation of the English philosophy of 'liberty' at this time. The vice president of the Board of Trade explained that it is not as important

> to urge the adoption of limited liability … (but to) argue in favour of human liberty that people may be permitted to deal how and with whom they choose without the officious interference of the state … every man has a right to choose for himself between the two principles, and it is ill advised legislation which steps in between him and the exercise of that right.[39]

These legislation reforms led directly to the doctrine of *Saloman v Saloman*[40] and the central tenets of company personality and the division between companies and shareholders, heavily supported by the judiciary and one of the obstacles for human rights activists trying to sue multinational companies in different jurisdictions. Joining the EU came as a shock because of the different philosophy in continental Europe. The fundamental principles of liberty, self-regulation and individualism, along with the importance ascribed to property rights at the core of the British company law edifice, came into conflict with the more communitarian approaches adopted at the other side of the Channel. Simultaneously, and against the EU's communitarian philosophy, the Margaret Thatcher administration embarked on a highly ambitious privatisation programme, offering shares of what had been up to then companies under state control to the general public; the government in Britain therefore intentionally promoted a widely diffused ownership structure of public companies. As we have seen, although privatisation was extremely significant in political terms, 'what really made a difference to corporate governance in the UK was the transition to widespread ownership of corporations by asset management firms: insurance companies, pension funds, and the unit trusts and investment trusts that provided individual investors with a way to diversify their portfolio through collective

---

38 Section 9, Partnership Act 1890.
39 HC Deb. 1 February 1856, v.140, Col.131.
40 *Salomon v A. Salomon & Co Ltd* [1897] AC 22.

investing'.[41] We have argued that dispersed ownership in the UK took place much later than in the USA and probably fully unfolded after 1970.[42] Interestingly enough, it followed a different trend; it followed the emergence of institutional investors, while in the USA the institutional investors appeared at a later stage after ownership had initially been dispersed to millions of individual shareholders. The divergence in historical trends and experiences underlines the notion that although literature uses the term 'outsider' model or the 'Anglo-Saxon' model of corporate governance for both jurisdictions due to their evident similarities and parameters which have been analysed throughout this book, they are in fact two distinctive models formed in the framework of different societies, and hence this categorisation does not entail any form of claim that the two countries employ an identical model of corporate governance. The UK corporate governance is based on contractual principles but the 'contract' of the articles is atypical, most importantly in the way that judges interpreted the contract. They insisted that there was a public interest to protect minority shareholders. Later the judges invented an insider-outsider distinction which they thought would protect vulnerable members. The extent of this right is still unclear.

In the UK directors owe their duties to the company exclusively, in contradiction of the corporate governance of the USA where the directors owe their duties to the company *and* to shareholders. However, even though the Companies Act 2006 enacted an apparently different structure of corporate governance by broadening stakeholders' rights, many commentators believe that the shareholder primacy model is still there. The telling point is that shareholders are still the only persons who can sue directors for their misdeeds. In the UK the remedies for breaches of directors' duties are woefully inadequate, fuelled further by the dispersed number of shareholders, allowing large constituencies. The unfair prejudice remedy is not often used by shareholders in a public company since they can sell their shares easily without recourse to litigation. The other pillar of remedies for directors' duties is the derivative suit, which is now completely convoluted involving several stages and significant judicial interventions.

The plethora of soft law is a particular aspect of the UK system partly because of the philosophy of individualism and also because of the power of the financial sector in the UK. We investigated the role of a number of

---

41 Nordberg, D., *Corporate Governance, Principles and Issues* (Sage Publications, London 2011), p. 80.

42 Cheffins, *Corporate Ownership and Control, British Business Transformed* (Oxford University Press, Oxford 2008), pp. 12–13.

Codes, and perhaps the most innovative factor of them was the approach named as 'comply or explain', a distinctive part of the UK corporate governance structure. The final corporate governance Code was promulgated in 2012. The Financial Reporting Council concluded that the final version of the Cadbury Code brought into force in 2008 was fit for purpose, but reform was now deemed necessary to attempt to respond to the challenges emerging from the financial crisis of 2008 which marked the City of London and exposed certain shortcomings of the UK corporate governance system, especially in relation to the board of directors and its effective monitoring along with the issue of directors' remuneration. It is not a coincidence that these issues were included in the 2010 Code as the centrepieces of the limited reform. One of the central parameters of the 2010 Code is leadership; the Code states that 'every company should be headed by an effective board which is collectively responsible for the long-term success of the company'. This is welcome, although there are a number of counterintuitive issues in the Code including the more stringent re-election regime. Although this arrangement can indeed enhance the accountability of directors as they will have to be re-elected on regular intervals on the basis of their performance, the assessment of their office on an annual basis is likely to encourage a short-term strategy undermining the previously defined necessity to pursue the long-term success of the company. A very necessary change is the inclusion of an element of diversity at the board level and more specifically gender diversity, although it is far from the Scandinavian model. New for this Code, it states that the board is responsible for determining the nature and extent of the significant risks it is willing to take in achieving its strategic objectives. In assessing risk, the board should maintain sound risk management and internal control systems. This might make risk assessment committees more rigorous. There is a new provision on the role of the senior independent directors who should provide a sounding board for the chairman and serve as an intermediary for other directors when necessary. Non-executive directors are now required to constructively challenge and help develop proposals on strategy; therefore it is evident that the wording employed by the 2010 Code is much stronger, clearly aiming at achieving a much more active involvement of the non-executive directors in the company. Furthermore, the 2012 Code now introduces the principle that all directors should be able to allocate sufficient time to the company to discharge their responsibilities effectively.

The issue of executive remuneration is a running sore in the media in the UK. As far as this issue is concerned, the Code now includes a new supporting principle according to which performance-related elements of executive director's remuneration should be designed to promote the long-term success of the company. Whether that is consistent with the annual re-election of the directors has to be seen. The Code has also been amended to make clear that any pay-outs under incentive schemes should be subject to non-financial performance criteria where appropriate and compatible with the company's risk policies and systems. Companies should give consideration to the use of provisions that permit the company to reclaim variable components in exceptional circumstances of misstatement or misconduct. Remuneration of non-executive directors should now not include any performance-related elements. It seems that it will not be effective enough to stop the arguments because it is inherent in the insider model of companies and the conflicts found in separating ownership and control. The UK Corporate Governance Code of 2012 is an expression of wishful thinking rather than a policy whose implementation is rendered imperative by the Code. We have seen the resurgence of inequality and the remuneration issues for directors, which is perhaps the most corrosive problem for corporate governance now, fuelled by the contractual model of companies and the neo-liberal agenda. The composition of the remuneration committee is of absolute importance since if it is dominated by executives who have an interest in setting each other's pay, the egregious imbalances in the economy cannot be reversed. Although there are small shareholders revolts against egregious remuneration packages for directors, these small outliers have not fired a revolution. If legislation is not put in place to introduce mandatory voting of shareholders and employees on the remuneration committee on the executive pay, inequality will be unstoppable.

The last of our case studies was Germany. This is necessary because it has gradually shaped a system of corporate governance which has proved to be particularly influential for countries seeking to make like-minded reforms. The corporate governance system in Germany took its current shape in the post-war period when successive governments made the conscious choice to construct an inclusive governance system based on consensus between its various constituencies. Cooperation as a concept is integral to the philosophical foundations of the German economy. Germany seems particularly attached to the notion of cooperation that will involve a major degree of consensus building. German company law and its orientation betray the origins of corporate governance which are deeply rooted within the national legislative tradition and social history, explaining its resistance to the forces of globalisation. The consensus model of corporate governance impacts upon the flexibility of the decision-making system and its ability to swiftly adapt to the outbreak of a crisis or to the rapid shift in the market conditions. We showed that

German corporate governance is less flexible and therefore managers need a greater range of skills to strengthen the durability of the economy. The history of corporate governance shows that network between banks and companies and the interrelation between the former and the latter remains a distinctive feature of the German corporate landscape even now. The concepts of 'cooperation', 'networks', 'close interaction', 'consensus' and 'long-term planning' seem to be monotonously repeated every time an analysis of the German corporate and economic model is written about, so it is clear that these are fundamental terms.

In 1720 the UK dealt with corporate fraud by sweeping reforms and legislation which restricted business as a whole; Germany dealt with corporate fraud by continuing to encourage corporate activities but focusing on placing the management under additional control. The supervisory board, which was recently enacted and was a part of the dual board structure that would emerge as one of the landmark features not only of the German corporate governance but also of the country as a whole, was about to assume a very significant role within this framework. In 1884 legislation changed the duties of the board members and of the shareholders' meeting. In particular they strengthened both the control duties and control powers of the supervisory board, and instituted director liability. The road had been paved for the creation of a corporate environment within the context of which a stakeholder-friendly approach would become the norm. During the Nazi era, corporate governance was shaped by centralisation by the government. We considered the paradox inherent in the National Socialists party by strengthening a stakeholder model allowing the *Reich* to be a stakeholder and therefore a sort of 'corporate democracy'. This degraded sort of democracy turned out to be highly anti-democratic for Germany because the state took control of the banks.

After the war ended, the Marshall Plan gave Germany significant aid to restore its infrastructure and consolidate the corporate governance structure. The system of cartelisation that already entailed a high level of coordination, synergies and cross-participations in the shareholding of a variety of companies on the basis of tight links between industry and government was thought to have also contributed significantly to the two world wars. It enabled Germany to avoid competition from abroad and therefore shielded its national industry from external pressures which could have either liberalised it or impaired its ability to engage in mass production of machinery which was crucial for the war. The system of cartels and corporate governance remained essentially the same during the war, strengthened by a constitution which highly protected human rights and the inception of the EEC. The new German corporate governance mix of human rights, and the relaxation of intensity between the state and the banks and a more dominant place for employees allowed Germany to devise a 'middle ground' between aggressive capitalism and strong socialism. The place reserved for labour within the administrative structure of the German company serves as the red line that utterly separates the US and UK corporate governance model with the German. The enhanced employee participation was upheld by Social Democrats and Christian Democrats alike guaranteeing the continuous support of the parties which formed the backbone of the governmental coalitions that ruled the country especially from the Second World War and onwards and until today. Already 'before the First World War, codetermination was developed by both liberal and Christian theorists as a process necessitated by industrialisation and as an acceptable alternative to revolutionary employee practices'.[43] Although codetermination was abolished by the Nazis, after the war the Allies and all sections of the German community were determined to make the country democratic and equal. The British believed that the incorporation of labour into the administrative structures of the German company would eliminate the possibility of a restive labour creating problems while it would ensure the administration of the German corporation on a more inclusive basis. However the theory was one thing, but at first there was significant resistance by management of big companies in Germany. They thought that it would be disastrous and said so, the Act was a 'horrified outrage. [They] … predicted that labour representatives would come blundering into management affairs like a herd of bulls in a china shop'.[44] Academia was about as sceptical about the change. A decisive Federal Constitutional Court judgment supported the legislation. By the 1970s the stability of German society became consolidated and codetermination was becoming an integral part of the German society and a landmark of its corporate governance model. Crucially German jurisprudence recognises significant limitation of property rights including an obligation to use property 'to serve the public good'.[45] The individual property rights in the UK and America are starkly dissimilar. Although some UK and American academics argue that property rights are limited, many individuals believe that they are inviolate. Property is a sacred right which should be

---

[43] Raiser, T., 'The Theory of Enterprise Law in the Federal Republic of Germany' (1988) *American Journal of Comparative Law*, p. 117.

[44] Vagts, F.D., 'Reforming the Modern Corporation: Perspectives from the German' (1966) 80 *Harvard Law Review* 23, p. 68.

[45] Basic Law for the Federal Republic of Germany, Grundgesetz; available at www.iuscomp.org/gla/statutes/GG.htm#14.

safeguarded against interventions. This means that shareholders own shares and therefore the company as a property right. Although this is bad jurisprudence, it has significant resonance in the Anglo–American corporate governance debate and contrasts with the German system which is a stakeholder model and rooted in a concessional understanding: since companies owe their historic success to the concessions granted consciously by the state, they ought to return part of the profit to the society at large.

In conclusion we believe that it is time that governments, academics and activists cooperated on changing corporate governance systems, allowing a flatter consensus model of companies which would allow stakeholders more power. We have seen the damage to equality, democracy and the environment which large company groups pose:

> globalization's effects are everywhere to be seen. The poor are getting poorer, the rich, richer … Mega-mergers leading to the establishment of giant oligopolies now control our marketplaces. These oligopolies, aided by loose government regulation, eliminate competition. Ignoring the cheerful, blind ideology of free marketers, they force up prices for vital goods like drugs, and capture disproportionably high profits … Elected democratic governments have been weakened, and lack the powers, resources and institutions to protect their citizens and firms and compensate citizens when shocks occur … leading to disillusionment with spineless parliaments; and with leaders that have given away to invisible 'markets' key powers to allocate resources.[46]

There is an imperative moral argument to design corporate governance not only for our own sake but for intergenerational reasons. Thomas Pogge believes that the rich have duties to the poor:

> moral norms, designed to protect the livelihood and dignity of the vulnerable, place burdens on the strong. If such norms are compelling enough, the strong make an effort to comply. But they also, consciously or unconsciously, try to get around the norms by arranging their social world so as to minimise their burdens of compliance.[47]

One of the most important devices that is used by the powerful is the limited liability company and the demands made on its managers to maximise the profits of shareholders. A common method of minimising

---

46 Pettifor, A., *The Coming First World Debt Crisis* (Palgrave, London 2006), pp. 51–2.

47 Pogge, T., *World Poverty and Human Rights* (Polity Press, Cambridge 2008), p. 5.

the burden of compliance is to interpose an agent to carry out reprehensible acts: Pogge gives the example of a lawyer to manage an apartment block. The most efficient use of the block would be to convert the flats into luxury accommodation and double the rent. Some of the flats are occupied by poor, elderly tenants who would be forced to leave and have difficulty finding accommodation elsewhere. The lawyer is appointed to manage the block 'efficiently', thus saving the owner from himself evicting the elderly residents. Pogge argues that this solution cannot absolve the owner of his moral responsibility.[48] Companies are used by rich societies in an exactly equivalent way, to be the agents carrying out reprehensible moral acts from which rich societies benefit. Companies are doubly useful in this respect as they can also be blamed for the reprehensible acts while those who invented them and profit from them can express moral outrage, thus feeling good about taking the moral high ground. Companies are used as providing ethical 'loopholes':

> Consider the ethical view that as a member of a social arrangement one may sometimes – when acting in behalf of other members or of the entire group – deliberately harm outsiders in some specific way, even though one may not do so when acting on one's own. Such views are, I believe, widely held. In the business world, those who implement a corporate policy that is harmful to consumers, employees, or to the general public often stress their status as managers and their obligations towards the firm's owners, whose financial interests they were hired to promote. How is this supposed to be ethically relevant? … Ethical views of this sort guide their adherents to form or join social arrangements in order to effect, through the special ties these involve, a unilateral reduction of responsibility toward those left out of these arrangements.[49]

This points up both the concept of exclusion; the company is an exclusive club; and hints at the mechanism by which the connection between 'ownership' of the company as property and the polarisation of income and power can come about because of the sloppy ethical understanding that creation of a corporation can, in some way, reduce ethical and human rights responsibilities. Pogge argues that where an ethic has fixed

> those basics that persons owe all others in the absence of any special ties and relations … [imposing an agent] should not enable persons unilaterally to reduce or dilute them. Specifically, it should not allow them, by forming or joining a social arrangement, to subject themselves to new, countervailing

---

48 Ibid., p. 77.
49 Ibid., p. 76.

> obligations to its members that may outweigh, trump, or cancel their minimal obligations to everyone else.[50]

As we have seen, companies are created by laws adopted by societies. Creating a company to obtain or manufacture goods cheaply and to provide investment opportunities means that rich societies are benefiting from the cheap prices obtained for resources from poorer societies, including labour resources. Creating a company to achieve objectives which would be ethically deplored in an individual means that we can conveniently blame others while reaping the reward of their behaviour. Ireland uses the image of a man lying on a sofa together with the assertion that he is 'working highly profitably' making money from his investments to reveal

> the irresponsibility that is built into the prevailing structure of corporate rights and the regulatory institutions that support them, for it is precisely the no-obligation, no-responsibility nature of corporate income rights which enables their owners to relax on sofas, blissfully ignorant of and uninterested in precisely how the dividends and interest accruing to them is generated.[51]

He also points out the wide complicity in corporate behaviour through the growth in private pensions. Using companies to generate our wealth and provide cheap food and commodities is the first moral deflection device.

A second such device comes into play when we vilify companies for their behaviour. This gives us the moral high ground while still living comfortably because of the benefits they provide. Moral indignation at the terrible behaviour of some corporations as discussed in Chapter 1 must not be allowed to obscure the fact that companies are designed by societies and their profits underpin much of our wealth. So when they strike bargains with evil regimes, repatriate their profits and sell us goods produced at low prices because of sweated or slave labour, this is not because of the inherent evil of the people that work in corporations but as a direct result of the legal design of corporations and the operation of the international legal system which provides them with many opportunities yet fails to regulate.

A variant of the second device is provided by the immense energy put into Codes of Conduct and Corporate Social Responsibility. Since these are voluntary and very liable to capture by the PR departments of

---

50 Ibid., pp. 78–9.

51 Ireland, 'Property and Contract in Contemporary Corporate Theory' [2004] *Legal Studies* 453 at 506.

companies, it is likely that a great deal of energy will be spent to little effect. The participants have a 'feel good' factor which deflects the more important structural issues causing the problems.[52] The avoidance of moral blame is assisted by the distortion of our understanding of companies by deconstructing their power and by a false understanding of their structure. The US/UK model has shareholders as the primary focus; the company must serve the interests of shareholders, and directors are appointed and dismissed by shareholders. Nevertheless directors are to act in the interest of the company and usually owe no direct duties to shareholders. This structure does not necessarily equate shareholders with the company, nor does it equate shareholder interests with 'profit maximisation' and impose a duty on directors to achieve such a goal. Nevertheless recent discourse has imposed the concept of profit maximisation on the assumption that this is what shareholders require, and the second assumption that shareholders and the company are one and the same thing. Such an understanding of corporate aims has wide implications for their behaviour since all considerations other than profit are seen as 'negative externalities' to be adhered to or to be bargained away if possible. It has also been one of the underlying causes of spectacular bankruptcies such as Enron and WorldCom. In terms of moral responsibility such a construct of corporations means that they become another method of moral deflection: because the purpose of corporations is to make as much money as possible, those who tolerate and profit from their existence have no responsibility for the methods they pursue. This ignores the fact not only that companies are structured by national laws but also that those who profit from an activity have a responsibility to prevent that activity harming others.

---

52 Fagan, A., 'Ethical Shopping and Trusting Morality' in B. Glanville and J. Dine (eds), *The Processes and Practices of Fairtrade, Trust, Ethics and Governance* (Routledge, London 2012), p. 246.

# References

## Books


Abelshauser, W., 'West German Economic Recovery 1945–1951: A Reassessment' (1982) 135 *Three Banks Review*, The Royal Bank of Scotland Group, p. 45.

Addo, M. (ed), *Human Rights Standards and the Responsibility of Transnational Corporations* (Kluwer, The Hague 1999).

Adger, W.N. and A. Jordan (eds), *Governing Sustainability* (Cambridge University Press, Cambridge 2009).

Aglietta, M. and A. Reberioux, *Corporate Governance Adrift* (Edward Elgar, Cheltenham 2005).

Andenas, M. and F. Wooldridge, *European Comparative Company Law* (Cambridge University Press, Cambridge 2009).

Anderson, S. and J. Cavanaugh, *The Rise of Global Corporate Power* (Institute for Policy Studies, Washington DC 1996).

Arnold, H. and F. Faurote, *Ford Methods and the Ford Shops* (The Engineering Managing Company, New York 1919).

Athukorala, P., *Crisis and Recovery in Asia: The Role of Capital Controls* (Edward Elgar, Cheltenham 2003).

Ayres, I. and L. Braithwaite, *Responsive Regulation* (Oxford University Press, Oxford 1992).

Bacon, F. in C. Hill, *Intellectual Origins of the English Revolution* (Panther, Oxford University Press, Oxford 1972).

Bainbridge, M.S., *The New Corporate Governance in Theory and Practice* (Oxford University Press, Oxford 2008).

Bakan, J., *The Corporation* (Constable, London 2005).

Bakan, J., *The Corporation: the Pathological Pursuit of Profit and Power* (Free Press, New York 2004).

Banner, S., *How the Indians Lost their Land* (Harvard University Press, Cambridge, MA 2005).

Barbier, E.B., *A Global Green New Deal* (United Nations Environment Programme (UNEP), 2010).

Barca, F. and M. Becht, *The Control of Corporate Europe* (ECGN, Oxford University Press, Oxford 2002).

Barker, R.M., *Corporate Governance, Competition and Political Parties, Explaining Corporate Governance Change in Europe* (Oxford University Press, Oxford 2010).

Beck, S., F. Klobes and C. Frank, *Surviving Globalisation?: Perspectives for the German Economic Model* (Springer, Dordrecht, The Netherlands 2005).

Beck, U., *Power in the Global Age* (Polity Press, Cambridge 2005).

Berle, A. and C. Gardiner Means, *The Modern Corporation & Private Property*, 10th edn (Harcourt, Brace & World Inc., New York 2009).

Berle, A., *Power Without Property* (Harcourt, Brace & World Inc., New York 1959).

Berle, A., *The Twentieth Century Capitalist Revolution* (Macmillan, London 1955).

Bernard, N., *Multilevel Governance in the European Union* (Kluwer, Dordrecht, Netherlands 2000).

Bernitz, U. and W-G. Ringe, *Company Law and Economic Protectionism, New Challenges to European Integration* (Oxford University Press, Oxford 2010).

Birch, K. and V. Nykhnenko (eds), *The Rise and Fall of Neo-liberalism: The Collapse of an Economic Order?* (Zed Books, London and New York 2010).

Blackbourn, D., *History of Germany 1780–1918: The Long Nineteenth Century* (Wiley-Blackwell, Oxford 2002).

Blair, M.M. and J.M. Roe, *Employees and Corporate Governance* (The Brookings Institution, Washington 1999).

Blair, M.M., *Ownership and Control* (The Brookings Institution, Washington 1995).

Boeger, N., R. Murray and C. Villiers (eds), *Perspectives on Corporate Social Responsibility* (Edward Elgar Publishing, Cheltenham 2008).

Bottomley, S. and D. Kinley (eds), *Commercial Law and Human Rights* (Dartmouth, Aldershot 2002).

Bottomley, S., *The Constitutional Corporation* (Ashgate, Farnham 2007).

Braithwaite, J. and P. Drahos, *Global Business Regulation* (Cambridge University Press, Cambridge 2000).

Braun, H.J., *The German Economy in the Twentieth Century, The German Reich and the Federal Republic* (Routledge, London 1990).

Brown, D., *Hear that Lonesome Whistle Blow* (Henry Holt and Company LLC, New York 2001).

Brown, L.R. et al. (eds), *State of the World* (Norton & co, New York and London 1991).

Brundtland, H., *Our Common Future* (Oxford University Press, Oxford 1987).

Brunsson, N. and B. Jacobsson, *A World of Standards* (Oxford University Press, Oxford 2000).
Burrows, P. and C. Velanovski (eds), *The Economic Approach to Law* (Butterworth, London 1981).
Cadbury, A., *Corporate Governance and Chairmanship* (Oxford University Press, Oxford 2002).
Cahn, A. and D.C. Donald, *Comparative Company Law* (Cambridge University Press, Cambridge 2010).
Cannon, T., *Corporate Responsibility, A Textbook on Business Ethics, Governance, Environment: Roles and Responsibilities* (Pitman, London 1994).
Carr, W., *A History of Germany, 1815–1990* (Bloomsbury Academic, London 1991).
Carter, G.R., *The Tendency Towards Industrial Combination* (Constable, London 1913).
Chandler, Jr, A.D. and H. Daems, *Managerial Hierarchies: Comparative Perspectives on the Rise of the Modern Industrial Enterprise* (Harvard University Press, Cambridge MA 1980).
Chandler, Jr, A.D., 'The Managerial Revolution in the American Business' in C. Thomas, *Theories of Corporate Governance, The Philosophical Foundations of Corporate Governance* (Routledge, London 2008).
Charkam, J., *Keeping Better Company, Corporate Governance Ten Years On*, 2nd edn (Oxford University Press, Oxford 2008).
Cheffins, B.R., *Company Law: Theory, Structure and Operation* (Clarendon Press, Oxford 1997 and 1999).
Cheffins, B.R., *Corporate Ownership and Control, British Business Transformed* (Oxford University Press, Oxford 2008).
Chew, D.H. and S.L. Gillan, *Corporate Governance at the Crossroads: A Book of Readings* (McGraw-Hill Irwin, New York 2005).
Chomsky, N., *Profit over People* (Seven Stories Press, New York 1999).
Chossudovsky, M., *The Globalisation of Poverty* (Pluto, Halifax, Nova Scotia 1998).
Circular to Bankers, February 1840 in J. Parkinson and A. Gamble, *The Political Economy of the Company* (Hart Publishing, Oxford 2000).
Clarke, T., *Theories of Corporate Governance, The Philosophical Foundations of Corporate Governance* (Routledge, New York 2008).
Clerc, C., 'Questioning the Legitimacy of Shareholder Power' in J.P. Touffut, *Does Company Ownership Matter?* (Edward Elgar, Cheltenham 2009).
Craig, A.G., *Germany, 1866–1945* (Oxford University Press, Oxford 1980).

Czinkota, M., I. Ronksinen and M. Moffett, *International Business*, 4th edn (Dryden, Fort Worth 1996).

Daems, H. and H. Van Der Wee, 'The Rise of Managerial Capitalism', in R. Tilly, *The Growth of Large Scale Enterprise in Germany since the Middle of the Nineteenth Century* (Martinus Nijhoff, Leiden, the Netherlands, Boston 1974).

de Jonge, A., *Transnational Corporations and International Law* (Edward Elgar, Cheltenham 2011).

Demb, A. and F.F. Neubauer, 'The Corporate Board: Confronting the Paradoxes' (1992) 25 *Long Range Planning* 3.

Dietmar, P., *Die Deutsche Wirtschaft in der Zweischenkriegszeit* (Steiner, Wiesbaden 1977).

Dignam, A. and M. Galanis, *The Globalization of Corporate Governance* (Ashgate, Farnham 2009).

Dine, J. and M. Koutsias, *Company Law*, 8th edn (Palgrave Macmillan, London 2013).

Dine, J., *Companies, International Trade and Human Rights* (Cambridge University Press, Cambridge 2005).

Dine, J., M. Koutsias and M. Blecher, *Company Law in the New Europe: The EU Aquis, Comparative Methodology and Model Law* (Edward Elgar, Aldershot 2007).

Dine, J., *The Governance of Corporate Groups* (Cambridge University Press, Cambridge 2000).

Doeker-Mach, G. and K.A. Ziegert (eds), *Law, Legal Culture and Politics in the Twenty-First Century – Essays in Honour of Erh-Soon Tay, Alice* (Franz Steiner Verlag, Stuttgart 2004).

Douzinas, C., *Human Rights and Empire: The Political Philosophy of Cosmopolitanism* (Routledge-Cavendish, Abingdon 2007).

Du Plessis, J.J., A. Hargovan and M. Bagaric, *Principles of Contemporary Corporate Governance* (Cambridge University Press, Cambridge 2011).

Du Plessis, J.J., B. Großfeld, C. Luttermann, I. Ingo, O. Sandrock and M. Casper, *German Corporate Governance in International and European Context*, 2nd edn (Springer, Heidelberg, Dordrecht, London, New York 2012).

Dunn, R., *Sugar and Slaves: The Rise of the Planter Class in the English West Indies, 1624–1713* (University of North Carolina Press, 1972 and 2000).

Eagleman, D., *Incognito: The Secret Lives of the Brain* (Cannongate, Edinburgh 2011).

Easterbrook F. and D. Fischel, *The Economic Structure of Corporate Law* (Harvard University Press, Cambridge MA 1991).

Edwards J. and K. Fischer, *Banks, Finance and Investment in Germany* (Cambridge University Press, Cambridge 1994).

Edwards, V., *EC Company Law* (Oxford University Press, Oxford 1999).

Ehrenreich, B., *Nickel and Dimed* (Granta, London 2002).

Ehrlich, E., *Fundamental Principles of Sociology of Law* (Harvard University Press, Cambridge MA 1936).

Elliott, L., *The Global Politics of the Environment*, 2nd edn (Palgrave Macmillan, Basingstoke 2004).

Eroglu, M., *Multinational Enterprises and Tort Liabilities* (Edward Elgar, Cheltenham 2008).

Esser, J., 'Bank Power in West Germany Revised' (1990) 13 *West European Politics* 4, 17.

Ezzamel, M. and R. Watson, 'Wearing Two Hats: The Conflicting Control and Management Roles of Non Executive Directors' in K. Keasey, S. Thompson and M. Wright, *Corporate Governance: Economic and Financial Issues* (Oxford University Press, Oxford 1997).

Fagan, A., 'Ethical Shopping and Trusting Morality' in B. Glanville and J. Dine (eds), *The Processes and Practices of Fairtrade, Trust, Ethics and Governance* (Routledge, London 2012).

Feldstein, M. (ed) *International Capital Flows* (University of Chicago Press, Chicago 1999).

Fleming, P. and S.C. Zyglidopoulos, *Charting Corporate Corruption* (Edward Elgar, Cheltenham 2009).

Fohlin, C., *Finance Capitalism and Germany's Rise to Industrial Power* (Cambridge University Press, Cambridge 2007).

Franco, A. and A. Colli, *Business History, Complexities and Comparisons* (Routledge, London 2011).

Freeman, R.E., *Strategic Management: A Stakeholder Approach* (Pitman, Boston, 1984).

Friedman, L., *A History of American Law* (Simon and Schuster, New York 1973).

Fullbrook, M., *A Concise History of Germany* (Cambridge University Press, Cambridge 1992).

German Federal Constitutional Court (*BVerfGE*) (1979) vol 50, 290.

Gillespie, J.G., *Transplanting Commercial Law Reform* (Ashgate, Farnham 2006).

Gillingham, J., *European Integration 1950–2003, Superstate or Market Economy?* (Cambridge University Press, Cambridge 2003).

Gitlow, L.A., *Corruption in Corporate America*, 2nd edn (University Press of America Inc, New York 2007).

Glinavos, I., *Neoliberalism and the Law in Post Communism Transition*, (Routledge, Abingdon 2010).

Gospel, H. and A. Pendleton, *Corporate Governance and Labour Management, An International Comparison* (Oxford University Press, Oxford 2005).
Gourevitch, A.P. and J. Shinn, *Political Power and Corporate Control* (Princeton University Press, Princeton NJ 2005).
Grear, A., *Redirecting Human Rights* (Palgrave Macmillan, Basingstoke 2010).
Green, D., *From Poverty to Power* (Oxfam, Rugby 2008).
Ha-Joon Chang, *23 Things They Don't Tell About Capitalism* (Allen Lane, Penguin, London 2010).
Halberstaum, D., *The Reckoning* (William Morrow, New York 1986).
Hall, A.P. and D. Soskice, *Varieties of Capitalism, The Institutional Foundations of Comparative Advantage* (Oxford University Press, Oxford 2001)
Hampden, T.C. and F. Trompenaars, *The Seven Cultures of Capitalism: Value Systems for Creating Wealth in the United States, Britain, Japan, Germany, France, Sweden, and the Netherlands* (Doubleday, New York 1993).
Harris, J., *Property and Justice* (Clarendon Press, Oxford 1996).
Harrison, P., *Inside the Third World*, 3rd edn (Penguin, Harmondsworth 1993).
Helm, D. and C. Hepburn (eds), *The Economics and Politics of Climate Change* (Oxford University Press, Oxford 2009).
Hertsgaard, M., *Earth Odyssey* (Abacus, London 1999).
Hertz, N., *The Silent Takeover* (Heinemann, London 2001).
Hill, C., *Intellectual Origins of the English Revolution* (Panther, Oxford University Press, Oxford 1972).
Hirst, P.Q., *Law and Ideology* (Macmillan, London 1979).
Horwitz, M., *The Transformation of American Law, 1780–1860* (Harvard University Press, Cambridge MA 1977).
Hudson, A., *Understanding Company Law* (Routledge, London 2012).
Hulme, M., *Why We Disagree about Climate Change* (Cambridge University Press, Cambridge 2009).
Hurst, J.W., *The Legitimacy of the Business Corporation in the Law of the United States, 1780–1970* (University Press of Virginia, Charlottesville 1970).
Hutton, W., *The World We're In* (Little, Brown, London 2002).
Irwin, D., *Free Trade Under Fire* (Princeton University Press, Princeton NJ 2002).
Jeffrey, C., N. Gordon, M.J. Roe, *Convergence and Persistence in Corporate Governance* (Cambridge University Press, Cambridge 2004).

Kamminga, M. and S. Zia-Zarifi (eds), *Liability of Multinational Corporations under International Law* (Kluwer, The Hague 2000).
Karliner, J., *The Corporate Planet* (Sierra Club, San Francisco 1997).
Kaufman, A., L. Zacharias and M. Karson, *Managers v Owners: The Struggle for Corporate Control in American Democracy* (Oxford University Press, New York 1995).
Kay, J. and A. Silberston, 'Corporate Governance' (2005) *National Institute Economic Review*, August.
Keasey, K., S. Thompson and M. Wright, *Corporate Governance: Economic and Financial Issues* (Oxford University Press, Oxford 1997).
Keasey, K., S. Thompson and M. Wright, *Corporate Governance, Accountability, Enterprise and International Comparisons* (John Wiley and Sons Ltd, Chichester 2005).
Keay, A., *The Corporate Objective* (Edward Elgar, Cheltenham 2011).
Keay, A., *The Enlightened Shareholder Value Principle and Corporate Governance* (Routledge, London 2013).
Keay, J., *The Honourable Company* (Harper Collins Publishers, London 1993).
Keynes, J.M., *Essays in Persuasion, The Collected Writings of John Maynard Keynes*, vol 9 (Cambridge University Press, Cambridge 1978).
Kieff, F.S. and A.T. Paredes, *Perspectives on Corporate Governance* (Cambridge University Press, Cambridge 2010).
Kitchen, M., *A History of Modern Germany 1800 to the Present* (Wiley-Blackwell, Oxford 2011).
Klein, N., *Fences and Windows* (Picador, New York 2002).
Klein, N., *No Logo* (Picador, London 1999).
Klein, N., *The Shock Doctrine: The Rise of Disaster Capitalism* (Allen Lane, London 2007).
Kogut, B., *The Small Worlds of Corporate Governance* (MIT Press, Cambridge MA 2012).
Korten, D., *When Corporations Rule the World* (Kumarian Press, San Francisco 1995).
Kraakman, R. et al, *The Anatomy of Corporate Law, A Comparative and Functional Approach* (Oxford University Press, Oxford 2009).
Kübler, F., *Gesellschaftsrecht*, 4th edn (C.F. Müller Juristischer Verlag, Heidelberg, 1994).
Kwarteng, K., P. Patel, D. Raab, C. Skidmore and E. Truss, *Britain Unchained* (Palgrave Macmillan, London 2012).
Larsson, T., *The Race to the Top; The Real Story of Globalisation* (Cato Institute, Washington 1999).

Licht, W., *Working for the Railroad* (Princeton University Press, Princeton NJ 1983).

Locke, J., *Two Treatises of Government*, P. Laslett (ed) (Cambridge University Press, Cambridge 1988).

Lowry, J. and A. Reisberg, *Pettet's Company Law: Company Law and Corporate Finance* (Pearson, Harlow 2012).

Macey, R.J., *Corporate Governance, Promises Kept, Promises Broken* (Princeton University Press, Princeton NJ 2008).

Macfarlane, A., *The Origins of English Individualism* (Basil Blackwell, Oxford 1978).

MacGregor, D.H., *Industrial Combination* (George Bell & Sons, Cambridge 1906).

Machiavelli, N., *The Florentine History*, vol 2 (Forgotten Books, Charleston, SC 2010).

Macmillan Patfield, F. (ed), *From Rights to Regulation: Perspectives on Company Law*, vol 2 (Kluwer Law International, London 1997).

Macmillan Patfield, F. (ed), *Perspectives on Company Law*, vol 1 (Kluwer Law International, London 1995).

Mallin, A.C., *Handbook on International Corporate Governance, Country Analyses*, 2nd edn (Edward Elgar, Cheltenham 2011).

Mäntysaari, P., *Comparative Corporate Governance, Shareholders as a Rule-maker* (Springer, Berlin, Heidelberg, New York 2005).

Marlowe, Christopher, *The Tragicall History of the Life and Death of Doctor Faustus* (1604).

McAllister, R., *From EC to EU, A Historical and Political Survey* (Routledge, London 1997).

McCahery, A.J. and P.M.E. Vermeulen, *Corporate Governance of Non-Listed Companies* (Oxford University Press, Oxford 2010).

McCahery, J., S. Picciotto and C. Scott (eds), *Corporate Control and Accountability* (Clarendon Press, Oxford 1993).

McKitrick, F., *The Stabilisation of the Mittelstand: Artisans in Germany from National Socialism to the Federal Republic, 1939–1953* (unpublished phd thesis, Columbia University).

McQueen, R., *A Social History of Company Law, Great Britain and the Australian Colonies 1854–1929* (Ashgate, Farnham 2009).

Meadows, D., J. Randers and D. Meadows, *Limits to Growth* (Earthscan, New York and London 2010).

Micklethwait, J. and A. Wooldridge, *The Company* (Phoenix, London 2005).

Monbiot, G., *Captive State: The Corporate Takeover of Britain* (Macmillan, Basingstoke 2000).

Monks, R.A.G. and N. Minow, *Corporate Governance*, 4th edn (John Wiley & Sons Ltd, Chichester 2010).

Moore, M., *World Without Walls* (Cambridge University Press, Cambridge 2002).
Morck, K.R., *A History of Corporate Governance Around the World, Family Business Groups to Professional Managers* (The University of Chicago Press, Chicago 2007).
Mount, F., *Mind the Gap* (Short Books, London 2004).
Muchlinski, P., *Multinational Enterprises and the Law* (Blackwell, Oxford 1995).
Nordberg, D., *Corporate Governance, Principles and Issues* (Sage Publications, London 2011).
Norton, J.J. and J. Rickford, *Corporate Governance Post-Enron, Comparative and International Perspectives* (British Institute of International and Comparative Law, London 2005).
Nozick, R., *Anarchy, State and Utopia* (Harvard University Press, Cambridge MA 1973).
O'Sullivan, M.A., *Contests for Corporate Control, Corporate Governance and Economic Performance in the USA and Germany* (Oxford University Press, Oxford 2001).
Ogus, A., *Regulation: Legal Form and Economic Theory* (Clarendon Press, Oxford 1994).
Orhnial, T., *Limited Liability and the Corporation* (Law Society of Canada, London 1982).
Owen, G., T. Kirchmaier and J. Grant, *Corporate Governance in the US and Europe, Where are we now?* (Palgrave Macmillan, New York 2005).
Oxfam, *Global Finance Hurts the Poor* (Oxfam America, Boston 2002).
Oxfam, *Global Finance, Tax Havens: Releasing the Hidden Billions for Poverty Eradication* (Oxfam America, Boston 2001).
Oxfam, *Oil, Gas and Mining: Poor Communities Pay the Price* (Oxfam America, Boston 2001).
Padgett, C., *Corporate Governance* (Palgrave Finance, London 2012).
Palast, G., *The Best Democracy Money Can Buy* (Pluto, Halifax, Nova Scotia 2002).
Parkinson, J. and A. Gamble, *The Political Economy of the Company* (Hart Publishing, Oxford 2000).
Parkinson, J.E., *Corporate Power and Responsibility: Issues in the Theory of Company Law* (Clarendon Press, Oxford 1993).
Pettet, B., *Company Law* (Pearson Education, Edinburgh 2001).
Pettifor, A., *The Coming First World Debt Crisis* (Palgrave, London 2006).
Pilger, J., *The New Rulers of the World* (Verso, London 2002).
Pilkington, C., *Britain in the European Union Today* (Manchester University Press, Manchester 1995).

Pinto, R.A. and G. Visentini, *The Legal Basis of Corporate Governance in Publicly Held Corporations* (Kluwer Law International, London 1998).

Pogge, T., *World Poverty and Human Rights* (Polity Press, Cambridge 2002 and 2008).

Posner, R., *Economic Analysis of Law*, 4th edn (Little, Brown, Boston 1992).

Postan, M.M, *The Medieval Economy and Society* (Weidenfeld & Nicolson, London 1972; Pelican, London 1975).

Postan, M.M., *The English Farmers of the Customs 1343–1352* (Transnational Royal Historical Society, 1959), fifth series, vol IX.

Redclift, M. and T. Benton (eds), *Social Theory and the Global Environment* (Routledge, London and New York 1994).

Revesz, R.L., P. Sands and R.B. Stewart (eds), *Environmental Law, the Economy and Sustainable Development* (Cambridge University Press, Cambridge 2000).

Riesser, J., *The German Great Banks and their Concentration* (The National Monetary Commission, Government Printing Office, Washington 1911).

Roe, J.M., *Political Determinants of Corporate Governance, Political Context, Corporate Impact* (Oxford University Press, Oxford 2006).

Rondo, C., *Banking in the Early Stages of Industrialisation: A Study in Comparative Economic History* (Oxford University Press, New York 1967).

Sandel, M., *What Money Can't Buy: The Moral Limits of Markets* (Allen Lane, Penguin, London 2012).

Sands, P., *Principles of International Environmental Law* (Cambridge University Press, Cambridge 2009).

Schlosser, E., *Fast Food Nation* (Penguin, London 2002).

Schmidt, H., J. Drukarczyk, D. Honold, S. Prigge, A. Schüler and G. Tetens, *Corporate Governance in Germany* (Nomos Verlagsgesellschaft, Baden-Baden 1997).

Schmidt, V.A., 'The Untold Story: The Impact of European Integration on France in the Mitterand-Chirac Era (1981–1997)', *European Community Studies Association Fifth Biennial International Conference, Seattle, May 1997* (University of Massachusetts Press, MA 1997).

Schmittoff, C. and K. Wooldridge (eds), *Groups of Companies* (Sweet and Maxwell, London 1991).

Schous, P.A., *Reasoned Freedom* (Cornell University Press, London 1992).

Schubert, W. and P. Hommelhoff, *Hundert Jahre modernes Aktienrecht* (Berlin 1985).

Sedgwick, P.H., *Christian Ethics* (Cambridge University Press, Cambridge 1999).
Seidl, D., 'Regulating Organisations through Codes of Corporate Governance', *Centre for Business Research, University of Cambridge, Working Paper Series* (December 2006).
Sharma, S., *The Asian Financial Crisis* (Manchester University Press, Manchester 2003).
Shleifer, A. and R.W. Vishny, 'A Survey of Corporate Governance' (1997) *Journal of Finance* 737.
Shue, H., *Basic Rights* (Princeton University Press, Chichester 1996).
Siebert, H., *The German Economy, Beyond the Social Market* (Princeton University Press, Princeton NJ 2005).
Siems, M., *Convergence in Shareholder Law* (Cambridge University Press, Cambridge 2008).
Simms, A. and D. Boyle, *Eminent Corporations* (Constable & Robinson Ltd, London 2010).
Sjafjell, B., *Towards a Sustainable European Company Law* (Wolters Kluwer, Alphen aan Rijn, Netherlands 2009).
Skidelsky R. and E. Skidelsky, *How Much is Enough?* (Allen Lane, London 2012).
Skidelsky, R., *Keynes; The Return of the Master* (Penguin, London 2009).
Smith, A., *An Inquiry into the Nature and Causes of the Wealth of the Nations* (Penguin, London 1999).
Smith, A., *The Wealth of Nations* (Prometheus Books, New York 1991).
Soederberg, S., *Corporate Power and Ownership in Contemporary Capitalism* (Routledge, London 2010).
Solomon, J., *Corporate Governance and Accountability*, 2nd edn (John Wiley & Sons Ltd, Chichester 2009).
Soros, G., *The Crisis of Global Capitalism: Open Society Endangered* (Public Affairs, New York 1998).
Stern, N., *The Economics of Climate Change: The Stern Review* (Cambridge University Press, Cambridge 2007).
Stiglitz, J., *Globalisation and its Discontents* (Allen Lane, Penguin, London 2002).
Stiglitz, J., *The Price of Inequality* (Allen Lane, Penguin, London 2012).
Streeck, W. and K. Yamamura, *The End of Diversity? Prospects for German and Japanese Capitalism* (Cornell University Press, New York 2003).
Sun, W., J. Stewart and D. Pollard, *Corporate Governance and the Global Financial Crisis, International Perspectives* (Cambridge University Press, Cambridge 2011).
Talbot, L.E., *Critical Company Law* (Routledge, London 2008).

Talbot, L.E., *Progressive Corporate Governance for the 21st Century* (Routledge, Abingdon 2013).

Tamanaha, B., *The Rule of Law* (Cambridge University Press, Cambridge 2004).

Tannenbaum, A.S., *Control in Organisations* (McGraw Hill, New York 1962).

Tawney, R.H., *Religion and the Rise of Capitalism* (Transaction Publishers, New Brunswick, NJ, 1998; originally published by Harcourt, Brace & Company Inc., New York 1926).

Taylor J., *Creating Capitalism: Joint Stock Enterprise in British Politics and Culture 1800-1870* (The Boydell Press for the Royal Historical Society, Woodbridge, Suffolk, 2006).

Taylor, L. and J. Eatwell, *Global Finance at Risk* (The New Press, New York 2000).

Tench, P. and L. Yeoman, *Exploring Public Relations* (Pearson, Harlow 2012).

Thankom, C. and A. Copinath, *Corporate Governance and Development, Reform, Financial Systems and Legal Frameworks* (Edward Elgar, Cheltenham, 2009).

Thomas, H., *The Slave Trade* (Picador, Phoenix, 2006).

Tilly, C. *The Growth of Large Scale Enterprise in Germany since the Middle of the Nineteenth Century* (Martinus Nijhoff, Leiden, the Netherlands, Boston 1974).

Tilly, C., *Democracy* (Cambridge University Press, Cambridge 2007).

Tooze, A., *The Wages of Destruction: The Making and Breaking of the Nazi Economy* (Penguin, London, New York 2006).

Toynbee, P., *Hard Work* (Bloomsbury, London 2003).

Traynor, J., *Mastering Modern German History, 1864–1990* (Palgrave, London 2007).

Trevelyan, G.M., *English Social History* (Penguin, London 1944).

Tricker, R.I., *Corporate Governance, Principles, Policies and Practices*, 2nd edn (Oxford University Press, Oxford 2012).

Tricker, R.I., *The Evolution of the Company, Corporate Governance: Practices, Procedures and Powers in British Companies and their Boards of Directors* (Gower, Aldershot 1984).

Turner, Jr, H., *German Big Business and the Rise of Hitler* (Oxford University Press, Oxford 1985)

Underhill, G. and Z. Xiaoke (eds), *International Financial Governance under Stress: Global Structures versus National Imperatives* (Cambridge University Press, Cambridge 2003).

Wearing, R., *Cases in Corporate Governance* (Sage Publications, London 2008).

Weiss, M. and M. Schmidt, *Labour Law and Industrial Relations in Germany* (Kluwer Law International, London 2008).

Weitzenboeck, E.M., *A Legal Framework for Emerging Business Models: Dynamic Networks as Collaborative Contracts* (Edward Elgar, Cheltenham 2012).

Westin, A.F., *Privacy and Freedom* (Atheneum, New York 1967).

Wiedermann, H., *Gesellschaftsrecht* (Beck, München 1980).

Wiesen, J., *Creating the Nazi Marketplace, Commerce and Consumption in the Third Reich* (Cambridge University Press, Cambridge 2010).

Wilkinson, R. and K. Pickett, *The Spirit Level* (Penguin, London 2009).

Wilkinson, R., *Mind the Gap: Hierarchies, Health and Human Evolution* (Wiedenfeld and Nicolson, London 2000).

Williamson, O.E., *The Mechanisms of Governance* (Oxford University Press, Oxford 1996).

Wilson, E.J., *British Business History, 1720–1994* (Manchester University Press, Manchester 1995).

Wright, L.B., *Middle Class Culture in Elizabethan England* (University of North Carolina Press, Chapel Hill 1935).

Zerk, J., *Multinational and Corporate Social Responsibilities: Limitations and Opportunities in International Law* (Cambridge University Press, Cambridge 2006).


## Articles, Papers and Reports


2010 UK Corporate Governance Code, Financial Reporting Council, June 2010, http://www.frc.org.uk/documents/pagemanager/corporate_governance/uk%20corp%20gov%20code%20june%202010.pdf

Ainger, Katherine, 'A Financial Coup D'etat: The Spanish government may be happy to sacrifice sovereignty for a bailout. But not the Indignos', *Guardian Wednesday*, 26/09/2012

Alchian, A. and H. Demsetz, 'Production, Information Costs, and Economic Organisation', 62 *American Economic Review*, 1972

Alldridge, P. and Anna Mumford, 'Tax Evasion and the Proceeds of Crime Act 2002', 25 *Legal Studies* 253, 2005

Attenborough, D., 'Giving Purpose to the Corporate Purpose Debate: An Equitable Maximisation and Viability Principle', 32(1) *Legal Studies* 4

Bainbridge Stephen, 'Director Primacy in Corporate Takeovers: Preliminary Reflections', 55 *Stanford Law Review* 791, 2002

Bale, B. Robert, 'Informed Lending Decision v Privacy Interests in Great Britain', 10 *Transnational Lawyer* 77, 1997

Basic Law for the Federal Republic of Germany, Grundgesetz, http://www.iuscomp.org/gla/statutes/GG.htm#14

Baun, Michael J., 'The Maastricht Treaty as High Politics: Germany, France and European Integration', 110 *Political Science Quarterly* 4, Winter, 1995–96

Belcher, Alice, 'The Boundaries of the Firm: the Theories of Coase, Knight and Weitzman', 17 *Legal Studies*, 1997

Black S. Bernard, 'Shareholder Passitivity Reexamined', 89 *Michigan Law Review* 520, 1990

Bolodeoku, Omotayo Ige, 'Economic Theories of the Corporation and Corporate Governance: a Critique', *Journal of Business Law*, 2002

Berlin, K. and T. Lang, 'Trade and the Environment', 16 *The Washington Quarterly* 4, 35–51

Campbell, D., 'Reflexivity and Welfarism in the Modern Law of Contract', *Oxford Journal of Legal Studies* 477, 2000

Cardonsky, B. Lauren, 'Towards a Meaningful Right to Privacy in the United Kingdom', 20 *Boston University International Law Journal*, 2002

Caspar, Rose, 'Stakeholder Orientation versus shareholder value: a matter of contractual failures', *European Journal of Law and Economics*, 2004

Clarkson, Max, 'A Stakeholder Framework for Analysing and Evaluating Corporate Social Performance', 20 *Academy of Management Review* 92, 1995

Coffee, John C., Jr, 'The Future of History: The Prospects for Global Convergence in Corporate Governance and its Implications', 93 *NwU Law Review* 641, 1999

Coffee, John, 'The Future as History: The Prospects for Global Convergence in Corporate Governance and Its Implications', 93 *Northwestern University Law Review* 654, 1999

Coffee John C. Jr., 'Dispersed Ownership: the Theories, the Evidence, and the enduring Tension Between "Lumpers" and "Splitters"', Columbia Law and Economics Working Paper No. 363, European Corporate Governance Institute, Law Working Paper No. 144/2010

Culpepper, D. Pepper, 'Institutional Change in Contemporary Capitalism, Coordinated Financial Systems since 1990', *World Politics* 57, 2005

Dean, Janice, 'Directors' Duties in Response to Hostile Takeover Bids', *International Company and Commercial Law Review*, 14(12), 2003

Dignam, Alan and Michael Galanis, 'Corporate Governance and the Importance of Macroeconomic Context', 28 *Oxford Journal of Legal Studies* 2, 2008

Dine, Janet, 'Jurisdictional Arbitrage by Multinational Companies: a national law solution', 3 *Journal of Human Rights and the Environment*, March, 2012

Directors' Remuneration, Report of a Study Group chaired by Sir Richard Greenbury, 17 July 1995, at http://www.ecgi.org/codes/documents/greenbury.pdf

Dodd Merrick, 'For Whom are Corporate Managers Trustees?' 45 *Harvard Law Review* 1161, 1932

Donaldson T. and L. Preston, 'The Stakeholder Theory of the Corporation: Concepts, Evidence, Implications', 20 *Academy of Management Review* 65, 1995

Dore Ronald, William Lazonick, Mary O'Sullivan, 'Varieties of Capitalism in the Twentieth Century', 15 *Oxford Review of Economic Policy* 4, 1999

DTI Report, Sir Roger John Laugharne Thomas and Raymond Thomas Turner, FCA, 2001, http://www.pixunlimited.co.uk/Media/pdf/mirror group.pdf

Easterbook, H. Frank and R. Daniel Fischel, 'The Corporate Contract', 89 *Columbia Law Review* 1416, 1989

Eberle, J. Edward, 'Human Dignity, Privacy and Personality in German and American Constitutional Law', *Utah Law Review* 963, 1997

Eisenberg, A. Melvin, 'The Conception that the Corporation is a Nexus of Contracts and the Dual Nature of the Firm', 24 *Journal of Corporation Law* 819, 1999

Evans, T. and A.J. Ayers, 'In the Service of Power; The Global Political Economy of Citizenship and Human Rights', 10 *Citizenship Studies* 239, 2006

Fama, Eugene, 'Agency Problems and the Theory of the Firm',99 *Journal of Political Economy*, 288, 1980

Fama, Eugene and Michael Jensen, 'Separation of Ownership and Control', 26 *Journal of Law and Economics* 301, 1983

Ferrarini, Guido and Niamh Moloney, 'Executive Remuneration and Corporate Governance in the EU: Convergence, Divergence and Reform Perspectives', *European Company and Financial Law Review*, 3, 2004

Ferrarini, Guido and Niamh Moloney, 'Executive Remuneration in the EU: The Context of Reform, European Corporate Governance Institute', Law Working Paper No. 32/2005

Financial Reporting Council, *The Combined Code on Corporate Governance*, 2008, http://www.ecgi.org/codes/documents/combined_code_june2008_en.pdf

Fisher Deryn, 'The Enlightened Shareholder – leaving Stakeholders in the Dark: Will Section 172(1) of the Companies Act 2006 make directors consider the Impact of their decisions on Third Parties?', *International Company and Commercial Law Review*, 2009, 20(1)

Freeman, Edward R., Andrew Wicks and Bidhan Parmar, 'Stakeholder Theory and the Corporate Objective Revisited', 15 *Organisation Science* 364, 2004

Fromholz, M. Julia, 'Foreign Law: a) Data Privacy: The European Union Data Privacy Directive', 15 *Berkeley Technology Law Journal*, 2000

Galanis, Michael, 'Vicious Spirals in Corporate Governance: Mandatory Rules for Systemic (Re)Balancing?', *Oxford Journal of Legal Studies*, 31(2)

Gelter, Martin, 'The Dark Side of Shareholder Influence: Managerial Autonomy and Stakeholder Orientation in Comparative Corporate Governance', 50 *Harvard International Law Journal* 129, 2009

Gelter, Martin, 'The Dark Side of Shareholder Influence: Toward A Holdup Theory of Stakeholders in Comparative Corporate Governance', Discussion Paper 17, Harvard Law School, Cambridge MA 02138, 7/2008

Gladstone, Julia, 'The impact of e-commerce on the laws of nations. The US privacy balance and the European Privacy Directive: Reflections on the United States privacy policy', *Willamette Journal of International Law and Dispute Resolution*, 7, 2000

Gomez, Pierre-Yves and Harry Korine, 'Democracy and the Evolution of Corporate Governance', 13 *Corporate Governance* 6, 2005

Greif, Avner and David Laitin, 'A Theory of Endogenous Institutional Change', *American Political Science Review* 98, November 2004

Gresser, E., 'Hidden Tax on the Poor: The Case for Reforming US Tariff Policy', Progressive Policy Institute Report, 25 March 2002

Grossfeld, B. and U. Lehmann, 'Management Structures and Workers' Codetermination in Germany with European Perspectives' (1994) 1 *Corporate Law Development Series*.

Grossman, Hugh Alexander, 'Refining the Role of the Corporation', 10 *Deakin Law Review* 572, 2005

Gunter, 'Enterprise Corporatism: New Industrial policy and the "essence of the Legal Person"' 36 *American Journal of Comparative Law* 130, 1988

Hale, B., 'Power Giant buys town to avoid pollution lawsuits', *The Times*, 14 May, 2002

Hampel Committee, Final Report, January 1998, at: http://www.ecgi.org/codes/documents/hampel23.pdf

Hansmann, Henry and Reinier Kraakman, 'The End of History for Corporate Law', Harvard Law School, John M. Olin Center for Law, Economics and Business Discussion Paper Series, Paper 280, 2000

Harper Ho, Virginia E., 'Enlightened Shareholder Value: Corporate Governance Beyond the Shareholder-Stakeholder Divide', 36 *Journal of Corporation Law* 1, 2010

Hart, Oliver, 'An Economist's Perspective on the Theory of the Firm', 89 *Columbia Law Review* 1757, 1989

Hart, Oliver and John Moore, 'Property Rights and the Nature of the Firm', *Journal of Political Economy* 1119, Vol.98, Number 6, December 1990

Hayek, Friedrich, 'The Use of Knowledge in Society', 35 *American Economic Review*, 519, 1948

Hessen, Robert, 'A New Concept of Corporations: A Contractual and Private Property Model', 30 *Hastings Law Journal* 1327, 1979

Hill, G. Jennifer, 'Subverting Shareholder Rights: Lessons from News Corporation's Migration to Delaware', 63 *Vanderbilt Law Review* 1, 2010

Hill, G. Jennifer, *The Rising Tension Between Shareholder and Director Power in the Common Law World*, European Corporate Governance Institute, Law Working Paper No.152/2010, Vanderbilt University School of Law, Law and Economics Research Paper No. 10-11 and University of Sydney Faculty of Law, Research Paper no. 10-34

Hill, G. Jennifer, 'Then and Now: Professor Berle and the Unpredictable Shareholder', *Seattle University Law Review* 1005, Vol.33, No.4, 2010

Hill, J. 'Visions and Revisions of the Shareholder', *American Journal of Comparative Law*, 39, 2000

Hopt, J. Klaus and Patrick C. Leyens, 'Board Models in Europe – Recent Developments of Internal Corporate Governance Structures in Germany, the United Kingdom, France and Italy', *European Company and Financial Law Review*, 2004

Ireland, P., 'Company Law and the Myth of Shareholder Ownership', 1999 *MLR* 62

Jeffrey, Gordon N., 'The Rise of Independent Directors in the United States, 1950-2005: Of Shareholder Value and Stock Market Prices', 59 *Stanford Law Review* 1465, 2007

Jensen, C. Michael and William H. Meckling, 'Theory of the Firm: Managerial Behaviour, Agency Costs and Ownership Structure', *Journal of Financial Economics*, 3, 1976

Joerges, C., 'Integration through de-legalisation? An irritated heckler', Paper given at the European University Institute seminar 'Governance, Civil Society and Social Movements', 30 June, 2007

Kamar, Ehud, Pinar Karaca-Mandic and Eric Talley, 'Going-private decisions and the Sarbanes Oxley Act of 2002: a cross country analysis', *Journal of Law, Economics and Organisation*, 9, 25(1)

Karliner, J., *The Corporate Planet*, 5; UNCTAD World Investment Report 1995: Transnational Corporations and Competitiveness, New York: United Nations Conference on Trade and Development, Division on Transnational Corporations and Investment

Karmel, S. Roberta, 'Implications of the Stakeholder Model', 61 *George Washington Law Review*, 1993

Keasey, K. and M. Wright, 'Issues in Corporate Accountability and Governance', *Accounting and Business Research* 291, 1993

Kerwer, D., 'Rules that Many Use: Standards and Global Regulation Governance' (2005) 18 *Governance: An International Journal of Policy, Administration, and Institutions* 4, October.

Kesan, P. Jay, 'Cyber Working or Cyber Shirking?: A First Principles Examination of Electronic Privacy in the Workplace', 54 *Florida Law Review*

Komo, Daniel and Charlotte Villiers, 'Are Trends in European Company Law threatening Industrial Democracy?', *European Law Review*, 2009

La Porta, R., F. Lopez de Silanes and A. Shleifer, 'Corporate Ownership Around the World', *Journal of Finance*, 54, 1999, 471–517.

La Porta et al., 'Law and Finance', *Journal of Political Economy* 106, 1113-1155, 1998

La Porta R., F. Lopez de Silanes, A. Shleifer and R.Vishny, 'Law and Finance', *Journal of Political Economy*, 106, 1998

LaPorta, R., F. Lopez de Silanes, A. Shleifer and R. Vishny, 'Legal Determinants of External Finance', *Journal of Finance*, 52, 1997

Lee, Joseph, 'Shareholders' Derivative Claims under the Companies Act 2006: Market Mechanisms or Asymmetric paternalism?', *International Company and Commercial Law Review*, 18(11), 2007

Leigh, David, 'How UK oil company Trafigura tried to cover up African pollution disaster', Guardian, 16/09/2009, http://www.guardian.co.uk/world/2009/sep/16/trafigura-african-pollution-disaster, accessed on 17/10/2012

Licht, N. Amir, 'The Maximands of Corporate Governance: A Theory of Values and Cognitive Style', 29 *Delaware Journal of Corporate Law* 649

Lord Gordon Slynn, 'The Development of Human Rights in the United Kingdom', 28 *Fordham International Law Journal* 477, 2005

Macey, R. Jonathon, 'Fiduciary Duties as Residual Claims: Obligation to Nonshareholder Constituencies from a Theory of the Firm Perspective', 84 *Cornell Law Review*, 1999

Mahoney G. Paul, 'The Common Law and Economic Growth: Hayek Might be Right', *Journal of Legal Studies*, Vol. XXX, 2001

Matheson, John and Brent Olson, 'Corporate Law and the Longterm Shareholder Model of Corporate Governance', 76 *Minnesota Law Review* 1313, 1992

Mayer, Colin, 'Corporate Governance, Competition and Performance', 24 *Journal of Law and Society*, 1997

McConvill, James, 'The Separation of Ownership and Control under a happiness based theory of the corporation', *Company Lawyer*, 2005, 26(2)

Mintzberg, Henry, 'Who should Control the Corporation', *California Management Review*, Vol. XXVII, 1984

Moravcsik, A. 'Negotiating the Single European Act: National Interests and Conventional Statecraft in the European Community' (1991) 45 *International Organisation*, 1, Winter

Morck, Randall K. and Lloyd Steier, *The Global History of Corporate Governance, An Introduction*, National Bureau of Economic Research, 2005, p. 9, http://www.nber.org/papers/w11062.pdf

Murray, N. Rothbard, 'Biography of Ludwig Von Mises (1881-1973)', Ludwig Von Mises Institute, http://mises.org/about/3248, accessed August 16, 2012

OECD data: http://www.oecd-ilibrary.org/economics/country-statistical-profile-united-kingdom_20752288-table-gbr

OECD data: http://stats.oecd.org/Index.aspx?DataSetCode=GOV_DEBT

OECD, *Principles of Corporate Governance*, OECD, Paris, 1999.

OECD, *Principles of Corporate Governance*, OECD, Paris, 2004.

Pulver, S, 'Making sense of Corporate environmentalism: an Environmental contestation approach to analyzing the causes and consequences of the climate change policy in the oil industry', *Organisation and Environment* 20, 2007, 1–40

Raiser, Thomas, 'The Theory of Enterprise Law in the Federal Republic of Germany', *American Journal of Comparative Law*, 1988

Randall, S. Thomas and Harwell Wells, 'Executive Compensation in the Courts: Board Capture, Optimal Contracting, and Officers' Fiduciary Duties', 95 *Minnesota Law Review* 846, 2011

Report of the Committee on the Financial Aspects of Corporate Governance, December 1992, 1.1., at: http://www.ecgi.org/codes/documents/cadbury.pdf

Report of the HIH Royal Commission, Vol I, Department of Treasury, 2003

Richards, A. 'Mitbestimmung: The Future of Co-determination in a Hostile World' (2007) 15 *Debatte*

Riley, A. C., 'Understanding and Regulating the Corporation' 58(4) *Modern Law Review* 595, 1995.

Roe, Mark J., 'A Political Theory of American Corporate Finance', 91 *Columbia Law Review*, 10, 1991

Roe, Mark J., 'Legal Origins, Politics, and Modern Stock Markets', 120 *Harvard Law Review*, 2006

Roe, Mark J., 'The Inevitable Instability of American Corporate Governance', 1 *Corporate Governance Law Review* 1, 2005

Roe, Mark J., 'The Shareholder Wealth Maximisation Norm and Industrial Organisation', 149 *University of Pennsylvania Law Review*, 2001
Roe, Mark J., 'Political Preconditions to Separating Ownership from Corporate Control', 53 *Stanford Law Review*, 2000
Roe, Mark J., 'A Political Theory of American Corporate Finance', 91 *Columbia Law Review* 10, 1991
Roe, Mark J., 'Chaos and Evolution in Law and Economics', 109 *Harvard Law Review* 641, 1996
Ross, A., "Tu-tu" 70 *Harvard Law Review* 625, 1957
Royal Commission on the Reform of Mercantile Law, Report, 1854
Royal Commission, *Directors' Duties and Other Obligations under the Corporations Act*, Background Paper 11, November 2001
Schwarz, Florian, 'The German Co-determination System: a model for introducing corporate social responsibility requirements into Australian Law?', Part 1, *Journal of International Banking Law and Regulation*, 23(3), 2008
Shankman, N.A., 'Reframing the debate between agency and stakeholder theories of the firm', 19 *Journal of Business Ethics*, 319, 1999
Singh, R. 'Privacy and the Media after the Human Rights Act' (1998) 6 *European Human Rights Law Review*, 712
Skolgy, S. and M. Gibney, 'Transnational Human Rights Obligations', *Human Rights Quarterly* 781, 2002
Smith, Thomas, 'The Efficient Norm for Corporate Law: A Neotraditional Interpretation of Fiduciary Duty', 98 *Michigan Law Review* 214, 1999
Teubner, Gunther, Vol. 61, *MLR*, p. 11, 1998
Teubner, G., 'The public/private dichotomy: After the critique?', Paper given at the European University Institute seminar 'Governance, Civil Society and Social Movements', 30 June 2007
The Times, December 1955 in one Hundred Years of Limited Liability in England, Lord Cohen of Walmer, Hebrew University, Jerusalem, 1957
The Tyson Report on the Recruitment and Development of Non-Executive Directors (June 2003), at: http://www.thecapability.uk.com/postboylbs/templates/non-personalised/documents/Tyson_Report_June_2003.pdf
Thomsen, Steen, 'Business Ethics as Corporate Governance', *European Journal of Law and Politics*, 2001
Turnbull, Shann, 'Corporate Governance: Its Scope, Concerns and Theories', *Corporate Governance: An International Review*, 5, 1997
UN Development Progress, Human Development Report, 1996, Oxford University Press, New York 1994; Third World Network, 'A World in Social Crisis: Basic Facts on Poverty, Unemployment and Social Disintegration', Third World Resurgence (No. 52), 1994

Vagts, F. Detlev, 'Reforming the modern Corporation: Perspectives from the German', 80 *Harvard Law Review* 23

Van der Weide, Mark E., 'Against Fiduciary Duties to Corporate Stakeholders' 21 *Delaware Journal of Corporate Law*, 1996

Wallman Steven, 'The Proper Interpretation of Corporate Constituency Statutes and Formulation of Director Duties', 21 *Stetson Law Review* 163, 1991

Walsh, J.P. and J.K. Steward, 'On the efficiency of the internal and external corporate control mechanisms', *Journal of Management Review*, 15, 1990, 421

Weiss, David C., 'The Foreign Corrupt Practices Act, SEC Disgorgement of Profits, and the Evolving International Bribery Regime: Weighing Proportionality, Retribution, and Deterrence', 30 *Michigan Journal of International Law*, 471, 2009

Weiss, Manfred, 'Convergence and/or Divergence in Labour Law Systems?: A European Perspective', 28 *Comparative Labour Law and Policy Journal*, 2007

Williamson, Oliver, 'The Modern Corporation: Origins, Evolution, Attributes', 19 *Journal of Economic Literature*, 1537

Worthington, Sarah, 'Shares and Shareholders: Property, Power and Entitlement: Part 1', *Company Lawyer*, 22(9), 2001

Worthington, Sarah, 'Shares and Shareholders: Property, Power and Entitlement: Part 2', *Company Lawyer*, 307, 2001

Yablon, Charles M., 'Overcompensating: The Company Lawyer and Executive Pay', 92 *Columbia Law Review* 1867, 1992

Yavasi, Mahmut, 'Shareholding and Board Structures of German and UK Companies', *Company Lawyer*, 22(2), 2001

Yohei, Suda, 'Monitoring E-mail of Employees in the Private Sector: A Comparison between Western Europe and the United States', 4 *Washington University Global Studies Law Review*, 2005

Zetzsche, Dirk A., *An Ethical Theory of Corporate Governance Theory*, CBC Working Paper, No. 6, 2007

# Index